Excavating Ships of War

Excavating Ships of War

edited by Mensun Bound

1998
The International Maritime Archaeology Series
Volume 2
Series general editor: Mensun Bound,
University of Oxford

Anthony Nelson

© 1998 Anthony Nelson and contributors respectively

Published in 1998 by Anthony Nelson
PO Box 9, Oswestry, Shropshire SY11 1BY England

ISBN 0 904614 53 0 (pbk)
ISBN 0 904614 64 6 (hbk)
ISSN 1356-983X

Designed by Harold Bartram
Typeset by Quetzal Communications
Printed by Redwood Books

Contents

For Yannis Costopoulos

Τούσδε ποτ᾽ ἐκ Σπάρτας ἀκροθίνια Φοίβῳ ἄγουτας
ἐυ πέλαγος, μία νύξ, εἶς τάφος ἐκτέρισευ.

SIMONIDES

Introduction and Acknowledgements

This book is intended as a companion volume to *The Archaeology of Ships of War*, volume I in *The International Maritime Archaeology Series*. Both books are based on a two day conference, 'The Archaeology of Ships of War', held at Greenwich on the 1st October and 1st November 1992, under the auspices of Oxford University MARE, the Nautical Archaeology Society, the National Maritime Museum and the World Ship Trust. However, only three of the chapters in this volume were presented at the conference, the remainder being reports and studies solicited by the editor and often representing work undertaken since the conference. Whereas Volume I concentrated as much upon ordnance and ship preservation as it did upon excavation, this volume concentrates almost exclusively upon excavations.

Once again it is a pleasure to be able to express my gratitude to those who made possible the conference from which this book derives: Tim and Katie Dingemans, Sarah Draper, Franco Fabri (who provided the funding), Gillian Hutchinson and her colleagues at the National Maritime Museum, the Management Committee of Oxford University MARE, the trustees of the World Ship Trust and the Council of the Nautical Archaeology Society. I am also indebted to Royston Raymond for his translation of the *Villefranche Sur Mer* chapter, to Peter Riou, Monique Meager and Kate Mallet for their translation of the *Slava Rossii* chapter, and, for editorial advice and assistance, to Liz Davy, John and Jean Yellowlees, Patrick Fischer, Patrick Lizé and Enrico Rampinelli. The National Maritime Museum showed great patience and professionalism in the help they gave with illustrations. Invaluable aid with the artwork was given by Chris Fitton, Henry Milner and Helen Ford. Others whose assistance I would like to record include David Taylor, Peter Winterstein, Francisco von Kuhn, Hector Bado, Carlos Coirolo, Sergio Pronczuk, Teddy and Sheila Neville-Jones, Max Meister and John Broadwater. My most heartfelt thanks however go to Mike Fischer of RM Plc whose generous donation was invaluable in the successful launch of this series.

Mensun Bound
St Peter's College, Oxford
(Triton Fellow in Maritime Archaeology at the University of Oxford)

Mensun Bound

British sea power: ships, armament, strategy and tactics[1]

'Whosoever commands the sea commands trade, whosoever commands the trade of the world commands the riches of the world, and consequently the world itself'; for the period covered by this book (16th century to 1945) there could hardly be a more apt or better construed truism of the sea. But then its author, that grand old Elizabethan adventurer and man of letters, Sir Walter Raleigh, knew a thing or two about ships, naval warfare and the wealth that might accrue from merchant enterprise. His words, however, might just as easily have been written by a Portuguese, a Dutchman, a Spaniard or a Frenchman - but it is only to the British, whose borders are the sea, that these precepts have a chiselled-in-stone, time-tested immutability. And it was only the British that ever came close to proving them, and this they did not by crude territorial conquest but by commanding the trades, which they did by commanding the seas, which they did by an adroit and sustained feat of sea power.

The reasons why such a large part of Britain's history has been so dominated by the sea are not hard to understand. Unlike its neighbours Britain did not have overland or inshore trade routes; for Britain its deep-water, seaborne commerce was everything. It was both the wealth and economic survival of the realm. To this day in Britain one can rarely look around and not see something that has been brought in by ship.

If, then, trade was so important to the realm, it follows that, like the realm, it had to be protected. The economic and sovereign survival of Britain has thus depended as much upon its navy as upon its merchant ships. From the time that Alfred met the Danes at sea in the mid ninth century and Harold sat in his ships off the Isle of Wight in the summer of 1066, right up until World War II, the period that ends this book, the foundation of British security and prosperity has been its ships and its ability to protect them, while at the same time suppressing those of its competitors and enemies.

Concerning World War II, Churchill wrote: 'Shipping' (meaning both merchant and naval), 'was at once the stronghold and sole foundation of our war strategy', words that might just as easily have been written by Lord Burghley in Elizabethan times or by Margaret Thatcher in 1982, or by any wartime leader in between.

After World War II Karl Doenitz, head of the German navy, wrote: 'Once Germany was committed to war with the United Kingdom, her whole naval effort was directed against British shipping and sea communications. If this campaign failed to achieve decisive results, then Germany's defeat, in whatever form it might happen to take, was inevitable'. Such remarks would have been just as apposite had they come from Philip of Spain in the 16th century or General Galtieri following his invasion of the Falklands, or by any wartime opponent of Britain during any period in between.

The lesson was simple: without its ships Britain could not survive.

The rise of the English navy

With the exception of those few wars that were inspired by no more than naked territorial expansionism, most of the conflicts in which Britain has been involved, were, at one level or another, to do with trade. Whatever the declared *casus belli* one does not have to scratch very deep to find trade. 'The trade of the world is too small for the two of us, therefore one must down', a Dutch captain told Pepys shortly before the second of the three short, sharp seaborne conflicts that characterized Anglo-Dutch relations during the third quarter of the 17th century.

Strange to say, it does not seem to have been until after the Anglo-Dutch Wars that the vital role of the navy in the survival and well-being of the nation was wholly understood. Certainly the Anglo-Dutch Wars saw an increase in professionalism and an improvement in ships, gunnery and tactical thought, but these are developments that would probably have happened anyway. Possibly it was the disaster off Dungeness (1652), the Four Days Battle (1666), the humiliation of seeing Dutch ships in the Thames (1667) and de Ruyter's success at Solebay (1672), together with the perspicacity and administrative genius of Pepys that shoehorned the English into a full appreciation of its fighting ships. In addition, the steady rise of the French navy in the 17th century could not have gone unnoticed and must have been a source of deep concern to the more sober minded. The navy which Richelieu had begun to build and organise in 1625 was completed under Colbert; by 1677 France had a fleet that could match that of England or the United Provinces. In addition the French were producing admirals like Duquesne and Tourville who were in every way the equal of Tromp and de Ruyter.

It is difficult to pinpoint exactly when maritime supremacy became a conscious goal of English government, but certainly the thinking was in place by the time of the great naval expansion of the 1690s. Whatever the chronological moment, if indeed there ever was one, the reality is that from Barfleur and La Hogue in 1692 (or perhaps more particularly from the capture of Gibraltar in 1704), to the Tokyo Bay treaty-signing on board the U.S. battleship *Missouri* in 1945, Britain enjoyed a sovereignty of the sea that at least from the guns of Trafalgar to those of August 1914 went virtually unchallenged.

But British supremacy at sea was never just a matter of having more and better ships. Frequently in fact, Britain was outnumbered, particularly during periods of Franco-Spanish alliance, and in 1689, at the beginning of the five Anglo-French wars that culminated in the great struggle against Napoleon, the English fleet was inferior in number to that of the French. Furthermore, although there was little difference in outward appearance between the ships of both sides, the French (at least during the late 17th century and first half of the 18th century) had a more scientific approach to ship design, and were held in such respect by the English that all French prizes were studied and measured with care (although it must be said that the French were often doing the same with the English). There is, in fact, no single factor that can explain the primacy of the Royal Navy during the period represented by the greater part of this book - but certainly guns and gunnery were significant contributors.

1 Henry VIII's Henri Grâce à Dieu. In her day the largest fighting ship in the world and one of the first in a long line of 'Great shypes' that ended with the battleships of World War II

2 An artist's rather fanciful recreation of the Battle of La Hogue (1692) in which some of the fighting took place in small boats. Barfleur and La Hogue mark the beginning of English naval supremacy

Guns and gunnery

The range, accuracy and efficacy of the stave-built wrought-iron guns of the early 16th century (best epitomized in this volume by the Villefranche ship see 38-50) left much to be desired, but by the time of the Alderney wreck in the late 16th century (see 64-83) both ships and artillery had reached a level of perfection that could not be much improved within the technology of the time. The *Mary Rose* of 1545 (ASW, 26-29) had sported some fine bronze muzzle-loaders while the vessel itself is traditionally believed to be the first ship with gun ports, thus heralding the bold new concept of ships that were purpose-designed to carry guns, from which there is but a small conceptual leap to the idea of formalized broadside discharges and line-ahead tactics. Henry VIII's bronze muzzle-loaders on the *Mary Rose* altered little during the following 250 years (particularly from the ballistic and manufacturing points of view), but bronze was an expensive material and gunsmiths, particularly English gunsmiths, turned to cast iron to meet the rapidly expanding need for heavy ordnance. The sakers on the Alderney ship illustrate the growth in the production of cast-iron guns that had taken place. In fact, by the time of the Alderney ship and after, English iron guns were so highly regarded that they were being exported in significant numbers to England's European neighbours.

The sakers that the writer was able to study on the Alderney wreck were relatively small guns, but on the Dutch East Indiaman *Nassau* (see 84-105), which was lost in the Straits of Malacca in 1606, shortly after the Alderney wreck, the writer found iron culverins which were dated to 1587 and displayed the cipher of Queen Elizabeth I. The culverin was a much longer and heavier gun that had proven its value against the Spanish Armada and which, according to Tudor ordnance specialist M.A. Lewis (1948, 426), had a point-blank range of about 330 yards. In cut-down form (made possible by the improved quality and quicker combustion of gunpowder), it was in effect, the forbear of the guns that were carried by, for instance, the *Dragon*, the *Stirling Castle* and the *Invincible* that feature in this book, or the Trafalgar gun that was raised from the *Agamemnon* during Oxford University MARE's 1997 survey of the vessel, which went down in the River Plate in 1809 (figs 11 and 12). [2]

The development, number and arrangement of artillery pieces within the purpose-built gun-ship helped bring in the rating system (which can also be seen as a reflection of the growing awareness - thanks to the Dutch Wars - that line-of-battle tactics required greater uniformity between the big ships and the exclusion of the less potent ones). During the reign of James I three or four loose 'ranks' of ships were recognized which seem to have become somewhat better defined under the Commonwealth and after the Restoration, so that, for example, a first-rate, of which there was only one, Peter and Phineas Pett's *Sovereign of the Seas* (later renamed *Royal Sovereign* by Charles II), was a three-decker with 100 fairly standardized guns (fig 3). It was not, however, until Lord Anson became First Lord of the

3 The *Sovereign of the Seas*, a 100 gun 1st rate, built by Peter and Phineas Pett and launched 1637. Renamed *Royal Sovereign* by Charles II. Fought at the battle of Kentish Knock, the St James Day Fight, the battle of Solebay, both battles of Schooneveld, the second battle of Texel, the battle of Beachy Head and the battle of Barfleur

Admiralty (1751) that a fully refined six-point classification system based on a vessel's dimensions, fighting capability and number of guns (in standardized batteries) was introduced.

By that time ships had evolved into great 200ft long floating strongholds with three tiers of heavy artillery. Gun technology, however, had not advanced significantly, so that although a first rate broadside could deliver half a ton of solid shot at a velocity of 120 feet per second, the results at a distance were not that destructive. Even in close, at a range where a 32-pounder could punch an 8 inch diameter hole through two foot of solid oak, such openings were easily plugged by experienced carpenters. In one of the eighteenth century wars against France not a single British ship was lost to enemy action, but during the same period, some 350 ships were wrecked by reefs, storms or adverse winds. [3]

The first fundamentally new gun to be introduced since the days of Henry VIII and the *Mary Rose*, was the carronade which was issued as an auxiliary armament to British ships during the French wars of the late 18th century, and was carried by such vessels in this book as the *Endymion*, the *Pandora*, the *Agamemnon* and the *St George*. It was a short, stubby gun with a wide bore that could, with relatively little propellant, dispatch an enormous 68-pound shot. At close range (i.e. up to 100 yards) carronades were devastating, for which reason they were popularly known as 'smashers'. They were also of moderate weight and thus could be mounted on the poop, quarter-deck and forecastle without destabilizing the vessel. For these reasons, and because they were easy to handle, did not compromise stowage space and were an excellent deterrent against pirates, they also found great favour with merchant ships. For example, in 1994 a carronade was recovered during the salvage of the *Diana*, an

English 'country' trader that went down in the Straits of Malacca in 1817 (fig 4).

The carronade was first put to the test in 1782 at the Battle of the Saints, the Royal Navy's most decisive victory since Hawk trounced the French at Quiberon Bay (1759) in the Seven Years War. The weapon proved a great success and the French (by the admission of their own officers) were completely outgunned. As a consequence of the Saints and of further experiments, the carronade was issued to almost every class of ship in the navy.[4] To be effective, however, battles had to be fought at close range - and they were.[5] Twelve years after the Saints, at the Glorious First of June, Howe's flagship, the *Queen Charlotte*, fired her first broadside when the French tricolour was brushing against her shrouds; in the same battle, HMS *Brunswick*, we are told, was so close to the French *Vengeur* that she could not open some of her gun ports and so simply blasted them away with a broadside. The situation was similar with Duncan at Camperdown in 1797 and with most of Nelson's victories. At the Nile, when Foley in the *Goliath* led the sweep behind the French, his follower, the American captain Ralf Miller in the *Theseus* was so close that his yards touched those of the French. At Trafalgar the *Victory* was in such near proximity to the *Redoubtable* that it could not fully run out its lower guns.

There were a number of factors other than the introduction of the carronade that, during Nelson's period, gave British ships a superior offensive capability. First there was better training; the British gun crews at the Nile, Copenhagen and Trafalgar had a much greater rate of fire and were generally more accurate. For instance, Cuthbert Collingwood's best gun crew could clean, load, aim and fire its cannon at the remarkable rate of three rounds every two minutes, whilst the slowest crew on the *Victory* could discharge theirs in less than two minutes. Second, there were the innovations of Sir Charles Douglas that gave British gunners a significant technological advantage. Not only did Douglas find ways to improve the mooring of a gun, dampen its recoil and reduce the clogging of the barrel from carbon deposits,[6] but, more importantly, he devised a way for traversing artillery. Since the Armada and before, battles at sea had been more a matter of aiming the ship than the gun, but with Douglas' method, oblique fire was at last possible; through an intricate block and tackle arrangement cannons could fire both 45 degrees before and abaft the beam. Finally, Douglas experimented with new ignition systems; first he used goose-quill tubes instead of loose powder to prime the vents, and then he re-introduced the flintlock and lanyard.[7] The charge had previously been ignited with a slow mach and linstock, a hang-fire method that involved a certain amount of presupposition as to when the gun might fire and where it might be pointing at that moment. With the flintlock, ignition was more spontaneous, so that at, for instance, the Nile, Copenhagen and Trafalgar, many of the gunners no longer had to anticipate the roll of the ship; what they saw when they squinted along their barrels, was very much what they got; gun laying was no longer a matter of guess-work.

4 A cannon of carronade type recovered in 1994 from the wreck of the *Diana* in the Straits of Malacca

A third factor that helped give British ships fighting superiority (particularly during the periods of the French Revolutionary (1793-1801) and Napoleonic (1803-1815) Wars), was the quality of their leadership and training which expressed itself in the discipline, skill and seamanship of their mariners and gun crews. The French and Spanish (in general) lacked admirals of the quality of Rodney, Howe, Jervis, Hood, Duncan or Nelson; or captains such as the 'band of brothers' who fought under Nelson. For instance, Admiral Brueys at the Nile made fundamental errors that gave the British their most devastating victory of the 18th century; and in the case of Admiral Villeneuve at Trafalgar, although he fully anticipated Nelson's tactics he still had no effective response. Unfortunately for France, three-quarters of its navy's officer corps had been guillotined or had fled into exile during the Reign of Terror (1793-94). Skills, maintenance, discipline and command structures collapsed in what was left of the once great French navy. Although under the Directory efforts were made to rebuild the fleet, the results were mixed; certainly the ships that participated in Napoleon's Egyptian campaign were suffering from neglect and Napoleon's reservations concerning the abilities of his naval officers were largely justified. In addition to that, there was the problem of Napoleon himself, who, like Hitler, never really understood the importance of naval strategy and the tactical detail of war at sea, and again and again denied his navy the resources and investment that were needed to maintain the fleets in full fighting condition. Furthermore, the successful blockade of French and Spanish ports meant that for years their crews were denied the vital training in seamanship and gunnery that the British received almost every day; as Nelson wrote, 'ships and seamen rot in harbour'.

One of the most telling vignettes of British naval superiority during this period came from Mathieu Prigny, Villeneuve's Chief of Staff at Trafalgar. Sometime after the battle he was asked by Vice-Admiral Sir William Henry Dillon what had been his greatest impression of the engagement. The answer was something of a surprise for it did not concern any aspect of conduct within the battle itself, but rather it focused upon the way in which the British seamen had comported themselves during the great storm that followed:

'The act that astonished me the most was when the action was over. It came to blow a gale of wind, and the English immediately set to work to shorten sail and reef the topsails, with as much regularity and order as if their ships had not been fighting a dreadful battle. We were all amazement . . . All *our* seamen were either drunk or disabled, and we, the officers, could not get any work out of them. We never witnessed any such clever manoeuvres before, and I shall never forget them' (Warner, 1959, 172)

In essence, the continental allies never stood a chance at Trafalgar - and both Nelson and Villeneuve knew it.

Tactics

The ascendancy of the Royal Navy was never just a matter of (generally) better gunnery, commanders and seamanship; it also had to do with such factors as ship construction, fleet administration, and, above all, sound strategy and tactical management.[8] Tactics are an issue which deserve special consideration here, for although they are at the heart of this book, regrettably, for reasons of space, they have had to be much ignored in the chapters that follow.

Battles at sea during the medieval era were usually close encounters in which slicing the cordage with shearhooks on poles, ramming, grappling and boarding were the primary tactical goals. The most famous English fleet action during this period was the bloody hand-to-hand victory over the French at Sluys (Flanders) in 1340. Close fighting remained the favoured form of engagement until well into the 16th century. We are given a sense of the closeness of post-medieval actions from the Villefranche wreck, which was well supplied with hand grenades (see 46-49), and the *Mary Rose* (ASW, 26-29), which, it will be remembered, was not only weaponed with the long bow, but was also covered with antiboarding nets. Clearly both ships were expecting close-quarter, if not hand-to-hand fighting of the kind that occurred in the famous action between the *Regent* and *Cordelière* off Brest in 1512 and which ended when both ships went down, still grappled together and on fire. By the time of the *Mary Rose* however, with its advances in gun technology (over the stave-constructed stone-throwers of the Villefranche wreck), a revolution in tactics was under way. In-fighting was becoming a thing of the past, while off-fighting, to the more visionary, was clearly the future: sea battles were becoming gun battles. With Henry VIII we have the beginning of a professional, permanent navy with properly issued ordnance and purpose-built fighting ships that featured rows of gun ports sited well down a carvel-laid hull which was starting to swell into what would become a well-pronounced tumblehome that provided the extra space which was necessary to work the vessel's heavier armament. By the time of Hawkins' navy we have the first galleons, vessels like Grenville's *Revenge* (b. 1577) which in many ways, although relatively small, were the first ships of the line, and which, in

their fundamentals, did not change much until the age of steam.

Comparisons between the fighting ships (like the *Mary Rose*) on the Anthony Anthony Roll of c. 1545 with their high forecastles (or those depicted by Pieter Brueghel the Elder a few years later), and the much more weatherly ship designs of Matthew Baker's drawings in the Pepysian Library of Magdalene College, Cambridge (or some of the ship illustrations on late Elizabethan maps), are extremely informative and reward careful study.

By this time (the last quarter of the 16th century) the English, and for that matter the Dutch, preferred to fight at a distance so that full use could be made of their superior ordnance and sailing capabilities. These in fact, broadly speaking, were the tactics used by the British in their confrontation with the Spanish Armada in July 1588. If the ultimate test of a warship and its most effective tactical usage, is battle, then the six day action against the Armada proved the efficacy of the new type of warship as well as its use of broadside and line-ahead formation. But as we see in the chapter on the Dutch East Indiaman *Nassau* (see 84-105), the Portuguese, another great maritime power of the 16th century, still favoured close battles in which they could deploy their galleys to maximum effect. In the Battle of Cape Rachado (1606) the Portuguese not only used their galleys as fast-attack craft, but also employed them to give their big ships superior positions on the wind, to manoeuvre them into a fighting posture when becalmed, and to extricate them from trouble when grappled engagements were not proceeding to plan. The *Nassau*, by contrast, favoured an arm's length gun battle for which she had the advantage, but once she was caught napping at anchor and such an engagement was out of the question, she was soon grappled and burned.

The Battle of Cape Rachado can also be used to illustrate the other common tactical mind-set of the day, which was to seek the advantage of the wind and then to fight it out in an uncoordinated manner, on an opportunity basis, within the unrestricted framework of a general mêlée.

The battle of Cape Rachado also in some ways marked the beginning of the Dutch Golden Age during which they dominated the South East Asian trades and built masterful ships, issued them with the best ordnance, and crewed them with skilled seamen under excellent leadership. Relations between the Dutch and British East India Companies had always been bitter but by the middle of the 17th century it was inevitable that the two great maritime nations of the period, who were both pursuing aggressively expansionist overseas trading policies, would come to blows.

It was during the three Anglo-Dutch wars (1652-1654, 1665-1667 and 1672-1674) that tactics began to formalize into a narrow set of procedures which, in the next century, would become almost rigid in their application. At the beginning of the wars the Dutch preferred to fight in groups,[9] as at the Battle of Kentish Knock (1652). In this action poor discipline and lack of cohesion (partly attributable to rivalry between the various maritime provinces) gave victory to the English, but fortunes were dramatically reversed later in the year when Marten Tromp decisively defeated the English under Robert Blake at Dungeness. Following this débâcle the English sought to strengthen their very mixed fleets by removing from them the clutter of unequal vessels that compromised the sailing efficiency of the big ships and weakened the combat prowess of the fleet in general. With the pruning of their ships and the regularization of their fleets into three squadrons (the van, the middle and the rear), the English were able to develop uniform ranks of heavy fighting ships and deploy them in regimented line-ahead processions when approaching and attacking enemy forces.

In its fully evolved state, the tactic consisted of a conterminous line of battle that would approach the enemy's windward side in close-hauled formation, with an interval of half a cable (100 yards) between the ships, and then - ideally - when the two vans were opposite and within range of the weakest guns, begin the action. In its essentials the new technique, which in broad terms can be called a British invention, was used after Dungeness at the first battle of Texel (Scheveningen) in 1653 (during which Tromp lost his life to an English bullet) and indeed, to a lesser extent, at the earlier English victories of Portland and Gabbard. Although Scheveningen was a decisive victory for the English, and although the tactic appears as the third fighting instruction of the period, line-battles were not without their detractors. In fact, it was not until 1665, during the Second War, that the method appears as a fully prescribed decree in the navy's *Fighting Instructions*. The leading proponents of formalized engagements were William Penn and the Duke of York (later James II). The critics were championed by Prince Rupert and General George Monck, Duke of Albemarle. The latter two felt that although there should indeed be an orderly linear approach, once battle had been joined there should be no more concerted tactical movements so that in the deregularized mêlée that would naturally follow, individual captains would be free to exploit opportunities as they arose.

By 1673 the formalist view had prevailed and for the remainder of the 17th and all the 18th century, these rules-of-engagement, with some minor modifications, became sacred writ within the Royal Navy. In fact, from 1691 (the year after the disaster at Beachy Head in which the Earl of Torrington broke his line), until the end of the American War of Independence in 1783, all tactics were governed by the *Fighting Instructions*, which although gave admirals considerable control over events, stifled initiative within the ranks of all officers below. Only with an enemy in flight, during the so-called General Chase (by which time the line had disintegrated) was there opportunity for enterprise and tactical imagination.

At first, the great actions of Barfleur and La Hogue (both 1692) followed by Rooke's victory of Malaga in 1704, seemed to justify this highly systematized method of fleet engagement, but as the century progressed, these great set-piece confrontations became increasingly ineffective and their outcomes indecisive. As maritime historians never tire

5 Comte de Grasse. Outsailed the British at Chesapeake Bay in 1781 but was decisively defeated by Rodney at the battle of the Saints in April 1782

of telling us, in the fifteen orthodox line-battles that took place between 1692 and 1782, not one enemy ship was sunk or captured. Not even in Sir Edward Hughes' five fierce actions against the famous French admiral Bailli de Suffren, during the period of the American Revolutionary War, was a single ship lost. By contrast, the six chases that took place during the same period (such as in the two battles fought off Finisterre in 1747, the first by Anson and the second by Hawk) all resulted in spectacular British victories.

By the American War of Independence (1775-82) it was becoming obvious to all but the most myopic that line-battles were not working. Never was this more evident than at the Battle of Ushant in July 1778 when Augustus Keppel (with his flag on the *Victory*), because of his insistence on fighting a traditional line-ahead engagement, was outsmarted, outmanoeuvred and tactically defeated (although no ship was lost or taken on either side) by the French admiral Comte d'Orvilliers who fought a hit-and-run action. In 1781 blind adherence to the line allowed Comte de Grasse (fig 5) to escape intact from what should have been the annihilation of his fleet at Chesapeake Bay. The failure of the Royal Navy at Chesapeake probably cost the British the Battle of Yorktown on land, and, because of that, the very war itself.

The success of the line-ahead formation depended to a remarkable degree upon the compliance of the enemy, and when they were not prepared to stand-up and fight (as at Ushant), or otherwise not co-operate (as at Chesapeake), the British did not have an answer.

After Ushant a young man called John Clerk, who had never been to sea, began to explore other methods of engagement. These he published in a series of tracts entitled

6 *Above* Sir George Rodney. Victor of the 'Moonlight Battle' in 1780 and the battle of the Saints in 1782

7 *Above left* First Viscount Hood. Admiral at the battle of the Saints and commander of the Mediterranean station during the first part of the French Revolutionary War

8 *Right* John Jervis, First Earl of St Vincent. Victor at the battle of Cape St Vincent in 1797

An Essay on Naval Tactics (1790 and 1797).[10] His main idea was to isolate part of the enemy force and then to overwhelm it by weight of numbers. It could take the van, or the remaining members of the enemy fleet, 30 to 60 minutes to come about or to wear, by which time half its force would have been crushed. In broad terms, these were the principles employed by Nelson at the Nile, Copenhagen and Trafalgar. At Trafalgar, for instance, it took some three hours for the French van to turn and join the fighting, by which time the battle had been won.[11]

It is not known if Rodney (fig 6) had actually read Clerk's book, but certainly he was well familiar with his ideas, and although he did not exactly follow Clerk's procedures when he met a Spanish squadron off Portugal in the late afternoon of 16 January 1780 (the 'Moonlight' Battle off St Vincent), he did none the less break naval etiquette by charging upon the enemy without letting his own fleet fall into line, or waiting for the Spanish to do likewise; he attacked immediately and won a resounding victory that helped relieve the beleaguered British garrison caught in the Great Siege of Gibraltar (1779-1783; see *ASW*, 64-76).

The real tactical turning point came in Rodney's famous battle with de Grasse (fig 5) in the West Indies, the so-called Battle of the Saints (1782), when the wind opened up a gap in the French line and Rodney (either on his own initiative, or at the urging of Sir Charles Douglas) deliberately broke from his own ordered file of ships to slice through that of the enemy. He then rounded upon the outnumbered French rear which was soon overwhelmed. Although the general chase that followed was not prosecuted as vigorously as it should have been, the Saints, none the less, was the most tactically significant battle since Barfleur and La Hogue, and helped to create a spirit in which admirals of that generation and the next, such as Howe, Jervis (fig 8), Duncan (fig 9) and, of course, Nelson (fig 10), could break with the old doctrinaire attitudes of the *Fighting Instructions* and perform feats of tactical finesse and daring that ended Napoleon's dreams of world conquest.

In addition to the new liberties that (thanks to the Saints) admirals were prepared to take for themselves, they were also content to allow their commanders a degree of flexibility that did not exist before so that in battle they might exploit tactical opportunities as they arose. A good example of this is the manner in which Nelson. when a captain under Jervis, on his own initiative, wore ship and broke the line at the Battle of Cape St Vincent in February 1797 to engage seven Spanish vessels (including the 130-gun, four-decker *Santissima Trinidad*, the biggest fighting ship of the day). A decade before this might have been a court martial offence, but as Nelson afterwards wrote, Jervis 'could not sufficiently thank me'.[12] Certainly initiative was something that Nelson was later to encourage within his own captains, so that, for example, at the Battle of the Nile when Foley ignored the battle plan and swept behind the enemy, he knew he could do so without fear of reproach from Nelson. The ultimate expression of this new freedom within the navy was Nelson's own crowning act of disobedience at Copenhagen in 1801 when he deliberately ignored Hyde Parker's signal to withdraw ('You know Foley, I have only one eye - I have a right to be blind sometimes').

In almost all the major sea battles following the Saints, the British appear to have been determined to avoid becoming enmeshed in any of the sterile broadside exchanges typical of those that took place under the old dogmas, but instead to smash through the enemy line as quickly and by any means possible, and then, to follow, as it were, Captain Locker's advice to Nelson, and lay the enemy alongside, in which position a British ship generally had the advantage. St Vincent (1797), the Glorious First of June (1794) and Camperdown (1797), and of course, Trafalgar (the final, conclusive end of all tactical line-engagements under sail), were all a vindication of this approach. And where it was not possible, as at Copenhagen in 1801, the

9 Admiral Adam Duncan, victor at the battle of Camperdown in 1797.

10 Lord Nelson, victor of the Nile, Copenhagen and Trafalgar.

British, though victorious, took a pounding. Even at the Nile where the French, under Admiral Brueys, drew up their ships into a static crescent-shaped 'redoubt' with their backs tight to the shoal, the British were able to avoid a line-against-line gun battle by 'leap-fogging' their vessels behind those of the French and then overwhelming their line section by section. The French admiral's great mistake was anchoring on one anchor, for when Foley, who was leading the British attack, saw this, he reasoned that if there was enough room for a 74 to swing, then there was enough room for another 74 to slip in behind. In this way the British sandwiched the enemy between two withering walls of fire.

Signals

We cannot leave the subject of tactics without considering the development of signalling. As in land battles, sound tactical movements at sea depend on good communications. Until the development of the radio, the navy's principal method of communication between ships was with flags. In its more evolved state and in the hands of skilled practitioners, the system worked to good effect, as in 1797 when Duncan with only two ships (the rest having deserted him to join the mutiny at Spithead and the Nore) successfully blockaded the Dutch at Texel by sending signals to an imaginary fleet over the horizon; or, on the eve of Trafalgar when vessels on picket duty off Cadiz were able to relay signal 370 ('enemy coming out of port') across fifty miles of ocean in two and a half hours. None the less, despite its many successes it was a clumsy system that was vulnerable to error and misunderstanding. Were space to allow, the history of poor signalling in sea battles would be an interesting subject to pursue with many illuminating case-studies to draw from, such as the contradictory signals at the Battle of Chesapeake Bay in September 1789 which helped give de Grasse the day, or the failings of the Grand Fleet under Jellicoe (who was labelled - with some justification - as 'the only man who could lose the war for Britain in an afternoon'). The action of December 1914, and of Dogger Bank in January 1915, were both characterized by appallingly inept signalling; and although the Battle of Jutland (May/June 1916) was a strategic victory for the British it was, none the less, a tactical débâcle because of (amongst other things) incompetent signalling from the flagship whose radio had been shot away.

It was the French who first saw the merit in developing a communication system between ships based on flags. By the 1690s they had an official signal book that, for its time, was remarkably wide in scope. In England the first flag-code was devised in 1647 and six years later an official set of signals based on five flags was issued to accompany the *Fighting Instructions*. With so few flags, however, intercourse between ships, however complex the situation, could consist of no more than a few simple injunctions or terse communiqués of fact. The first published code appeared in 1714, but in general it was left to individual commanders to develop their own systems. Richard Kempenfelt, the seaman-scholar, who died prematurely on the *Royal George* when it turned over and sank during cleaning off Spithead, contrived a tabular system which was adopted and developed by Howe, who issued it for ships under his command in 1776. Although Howe's system of signals was less elliptical than anything that had gone before, it was still a long way from an organic flag-language. An example of its limitation can be taken from the Battle of the Saints when Rodney decided to peel off from his own line and drive through that of the French. Once he had embarked upon this course of action, there were several uncomfortable minutes while he waited to see if those behind him would interpret his intentions correctly and follow-the-leader. Although Rodney had forty-three different signalling flags which could be flown from eight different points aloft, giving him a repertoire of over three hundred messages to draw from, he still did not have a specific flag (or combination of flags) that he might use to instruct the others to break the line; nor did he have a method that would allow him to spell out his wishes. Fortunately for Rodney the other ships understood his intentions and followed.

A more fully evolved version of Howe's signals became official navy issue in 1790, but it was not until 1800 that flag-signalling reached is orthographic and syntactical peak when Sir Home Popham devised a method that allowed words to be spelled out when the need arose. It was this code that gave Nelson the facility at Trafalgar to burnish the moment with one of the most self-consciously contrived bits of whimsy in history. At 1135 hours - just fifteen minutes before the first guns fired - he ordered his signal officer, Lieutenant Pasco, to express to the fleet: 'England confides that every man will do his duty'.[13] Pasco thought about it for a moment then asked if he might replace 'confides' with 'expects' since the latter was in Popham's signal book, but 'confides' would have to be spelt. Nelson agreed.

By Trafalgar, however, Nelson had taken fleet-communication one step further than flags by holding regular briefings with his captains so that they were not only familiar with his general way of thinking but also with the detail of his tactical thought. Because of this Nelson could afford to be remarkably taciturn when it came to signals. At the Nile, after he had issued his favourite signal (no. 16; a red pennant over a blue flag) 'Engage the enemy more closely', he flew no more orders. Similar happened at Trafalgar.

Display

We have now explored British sea power under sail from the points of view of artillery and tactics. But there are several other aspects that should be mentioned before examining the Royal Navy during the age of mechanical propulsion. The first is the British use of its navy as a potential weapon, or as a 'navy in waiting'; second, its use of geography, and third, Britain's vulnerability to economic warfare.

The tactical value of a fleet 'in being' has been appreciated since antiquity. Once Rome (after, let us say, Actium in 31 BC) understood the importance of a standing navy that could patrol and be seen, it was able to maintain a hold on the Mediterranean that lasted 250 years. Again and again throughout history we see how no more than the presence of a fleet (or even just a single ship) is enough to discourage any bellicose, or otherwise unwanted activity during peacetime, and confuse or tie up an enemy's resources during periods of war. In the 17th century, for example, the French admiral Jean Bart was able to keep more than fifty Dutch and English ships at sea with only five frigates. The best example of how no more than the threat of a powerful vessel can incite consternation within a superior enemy navy, is that of the *Tirpitz* in World War II. Her very existence in Norwegian waters was such a source of alarm to the Admiralty that it ordered the dispersal of Convoy PQ 17 which led to one of the greatest disasters in British naval history when 23 of the original 36 merchant ships were sunk by either aircraft or submarines. A more recent and extreme example of the strategic value of a single ship is that of HMS *Endurance*, an ice-patrol ship armed with only two 20mm Oerlikon guns, whose main purpose 'in being' (though not everybody would agree with this) was as a symbol of British resolve to protect its interests in the South Atlantic. The move to withdraw the *Endurance* was misunderstood and, as a result, South Georgia and the Falkland Islands were invaded by Argentina. It is not a mistake that Nelson would have made; in a letter to a friend he wrote: 'I hate your pen and ink men, a fleet of British ships are the best negotiators in Europe'.

Despite such notable failures, it was, none the less, the British who, in the 19th century, raised the concept of 'fleets in being' to a diplomatic art form. The Royal Navy was never just there to fight battles and defend the realm, it was also there to express capability or intent, or, put another way, to intimidate and coerce. This carefully contrived display of muscle was also used to cement together a network of friendly countries (sometimes called the 'unofficial' empire) that helped buttress and protect the actual empire.

Geography and empire

This brings us to the matter of geography, in which regard our discussion can be divided into two parts: Britain's exploitation of the passive geographic realities at home and its creative use of geography abroad.

The natural geographic features and, to a certain extent, meteorology of Great Britain conferred upon it certain advantages. Britain's neighbours had long vulnerable borders which meant they had to invest a large part of their resources in a standing army, whereas Britain, by contrast, could concentrate a far greater proportion of the nation's wealth upon its navy. Moreover, Britain had better ports than those of Western France or Spain and, in addition, there was the manner in which the island of Britain itself acted as a physical barrier between the nations of Northern Europe and the Atlantic. All North European ships had either to pass through the English Channel or to sail around Scotland. This stranglehold, which was especially irksome to the Dutch, was a major influence on both strategy and tactics in many of Britain's wars with its neighbours,

particularly the Anglo-Dutch Wars of the 17th century.

Britain also had the advantage in blockading operations. During the age of sail it was far easier for Britain to pinion its enemies than vice versa. For instance, the westerlies that might force a British blockading fleet to withdraw to the shelter of England would also serve to confine the enemy to port; and when the winds had abated or changed, the British would be back on station before the French had time to mobilize.

Obviously Britain's proximity to France, Spain and Holland helped in blockading operations, but it also had its disadvantages. For instance, were the navy to let down its guard for but an instant, a poised invasion force could be in London within several days. As Napoleon observed, 'The Channel is but a ditch and will be crossed as soon as someone has the courage to attempt it'. In 1804, he said, 'Let us be master of the straits for six hours and we shall be masters of the world'. This meant that in Britain's wars with its neighbours part of its strategy had always to be defensive.

Just as distance made Britain vulnerable to attack from France, so too was it a major consideration in Britain's strikes against the continent. Never was this more critical than in the planning for D-Day. The obvious place for the Allies to land was Pas de Calais (from where just two months before Trafalgar, Napoleon planned to pounce with his 161,000 troops and 2,300 boats), but, as the Admiralty soon pointed out, there was not enough sea room in the Straits of Dover for the invasion fleet of 1,213 warships and 4,126 landing and support vessels to operate, not to mention the prodigious logistics train that had to follow. Only off the south of England was there adequate room spread over a distance that an armada might cross undetected in a single night. It had to be Normandy.

In all Britain's conflicts with Europe, controlling the Channel and often the North Sea approaches, was fundamental to a successful outcome. Never was this more important than during World War I when Britain was able to close down the Channel so successfully (with mines and patrols) that the only navigable seaway left was that between the Kent coast and the Goodwin Sands, a passage that no enemy ship would hazard. In the north, Britain was able to choke off all Germany's trade routes (with the notable exception of that with Sweden) by patrolling the 300 miles between the Shetlands and Norway and also the waters between Scotland and Greenland.[14] The effect on the Central Powers was so catastrophic, that, in the end, it was not the armies that collapsed, but Germany itself.

A more remarkable achievement, however, was Britain's 'creative' use of geography, for it was through this that she fulfilled the prophesy which opened this essay, and which, by extension, left an indelible mark upon the globe in the form of the English language, the lingua franca of the modern age.

Through the naked and unabashed use of sea power, Britain grew to dominate the principal seaways of the world. Control of the web depended upon a nexus of friendly ports or outposts that included such places as the West Indies, St

Helena, Ascension, the Falklands, Cape Town, Freetown, Mombassa, Suez, Aden, the Persian Gulf, Ceylon, Singapore, Hong Kong, Australia, New Zealand, Gibraltar, Malta and Port Said. Wherever the sea-lanes converged, more often than not they were held by the British. From such bases and dependencies British influence frequently swept the hinterland. It was the biggest empire in history. By the time of the Great Queen's death in 1901, she was mistress of over a quarter of the world's population and almost a quarter or its land-mass. But despite the surface area that came under British hegemony, the Empire in its essentials, was a maritime empire which, to protect, service and exploit, depended on a large, well organized navy that could replenish and function efficiently in self-contained units for long periods far distant from home. That, for instance, two of the Royal Navy ships which feature in this volume, ended up in such remote parts as the River Plate and Patagonia, is no mystery; they were simply on the South American station at the time, helping to protect Britain's trade and performing their part in the role of the world's self-appointed policeman.

It cannot be denied that British imperialism was motivated by self-interest, but equally it cannot be denied that there was a keen awareness in Britain that they could and should, and by and large *did*, operate as a force for good on the globe. Certainly the British Empire, through the exercise of its maritime might, framed an unprecedented period of world peace - the Pax Britannica - during which time its fighting ships, amongst other things, single-handedly eradicated slavery (an achievement for which the Royal Navy never seems to receive any credit).

Economic warfare

Being an island with a far-flung empire meant that both Britain and its holdings were vulnerable to 'economic warfare', or what the French call *guerre de course*, commerce destruction. Never was this more evident than during the World Wars when, for instance, in 1939, a single German surface raider, the *Graf Spee*, operating in the South Atlantic could hold the Royal Navy to ransom for two and a half months.[15] Similarly, in 1941, no less than forty-eight warships had to be taken off other duties to hunt down and destroy the *Bismarck*.

In both World Wars it was the German U-boat fleet that came closest to defeating Britain through its rigorous prosecution of economic warfare. After Jutland in World War I the Germans concentrated on submarines. Soon Britain was in crisis. Ships that had travelled from some distant dot of empire on the other side of the world were being sunk within sight of their destinations. The low point came in April 1917 when 430 ships were lost. Almost too late Britain rediscovered the convoy system, a solution that had proven itself during the Revolutionary and Napoleonic wars, but which somehow had slipped from naval memory during the age of the mechanized fighting ship. Instead of many opportunities to strike against many 'sitting ducks' the U-boats now had only one target and few offensive opportunities, and when they did attack there was now always the counter-attack.

11 In March 1997 Oxford University MARE in collaboration with the Uruguayan navy and the National Department of Heritage recovered an iron gun from the wreck of HMS *Agamemnon* in the River Plate. The *Agamemnon* had been commanded by Nelson during the French Revolutionary War. It was his favourite ship. Here, vessels from the Uruguayan navy prepare to raise the gun

18

12 The gun on deck. The *Agamemnon* fought in Nelson's column at the battle of Trafalgar. This is the only securely identifiable gun to have been fired at the battle

In World War II Britain's principal naval objective was once again to blockade Germany and to defeat the submarine menace with the convoy system. Britain, however, had been slow to rearm, and, as a result, had less than thirty escorts to protect its convoys in the Western Approaches. In the end it was Germany which, through a well orchestrated submarine

13 The paddle-driven warship *Terrible* at Woolwich. The paddles made such vessels vulnerable to cannon fire and compromised the space that was available for the broadside batteries

campaign, blockaded Britain. Doenitz had wanted to start the war with 300 U-boats that could operate in co-ordinated packs; he was, however, given only 56. If Hitler had been a better admiral and had given Doenitz his submarines, there can be little doubt that Britain, whose navy was woefully unprepared for war, would soon have been forced to the negotiating table. In the end it was Japan, which had the best navy in the world, that suffered the fate that could have been Britain's. Like Britain, Japan was an island that was totally dependent on its mercantile fleets. After Pearl Harbor the United States began a campaign of unrestricted submarine warfare that soon established an economic blockade of the island which held until America was ready to assume the offensive and begin its conquering sweep of the Western Pacific. By the time of the Iwo Jima and Okinawa landings Japan's industry and resupply capability had been bled to exhaustion and its merchant fleet had been virtually annihilated. It was the most complete and successful example of economic warfare that the world had ever seen.

Powered propulsion and ironclads

Although the main focus of this essay has been the Royal Navy under sail, the following few, brutally compressed paragraphs, will, for the sake of thoroughness, attempt to summarize developments through to World War II, the period that both ends this book and sees the demise of British sea power.

Trafalgar was the last great wind-driven fleet action. The age of fighting sail was over. Within seventeen years the navy had commissioned its first steam powered vessel, the

Comet. The rate at which technical innovation followed was bewildering. Materials, propulsion, armour, armament and tactics affected each other as never before. Ships were sometimes out of date even as they slid from the stocks. Weapon systems were frequently obsolete before ever having been tested in battle. Whereas a captain of Trafalgar would have understood and been at home in a ship of three hundred years before, he would have been confused and helpless in a ship of fifty years later.

The Admiralty was slow to grasp the implications of the Industrial Revolution that was taking place within their own backyard and which was, within a few years, to change utterly the nature of naval warfare. It was, in fact, the Americans who launched the first steam-driven warship, the *Fulton* (ex-*Demologos*), in 1814, to protect New York from the British during the war of 1812.[16] In 1821 the navy purchased the 212 ton *Monkey* and the following year launched its first paddle-wheeler the *Comet*, the principal purpose of which was to function as a tug. However, paddles were vulnerable to gunfire, and, together with their sponsons, occupied nearly a third of the vessel's length thus limiting the number of side-guns that could be carried as well as their arcs of fire (fig 13). Paddle warships never fought a major action but the armed East India Company paddle steamer *Diana*, did play a successful role in the first Burma War (1824-1825) owing, in large part, to its captain, Frederick Marryat, who was in charge of the naval side of the conflict but who now is better remembered for his literary achievements. Later, in 1827, during the Greek War of Independence, the paddler *Karteria* (ex-*Perseverance*) devastated enemy ships with red-hot shot fired from her 68-pounders.

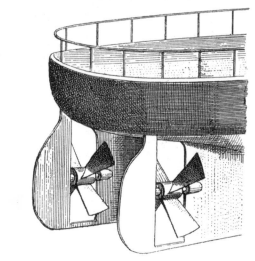

With their usual plodding circumspection (laced with an equally typical frugality) the Admiralty was slow to appreciate the thrust that a helical blade immersed at the stern might impart to a hull (fig 14). In 1843 the Americans once more led the way with the launch of their 10-gun, screw-driven sloop *Princeton*. The following year the *Dauntless* was laid down, the first British naval fighting ship powered by steam. The *Dauntless*, however, was not a successful design; her speed was disappointing and although her propeller was beyond the reach of shot the device itself was not well pitched and the full-bodied stern prevented the flow of water that was necessary to give the propeller effective bite. In addition, vibration caused difficulties.

By 1852, with the launch of the 91-gun *Agamemnon* (not to be confused with Nelson's *Agamemnon* of pages 249-257), the problems of screw propulsion were beginning to be resolved. The *Agamemnon* was the first British capital ship to be design-fitted with screw propulsion, but this, however,

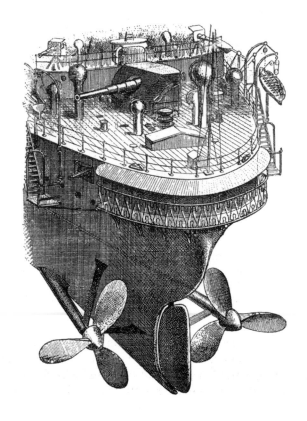

14 The first patent for a method of propelling ships with a revolving 'screw' was taken out in 1785 but it was not until 1844 that the Admiralty ordered the *Dauntless*, the first Royal Navy ship that was designed to fight under screw-propulsion. To begin with there were many problems with the shape of the stern, slip and pitch, but by 1899 early destroyers like the *Viper* (the first British warship to be fitted with steam turbines), could command speeds of 34 knots

15 *Top* HMS *Agamemnon* was the first 'line' ship designed to take steam machinery. She was in every other respect a sailing vessel. Her great broad stern was ill-suited for screw propulsion. She distinguished herself at the bombardment of Sebastopol where she led in the English squadron and with her large pivot gun bombarded the shore batteries from a range of only 750 yards

16 *Above* In 1853 the greater destructive power of shell-fire over solid shot was demonstrated at Sinope where a Turkish fleet was destroyed by a smaller Russian squadron

was seen as no more than an auxiliary power source, for in every other respect she was a traditional sailing ship. None the less, she was a successful design and at the bombardment of Sebastopol in 1854 she acquitted herself with distinction by being able to manoeuvre herself closer to the enemy than any of the sailing ships, from which position she was able to lay down a more effective spread of fire (fig 15).

Together with the radical changes in propulsion there was a concomitant revolution in the design of artillery and projectiles, which led to the introduction of the ironclad. In its early form, as its name implies, this was simply a wooden hull sheathed in iron. The first ironclad was the French warship *Gloire* completed in 1859, but, as befitting the 'workshop of the world', Britain was not slow to respond and the following year launched the metal-hulled *Warrior* (see ASW, 155-165).

Artillery

In many ways the first step away from the traditional cannon that fired solid round shot, came with the introduction of shell-fire. Explosive shells and 'carcasses' [17] had proven their value in 1788 when, in the Sea of Azov, a squadron of Russian long boats, that had been armed and equipped by Sir Samuel Bentham, devastated a much larger force of Turkish ships. The technique and theories of shell-fire were developed further by the French artillery expert Henri-Joseph Paixhans in the 1820s, but they were not put to the test until 1853 when, at Sinope, a smaller Russian squadron once more destroyed a larger wooden Turkish fleet that was radiating conventional fire (fig 16). Two years later the French, in four hours, devastated the Kinburn forts at the mouth of the Dnieper with a flotilla of specially designed, armoured, steam-powered, shell-firing, floating batteries.

By that time it was evident that a small number of large calibre guns, particularly shell-firing guns, had greater destructive and incendiary power than a large number of traditional, small, smooth-bore, muzzle-loading cannon of the type featured in fig 17. The existing offence-defence equilibrium had been upset. Timber was no longer offering adequate protection; worse, it had become a liability. Britain's wooden walls that had served so well for so many centuries, had now to be encased in protective armour against which round shot was ineffective. To overcome this

17 A traditional smooth-bore, muzzle-loading, spherical shot cannon. Improvements in armour protection and warship design made it obsolete

metal cladding, the penetrating and destructive power of shipborne ordnance had to improve.

The first rifled cannons were issued soon after the Crimean War. At the same time spherical shot and shells were replaced by cylindrical projectiles. The reduced air resistance resulted in a lower trajectory and improved accuracy, range and striking velocity. As with shell fire, France again led the way, but soon Joseph Whitworth and Sir William Armstrong were producing outstanding rifled artillery. One Whitworth naval gun in the early 1860s was able to fire shot five and a half miles. By then guns were no longer being cast as a single piece but rather were much stronger composite constructions made up of hammer-welded components. Amstrong's gun, which featured polygroove rifling, was particularly interesting for its breech-loading mechanism (fig 18). In 1863 a gun of this type, loaded with an explosive shell, was tested successfully against a target off Shoeburyness that had been modelled on a section of the *Warrior* (fig 19). None the less, controversy between muzzle- and breech-loading raged and in 1864 Britain reverted to muzzle-loading which it retained until an explosion within the barrel of a 12-inch rifled muzzle-loader (RML) on HMS *Thunderer* in 1879 led to the reintroduction of the breech-loader.

One of the most important innovations of the 1860s was 'Palliser shot' (after Sir William Palliser). With these cylindrical projectiles the core was filled with explosive that was ignited by the shock of impact and burst immediately after penetration. Another major advance took place in the 1880s with the introduction of 'fixed' rounds, that is to say brass cartridges with the projectile attached, which, together with the new sliding breach block, led to the development of the quick-firing gun. Further developments occurred in 1885 with compound armour piercing shells, and in the 1890s with new propellants such as cordite and, in the same decade, with armour piercing shell caps and base fuses that

Cartridge for smooth bore Gun

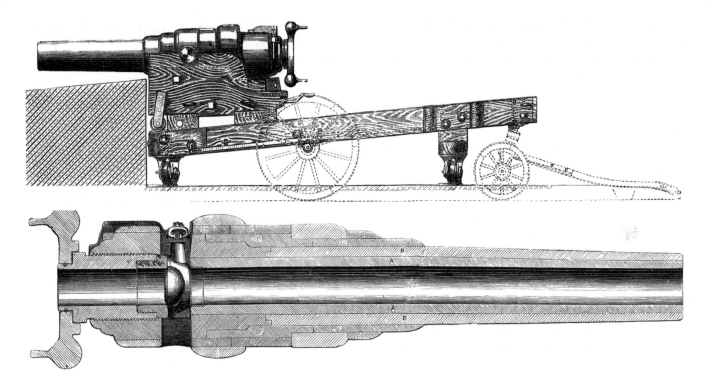

18 An Armstrong gun

ignited the high explosive contained within the body of the shell. By the end of the century naval guns had reached a level of technology that did not change significantly until after World War II. The changes that did occur mostly had to do with loading, sighting, range finding and other fine points of gun laying.

The extended range and greater potency of the big guns meant that shells were following a longer trajectory that ended in a fairly low parabolic curve. Shells were not, therefore, making right-angle contact with their targets, but rather were hitting at fairly oblique angles which compromised their penetrative capability. It was the Germans who perfected a new kind of capped armour-piercing shell with a reliable base fuse that could both penetrate and devastate an enemy ship from a 15 degree angle of attack. A good example of the destructive power of the new generation of shells can be taken from the Battle of the River Plate in 1939, the last broadside battle. In this engagement the German 'pocket' battleship *Graf Spee* was able to open effective fire on the British cruiser squadron at a distance of 11 miles. At that range an 11-inch, base-fused 670 pound shell was in the air for over a minute. One such shell from the *Spee* entered the deck of HMS *Ajax* at an angle of 35 degrees. It first ripped through three cabins, then smashed its way across the ammunition lobby of X turret (where splinters killed four men and wounded five) before slamming off the angle irons which drove it upwards through the gun's working chamber (where it killed two more), from where it ploughed through more bulkheads before finally exploding in the admiral's cabin. In the meantime the shell's base plug had been blown aft where it jammed Y turret and gave off a spray of splinters which

sliced through the main power circuits causing loss of light and flooding [18] (Pope, 1989, 38). Artillery had come a long way since the solid, round-shot of Nelson's day.

From the Crimean War up to the sinking of the *Hood* in World War II it had been clear that big guns sank ships, but thereafter the age of the big gun had passed to be replaced by aircraft, torpedoes and missiles.

New types of fighting ships
While these developments had been happening significant changes had also been taking place with regard to the manipulation and disposition of heavy shipboard ordnance which meant departing from the traditional arrangement of broadside batteries. The 1862 Battle of Hampton Roads, during the American Civil War between the *Monitor* and *Merrimack* (see 287-293), was a revelation for Britain and the other European countries that had been without a good stand-up fight of their own in which to test the recent developments in plating and armament. One result of Hampton Roads in the Royal Navy (drawing its inspiration from the *Monitor*), was the concentration of a small number of powerful, turret-mounted guns in a 'citadel' amidship. The finest exponent of this new type of vessel was the *Inflexible*, laid down in 1874 (fig 21). The problem with such designs, however, was that the arc of fire was limited by masts, rigging, breastwork and general superstructure. Experiments followed with indented side-emplacements, ahead-firing bow guns and superimposed central batteries. Owing in part to the influence and inventive genius of Captain Cowper Coles, all-round turreted fire slowly became accepted (fig 23) and in 1873 the navy's first modern battleship, the *Devastation*, was launched. In

23

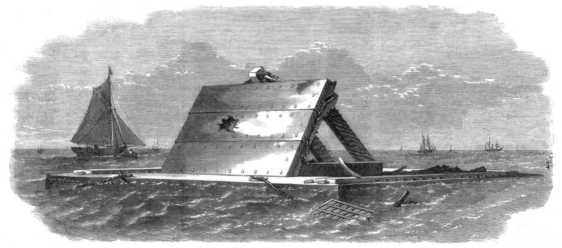

19 *Opposite* In 1863 Sir William Armstrong's shunt-gun (Big-Will), loaded with a 600-pound shell, was tested off Shoeburyness. The floating target, which had been constructed to represent the side of the *Warrior*, consisted of 4 1/2 inch thick iron plating bolted to 18 inches of teak and another iron plate. The cylindrical shell had a thin cast-iron nose with solid iron at rear. On striking, the nose (which contained a charge of powder) was crushed and ignited the charge. Because of its size the shell was visible during flight. The Times reported that 'the plates of the target (were) so torn and rent, and the timber backing so much shivered, that no repairs will ever render it fit to be again experimented upon'. (*Illustrated London News*, Dec. 26, 1863 and Jan 9, 1864)

20 In March 1997 Oxford University MARE in collaboration with the Uruguayan navy and National Department of Heritage recovered a 150mm gun from the wreck of the German 'pocket' battleship *Graf Spee* which was scuttled in the River Plate in December 1939 following a battle with the Royal Navy cruisers *Exeter, Ajax, Achilles*. In the first illustration the great lifting barge *Triton* moves out of Montevideo to take up station over the battleship. The following two illustrations show the gun raised from the sea

addition to her 12-inch muzzle-loading, centre-line, end turrets she was iron-hulled and fully steam driven (without any auxiliary sail capability). The 1870s, which had seen much thought concerning the nature of big fighting ships and their tactical deployment, culminated in the *Collingwood*, one of the most successful big-gun ships of the era and one which became the basis of several future classes of warship (fig 22).

This period was also characterized by the advent of the mine (fig 24), the torpedo and the submarine. These led to new classes of ships and to a completely new doctrine of tactics. The first mines (then called torpedoes) were used in 1855 by the Russians in the Baltic. In 1866 Captain Luppis of the Austrian navy produced the locomotive torpedo and although they were launched in anger by the British in 1877,[19] it was not until the following year that they were employed with success by the Russians against the Turks in Batum Harbour; but they were a long way from perfection

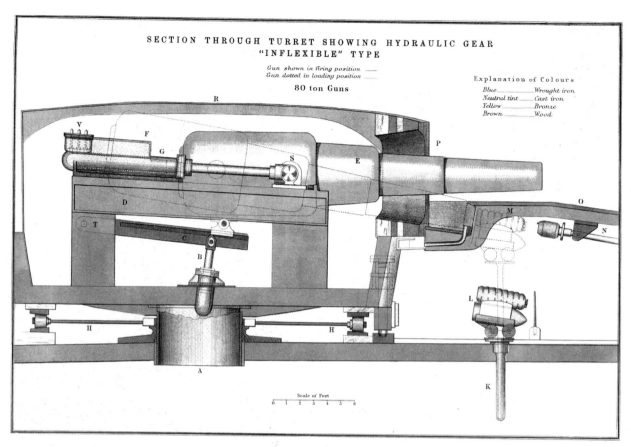

SECTION THROUGH TURRET SHOWING HYDRAULIC GEAR
"INFLEXIBLE" TYPE

Gun shown in firing position ———
Gun dotted in loading position ——————

80 ton Guns

Explanation of Colours

Blue	Wrought iron
Neutral tint	Cast iron
Yellow	Bronze
Brown	Wood

Scale of Feet
0 1 2 3 4 5 6

W.E.A

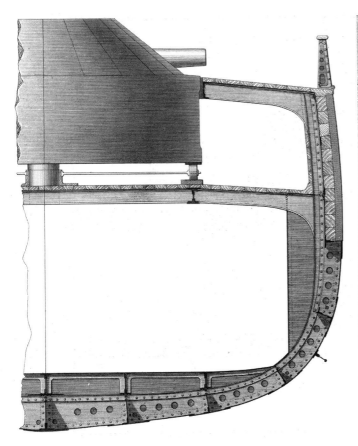

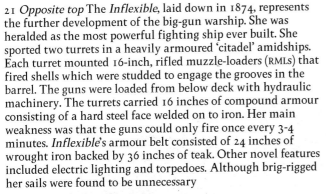

21 *Opposite top* The *Inflexible*, laid down in 1874, represents the further development of the big-gun warship. She was heralded as the most powerful fighting ship ever built. She sported two turrets in a heavily armoured 'citadel' amidships. Each turret mounted 16-inch, rifled muzzle-loaders (RMLs) that fired shells which were studded to engage the grooves in the barrel. The guns were loaded from below deck with hydraulic machinery. The turrets carried 16 inches of compound armour consisting of a hard steel face welded on to iron. Her main weakness was that the guns could only fire once every 3-4 minutes. *Inflexible*'s armour belt consisted of 24 inches of wrought iron backed by 36 inches of teak. Other novel features included electric lighting and torpedoes. Although brig-rigged her sails were found to be unnecessary

22 *Opposite bottom* The *Collingwood* not only represents the total abandonment of sail propulsion, but was also the first of a new type of battleship to emerge in the 1880s which became the basis of many future classes of warship including the all-big-gun dreadnoughts. Her principal artillery consisted of twin guns fore and aft on unarmoured barbettes with medium size broadside armament in between (from *The Graphic*, 8 May, 1886)

23 *Above* In Britain Captain Cowper Coles was more responsible than any other for the introduction of the armoured turret

24 *Above right* The 1850s to 1870s saw much experimentation with mines and later, torpedoes

and even by the Battle of Tsushima in 1905 they still had not proven their worth. None the less, fast-attack torpedo boats were a source of concern and led in 1893 to the first destroyers. Over time they evolved into the well-known destroyers of our own era which had their finest hour under

Halsey, in October 1944, at the Battle of Leyte Gulf in the Philippines; in terms of the sizes of the two opposing fleets and the area over which the fighting ranged, this was the biggest sea-battle in history. As a class of ship, the destroyer was only relegated from the Royal Navy in the 1990s.

The submarine, at first no more than an object of curiosity, was soon taken seriously after one of the midget 'Davids' sunk the *Housatonic* in 1864 during the American Civil War. In 1776 one of Bushnell's crude submersibles, the *Turtle*, nearly sank Howe's flagship, the *Eagle*. By the 1890s, John Philip Holland had lifted the development of the submarine to such a level that in 1901 the Admiralty were sufficiently confident to order five submarines of the Holland type.

Another class of vessel, the cruiser, was also in many ways a child of the American Civil War. The Royal Navy laid down its first cruiser in 1866. Over the next twenty years, they became larger, faster and more heavily gunned, evolving first into 'armoured' cruisers and then 'battle' cruisers. They were, essentially, reconnaissance vessels that could locate battle fleets and be swift enough to escape and report back their position. By World War I they were used for both convoy protection and attack. In groups it was found that they could engage a strong enemy. In 1914, after German dreadnoughts sank the British pre-dreadnoughts, *Good Hope* and *Monmouth* off Coronel, Chile, the German squadron was hunted down and destroyed by a posse of British cruisers at the Battle of the Falklands on 14 December 1914 It was also a British cruiser force (Force G: *Exeter*, *Ajax* and *Achilles*) that cornered the German pocket battleship *Graf Spee* in the opening months of World War II.

25 The German High Seas Fleet was interned at Scapa Flow after World War I. On 21 June 1919, the fleet scuttled itself. Of the 52 warships that went to the bottom, 45 were later salvaged. None the less, Scapa Flow remains the finest underwater graveyard of dreadnoughts, pre-dreadnoughts and cruisers in the world

The most famous form of warship to evolve at this time was the dreadnought. The *Devastation* and *Inflexible* had signalled the move away from fighting ships of monitor type towards the modern all-big-gun battleship best epitomized by the *Dreadnought*, the first of its class that was launched in 1886. In the quarter century since the 8-inch, smooth-bore muzzle-loaders of the *Warrior* (1860), both artillery and attitudes had changed dramatically. It was by then fully accepted that bigger and more powerful guns could deliver with more piercing and explosive power over a greater range, than secondary, medium-bore side ordnance which, except for anti-torpedo and, later, anti-aircraft purposes, had become somewhat redundant. In addition, uniform salvo-firing big guns also made range-finding easier, and of course, being able to fight at long distance, largely negated the threat of torpedoes. Twelve-inch guns, such as were on the *Dreadnought*, thus became the norm for big ships.

Just as the *Dreadnought* could outshoot any other vessel, so too could it outsteam anything else then afloat. Being the first large warship to be fitted with turbines, she could reach a speed of about 21 knots. This was an important tactical

consideration for the new generation of big ships, for not only did the faster vessel have the option of declining an action, but also, to a certain extent, it could choose the range. Never was speed and superior firepower more important than at the Battle of Tsushima during the Russo-Japanese War of 1904-5, the first great ironclad engagement in which the Russian navy was annihilated (14 battleships and 5 armoured cruisers sunk) by the 12-inch guns of Admiral Togo. Furthermore, because of its greater speed the Japanese navy was able to stay in contact with the Russian fleet after it withdrew.

The battleship, which was born with the 20th century, died with the 20th century. Its reign was short and ended with the Battle of Jutland in 1916. In World War II battleships performed something of a secondary role; certainly they played an important part in the fighting around the Marianas in 1944, but they were mainly used to provide cover for convoys and aircraft carriers and to lay down pre-invasion bombardment and close support fire once the troops were ashore. Although bombers could deliver a greater weight of explosive, the big naval guns were more accurate. In this latter role battleships were vital at Salerno and at Anzio where they broke up enemy counter-attacks, at the Normandy landings (particularly on Omaha Beach) and in the Pacific where they were invaluable in the long-drawn fighting at Guadalcanal in the Solomons.

One problem of the battleship was that, for such an expensive vessel, it presented a fat and sometimes relatively easy target. Its vulnerability to torpedo attack was first demonstrated in 1914 when the British submarine *B11* passed under five rows of mines in the Dardanelles to sink the Turkish battleship *Messudieh*. During World War II midget submarines destroyed the *Tirpitz* whilst a conventional submarine, Gunther Prien's *U-47*, managed to infiltrate Scapa Flow and sink the *Royal Oak*. The most recent example of big ship vulnerability came from the Falklands War when the British submarine *Conqueror* easily sank the *Belgrano* (formerly the *Phoenix* that had survived the attack on Pearl Harbor and fought with distinction in the Battle of Leyte Gulf). Battleships were equally assailable from the air. In South East Asia Japanese planes quickly dispatched the British battleships *Prince of Wales* and *Repulse*; in the Atlantic aircraft crippled the *Bismarck*, and in the Mediterranean Cunningham's aerial assault on big ships in Taranto Harbour bludgeoned the Italian navy into a virtual state of surrender. In the attack on Pearl Harbor no less than seven battleships were sunk by Yamamoto's pilots.

After World War II, battleships played a much reduced role. They pounded shore-based stations in Korea and Vietnam and in February 1991, during 'Desert Storm', the World War II battleship *Missouri* (upon which the Tokyo Bay treaty had been signed) bombarded Kuwait and Khafji in Northern Saudi Arabia and fired tomahawk missiles at Iraq. The United States is now the only nation still operating battleships. Britain's last one, the *Vanguard*, (in fact the last one to be built anywhere in the world) was scrapped in 1960, thus ending a tradition of 'Great Shypes' that went all the way back to the *Henri Grâce à Dieu* of Henry VIII (fig 1).

At the beginning of World War II the battleship was still viewed as the 'Queen of the Fleet' but by 1941 the aircraft carrier had become, and has been ever since (together with the missile), 'the pre-eminent battle-winner at sea'. The Battle of Cape Matapan had pointed the way, and the carrier-borne attack on Pearl Harbor had confirmed what naval theoreticians had been thinking, but the real turning point came in May 1942 with the battle of the Coral Sea in which an American carrier fleet won a strategic victory over a similar Japanese force without either side ever coming within sight of the other. The following month the two sides met again at the battle of Midway. Again it was fought from over the horizon, but this time it was a decisive American victory; four Japanese carriers went down. Since World War II both naval operations as well as land-based campaigns have depended for their success upon air supremacy over the theatre, thus the role of the carrier has remained one of foremost importance. Carriers have played a fundamental part in almost all the major engagements since 1945, for example they were essential in the Gulf War and, of course, they were the knuckles of Britain's long strike against Argentina in 1982.

Once the United States had shaken itself free of the paralysis that followed Pearl Harbor, it focused its wealth and almost infinite resources upon the creation of a navy the like of which the world had never seen before. By 1943 it was completing one destroyer every three days. By the end of the war it had 23 carriers in commission and almost as many again on the stocks. The United States' navy came out of the war much stronger than when it went in. Britain, by contrast, had been left exhausted and impoverished by the defeat of the Axis powers. During the infamous winter of 1947, Britain's operational home-waters fleet consisted of no more than one cruiser and three destroyers. Thus, after two and a half centuries the mantle of sea power had passed to the Americans.

Afterword

As this book goes to press (1997) it is exactly one hundred years since Queen Victoria reviewed the fleet at Spithead to mark her Diamond Jubilee, 'Sixty glorious years'. It was the largest and finest collection of fighting ships that the world had ever seen under one flag. 165 warships stretched over five miles. And this was only half the fleet. Today Britain's surface navy numbers no more than 35 frigates and destroyers and three small carriers. True, the Empire now represents no more than 180,000 souls, its merchant fleet has been allowed to perish and the Cold War is over, but none the less, Britain is still an island with shores to safeguard, it still has overseas responsibilities and duties within NATO, there is still terrorism, and there are still trade-lanes, fisheries and oil fields to protect. Above all, there are still ideologically and territorially predatory nations in the world.

Also as this book goes to press it is exactly two hundred years since Sir John Jervis triumphed over the Spanish off Cape St Vincent. These days the battle is remembered as just another in a line of spectacular British naval victories of the period, but behind this one was something altogether more sinister. The Spanish squadron was on its way north to join the combined fleets of France and Holland for an intended invasion of England. Since then there have been two more planned invasions, and of course numerous other conflicts around the globe that have involved Britain. In fact, the 20th century has seen more wars and greater wars than any other. To think that war cannot again touch Britain is foolish in the extreme. Yet this year (1997) the Prime Minister was reported as saying, 'Mine is the first generation able to contemplate the possibility that we may live our entire lives without going to war, or sending our children to war'. To any student of history such thoughts of peace in our time are icily familiar. In 1792 Pitt the Younger made a similar boast, yet the following year Britain was locked in a struggle with Revolutionary France that lasted a quarter of a century. In 1914 Britain was again caught unprepared, as it was once more in the 1930s. It is a habit of international conflicts, that they rise quickly and often from unexpected quarters. Even when the enemy is screaming out its intentions (as with Hitler in the 1930s and the Argentine generals before the Falklands War) the politicians still cannot see, or do not want to see, where events are leading. In 1981 there was a Defence Review Committee, which, with almost criminal lack of judgement, made cuts to the navy which precipitated the Falklands War. Dangerously ill-equipped because of previous Defence Reviews, an essentially anti-submarine fleet travelled 8,000 miles to mount the largest amphibious assault since World War II against an overwhelmingly superior hostile air power. It had two flawed missile defence systems and no AEW (Airborne Early Warning). Only 19 Sea Harriers stood between the Task Force and disaster. That they succeeded was a tribute to the men rather than the machines.

We are currently in the middle of another Defence Review. There is good reason to worry: politicians are never so dangerous as when they cannot see the enemy. To down-grade and down-size is quick and easy; to rearm (as was found to the nation's cost in the 1930s) takes years. Although the whole nature of warfare has changed and even though Britain is currently at peace, history tells us that this cannot last. Albion still requires its chariots of fire - a fleet of strong and versatile fighting ships.

Notes

1 Over half the fighting ships in this and its companion volume, *The Archaeology of Ships of War* (ASW), are Royal Navy vessels, an unintended imbalance but one that reflects the size and world-wide activities of the Royal Navy since Elizabethan times. Because this is an archaeology book the individual chapters have had to concentrate mainly upon the ships as artefacts rather than as functions of history. The primary purpose of this chapter is to help fill that gap by providing a back-drop against which these ships, particularly the British ships, but also some of the non-British ships, can be better understood.

2 The old medieval names for ordnance, such as minion, saker and culverin, remained in use until the second half of the 17th century by which time guns were being described by the weight of the shot they fired (e.g. 24-pounder, 32-pounder, etc.).

3 In fact, of all the Royal Navy ships featured in this volume and its companion volume, *The Archaeology of Ships of War*, not one was lost to cannon fire.

4 The French did not devise anything of comparable destructive power until 1799.

5 Though not always, of course, because of the carronade.

6 This virtually eliminated the time-consuming process of 'worming' to extract the debris.

7 A good example of a flintlock and lanyard on the breach of a naval cannon can be seen in the famous painting in the National Portrait Gallery, London, of Nelson receiving the French colours after the Nile. The painting, by Guy Head (1753-1800) who met Nelson in Naples after the battle, was given by Nelson to Lady Hamilton.

8 Though these were all factors that vacillated enormously during different periods of the Navy's history.

9 Remembering perhaps battles like that of Cape Rachado, in which isolated ships, such as the *Nassau*, were simply overwhelmed and destroyed.

10 Although it was never acknowledged, Clerk must have been familiar with the tactical thought of the Abbé Hoste and Bigot de Morogues whose works were available in English translation in the 1760s.

11 Interestingly, Clerk considered Nelson's tactics at Trafalgar to have been suicidal.

12 It is, however, a little known fact that Jervis gave the signal to 'Engage enemy as arriving up in succession' just seconds before Nelson began to wear ship. Clearly, the same thought was in both men's minds (Kemp, 1976, 431).

13 The original message had been '*Nelson* confides that every man will do his duty'.

14 While also, of course, cordoning off the Mediterranean routes.

15 Nine hunting groups comprising 20 ships were dispatched to find and destroy the *Graf Spee*.

16 The war, however, was over before it could be used.

17 'Carcasses' were lightweight spheres filled with incendiary material.

18 As in Nelson's day it was often the splinters that did the worst damage.

19 By the frigate *Shah* against the Peruvian Monitor *Huascar*.

Further reading

Bound, M. (ed.), 1995 *The Archaeology of Ships of War*, International Maritime Archaeology Series 1, Anthony Nelson, Oswestry.

Caruana, A.B., 1994, *The History of English Sea Ordnance 1523-1875*, vol I, Jean Boudriot publications.

Corbett, J., 1905, *Fighting Instructions, 1530-1816*, Navy Records Society, London.

Cowburn, P., 1966, *The Warship in History*, MacMillan, London.

Hill, J.R. (ed.), 1995, *The Oxford Illustrated History of the Royal Navy*, Oxford University press.

Kemp, P.K., 1976, 'Jervis, John', *The Oxford Companion to Ships and the Sea*, Oxford University Press, 430-431.

Kennedy, P., 1976, *The Rise and Fall of British Naval Mastery*, New York.

Lewis, M.A., 1948, *The Navy of Britain*, George Allen & Unwin, London.

Lewis, M.A., 1961, *Armada Guns*, George Allen & Unwin, London.

Mahan, A.T., 1898, *The Influence of Sea Power upon History, 1660-1783*, Boston.

Marcus, G., 1960, *Heart of Oak*, Oxford University Press.

Pope, D., 1989, *The Battle of the River Plate*, London.

Richmond, H.W., 1946, *Statesmen and Sea Power*, Oxford University Press.

Roskill, S.W., 1954, *History of the Second World War: The War at Sea, 1939-1945*, HMSO, London.

Warner, O., 1959, *Trafalgar*, B.T. Batsford, London.

Manuel Martin Bueno (University of Zaragoza)

Cavoli: A 15th century shipwreck off Sardinia

The development of Medieval and Post-Medieval maritime archaeology in the Mediterranean lags behind that of the earlier periods. None the less, in recent years the balance has begun to improve with serious scholarly investigations taking place on a number of wrecks of the Post-Roman era off the coasts of Italy, France and Spain. Little by little our knowledge of ship construction, navigation and trade during the Medieval and early Post-Medieval periods is expanding.

The excavation carried out by our team on the remains of a ship in Italian waters off Southern Sardinia has added significantly to the picture by providing a valuable insight into seafaring and life at sea in the 15th century. It was a complicated site, but none the less, much was learned about the ship and its contents and we have been able to assemble some of the details of its last voyage, including its port of origin, and the destination it never reached.

Our background understanding of this wreck is set within the Golden Age of Aragon in the 14th century. It was a period in which the Crown of Aragon enjoyed a substantial presence in Southern Italy and the islands of Sicily and Sardinia. Its further control of such strategic locations as Malta, Gozo, Gelves, Querquenas and Rhodes, and its protectorate relationship with several North African nations meant that Aragon rivalled Genoa, Venice, the Papal States, and even the Islamic territories, for power and influence within the Mediterranean. In the 15th century, however, the situation changed, and instead of further territorial aggrandizement the policy of the Aragonese monarchs became one of consolidation and stabilization, but it was not easy and they frequently found themselves in disagreement with either the Papacy, Genoa, Pisa or Venice; the control of the maritime routes being a particular focus of contention.

The Cavoli ship is directly connected with the historical panorama just outlined. Its presence on this vital strategic and commercial route confirms the privileged trading relations between the Spanish Mediterranean ports of Barcelona, Tarragona, Tortosa, Valencia, Mallorca, etc., and those of Naples and Palermo and the intermediary stations of Alghero and Cagliari in Sardinia.

The location, discovery and disposition of the wreck

The wreck is situated off the islet of Cavoli at the southern end of Sardinia, near Cabo Carbonara (fig 1). Apart from light occupation during the Prehistoric era, the island appears to have been uninhabited except for occasional

1 Site of the Cavoli shipweck

fishermen, and, in more recent time, a family which tended the lighthouse until its automation.

The geographic location of the island at a point where several routes converged, and the exposed and hazardous nature of its shores when the 'Mistral' and 'Greek' winds blow, means that numerous shipping losses have occurred there during history.

The wreck remains that are the focus of this paper were found off the north of the island sometime in the early 1970s. We know, for instance, that in 1974, a group of British military divers recovered a considerable amount of material without proper archaeological care or authorization. The present whereabouts of this material is unknown, but it was classified as pottery from a 'Hispanic-Moresque' boat (Fennel, 1974, 331-2). In 1986 a group of Italian divers relocated the site and the following year recovered a considerable number of items, most of which can be classified as cargo or armament. These finds allowed the vessel to be dated to the Medieval period (Martin-Bueno, 1993, 39 ff). The majority of these objects, particularly the breech-loaders and earthenware objects, were stored without regard for conservation and thus have suffered significant, and in some cases irreversible, deterioration.

An excavation was carried out between 1990 and 1991 by a team from the University of Zaragoza with the assistance of the University and Superintendency of Archaeology for Cagliari. The objectives were to determine the state of preservation of the submerged remains and to begin their excavation in a controlled manner with all the proper

conservation facilities (provided by the Italian archaeological authorities) and other skills at hand. The study of the remains was also, of course, an essential part of the programme. Archive research, environmental studies and sediment analyses were also carried out before excavation proper began, and in addition, magnetometer and metal detector surveys were conducted. A full record of the site and the campaign in general was made on video and 16mm celluloid. In all these matters we received vital help from our Italian collaborators.

Headquarters were established in the mainland town of Villasimius, from where the team commuted to Cavoli in light boats. With the help of a helicopter a small laboratory was also set up on the island for immediate conservation care.

A light PVC grid was constructed over the irregular seabed. Dredges were used to remove the sand. Technically speaking, Cavoli was not a difficult excavation, the depth was fairly shallow (12-18m) and sea conditions were generally favourable. The main problem was the posedonia grass that covered most of the timberwork and other principal deposits to a depth of a metre or more. Fortunately, on the western side of the site from where most of the pottery had come, the posedonia thinned to almost nothing.

There were two main concentrations of material separated by about 50m of seabed but none the less linked by a debris trail of ceramic fragments (fig 2). The division between these two areas has lead some researchers (D'Agostino, 1987, 1988)

2 *Above left* Ceramic remains

3 *Top right* Hull timbers

4 *Above right* Timbers prepared for lifting

to propose that the Cavoli remains represent two separate wrecks (and to speculate further that they might have been galleys lost as the result of piratical activities). Our studies of the materials and the manner of their dispersal, confirm, however, that these deposits are from a single shipwreck and seem to prove that the hull broke into at least two separate sections after she struck the rocks.

Relatively little of the hull survived. Several concentrations of timbers were found, but in each case the wood was much fragmented and in an advanced state of deterioration. Presumably the relatively shallow disposition of the remains meant that they were vulnerable to wave and current action; and it may be that salvage work soon after the vessel's loss was also massively destructive. The lesser deposits had evidently experienced post-depositional movement along the seabed, and this had clearly contributed to their more advanced decay.

The principal hull assemblage, situated within the main wreck deposit, covered about 12 square metres (fig 3, 4, 5 and 6). These timbers came from the vessel's lower hull and consisted of frames, futtocks, flooring, ceiling and exterior cladding. Some smaller timber pieces were used to buttress

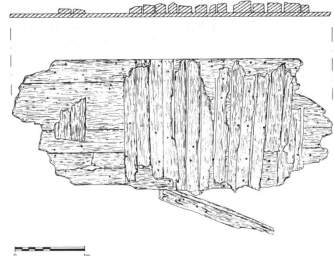

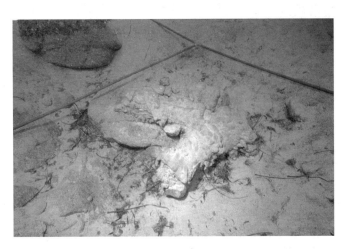

5 *Above* Raising the timbers

6 *Top right* Drawing of hull timbers

7 *Lower right* Concreted iron cannon

and reinforce the frames. The fastening of the timbers was achieved by dowels and wrought iron nails whose heads were covered in lead to discourage oxidation. Analysis revealed that the wood was of Spanish Mediterranean origin.

From the same zone came several concreted pieces of wrought iron heavy ordnance, two breech-chambers and two smaller deck pieces (fig 7). Concretion and general poor preservation prevented their typological identifications. Swords, crossbow fragments and some earthenware sherds came from the same area.

The other principal area of seabed investigation (to the west) consisted almost entirely of ceramic remains. These pieces had been much dispersed and abraded, both in the distant past and more recently. They comprised wall and floor tiles and a remarkable number of fragments from storage jars and kitchenware; clearly there were far too many containers on board for the requirements of the ship and its crew.

Ordnance and conservation

During the campaigns preliminary conservation was given by the team (Martin-Bueno, 1993, 67 ff). A programme of

sampling was carried out to determine the best procedures for each category of object. It had been our original intention to recover the main timber assemblage and artillery pieces and administer their conservation in existing specialist facilities at the University of Zaragoza. In the end the responsibility for this was assumed by the Superintendency of Archaeology for Cagliari, but nothing has yet been done and the remains are still on the seabed protected by a covering of sand. Some of the ordnance-related items recovered by the Italian authorities in 1987 (Soprintendenza, 1991) have, however, been gathered together, but their previous neglect has meant that the results of the care they have now received are not ideal. Better results have been achieved with the conservation of the ceramic material and some of the small objects.

The ordnance consisted of wrought iron bombards, their main component parts being the barrel and a breech-chamber which took the charge and the shot. Six of the guns were over 3m long, two measured between 2.45m and 2.60m, and there were several smaller pieces, almost certainly falconets. Surprisingly little shot was recovered (certainly nothing approaching the official issue of 20

33

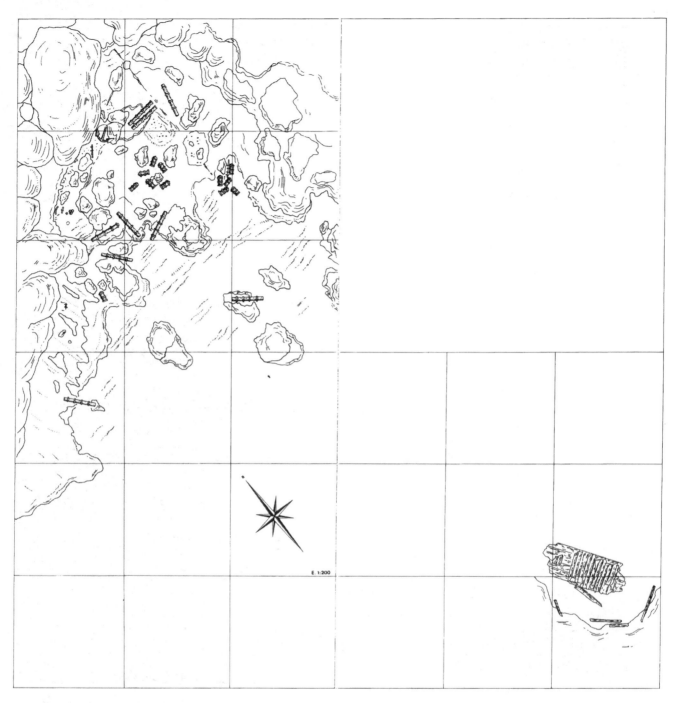

E. 1:200

8 Distribution map of the guns from the Cavoli ship

charges per gun); or it is possible that much of this was salvaged soon after the vessel's loss, or was taken by aqualung divers during recent times. The shot we ourselves recovered was both of stone and iron and reflected a variety of bores. Small-bore lead shot was also found; this came from muskets and perhaps also pistols.

Ceramics

The ceramics, which represented a considerable part of the cargo, have provided a secure means of dating the ship. The tiles, because of the heraldic devices which some of them displayed, were evidently intended for the ornamentation of

a palace belonging to the Becadelli family who served the Aragonese monarchs in the 15th century. The device consisted of a three winged crane's feet (fig 9). In 1450 the family was permitted the right to place their coat of arms alongside that of their Royal patron. The absence on the tiles of the Aragonese coat of arms gives a *Terminus ante quem* for the wreck of 1450. The activities and positions held by the family in Naples and Palermo during the Aragonese consolidation of their Italian territories, give us a lower chronological bracket for the wreck of 1425. Antonio Becadelli, the most important member of the family during this period, enjoyed the trust and favour of

Manises provenance. Archive documents exist which record orders for tiles decorated with the royal coat of arms of Aragon and the Two Sicilies, or the Kingdom of Naples, for rooms at the Palace of the King of Naples who even hired a master-tiler to oversee their installation from May to September 1447. The consignments of tiles for the Neapolitan Court lasted until the death of King Alfonso V in 1458 (fig 10). It would therefore seem that the Cavoli ship was one of the vessels involved in this rather unusual one-way royal trade.

9 Tile with the arms of the Becadelli family who served the Aragonese monarchs of the 15th century

10 Naples in the 15th century

King Alfonso the Magnanimous of Aragon who bestowed on him ecclesiastical appointments, such as the cardinalship of Palermo, which he later abandoned to return to his function as Secretary of the Royal Chancellery in Naples.

The tiles, including the table ware, have their origin in the 15th century Valencian workshops of the Manises area. It is known that much of the ceramic trade from that period and place was produced to order, the customer presented the design he desired, and the manufacturer undertook its production (Lopez Elum, 1984). The 'ruedavientos'-type designs on the 160mm x 160mm floor tiles can also be dated to the first half of the 15th century and further support a

The tableware on board included forms glazed in cobalt blue and gold veneer. Most of these pots were open shapes, i.e. bowls, dishes, plates and basins, but also there were beautifully painted water jugs, candlestick holders and several ornamental pieces (Martin-Bueno, 1993, 77 ff). There were also some plain or plain-glazed earthenware forms, cooking pots and storage containers which presumably came from the ship's galley. Of particular note in this category were mortars (fig 13), albarelli (fig 14), large vats and a series of glazed bowls and pitchers. All these pots date from the second half of the 14th century to the end of the first half of the 15th century.

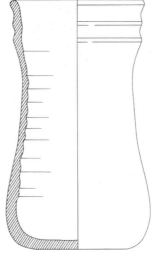

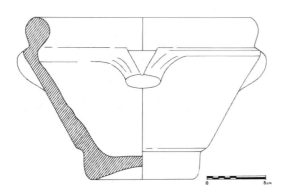

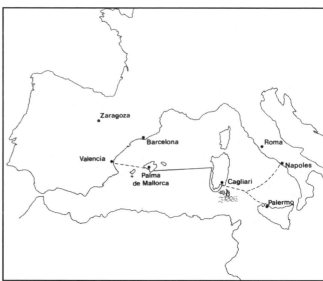

11 *Top left* 15th century Manises pottery

12 *Above left* 15th century pottery from Manises (Valencia)

13 *Left* 15th century mortar from Manises (Valencia)

14 *Top right* 15th century albarello

15 *Above* Route of the Cavoli ship from Valencia

A lead seal used for consignments of textiles, and bearing the city arms of Mallorca, is a certain indication that the vessel was also carrying bales of cloth. This item can be dated to the same period (Martin-Bueno, 1993, 86).

Route and conclusion (fig 15)

We cannot be certain what type of vessel the Cavoli ship represents, but the finds do allow us to trace its route. The evidence suggests that it began its voyage from a port on the Spanish Levant, almost certainly in Valencia where the tiles

bearing the arms of the Bacadelli family were loaded. It then made a stop at Mallorca (fig 16) to take on textiles before departing for the Aragonese port of either Alghero or Cagliari, from whence it would have continued to Palermo. While rounding Cabo Carbonara, however, she ran into adverse weather conditions which caused her to seek shelter between the two headlands which shape the islet of Cavoli. Here she hit the rocks with such violence that she took the sea and sank. The hull split in two; one half, which bore the artillery and part of the cargo, remained near the shore close

16 Mallorca in the 15th century

to where she struck; the other part, which carried most of the ceramics, was moved by the sea some 50m in a westerly direction before settling in 12m.

Relatively little is known of Medieval ships; few wrecks have been discovered, and even fewer have been examined in a responsible archaeological manner. The Cavoli excavation represents a small but important step in the right direction. In particular the Cavoli wreck provides valuable knowledge on early ordnance in the age of gunpowder, but it also gives a precious insight into the methods and means by which the Aragonese Crown supplied and consolidated its overseas territories. Probably most important of all is the information this wreck gives on ship construction of the period, for the 15th century was a period of great change and improvement in naval design and construction. It was these ships, in more evolved form, that would dominate the coming century of exploration and discovery.

References

D'Agostino, M., 1987, *Una nave catalana del XV-XVIsecolo, IV Rassegna di Archeologia Subacquea II premio Franco Papo,* Giardini Naxos, 187-192

D'Agostino, M., 1988, Il relitto B dell'Isola del Cavoli. Nota preliminare. *Quaderni della Soprintendenza Archeologica per le Province di Cagliari e Oristano,* Cagliari

Fennell, J.R., 1974, *Sardinia: Cap Carbonara,* IJNA, 3, 331-332

Lopez Elum, P., 1984, *Les origenes de la ceramica de Manises y Paterna (1285-1355),* Valencia

Martin-Bueno, M. (ed.), 1993, *La nave de Cavoli y la Arqueologia Subacuatica en Cerdena,* Zaragoza.

Soprintendenza Archeologica per la Toscana, 1991. Informe sobre el relitto dell'Isola del Cavoli. Ipostesi de intervento conservativo e restitutivo de alcuni cannoni ritrovati in mare e rimasti esposti all'aperto per 5 anni

Max Guérout (Groupe de Recherche en Archéologie Navale)
and Eric Rieth (Centre National de la Recherche Scientifique)

The wreck of the *Lomellina* at Villefranche sur Mer

The Villefranche sur Mer wreck is probably that of the *Lomellina*, a Genoese *nave*[2] which sank in 1516. It was discovered in April 1979 by Alain Visquis. Since 1982 nine consecutive years of excavation, representing a total of nearly 4,750 dives, have taken place. The team, which over this period, numbered nearly one hundred, was directed by Max Guérout and included the ship construction specialists Eric Rieth and Jean-Marie Gassend of the CNRS.

The site

The Bay of Villefranche sur Mer (fig 1 and 2) is situated near Nice, between the headlands of Mont Boron and Cap Ferrat, in the French department of Alpes-Maritimes. It is oriented north-south, has a length of 2,000m and a surface area of 346 hectares. It is well sheltered but vulnerable to the southeasterlies, particularly in winter when a building sea can turn it into a dangerous anchorage. Its merits, however, far outweigh its occasional hazards for which reason it has always been a popular roadstead, particularly with the French and foreign wind-fleets of the 19th century for

2 The Bay of Villefranche with the excavation barge over the site (*J.L. Pereyre*)

whom sea-room in a haven was just as important as shelter. Its frequent naval use, however, meant that it was regularly dredged. From the archaeological point of view this not only destroyed wrecks and removed isolated artefacts but also it compromised the stratigraphic value of the upper sediments.

1 Villefranche on the coast of Southern France (*Chris Fitton*)

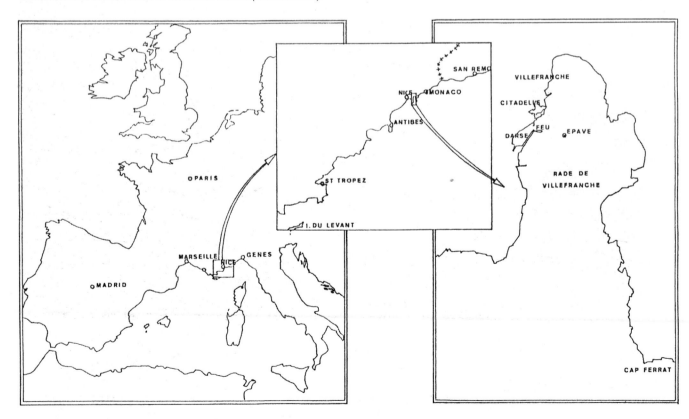

The wreck

The wreck is situated in 18 metres of water on a mud-sand bottom that slopes gently towards the south. A substantial portion of the hull still survives. It is situated at angle of 45 degrees to port and covers an area of 10m x 35m. Although the midships and areas aft have much deteriorated above keel level, the forward sections of the vessel are well preserved and include parts of the orlop and main decks.

The excavation (fig 3)

As a result of the 1982 survey it was decided to proceed with excavation. The idea of recovering the hull was put aside in favour of an *in situ* investigation. The principal research aims were: a written and diagrammatic record of her hull, a reconstruction of her lines and a study of her assembly and the tooling of her component parts. From this it was hoped to be able to draw some conclusions regarding her sailing

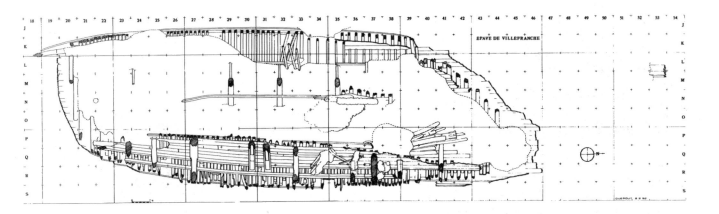

3 *Top* Plan of the site made during the 1982 season
(*M. Guérout*)

4 *Above* Artists view of the wreck
(*by Noel Blotti, copyright Geo Magazine/N. Blotti*)

qualities and general performance. With most wrecks usually only a few of the bottom timbers survive which give but small idea of the vessel's structure, but with the *Lomellina* there was a major part of hull that included two levels of deck (fig 4). Although the information value of such an assemblage was considerable, the sheer size and complexity of the structure prevented us (for technical and financial reasons) from dismantling the remains for the completion of an exhaustive study. We did, however, initiate a series of selective deconstructions which allowed for a fairly complete analyses of the hull.

The only logical way to cope with the underwater study of such a large construct was through a series of transverse trenches (each roughly 4m x 10m) starting at the stern. The main drawback to this approach was that it took nine years of excavation to comprehend fully the ship's design. In addition to the survey of the hull, equal importance was given to the vessel's rigging, fittings, equipment and armament, as well as all the everyday items that make it possible for a community to survive at sea.

Dating and identification of the wreck

The dating of the wreck was obtained from a series of coins which gave a *terminus post quem* of 1503. These included a Milanese lira struck in 1474 with the effigy of Galeas Marie Sforza; two French crowns struck in the reign of Charles VIII and dated 1483 and 1498; a Milanese testa with the effigy of Louis XII struck between 1500 and 1512, and a cornutus of the Marquisate of Casale Monferrat with the armorial bearings of William II Paleologous (1494-1518). In this regard mention should also be made of three credit pieces known as 'Nuremberg tokens'. Also of help with the dating was a majolica dish from Montelupo in Tuscany. All these elements gave us a chronology for the wreck that was somewhere around the middle of the first quarter of the 16th century.

These dates, together with the evidence of the hull, indicate that the wreck was that of a great 'round ship' of the Mediterranean 'nao', 'nef' or *'nave'* type which implies that it was probably built in the region of Venice, Ragusa, Genoa or Barcelona.

The origins of the wreck were first researched by analysing the geographical provenance of some of the objects on board (coins, ceramics and weights). They pointed to an area centred on Northern Italy (the Liguria region and the Province of Milan). A second line of inquiry involved identifying the principal timber species used in the vessel's construction (oak, beech, elm, poplar, aleppo pine (*pinus halepensis*), maritime pine (*pinus nigra*), stone pine (*pinus pinea*) and Scots pine (*pinus silvestris*) and then mapping their growth zones. This approach had to be treated with some caution as certainly there was a Mediterranean-wide trade in shipbuilding timber, but none the less, it did point to two likely areas: first, Liguria and the Gulf of Genoa, and secondly, the region of Barcelona Finally we undertook an analysis of the origin of the rock used for the ballast and stone cannon balls. This defined a zone stretching from

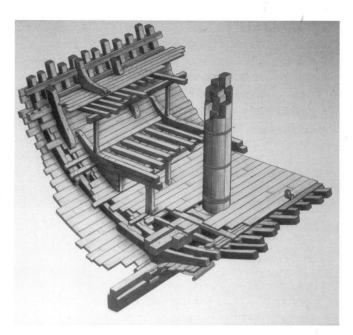

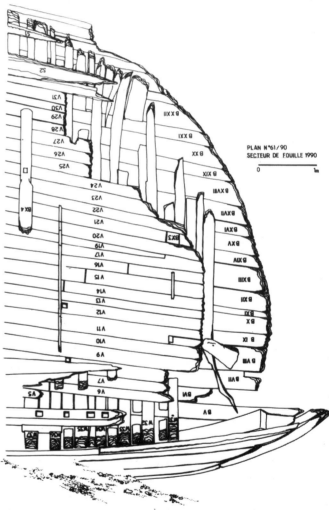

5 *Top* Hull reconstruction in the area of the mainmast (by Noel Blotti, copyright *Geo Magazine/N. Blotti*)

6 *Above* Plan of the forward end of the hull showing the lower stempost. 1990 season (*M. Guérout*)

50km west to 100km east of Genoa. All things considered, the Genoese origin of the ship seemed beyond doubt.

While all this was going on we were also pursuing archive research. Of key importance was a document from the state archives of Genoa recording a session of the Council of Elders. This indicated that our vessel might be the *nave Lomellina*. Testimony by several other chroniclers of the time supported this. Although we lack absolute proof that this is the *Lomellina*, the weight of the documentary and archaeological evidence is such that it would be unnecessarily perverse to think of this as any other vessel.

From the archives we know that the *Lomellina* sank in the Bay of Villefranche during a hurricane of exceptional violence on the 15 September 1516. It is safe to assume that she was named after the Lomellini family who undoubtedly were also her principal shareholders. The Lomellini were Genoese, originally from Lombardy, who at the end of the 14th century, created a bank which became the backbone of an immense business network that had connections throughout Europe. During the course of its history members of the family occupied numerous positions of influence and power: captains, admirals, consuls, ambassadors, commissaries of Corsica and twice doges of Genoa.

The keel

The excavation's most important contribution to learning concerns the vessel's construction. The following section, however, will concentrate mainly on those aspects which have not been discussed in detail elsewhere (Guérout, Rieth, Gassend, 1989; Rieth 1991a, 1991b).

The keel (fig 5), of oak (*chêne à feuilles caduques*), is preserved to a length of 34.18m (from the aftermost part of the skeg to the forward end of the stempost and its supportive assembly). The length of the keel proper (which is important for calculating tonnage) is 33.38m. This by itself reveals the importance of the *Lomellina*. Such dimensions can be compared to a 17th century French East Indiaman of about 600 tons burthen.

The keel of the Villefranche wreck is made up of four lengths, the shortest of which (the aftermost) is 6.90m, and the longest (the forwardmost) is nearly 10m. It has an average depth of 70cm, and an average width at the bottom of 35cm. The rabbets are L-shaped, 6cm to 7cm deep; on average they are 28cm from the bottom of the keel. The angles between the two faces of the rabbets changes very slightly along their length (from 110° to 115°); their vertical faces remain constant, only the lower faces vary their angle.

The forward and after extremities of the keel have a comparable morphology: both ends curve up naturally (this probably reflects the beginning of a large branch) to form an angle of about 35° with the horizontal base of the keel. This was a North European shipbuilding characteristic that had been common practice since the Middle Ages (in cogs for example) and which is still found today in both the East and West Mediterranean, but always limited to vessels of much lesser tonnage.

A	SEMELLE
B.C.D.E.	SAFRAN
F	BROCHE
G	FERRURE
H	RENFORT

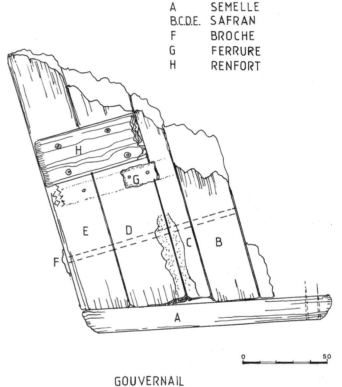

GOUVERNAIL

7 *Top* Forefoot and lower stem. Compare with figure 6 (*copyright* GRAN/CNRS *J.C. Hurteau*)

8 *Above* Plan of lower rudder (*E. Rieth*)

The stem

The stem is preserved over a length of 2.25m (figs 6 and 7). The exterior surface presents a slightly convex profile. It has a fore-and-aft thickness of 27cm where it joins with the keel, which broadens to 34cm at its broken upper end. The lower end of the stem forms a 61cm long scarf where it joins the forward end of the keel. Three iron fastenings (of 3cm to 4cm diameter) riven through at right angles to the grain of the wood, make fast the join between the foot of the stem and the keel. These through-fastenings have their lower ends riveted over a metal rove which has been countersunk into the outside edge of the stem.

41

9 *Above* After extremity of the keel and the remains of the rudder *(copyright GRAN/CNRS, J.C. Hurteau)*

10 *Left* General view looking down past the main deck towards the orlop deck. Note the channels for the discharge of bilge water and the gun carriage wheels below *(copyright GRAN/CNRS, J.C. Hurteau)*

The rudder (figs 8 and 9)

The lower part of the stern-hung rudder (preserved to a height of 1.55m) was found about 20cm from the skeg. This was an exceptional find. It consists of an oak foot, 1.45m long, on which was attached the pintle (or pivot) that no longer survives, and the blade, part of which fortunately does. The latter is made up of four lengths of poplar set with a rake of about 78°. This angle which is close to that formed by the horizontal axis of the keel and the vertical surface of the rebate in the skeg (75°), allows us to give the stern post an estimated rake of between 75° and 78°.

The keelson

Two lengths of the keelson are preserved; one (see fig 5) beneath the step of the mainmast (3.70m long), and the other at the forward end of the keel (5.35m long). They are rectangular in section with a width of 28cm beneath the step of the mainmast that diminishes to 24cm at the stem. Depth diminishes from 25cm at the step to 17cm at the forward end.

The lower surface of the keelson has a series of notches (between 1.5cm and 5.0cm deep) which fit over the backs of the horn-like floor timbers. At the extreme forward and after ends of the keelson, there are no notches; in these areas the keelson is set flat across the necks of the floors.

Regarding the fastening of the keelson to the floor frames and keel. In the area of the mainmast the keelson is joined to each floor timber (except one) by an iron fastening of 3cm average diameter. Such reinforcement is necessary because it is here that the mechanical strains imposed by the mainmast are at their greatest. Forward of the mainmast step, however, the pattern is different, here the keelson is fastened to every other floor frame.

The upper surface of the keelson has been given a series of rectangular mortises designed to receive, for the most part, the heels of the central pillars.

The frames

The frames (figs 4 and 5), made of oak(*chêne à feuilles caduques*), are preserved to four levels starting with the floors. They are somewhat irregular in section and relatively narrow, their average widths being no more than 19.0cm to 23.5cm. The space between them is almost equal to the width of the floors, a rhythm which is quite different from usual Mediterranean shipyard practices.

The various components (floors, first futtocks, second futtocks, etc.) are of apparently different cut and do not follow strict installation patterns; they seem to relate only to the most economic use of the available timber. Furthermore, when the dimensions of a timber seem too weak, or the length too short, packing pieces are installed; sometimes they are no more than jammed into position. Recycled timbers were also used.

The floor timbers lie without notches over the top of the keel. They are joined to the keel and the keelson with iron fastening in the pattern described in the section above. The heel of each floor is usually pieced by two circular limber holes. With the exception of floors W70 (situated 13m from stern) and W59 (situated 13m from the bow), which are bonded to futtocks on both their fore and aft sides, only one futtock is joined to each floor.[3] The lateral connection is made by means of dovetail joints of average 2cm depth.[4] The junction between futtocks follows the same lateral overlap principle. The use of angled joints (whether dovetailed or plain) is also used to bond the frame components above futtock level.

The planking (fig 5)

The outboard planking, of which 30 strakes are preserved from the garboard up, is made from aleppo pine (*Pinus halepensis*), stone pine (*Pinus pinea*) and oak. The average thickness of the lower fifteen strakes is 12cm, that of the upper strakes approximately 10cm. There are, however, three exceptions to the upper: two strakes are of 12cm and one is of 19cm. The latter very likely acted as a protective stringer or wale. The widths of the planks vary between 18cm and 34cm. They are carvel set and joined to the frames with only iron nails.

From the garboard to the 26th strake (which probably marks the water-line) the hull is pitched then sheathed in lead several millimetres thick. The sheathing is attached with a dense spread of tacks.

The oak clamps, on average 18cm wide by 15cm deep, are imbedded into the inboard surface of the frames. They are set in pairs according to the positions of the beam-ends and their associated timbers.

The ceiling planking, which is of oak and beech, lies flat upon the frames and covers the entire inboard framework from the very bottom to the main-deck beam clamps.

The garboard which has a pentagonal cross-section at its forward and after extremities, and a hexagonal cross-section at the centre, has been virtually sculpted into place. Its section changes according to the shape of the lower hull. The rabbet, by contrast, retains the same cross-section along the whole of its length. This changing garboard and unchanging rabbet are completely opposite to later known practices where typically the cross-section of the garboard remained the same while that of the rabbet altered. Moreover, the way the broad 'sculpted' garboard becomes, so to speak, a massive single unit with its keels, recalls the monoxyle keel/garboard design that was found on the mid 16th century wreck of a whaler in Red Bay, Labrador.

The planking, clamps, waterways and ceiling of the *Lomellina* are all fastened to the frames by the same method of nailing. In this way the internal and external planking play a major role in the structural integrity of the hull. The oak planking and clamps further stiffen and strengthen the assembly. These latter two longitudinal components, which from the structural point of view are more rigid than the others, also serve to provide cohesion for the vessel's primary thwartship timbers The essential contribution of these longitudinals to the integrity of the hull is an interesting variation on the accepted 'frame-first' approach to wooden ship-building. Clearly the design and assembly of the primary hull during this period are more complex than hitherto thought.

Beams and decking (figs 5 and 10)

The orlop deck is made up, in its central section, of five double beams, or pairs of beams, that are laid one over the other.

The beam-ends (on average 20cm deep, with a comparable fore and aft width) are fastened to the sides by means of notched joints which lock over the clamp and waterway longitudinals (fig 5). Several pillars, or stanchions, with an average section of 17cm x 17cm, are situated between the under-surface of the lower beam and the frames. In addition to their support function and the transfer of forces towards the bottom of the hull, these pillar act as vertical supports for the attachment of bulkhead planking.

Between the two double-beams that are situated fore and aft of the mainmast are six single cross beams of rectangular section (13-15cm deep and 14-18cm wide) which pass over a fore and aft timber that is notched to receive them.

The foremost purpose of the orlop deck (which, interestingly, was unplanked) is to provide thwartship reinforcement by bonding and stiffening the lower hull and to help with the distribution of stress and weight to the fore and aft assembly. More obviously the orlop deck functions as a storage platform for heavy gear. For instance, the shank of an anchor, the halyard blocks and their shaft (dismantled into three sections), casks and a cannon, were found lashed to the orlop deck.

The main-deck, which is situated at about water-line level, has a very different structure to the orlop deck. It is composed of a series of beams (noticeably lighter than those of the orlop deck) of varied width (between 10cm and 20cm) placed at remarkably irregular intervals (between 10cm and 60cm). The beam-ends are dovetailed into a sturdy clamp (20cm wide by 22cm deep). Heavy hanging knees that pass over the beams and decking are the final components that lock the deck assembly to the ship's side.

The discovery of the mainmast halyard blocks and their 8.22m shaft allows us to hypothesize with complete confidence the existence of an upper deck whose height above the keel can be estimated at 7m.

The stepping of the mainmast (fig 5)
The method of stepping the mainmast involved four elements:
- The keelson which, in this area, is at its heavies (25cm deep by 28cm wide)
- Two side-keelsons arranged on either side of the main central keelson. The one on the portside (the only one preserved) is over 5m long and has a section that is greater than that of the keelson itself (40cm deep by 30cm wide). The side-keelsons rest without fastening across the upper surfaces of the floor timbers.
- Two short thwartship timbers with dovetailed ends, set fore and aft of the mast. These act to bond and reinforce the side-keelsons.
- Chocks situated between the side-keelsons and thickstuff. Essentially these serve as filling to prevent any lateral movement of the mast heel.

This arrangement clearly derives from a specifically Mediterranean tradition of shipbuilding that is quite different from 'Atlantic' practices, which at this time, were characterized by the mainmast being stepped directly into the keelson. The stepping of the mainmast in the *Mary Rose*, a vessel of similar dimensions to the *Villefranche* ship, is representative of this 'Atlantic' tradition.

Conclusions regarding design
The main dimensions of the *Lomellina*, according to the archaeological evidence and written sources, can be hypothetically restored as follows:
- keel length: 33.80m
- beam at the midships: 14m
- depth (from the top of the keel to the underside of the main deck beam): 4.40m
- rake of stem: 10.50m
- rake of sternpost: 2.15m
- length from stem-head to sternpost: 46.45m

The above dimensions, when applied to French formulae for calculating tonnage (based on the naval regulations of 1681), give a carrying capacity of 829 tons, or about 810 modern tons.

Complementary discoveries
In addition to the features described above, several further discoveries have been made that relate to the vessel's construction. They include:
- A semi-intact capstan.
- A halyard block and shaft whose dimensions indicate that it was installed on the upper deck while the bottom of its trunk was fastened to the keelson.
- Part of the vessel's pump system. Bilge-water was discharged by way of channels across the main deck (fig 10).
- Two ports, in the side at maindeck level. These were most likely for lading and perhaps also the discharge of artillery.
- The powder room, situated at the forward end of the hold. This conforms to contemporary practice as attested by surviving builder's contracts of the period.
- The mast cap (figs 10 and 11). Made of elm, typically Mediterranean in design.

The weaponry
The investment involved in the construction and fitting-out of a ship, as well as its operational and maintenance costs, were considerable, and consequently owners could not afford to neglect the defence of their vessels. The 16th century commercial *nave* possessed almost all the constructional characteristics of a warship: raised bulwarks, castles fore and aft that were veritable defensive towers and circular crow's-nests that were armed like the 'donjon' of a castle. At the beginning of the 16th century, however, there were no structural differences between an armed merchant *nave* and an armed *nave* of war; the only distinction was that the latter had more artillery and carried a contingent of fighting men. Later, the principal visual distinction between a vessel conceived as a fighting ship and that intended for merchant use, was the presence of ports at 'tween deck level.

11 Mast cap. Found stored on the orlop deck
(copyright GRAN/M. Guérout)

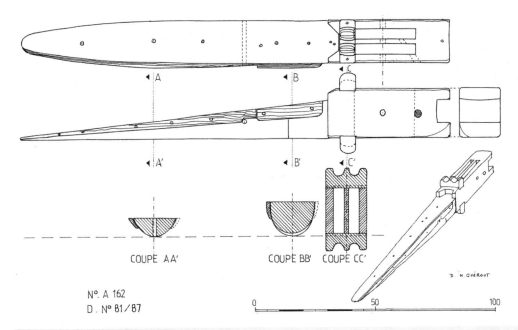

COUPE AA'   COUPE BB' COUPE CC'

Nº. A 162
D. Nº 81/87

0   50   100

D. M. GUÉROUT

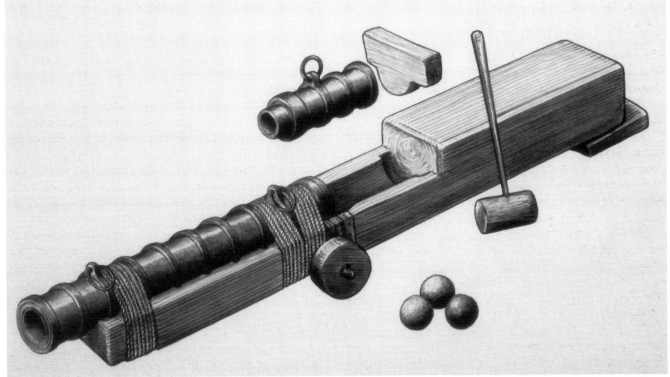

However, the below-deck space necessary to house and work heavy ordnance compromised the area available for cargo stowage and required significant additional constructional costs. On top of this there was, of course, the expense of the guns themselves and the additional pay required to employ gun crews. All these factors made it difficult, if not

12 *Top* Technical study of mast cap in figure 11 (M. Guérout)

13 *Above* Reconstruction of wrought iron gun and stock
(by Noel Blotti, copyright Geo Magazine/N. Blotti)

14 *Right* Wrought iron gun and stock *in situ*
(copyright GRAN/CNRS, J.C. Hurteau)

15 The same gun after conservation by the Archéolyse International Laboratory *(copyright Norbert Genetiaux)*

impossible, for a well armed merchant ship to operate in profit, and so evolved specialized fighting ships and professional navies as a means of protecting the commerce and other interests of the emerging powers of the day.

The ordnance recovered from the *Lomellina* (figs 12, 13 and 14) comprised a bronze arquebus, breech-loading cannon, breech chambers, gun carriages, wheels and axles. Accessories consisted of powder barrels, powder scoops, rammers, linstocks and shot moulds. The shot itself was made of iron, lead and stone. Only four of the observed thirteen guns have been raised, two of which are undergoing conservation (Guérout, Rieth & Gassend, 1989).

The two pieces currently being conserved (figs 13 - 14) are forged iron, stave-built guns of 240mm and 177mm bore. The first very likely fired stone shot, the second was probably intended for iron shot of 165mm diameter and approximately 34 French pounds. The general design and construction of such pieces are now fairly well known. Their barrels were made up of iron staves forged together along their longitudinal seams to form tubes which were reinforced with iron hoops that had been forced over the barrels when they were in red-hot expanded state. These hoops were of different sizes and two held lifting rings. The removable breech chambers were similarly forged and reinforced with hoops; one of the latter also featured a lifting ring.

One of the recovered cannons (figs 14 and 15) was bedded into a single length of heavy timber and held in place with multiple turns of rope. A cutting on the underside of the timber indicates the position of an axle, a complete example of which was found separate from the mount.

A large amount of shot was also recovered. It is interesting to note that, if the arquebus and musket projectiles are included, a maximum of 25 different calibres were identifiable.

Our understanding of the *Lomellina*'s ordnance is vexed by the fact that she was also carrying artillery which perhaps was intended for land-based operations that were taking place at the time. Six different types of wheel (some banded in iron) were found, two of which were unsuitable for shipboard usage, but ideal for landed transports or gun carriages. Further complications to our understanding arise from the fact that at least two salvage operations have taken place on the wreck: the first, in 1516, was conducted by officials from the Office of the Marine employed by the Council of Elders from the town of Gênes; the second, in 1531, was undertaken by private individuals from Villefranche (Archivio di Stato, Torino, Citta e Contado, Porte de Villefranche, Mazzo 11, no. 71).

Although it may not be possible to distinguish with certainty the vessel's own armament from artillery being transported as cargo, there can be no doubt that, because of their early date, studies of the individual pieces, backed-up by inventory information from the Turin archives, will prove rewarding.

Pine cone grenades

One of the most interesting items in the vessel's arsenal was a single hollowed out pine cone (fig 16), which was quite distinct from the numerous other complete pine cones that were found and which were no doubt intended for kindling or as a source of pine kernels for consumption. The hollowed pine cone was probably filled with powder, sealed with wax and used as a primitive kind of incendiary grenade. In contemporary Italian *pigna* means 'pine cone', from which derives the term *pignatta* which is found in the inventories of *naves* and which refers to incendiary grenades.

Fire pots

The largest of the ceramic fire pots was like a small amphora (figs 17 - 19). It had a long neck of 9cm, two handles, a flat bottom, a height of 30.5cm and a maximum body diameter of 19.5cm. Its grey-black body had been deliberately furrowed and its small handles had apparently not been designed to be grasped by hand. The upper part of the neck still had traces of a wax or pitch sealant (fig 18) and the interior contained a residue of powdered charcoal. This pot was probably an incendiary projectile that had been fused and then sealed with wax. Its weight and awkward shape suggest that it was not for throwing at deck level, but it might well have been hand-launched (or perhaps sling-cast) from a crow's-nest or ship's castle.

There is no explicit mention of this type of projectile in the contemporary inventories that we have been able to consult, but descriptions of *pots à feu* or 'firepots' can be found in numerous treatises and memoirs written during the second half of the sixteenth and early seventeenth centuries (Cataneo, 1571, 25; Collado, 1592, 83; Boillot, 1603, 150; Ufano, 1614, 155). Such pots were used either as incendiary devices that ignited on rupture or as explosive-type grenades. A large variety of pyrotechnic mixtures was available, the main components of which were gunpowder saltpetre and sulphur. For example, the recipe recommended by Diego Ufano consisted of 8 parts gunpowder 8 parts sulphur, 8 parts saltpetre, 8 parts sal ammoniac, 2 parts camphor and one handful of common salt, all of which were mixed together with liquid pitch or oil of stone or linseed. To make explosive pots the proportion of gunpowder was increased and iron dice or lead bullets were added. The small handles were used, when necessary, to fasten a slow match which functioned as a fuse. Fire pots of

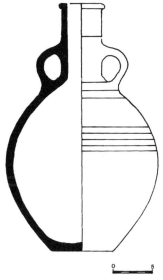

16 *Pignatta (copyright GRAN/C. Petron)*

17 Powder pot *(copyright GRAN)*

18 Detail of figure 17 showing the pitch around the neck *(copyright GRAN/C. Petron)*

19 Profile drawing of the powder pot in figure 17 (M. Guérout)

this type (although of smaller size) with similar handles were found on the wreck of the *San Antonio de Tanna*, near Mombassa, Kenya (Piercy, 1977, 346).

23 Type 3 hand grenade *(copyright GRAN/C. Petron)*

Balles à main, pignates or alcancias

Other ceramic incendiary pots of a more canonical form were found in fairly large number (almost a hundred intact or fragmented examples). Their dimensions, form and weight confirm that they were intended for use as grenades. Their shapes are not precisely standardized; heights vary from 10cm to 11cm, maximum diameters are 11cm, base diameters range from 6cm to 8cm and body walls are about 0.8cm thick. Their clay is coarse and unglazed and varies in colour from pink to pale red. They can be divided into three types distinguished less by size and capacity than by the form of their mouths.

Type 1 (figs 20 and 21) has a neck or rim that is either straight or slightly flared with an exterior diameter of 3.6cm. Traces of wax or pitch can sometimes be found over the entire exterior surface. Only grenades of this type were found still to contain the remains of their original contents, a black powder which analysis has shown to be charcoal.

Type 2 (fig 22) has a straight-sided rim with an exterior diameter of 52mm.

Type 3 (figs 23 and 24) has a flared rim with an exterior diameter of about 6cm.

The type 1 pot is shaped like the pomegranate fruit, the word for which in French and Italian is *grenada*. The etymology of the word 'grenade' is thus clear. Type 1 pots appear to have been known by several names. Ufano (1614, 144) speaks of *balles à main*, Collado (1592, 83) mentions *alcancias* and Gentilini (1598, 74) talks of *pignatta artificiata*. Borghesi (1970, 170) describes forty *pignatte di fuoco* being issued to one of Andrea Doria's galleys while records in the archives of Bouches-du-Rhône (B1260, f385) lists 110 *pignates de feu* on the *'nef du Roy'*, *Marguerite*. One of the earliest mentions of such items (1436) comes from the inventory of a vessel belonging to the Duke of Burgundy in which are described *petits pots de terre ronds a mettre poudre et croye pour gicter a combattre sur vasseaux de mer* (Paviot, 1995, 301). An archaeological reference to

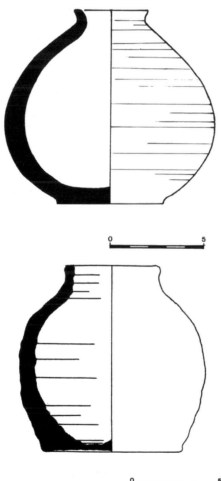

20 Type 1 hand grenade *(copyright GRAN)*

21 Type 1 hand grenade, as in figure 20 *(M. Guérout)*

22 Type 2 hand grenade *(M. Guérout)*

48

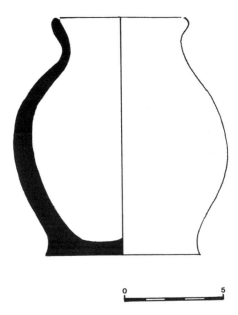

24 Type 3 hand grenade, as in figure 23 *(M. Guérout)*

alcancias of pinched-waist shape (different from type 1) came from the excavation of the Armada ship *Trinidad Valencera* (Martin, 1994, 208; see also Glover in this volume).

Type 2 and 3 recall pots mentioned by Eustache Lemoine in 1216, that could be filled with quick lime (*pots de terre à mettre chaux vive*) (Paviot, 1995), green soap, or other products harmful to the enemy.

Conclusion

The Villefranche wreck is very likely a Genoese *nave* (to use the term employed by the documents of the day). According to what we know of ship types of the time, this kind of heavy burthen vessel belongs to the Medieval tradition of ship construction that was much favoured by the great maritime cities of the Mediterranean, in particular Genoa. These capacious, deep-water armed merchantmen were mainly intended for the transport of heavy, bulk materials. Especially useful contributions to our understanding of this type of vessel have been made by Italian scholars (d'Albertis, 1893; Calegari, 1970; Gatti, 1975 and Campodonico, 1991). There is also a wealth of primary source material (mainly in the archives of Genoa) that includes manifests, indexed manuscript documents, timber purchase agreements and shipbuilding contracts. In addition there is a rich iconographic record of the *nave* which though requiring a rigorously critical approach is, none the less, very helpful. The full exploitation of these sources together with the archaeological data should allow us to identify with greater precision the characteristics of this type of vessel which was the backbone of one of the great maritime states of the day.

Probably more important than our improved understanding of the Genoese *nave*, is the manner in which our work, in a broader sense, has illuminated the purely Mediterranean tradition of 'round ship' construction. We have seen that several structural characteristics as well as certain parts of the rigging of the *Lomellina* were typically Mediterranean, and furthermore, some of the contracts for the building of Genoese

naves that we consulted made it clear that certain of the constructional techniques used were identical to those employed in the building of galleys (the same technical terminology was used for both types of vessel). In other words, there were aspects of Mediterranean shipbuilding that cut across the broad typological gaps of the time. These techniques no doubt persisted until the end of the 'round ship' in the 17th century and the demise of the galley in the 18th century; at this point traditional methods which had been idiosyncratic to Mediterranean yards were overtaken by 'Atlantic' traditions of design and construction. The precise detail of these contrasting practices and the nature of the transition that took place within the Mediterranean yards, is an area of study which, as far as we are aware, has been almost totally ignored.

Notes

1 The author and editor would like to express their sincere gratitude to Mr Royston Raymond for translating this chapter from the original French.

2 '*Nave*' has been left in an untranslated italics to remind the reader that although it is a generic term, it also connotes a specific type of ship, particularly at the beginning of the 16th century.

3 The frames precisely mirror each other on either side of double-futtocked floor timber W59. Forward of this presumed midships floor, the futtocks are joined to the after side of the floor timbers, and aft of W59 the futtocks are joined to the forward side of the timber. Such a pattern does not follow any previously known practice.

4 This method of joining floors and futtocks is very different from the mortise and tenon method of assembly that has been traditionally associated with Mediterranean shipyards. The use of dovetail joints seems, as far as present archaeological knowledge for the periods allows, to be a feature that is perhaps characteristic of the Atlantic yards.

References

Boillot, J., 1603, *Artifices de feu et divers instruments de guerre*, Strasbourg

Borghezzi, V., 1970, Informazioni sulle galee di Andrea Doria nelle carte strozziane (1552), in *Miscellanea storica Ligure, Guerra e commercio nell'evoluzione della marine genovese tra XV e XVII secolo*, Genova, 117-206.

Borghezzi, V. & Calegari, M., 1970, La nave Bertorota (1547-1561), in *Miscellanea storica Ligure, Guerra e commercio nell'evoluzione della marina genovese tra XV e XVII secolo*, Genova 95-116.

Calegari, M., 1970, Navi e barche tra il XV e il XVI secolo, in *Miscellanea storica Ligure, Guerra e commercio nell'evoluzione della marina genovese tra XV e XVII secolo*, Genova, 13-55.

Campodonico, P., 1991, *Navi e marinai genovesi nell'età di Cristoforo Colombo., Genova*.

Cataneo, G., 1571, *Dell'arte militare*, Brescia.

Collado, L., 1592, *Pratica manuel de artilleria*, Milan.

d'Albertis, A., 1893, *Le costruzioni navali e l'arte nautica ai tempi di Colombo*, Roma.

Gatti, L., 1975, Costruzioni navali in Liguria fra XV et XVI secolo, *Studi di storia navale*, Firenze, 25-72.

Gentilini, E., 1598, *Instruttioni di artiglierie*, Venice.

Guérout, M., Rieth E.. & Gassend, J.M., 1989, *Le navire genois de Villefranche, Un naufrage de 1516?*, Archeonautica, 9, CNRS, Paris.

Martin, C.J.M., 1994, Incendiary weapons from the Spanish Armada wreck *La Trinidad Valencera*, 1588, *International Journal of Nautical Archaeology*, 23, 3, 207-217.

Paviot, J., 1995, *La politique navale du Duc de Bourgogne, 1384-1482*, Lille.

Piercy, R.C.M., 1977, The Mombassa wreck excavation: preliminary report, *International Journal of Nautical Archaeology*, 22, 257-265.

Rieth, E., 1991a, L'épave du début du XVIème siècle de Villefranche-sur-Mer, *Carvel Construction Technique*, Oxbow Monographs, 12, Reinders, R. & Paul, K. (eds.), Oxford 47-55.

Rieth, E., 1991b, L'emplanture du grand-mât de L'épave du début du XVIème siècle de Villefranche-sur-Mer: un exemple d'emplanture de tradition méditerranéenne, *Medieval Ships and the Birth of Technological Societies*, vol. II, Villain-Gandossi, C., Busutti, S. & Adam, P. (eds.), Malta, 179-196.

Ufano, D., 1614, *Artillerie*, Frankfort.

Winifred Glover (Curator, Ulster Museum)

The Spanish Armada wrecks of Ireland

The Spanish Armada of 1588 was one of the most ambitious naval undertakings of the sixteenth century. Even by modern military standards the plan to crush England with a large Armada in conjunction with a mighty army that had to move through Europe to rendezvous in Flanders, would be hazardous to execute. Poor communications and the

1 Detail from an engraving by John Pine showing a galleass in the foreground (Ulster Museum)

inevitable difficulties and delays between the naval and land commands were to seal the fate of the endeavour and give the advantage to the mobile defender.

The idea of invading England with a vast Armada of ships was planted in the mind of Philip II of Spain by his veteran naval commander, Don Alvaro de Bazan, Marquis of Santa Cruz. Santa Cruz had taken Spain to victory in July 1583 at the great sea battle of Terceira, one of the islands in the Azores. This archipelago, strategically placed in the mid-

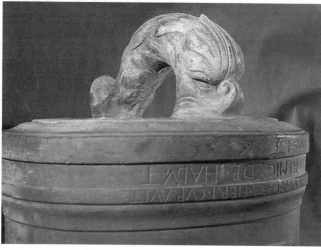

2 *Top* Siege gun mounted on replica gun carriage. Copyright Mike Bartley, Plymouth *(Ulster Museum)*

3 *Above* The 50lb bronze siege gun from *La Trinidad Valencera* showing the maker's mark, Remigy de Halut 1556. It was one of a Royal Siege-train of 54 pieces cast for Philip II *(Ulster Museum)*

Atlantic, was the last surviving part of the Portuguese Empire. By defeating a combined Franco-Portuguese force, Santa Cruz gave Spain control over all Portugal's colonies in the Pacific and Atlantic as well as her profitable trading routes.

The acquisition and organization of such an enormous fleet as the Armada was a formidable undertaking. Before the defeat of the Portuguese, Spain did not have a significant naval force of her own, except, that is, for her galleons in the Mediterranean. The conquest of Portugal had provided her with a useful squadron of galleons to which four large galleasses from Naples squadron provided

a useful addition. The remainder of the force was to be made up of ships from all parts of the Spanish Empire and whatever other vessels could be chartered or commandeered from the rest of Europe. *La Trinidad Valencera*, for example, one of the largest, was a heavily armed Venetian merchant ship.

The first plans drawn up by Santa Cruz were remarkably ambitious; 556 ships with 30,000 crew and an invasion force of 64,000 soldiers (Flanagan, 1988, 10). The costs, however, were prohibitive and the requirements impossible to meet. Philip studied the plans carefully and the resultant Armada was on a smaller scale. To avoid the need for transporting a huge invasion force, Philip planned to join forces with the battle-hardened Spanish troops who were already based in Holland under the command of the King's nephew, Alexander Farnese, Duke of Parma.

Although the assembly of the great fleet began in the spring of 1586, by 1588 it was scarcely ready. Sir Francis Drake had mounted a damaging attack on the fledgling Armada at Cadiz on 29 April 1587, destroying 24 ships. None the less, on 28 May 1588 a fleet of 130 ships carrying 29,453 men sailed from Lisbon with the intention of invading England and bringing it again under Catholic domination. Santa Cruz did not live to see it sail; he died suddenly of typhus on 9 February 1588. His place as Commander was reluctantly undertaken by Don Alonzo Perez de Guzman, Duke of Medina Sidonia. He was a military commander not a naval one and his successes had all been on land. However, Philip considered him to have the necessary leadership qualities and insisted he assume command.

The 130 ships consisted of galleons, hulks, despatch vessels, zabras ,galleasses and galleys, as well as 10 caravels and 10 fellucas[1]. The ships were in nine squadrons. They ranged in size from a fast-sailing patache (60 tons; 9 guns), used for conveying information throughout the fleet, up to the huge flagship *Santa Ana* of 1,250 tons and 47 guns. Altogether the Armada carried 29,453 soldiers and mariners and 2,241 guns of all types and sizes (Martin & Parker, 1988, 63).

The excavations of the *Girona* and *La Trinidad Valencera* both produced many examples of the arms used in sixteenth century naval and land warfare. There were muskets, arquebuses, daggers, swords and grenades as well as swivel guns which were anti-personnel weapons mounted on deck for close-in attack on the enemy. *La Trinidad Valencera* even carried enormous bronze siege cannon to lay waste any English towns that might be tempted to resist (figs 2 and 3).

Forty of the Armada ships failed to return to Spain and of this number, over twenty were wrecked off the North and West Coasts of Ireland. O'Danachair (1954-6, 329) lists twenty-four ships using information from the Elizabethan State papers of Ireland and other documentary sources. He indicates that there may have been a twenty-fifth, one of the Baltic hulks, which perished in Donegal Bay (State Papers Ireland, 1588-92, 64). Flanagan's map (1988, 26) shows fourteen locations of named ships and the probable locations of two unnamed ones, making a total of sixteen.

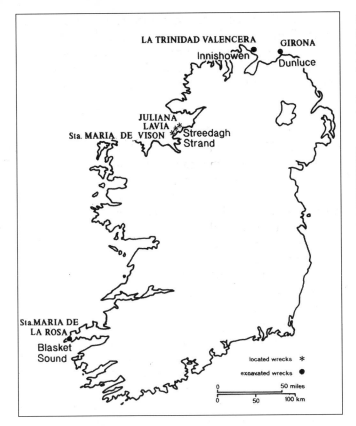

4 *Above* Armada shipwrecks around Ireland

5 *Above right* Bronze breech-loading *esmeril* from the *Girona* bearing the arms of Philip II on the octagonal barrel. These were mounted along the side of the galleass on walkways above the rowing benches and were designed for rapid shipboard firing. The bronze breech block is in position and other breech blocks and iron and stone shot are shown beside it *(Ulster Museum)*

The map in Martin & Parker (1988, 243) gives the locations of thirteen named ships and indicates the probably location of six others.

The Ulster Museum houses the excavated remains of three Armada ships: the galleass *Girona* wrecked at Lacada Point, Co. Antrim on the morning of 26 October 1588; *La Trinidad Valencera* a refurbished Venetian merchantman wrecked in Kinnagoe Bay, Co. Donegal on 16 September 1588 and the *Santa Maria de la Rosa*, a vice-flagship which suddenly sank in Blasket Sound, Co. Kerry on 21 September 1588. Three other wrecks have been located on Streedagh Strand, Co. Sligo, the *Juliana*, the *Lavia* and the *Santa Maria de Vision* (fig 4).

The galleass *Girona* had been built at Naples which at that time was under Spanish rule. She was one of four vessels of this type (see fig 1) under the command of Don Hugo de Moncado. Having the advantage of being both sail and oar-powered they performed the essential role of support ships. They had also played an important part in the battle of Lepanto, off western Greece, in 1582. In this engagement six of them had fought on the Christian side (represented by the fleets of Spain, Venice and the Papal States) against the Ottoman Armada. In the Ionian Sea they had performed well, but in Atlantic conditions off Western Europe they proved unwieldy and unreliable.

When the contents of the *Girona*'s wreck were recovered from the seabed at Lacada Point, the ship itself had broken up completely and so information on her size and construction have had to come from written sources which only describe galleasses in general. We know that she carried a complement of 50 cannon, most of which was jettisoned to make room for extra crew and soldiers before she left Killybegs harbour on her last fatal voyage. Captained by Fabricio Spinola of Genoa, she carried a total crew of 500 men made up of 121 officers and men, the remainder being oarsmen who were either convicts, slaves or, surprisingly, volunteers - of whom there were 63 (Scandurra, 1972, 213). In addition to the cannon on board were 8,000 cannon balls of iron and stone (fig 5). The foodstuffs were as follows: 750 pieces of hard tack, 100 casks of wine, 62cwt of lard, 62cwt of cheese, 60 casks of tuna fish, 40 casks of sardines, 15cwt rice, dried beans and pulses, raisins, oil and vinegar, sugar, salt and semolina.

The oarsmen were seated beneath the deck on which the cannon and other weapons were mounted. They had three masts, each carrying lateen sails. Pietro Martire d'Anghirera, who sailed in one at the beginning of the sixteenth century, said that they had 150 oarsmen seated at 25 banks on each side of the ship (cf. fig 1). Fifty sailors were assigned to handle the running rigging from the decks while twelve others went aloft and along the yards to take in sail when required. The latter also took care of the rudder.

In 1530 a decree of the Venetian senate had said that every galleass must be 47m long, have a beam of 8m and a stanchion of 3.20m (Scandurra, 1972, 211-2). The galleass *San Lorenza* which ran aground at Calais was boarded by Richard Tomson, an English seaman, who described her as being about 50m long with 25 oars on each side (Flanagan, 1988, 43).

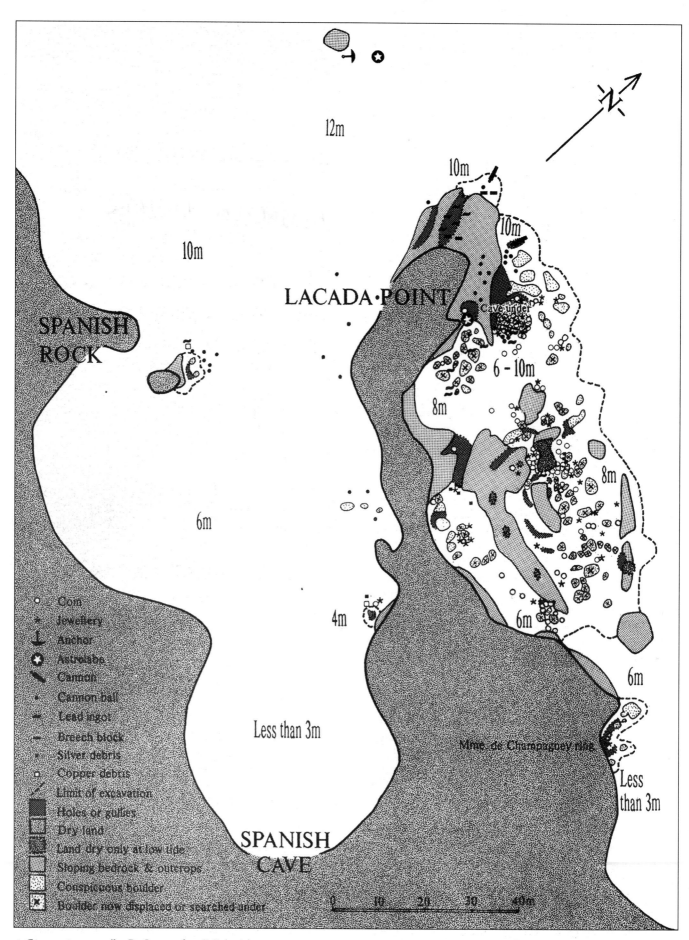

12m

10m

10m

10m

SPANISH
ROCK

LACADA·POINT

Cave under

6 - 10m

8m

8m

6m

6m

4m

Less than 3m

Mmc de Champaguey ring

Less
than 3m

Coin
Jewellery
Anchor
Astrolabe
Cannon
Cannon ball
Lead ingot
Breech block
Silver debris
Copper debris
Limit of excavation
Holes or gullies
Dry land
Land dry only at low tide
Sloping bedrock & outcrops
Conspicuous boulder
Boulder now displaced or searched under

SPANISH
CAVE

0   10   20   30   40m

6 *Girona* site-map *(by D. Crone after R Sténuit)*

The best illustration of a galleass in the Armada fleet comes from the John Pine engravings which were copied in the 18th century from tapestries woven by Francis Spiernig about 1589. These show a galleass as a three-masted ship with 20 to 22 oars each side.

After a first engagement in the English Channel, followed by another attack off Portland Bill, the Armada's Commander, Medina Sidonia, decided that the Fleet should anchor at Calais. Fire-ships sent in by the English forced the Spanish to cut their cables and scatter, so losing their usual effective crescent fighting formation. Another very damaging encounter took place off Gravelines after which the decision was taken to abandon the enterprise and head home. Medina Sidonia ordered that they return home via the north of Scotland and along Ireland's Atlantic coast. He specifically exhorted his Commanders to 'take great care lest you fall upon the Island of Ireland, for fear of the harm that may befall you on that coast' (State Papers Eliz. Ireland, cxxxvii, 1, ii). Unfortunately the autumn storms of 1588 went on record as the worst known and, as the Armada valiantly attempted to return to Spain, the ships were scattered and blown off course.

The *Girona* sank on 26 October 1588, off Lacada Point, near the Giant's Causeway on the North Antrim coast. She had previously been forced into Killybegs harbour, Co. Donegal to repair her rudder and sails. News of this reached the survivors of two other ships, the *Duquessa Santa Ana* which ran aground at Loughros More, Co. Donegal and the *Santa Maria Encoronada*, which had been wrecked in Blacksod Bay, Co. Mayo. The leader of the two groups of survivors was Don Alonso Martinez de Leiva, Commander Designate of the Armada. Though wounded in the leg after his second shipwreck and carried on a litter to Killybegs, he still made determined efforts to get his men safely back to Spain. When the *Girona* was repaired, she set sail with one thousand three hundred men aboard. To accommodate them on a ship originally intended for 500 men, forty-five pieces of ordnance were jettisoned. Despite all efforts the ship was lost. Only five men survived. The wreck of the *Girona* lay undiscovered until 1967 when the first artefacts were discovered along the eastern face of Lacada Point by the Belgian nautical archaeologist, Robert Sténuit (fig 6).

Sténuit had spent many years consulting Spanish and English archive documents. He also took note of local names and traditions concerning the whereabouts of the Spanish wreck. He found the first sign of the *Girona* at a depth of 25-33ft. The first object he located was a boat-shaped lead ingot. In all, twenty-seven complete, and one half ingot were recovered. There were also sixty-two flat, roughly rectangular lead ingots that had been perforated with various round, square and star-shaped holes. The lead was not carried as ballast because piles of stones were found on the ocean bed which served that purpose. Similar piles of stones were found round the remains from the *Santa Maria de la Rosa*. The ingots were used for fire-arms shot and sheeting for hull repairs.

In the excavations which commenced in 1968 and were completed in 1969, a dazzling amount of treasure was

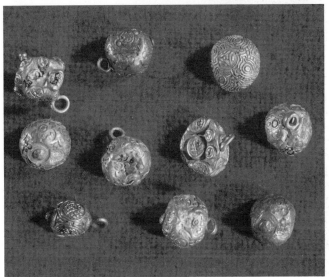

7 *Top* Treasures from the Armada showing the salamander, Cross of the Order of a Knight of Santiago, a section of a composite gold chain inset with pearls and rubies, a gold cross, a gold pendant set with amethyst on a background of silver *reales* (Ulster Museum)

8 *Above* Gold buttons from the Galleass *Girona* (Ulster Museum)

recovered in the form of coins and Renaissance jewellery (fig 7). The reason for the presence of such finery was because the officers of the Armada had been chosen from the noblest and wealthiest houses in Spain. In fact the *Girona* was carrying the officers of three Armada ships when she sank. They all dressed as if they were attending Court, complete with gold buttons (fig 8), gold chains, gold rings (fig 9), orders of chivalry and glittering diamond rings. They were also carrying some of their personal fortunes with them in coinage. James Machary was an Irishman who had been conscripted in Lisbon to join the Armada. He was left behind when the *Girona* sailed out of Killybegs. When he was subsequently examined by Sir William Fitzwilliams,

9 *Left* Gold ring of a hand holding a heart with the inscription 'No tengo mas que dar te' I have nothing more to give you *Girona (Ulster Museum)*

10 *Below left* One of a set of eleven gold cameos set with lapis lazuli and surrounded with pearls. This is the most complete found on the *Girona (Ulster Museum)*

Lord Deputy of Ireland he said that after de Leiva was shipwrecked for the first time (from *La Rata Sancta Maria Encoronada*) and he and his men were taken aboard the *Santa Ana*, they took with them 'all the goods they had in the shypp of any valewe, as plate, apparell, monie, iewells, weapons, armor etc.' (State Papers Ireland, No. 25 i, f.83).

As well as sailors, soldiers and armaments, the *Girona* carried clerics because Philip was a very devout monarch and viewed the Armada as a religious undertaking. Before it set sail, *La Felicisima Armada* was blessed and all on board received religious medals of copper, pewter or lead. The finds from the *Girona* included crosses of gold, silver, bronze and lead, religious medals, a gold *Agnus Dei* reliquary (fig 11) and a heavy gold ring engraved with the initials IHS, the sacred monogram of the Jesuits and undoubtedly the property of a cleric on board (fig 12).

The golden jewellery recovered comprised orders of chivalry, religious orders and decorative personal items such as gold chains and gold buttons. Hundreds of gold and silver coins were recovered, as well as silver candle and taper sticks (fig 13) and the remnants of silver-gilt tableware designed to grace the tables of the noble ship's officers.

Many of the jewels reveal facets of sixteenth century Spanish history. The orders of chivalry of Compostela and

11 *Top right* Gold *Agnus Dei* reliquary from *Girona*. The reliquary is in the form of a book with a depiction of St John the Baptist on the front. Inside are five circular compartments which contained wax tablets, *Agnus Dei* made from the wax of Paschal candles, blessed by the Pope. *(Ulster Museum)*

12 *Above* The Sacred Monogram IHS on the bezel of a gold ring from the *Girona*. This may have belonged to a Jesuit on board *(Ulster Museum)*

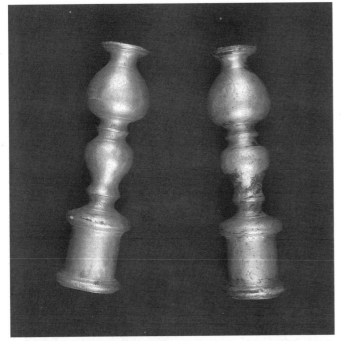

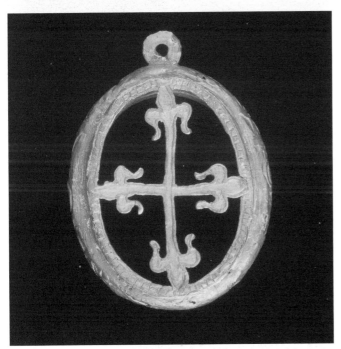

13 Above left Silver candlesticks *Girona (Ulster Museum)*

14 Left Front part of the gold Cross of a Knight of Alcantara *Girona (Ulster Museum)*

15 Top right Gold cross of a Knight of St John of Jerusalem set on gold chains *Girona (Ulster Museum)*

16 Above Gold one-escudo and two-escudo pieces minted in Seville *Girona (Ulster Museum)*

Alcantara were originally founded as religious military orders whose purpose was to fight the Moors in Spain (fig 14). The Cross of a Knight of Santiago of Compostela belonged to Don Alonso Martinez de Leiva and was one of the highest orders of Chivalry.

The gold and silver coins (fig 16) show the close connection between medieval Spanish wealth and her conquests in the New World. They also reflect the extent of her Empire at that time. The 414 gold coins, 789 silver and 122 copper coins had been minted in six different countries, Spain, Portugal, the Kingdom of the Two Sicilies, the Republic of Genoa, Mexico and Peru. Although the Spanish had established mints at Mexico, Lima and Potosi, almost

85% of the gold coins had been minted at Seville. Situated at the head of the great Guadalquivir River it was the centre for incoming gold from the New World.

Other finds illuminate more aspects of sixteenth century Spanish life. Among the hundreds of pieces of metalwork were copper pot handles, lead seals for jars, copper nails, many tiny fragments of gilt bronze vessels, the top halves of at least six silver perfume flasks, the arm of another set of navigational dividers (five complete but bent pairs were recovered), the trigger guard from a musket and a small gilt bronze disc. Unfortunately the latter was much corroded but sufficient numbers and letters were visible to confirm that it was part of a navigational instrument similar to an

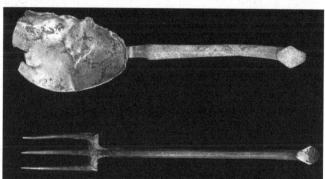

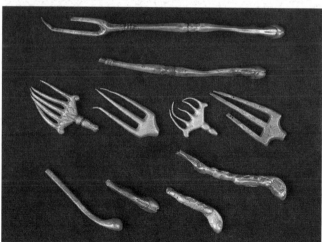

17 Bronze astrolabe from *Girona* which was used for establishing the ship's latitude. The ring should be calibrated round the edge and at the centre a sight-rule or alidade would pivot but these features have been obscured by sea action *(Ulster Museum)*

18 Silver fork with the initials 'SM' and a silver spoon *Girona (Ulster Museum)*

19 Different types of silver forks from the *Girona* for the officers on board *(Ulster Museum)*

20 Small bowl of casting metal made to commemorate the Marquis of Santa Cruz's victory at Terceira in 1583 *La Trinidad Valencera (Ulster Museum)*

21 Gunner's equipment from *La Trinidad Valencera*. A bronze bucket stands behind a wooden sponge head for cleaning out the gun barrels. In front there are a copper powder scoop, stone and iron shot, three wooden shot gauges and a wooden linstock in the form of a clenched fist *(Ulster Museum)*

astronomical compendium.

The great value of the finds from the three Irish Armada wrecks is that they provide a closely dated context for navigational instruments of the day (sounding leads, astrolabes (fig 17), navigational dividers); information on how a naval and land campaign was waged (campaign tents, spiked stakes for building defences), and the domestic and combat equipment carried on board a fighting ship. They also illuminate how life was lived on board by both the noble leaders and the ordinary infantryman and seaman.

The seabed round the North Coast of Ireland is a constantly shifting place (Flanagan, 1988, 27) and since the *Girona*'s original excavations several more pieces have been found near the wreck site. One of these was de Leiva's order of chivalry, the Cross of a Knight of Santiago. The other was an unusual fork, surprisingly modern in appearance (fig 18) with the initials SM at the end of the handle. Other silver forks (fig 19) recovered were exotic types with two to five tines and the handles terminating in cloven hooves, men's torsos, clubs and serpents. While the initials could be its owner's (and from the wreck of the *Santa Maria de la Rosa* we know that Captain Francisco Ruiz de Matute, captain of Infantry, had two pewter plates bearing his name) there could be another explanation. From Dr Colin Martin's excavation of *La Trinidad Valencera* came a small metal bowl commemorating Santa Cruz's victory at Terceira in the Azores (fig 20). Another of his victories within this archipelago was at the Island of Sao Miguel, and this fork, so dissimilar to the others found, may also commemorate this success.

Running before the storms the 42 gun, 1,100 ton merchantman *La Trinidad Valencera* was badly damaged on 12 September She took in so much water her pumps could not cope and, seeking shelter, she ran aground on a reef in Kinnagoe Bay, at Malin Head in north Donegal (fig 4). Her remains were discovered in February 1971 by members of the City of Derry Sub-Aqua Club who found one of her guns. Other guns were found and anxious that the best and most scientific means of recovery should be employed, Dr Colin Martin, one of Britain's foremost nautical archaeologists, was requested to direct the excavations.

The results were spectacular; a battery of great guns was recovered. It included three siege-guns (figs 2 and 3) from the Royal train of Philip II, made for him in Malines in 1556, and, from the ship, two Venetian bronze guns, and a bronze and iron swivel gun. Gunner's equipment, consisting of three shot gauges, pieces of a gunner's rule, a copper powder scoop and stone, lead and iron shot of different calibre provided more information on sixteenth century Spanish armaments (fig 21).

Most significantly *La Trinidad Valencera* yielded a highly important number of organic items such as a portion of anchor cable, wooden barrel staves, wooden bungs from casks, wineskin stoppers, wooden pegs from musical instruments and many other pieces of turned wood. Of particular interest was the fingerboard of a musical instrument, suggested by Martin & Parker (1988, 139) to be

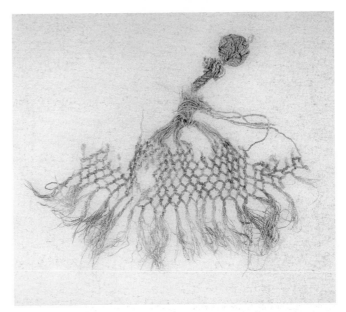

22 *Top* Silk tassel recovered from *La Trinidad Valencera* which may have hung from the belt of a musketeer (*Ulster Museum*)

23 *Above* Olive jar from *La Trinidad Valencera* (*Ulster Museum*)

a cittern. The 400 pieces of textile included a silk tassel (fig 22), a velvet collar, a woollen sock and the remnants of a campaign tent. Many soles and upper parts of leather shoes were recovered, similar in type to those from the *Girona*. More information was revealed about foodstuffs on board when the contents of an 'olive' jar (fig 23) were seen to be

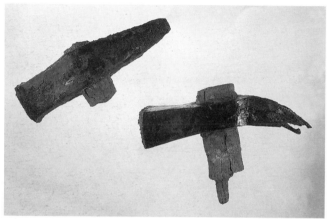

27 Green-glazed pottery jug and plates for the ordinary soldier and infantryman. *La Trinidad Valencera (Ulster Museum)*

28 Wooden bowl and spoon for the ordinary soldier and infantryman. *La Trinidad Valencera (Ulster Museum)*

24 One of several pine cones from *La Trinidad Valencera (Ulster Museum)*

25 Iron spall-hammer and iron claw-hammer with portions of surviving wooden handles *La Trinidad Valencera (Ulster Museum)*

26 Pewter jug and goblet for the ship's officers *La Trinidad Valencera (Ulster Museum)*

lentils. Three pine cones (fig 24) and a bay leaf provided further insights on the diet available. A plum stone from the *Girona* and a Brazil nut from the *Santa Maria de la Rosa* indicate that some effort was made to provide fresh food for the crews.

Two giant iron-shod wooden wheels (1,520mm diam) from a gun carriage were part of the dismantled sections of six carriages to be used in a siege train. Many wooden pulley blocks, bronze breech blocks and several different types of ship's hammer (fig 25) were recovered. Caulking hammers were essential in rendering the seams between wooden plank-built boats watertight. Padfield (1988, 71) mentions that the Portuguese and Spanish used a mixture of tallow, lime, sulphur or fish oil on the wooden timbers of the underwater hulls in an attempt to discourage the toredo worms which were so damaging in tropical waters. One giant single block (hgt 650mm) and sheave from *La Trinidad Valencera* showed massive toredo worm erosion (Flanagan, 1988, 45, 4.3).

A wide range of damaged pewterware items (fig 26) was salvaged from *La Trinidad* and, after considerable

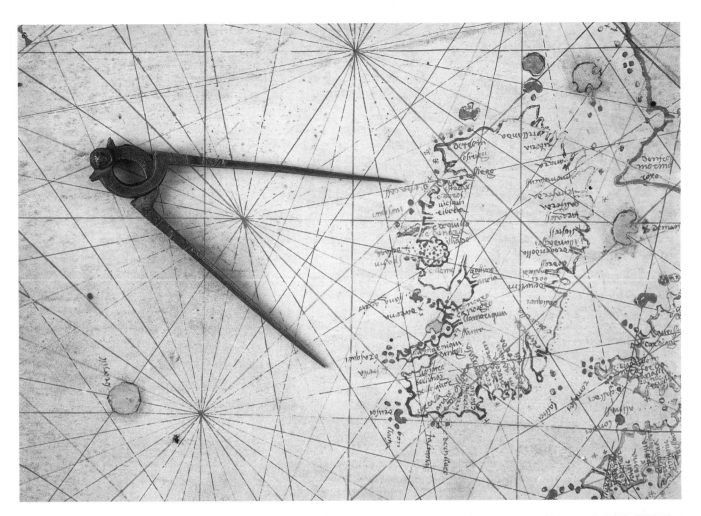

conservation work had been completed, they emerged as fine goblets, several large bowls, many plates of varying sizes, spoons, a jug and an interesting open-bodied container with a spout and suspension ring which may have served for feeding invalids (Flanagan, 1988, 129 9.32). The ordinary soldier and mariner made do with pottery jugs and wooden bowls and spoons; their plates were either ceramic or wooden (figs 27 and 28).

The third Armada ship to be excavated was the *Santa Maria de la Rosa*. She was 945 tons, carried 250 men, was armed with 26 guns and was the vice-flagship of the Guipuzcoa squadron under the Command of Miguel de Oquendo. Her whereabouts were known since there were eye-witness accounts of her sudden sinking (de Arumburu in Duro, 1884-5, II, 315-26) and there was one survivor, Giovanni de Manona, who was the son of the ship's pilot. She had been holed four times but her eventual fate was sealed when the bottom was lacerated on a reef at the neck of Blasket Sound, Co. Kerry on 21 September 1588. Her single anchor still lies on the northern edge of the reef (Martin & Parker, 1988, 238).

There are six iron anchors lying in Blasket Sound which belong to Armada ships, but to which is still unclear (Flanagan 1988, 39). From the three located by Sidney Wignall and the one recovered from the *Girona*, it can be seen that sixteenth century Spanish anchors had a straight

29 Set of navigational dividers from *La Trinidad Valencera* placed on a sixteenth century navigational chart showing Ireland. The chart is by the Genoese map maker Battista Agnese *(Ulster Museum)*

30 Ceramic fire pot from *La Trinidad Valencera* designed to be filled with flammable material and thrown on board an enemy ship *(Ulster Museum)*

metres long. Three other anchors were also discovered. The actual wreck lay about 200 yards to the southeast of a submerged reef known as Stromboli (fig 32). The site was marked by a large ballast mound of stones, iron shot, lead musket balls and six large lead ingots similar to the *Girona*'s (Wignall, 1968, 74-6). The finding of two pewter plates with the name 'Matute' underneath the rim proved that this was indeed the *Santa Maria*. Documentary sources confirmed that Francisco Ruiz Matute had been a captain of infantry on board the ship.

31 *Left* Iron rigging shackle *La Trinidad Valencera* (*Ulster Museum*)

32 *Below* Site plan of *Santa Maria de la Rosa* (*Courtesy of C. Martin*)

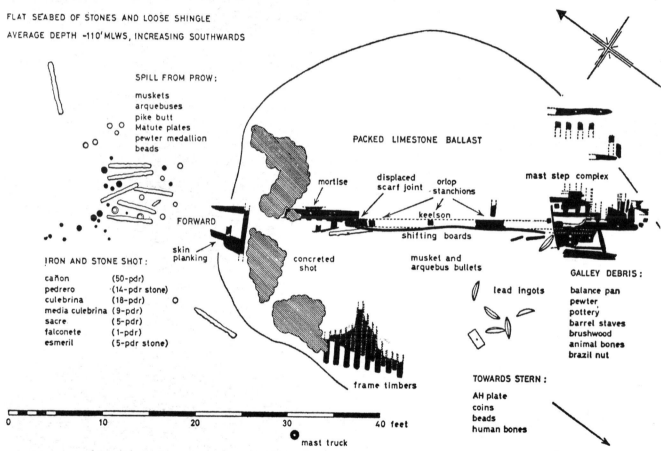

FLAT SEABED OF STONES AND LOOSE SHINGLE
AVERAGE DEPTH ~110'MLWS, INCREASING SOUTHWARDS

SPILL FROM PROW:

muskets
arquebuses
pike butt
Matute plates
pewter medallion
beads

PACKED LIMESTONE BALLAST

FORWARD

mortise

displaced
scarf joint

orlop
stanchions

mast step complex

keelson

shifting boards

skin
planking

concreted
shot

musket and
arquebus bullets

GALLEY DEBRIS:

balance pan
pewter
pottery
barrel staves
brushwood
animal bones
brazil nut

IRON AND STONE SHOT:

cañon	(50-pdr)
pedrero	(14-pdr stone)
culebrina	(18-pdr)
media culebrina	(9-pdr)
sacre	(5-pdr)
falconete	(1-pdr)
esmeril	(5-pdr stone)

lead ingots

frame timbers

TOWARDS STERN:

AH plate
coins
beads
human bones

0   10   20   30   40 feet

mast truck

shank and curved arms ending in two flukes. One of the flukes of the *Girona*'s anchor was badly damaged; this seems to have been a weak point as a similar damage occurred on two of the other anchors. Another weak point was the ring at the top of the shank. An anchor ring covered in concretion was recovered from *La Trinidad Valencera* (Flanagan, 1988, 45, 4.2).

Locating the *Santa Maria de la Rosa* was fraught with difficulties. Desmond Brannigan led a preliminary search in 1963 but it was not until 1968 that a diving team led by Sidney Wignall, and assisted by John Grattan and a team of service divers, located the first real clue: a large anchor four

The *Santa Maria* was a vice-flagship and it was supposed that she might have had much treasure on board. De Aramburu mentions that she was carrying a fortune in gold and plate (1984-5, II, 320). None of it, however, has been recovered. The finds included iron shot, timbers, iron nails, lead shot, lead ingots, pot sherds, a Brazil nut, pieces of animal and human bone and the Matute plates. Some of the finds did not survive their removal from the water.

Unlike the *Girona* a considerable portion of the ship's timbers survived underneath the ballast mound. From this it was possible to determine that the hull structure of the vessel, the most complete part surviving, was a light construction and unsuited to the rough conditions of the Atlantic seas off Ireland.

As in land archaeology, the more meticulous and scientific the excavation, the greater the material and scientific value which results. The provision of skilled conservation facilities is absolutely essential in all excavations. Conservation provided by the Ulster Museum has ensured that the objects excavated from the *Girona* and *La Trinidad Valencera* have been preserved as a permanent record of a momentous event. They are a continuing source of historical information, for both scholars and public alike, about many aspects of sixteenth century Spain.

Acknowledgements

I am grateful for the assistance of the following: Mrs D. Crone of the Dept. of Archaeology and Ethnography, the Ulster Museum, for her re-drawing of the site plan of the *Girona* after Sténuit , 1972; Dr Colin Martin, Director of the Institute of Maritime Studies, St Andrews University, for permission to use his site plans of the *Trinidad Valencera* and *Santa Maria de la Rosa* excavations.

Notes

1 Padfield (1988, notes chap. 4, 20) refers to 'Full statement of the Armada sailing from Lisbon' 9 May 1588. Medina to Philip Sp. pp. 280 ff.

References

de Arumburu, M. in Duro, C.F., 1884-5, *La Armada Invencible* I, II, Madrid.

Flanagan, L.N.W., 1988 *Ireland's Armada Legacy*, Dublin, Gill & Macmillan.

Martin, C.,1979, 'La Trinidad Valencera', *Int. J. Nautical Archaeol.* Vol. 8, I, 13-38.

O'Danachair, C., 1954-56, 'Armada Losses on the Irish Coast', *The Irish Sword* II (9): 321-331.

Padfield, P., 1988, *Armada*, London: Victor Gollancz

Scandurra, E., 1972, 'The Maritime Republics: Medieval and Renaissance ships in Italy' in Bass, G.F. (ed), *A History of Seafaring*, London: Thames and Hudson

Sténuit , R., 1972 *Treasures of the Armada*, London: Thames and Hudson.

Wignall, S., 1968, *The Spanish Armada Salvage Expedition (1968): a progress report on seven years' research and underwater investigation into the sinking of the Santa Maria de la Rosa* (privately circulated).

Mensun Bound (Oxford University MARE)

A wreck off Alderney from the late Elizabethan Period: An Analysis of the Artefacts[1]

In Volume I of this series, *The Archaeology of Ships of War*, there was a preliminary presentation on the Alderney wreck and its contents by Davenport and Burns (1985). Since that article was written, two seasons of survey (1993 and 1994) have taken place on the site under the technical direction of Michael Bowyer and the archaeological

1 Aerial view of the main harbour area of Alderney. The wreck is situated directly out to sea from the lighthouse in the top left of the picture. The coast of France can be seen in the background (*courtesy Guernsey Press*)

direction of Mensun Bound. Although little significant progress has been made on the understanding and mapping of the site, considerable advances have been made on the recording and study of the artefacts raised from the wreck by the divers of the Alderney Subaqua Club. The present writer, in addition to having examined the site under water, has carried out a study of the artefacts and closely supervised their documentation. The purpose of this chapter is to give a more detailed presentation and analysis of the material recovered, and to speculate upon the nature of the ship and her loss.

Location and nature of the site

The wreck is situated in 26-28.5m of water on a mixed rock and sand bottom, half a mile to a mile north-east of Alderney Harbour (fig 1 and 2). Although visibility is fair, currents are generally strong which means diving (average duration of dive, 20 minutes) can only take place at slack water, a 'window' of about 40 minutes. Most of the finds have come from an open sandy area about 35m across (fig 3). There are, however, many artefacts in the rocky margins surrounding the sand patch.

Ship's timbers

In the rocky areas to the north and west of the main site the writer saw some 20 or more broken timbers. Although it was obvious that some of these pieces represented the ship's contents or other non-pressure-bearing elements, it was equally evident that other pieces were from the vessel's

2 Alderney Harbour. Returning divers unloading their equipment (*Paolo Scremin*)

3 Plan of the site. One of the cannon at the top of the map was raised during the 1994 season. Note the remains of the vessel's rudder in the lower right (*Chris Fitton*)

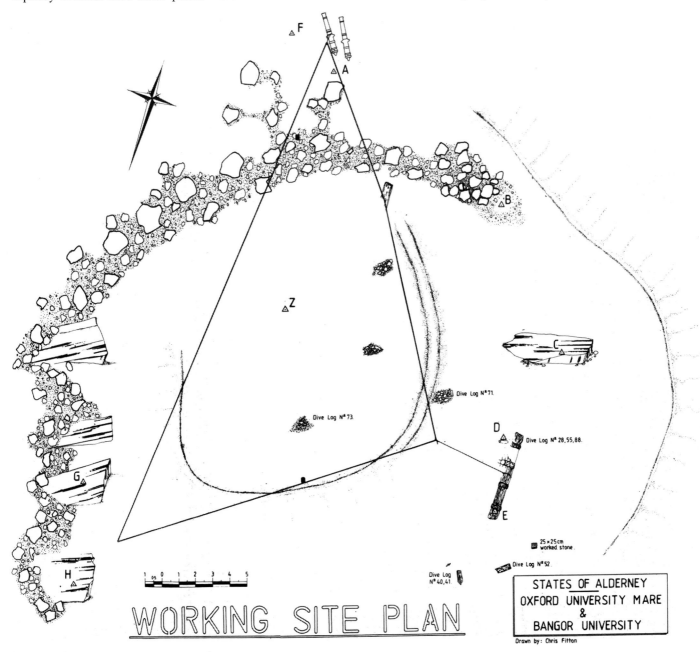

WORKING SITE PLAN

Dive Log Nº 71.
Dive Log Nº 73.
Dive Log Nº 28,55,88.
Dive Log Nº 52.
Dive Log Nº 40,41.

25×25 cm
worked stone.

STATES OF ALDERNEY
OXFORD UNIVERSITY MARE
&
BANGOR UNIVERSITY

Drawn by: Chris Fitton

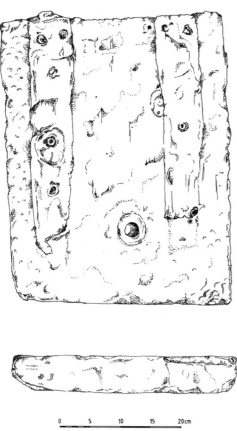

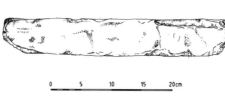

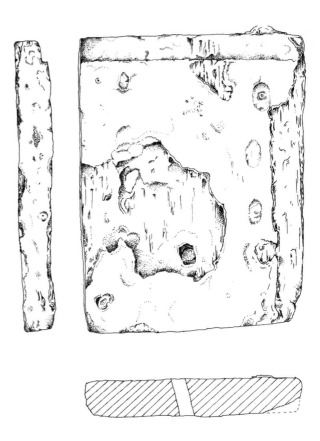

4 Gun port

primary structure or cladding. Most were in poor condition. An exposed assemblage of timbers on the east side of the sandbank has been identified as the ship's rudder. Probing has revealed further timbers beneath the sandbank.

Two rectangular ports were recovered by the Alderney Subaqua Club, one of which (145; fig 4) was certainly a gunport. It had been hung vertically with twin hinges and measured 371 x 462mm. Its thickness diminished from 63mm at the top to 48mm at the bottom. The sides were slightly bevelled so as to provide a better sealing surface and a rebate had been cut along the top edge. A hole of 21mm diameter passed through the port 102mm from its lower edge. The impression of a collar, or washer, in the wood indicated that there had once been an eye-bolt at this point which would have taken the rope that served to raise and lower the port. Indeed, in photographs taken soon after its recovery such a feature is clearly visible. This is one of many examples of how the artefacts have deteriorated or been damaged in recent years by repeated handling and the absence of conservation.

The second port (103) was 363 x 467mm, had a thickness of 48-52mm and appears to have been hung horizontally. It features a hole (diam. 20mm) which has been countersunk on one side to take (presumably) an eye-bolt. It is not certain that this was gunport; it might have been a small hatch or cover.

In 1995 the vessel's rudder and part of the sternpost were raised. They were held together by four gudgeons and pintles. The surviving length of the assembly was 15ft.

Iron fastenings, fittings and accoutrements

Two large, mushroom-headed fastenings were recovered (306 and 393), they had rounded shanks and surviving lengths of 634mm and 344mm respectively. Three of the fastenings (219, 221 and 220) had disc-shaped heads and washers. They had surviving lengths of 410mm, 459mm and 246mm respectively. Three of the iron fittings had eyes at one end: the first (4) had a four-sided shank and a flattened end; the second (225) was 505mm long and diminished to a point; the third (224) was 366mm long and had a roughly oblong hole through the penetrating end of its shank. Six badly eroded bars were recovered which, presumably, had originally been headed. Two of them had washers on their shanks. Other iron fittings and accessories included three hooks (6, 304 and 226), two hinges (227 and 228) and three rings (350, 369 and 370) of varying diameter.

Of particular interest was a pump handle (283; fig 5).

The remains of two anchors survived on the site; one (600; fig 6) comprised the shank, the ring and the remains of both arms and the stock; the other (601) consisted of only the ring and the shank which appeared to be broken at the trend.

Lead fittings and accessories

Two lead scupper linings (299 and 300) were recovered; they had lengths of 285mm and 329mm and diameters of approximately 65mm and 78mm respectively. Both were flared at one end, especially 299.

Two sheets of folded lead were recovered. One (218), folded nine or ten times, had an estimated length of 1970mm and

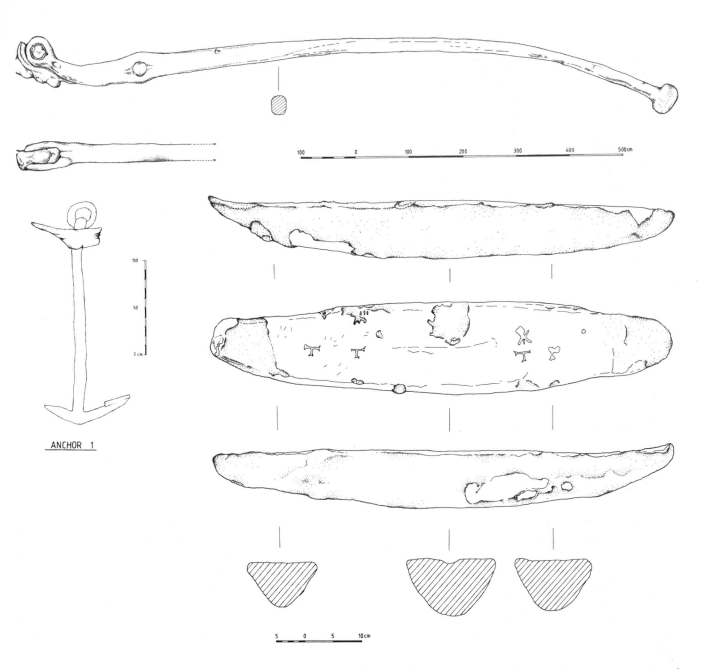

ANCHOR 1

5 *Top* Pump handle

6 *Above left* Tracing made under water of one of the ship's anchors

7 *Above right* Lead ingot

a width of 705mm; the other (301) had been folded three times.

One piece of badly crushed lead (302), approximately 467mm long, contained 26 tack holes. It may have been a repair tingle.

One boat-shaped lead ingot (5, fig 7) was found which is presumed to have been part of the ship's supplies. It was 825mm long, weighed 57 kilos and its flat upper surface was stamped with marks that resembled a capital T.

Cordage and related accoutrements

14 short lengths of cordage were recovered. The majority had been hardened by iron migration and many still smelt of pitch.

Three distinct diameters were observed: 25mm, 16-17mm and 6-7mm. The majority, if not all, were triple-stranded, right-handed, hawser-laid. Those pieces in better condition showed that each strand (left-hand twisted) comprised twelve right-hand spun yarns. One piece of particular interest (483) seemed to have been spliced into a grommet within which were the remains of a concreted iron eye or thimble.

One drop-shaped deadeye with five lanyard holes was recovered from concretion (303; fig 8).

Cooperage, tools, navigational aids and weights

One 703mm long barrel stave was recovered (294). It had been triple crozed at one end. One of its chimes was badly eroded. Examples of white cooperage were also seen on the sea-bed by the writer.

Remains of two tools were found; a concreted saw-blade (82 and 436) and an ash shaft with an oblong head that may have functioned a serving mallet (351).

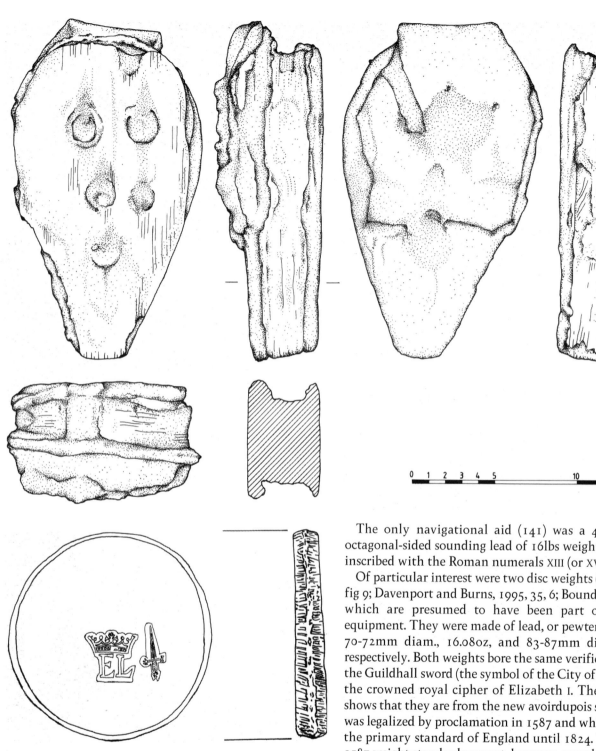

8 *Top* Deadeye still partially covered in concretion

9 *Above* Disc weight stamped with the Guildhall dagger and the crowned cipher of Elizabeth I

10 *Opposite page, top* Photomosaic of iron cannon on sea-bed. Length of cannon in concretion 2.31m.

The only navigational aid (141) was a 437mm long, octagonal-sided sounding lead of 16lbs weight. It had been inscribed with the Roman numerals XIII (or XVI).

Of particular interest were two disc weights (500 and 501; fig 9; Davenport and Burns, 1995, 35, 6; Bound 1995, 14, 13) which are presumed to have been part of the ship's equipment. They were made of lead, or pewter, and were of 70-72mm diam., 16.08oz, and 83-87mm diam, 32.08oz respectively. Both weights bore the same verification marks, the Guildhall sword (the symbol of the City of London) and the crowned royal cipher of Elizabeth I. The crowned EL shows that they are from the new avoirdupois standard that was legalized by proclamation in 1587 and which remained the primary standard of England until 1824. Work on the 1587 weight standard was not, however, completed until the following year, 1588, the year of the Armada. 1588 is thus the *terminus post quem* for the wreck.

Heavy ordnance and shot

Reports vary but there appeared to be a minimum of six to eight iron cannon on the site, all apparently (judging from the shot and the two cannon investigated) of 3½ (89mm) bore.

In a controversial move in 1994, one of the cannon (1000) and part of its carriage was raised to create a media event which, it was hoped, might help with fund-raising (figs 10,

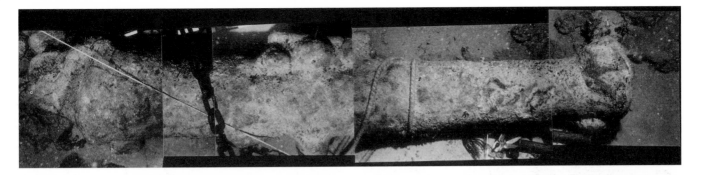

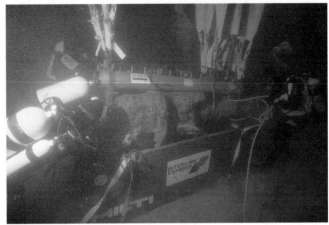

11 Recovery of iron cannon: a) cannon raised from *situ* with lifting-bags b) neutrally buoyant the cannon is walked along the sea-bed to the recovery-tank c) cannon manoeuvred into position over the tank d) lowered into the tank for recovery (*Tim Dingemans*)

a

b

d

11 and 12; Dingemans, 1996). The cannon was first placed in a heavy, unpadded, unlidded iron box and then raised in an uncontrolled manner with lifting bags. During the first attempt one of the bags deflated on the surface and the box and cannon sank back to the sea-bed. It narrowly missed one of the divers, but hit another cannon and ruptured its covering of concretion thus exposing it to severe secondary corrosion[2].

A second attempt to recover the gun was more successful. It was later taken for treatment to the conservation centre of the York Archaeological Trust. During the removal of the concretion it was found that the tampion was in place and that there was a shot within the breech. Its barrel was without any decoration but displayed the number 1400 (its weight in pounds) and it had a bore of 3⁹⁄₁₆ in (91mm), thus making it a saker[3].

The gun hit by the falling cannon had had its muzzle exposed by the impact. On the sea-bed the writer removed the loose pieces of concretion to establish its bore before all definition was lost to secondary corrosion. It was found to have

69

12 *Left* The recovered cannon on a fork-lift carrier

13 *Below* 'Star'-shot

14 *Bottom* Musket with the remains of a pintle on its underside; presumably for shipboard use *(D. MacElvagne)*

15 *Opposite top* Concretion containing five bar-shot

16 *Opposite bottom* Stock fragment showing the recess for the lock mechanism and the faceted groove to seat the barrel

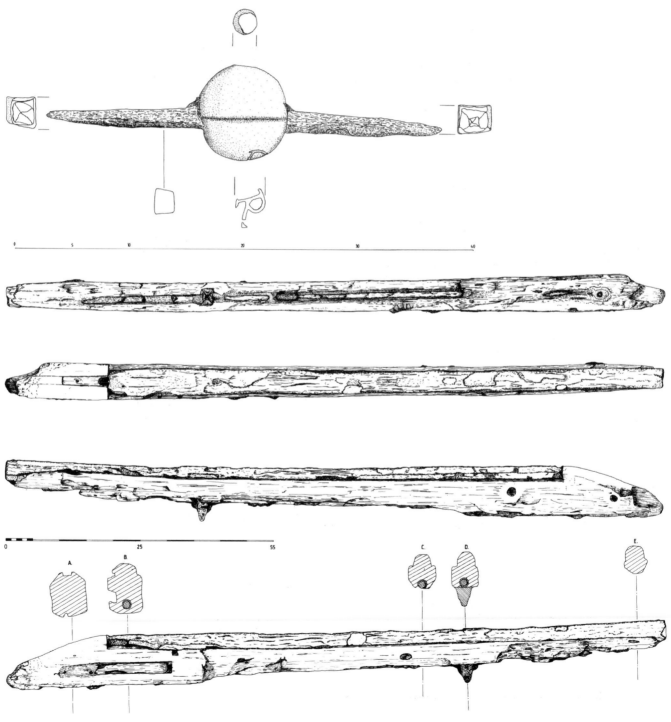

three muzzle rings and a bore of $3\frac{7}{16}$ in (87mm), making it a close reflection of the cannon that had been raised.

41 pieces of round shot, 10 pieces of so-called star-shot and 5 pieces of bar-shot were recovered. The round shot was of $3\frac{1}{8}$ in (79-80mm) diameter. The star-shot (fig 13) consisted of two iron hemispheres cast over an iron bar which drew to a point at each end. In addition to the physical havoc that these latter items would have inflicted upon both men and ship, they were also used at times to carry incendiary material. Each ball was of $3\frac{1}{8}$ to $3\frac{1}{4}$ in (79-81mm) diameter. The longest surviving projection was 131mm, the majority were considerably shorter. The star-shot had suffered more than most artefact groups from deterioration and neglect.

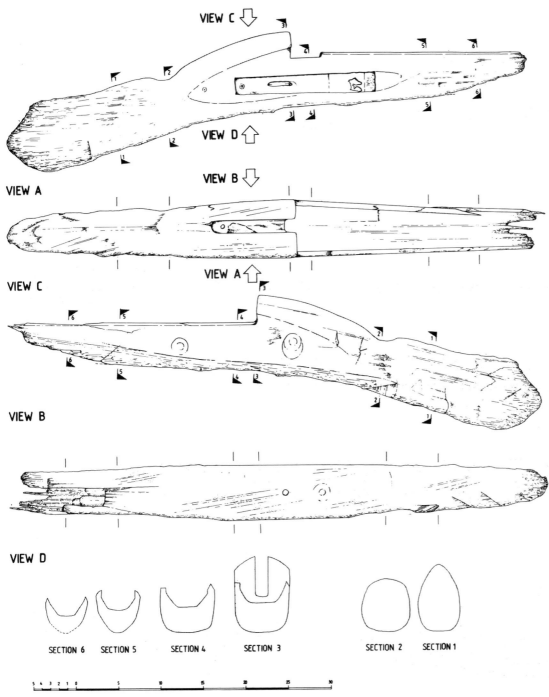

The bar-shot, which were recovered as a single piece of concretion (fig 15), consisted of two iron hemispheres on the ends of an iron bar. Two independent hemispheres were also recovered, one of which appeared to be of lead, or, possibly, iron covered in lead. A further example was seen by the author on the sea-bed but was not recovered. The diameters of the hemispheres were 3 to 3 1/16 in (76-78mm). One void concretion suggested that the ship was also carrying shot of dumb-bell shape. Allowing for windage, all the shot was of a diameter suitable for both the raised and damaged guns (see note 3).

Firearms

45 musket[4] fragments were raised. These consisted of 2 semi-intact stocks and barrels, 26 stock fragments without barrels, 15 barrel fragments and 2 lock fragments. Most, if not all, had been extracted from concretion. All the butts were missing from the stocks and in all cases the lock mechanisms had disintegrated. From the shape of the lock recesses it was evident that nine of the pieces were from matchlocks and one from a possible wheel-lock or snaphaunce. One of the matchlocks, which was much heavier than the others and featured a pintle on the underside of its forestock, had most likely been for shipboard use (391; fig 14).

All the barrels had milled octagonal flats. Frequently the vertical fasciae were wider than the others in order to provide a greater attachment area for the flashpan and baffle. The flats narrowed with the diminution of the barrel and at a certain point the majority, if not all, became rounded. Barrel grooves in the forestocks were cut to reflect the flats (fig 16). A typical barrel was held in position with perforated lugs which had been welded to its underside; these passed through oblong cuttings in the lower side of

the forestock where they were cottered into place with pins that passed horizontally through both the lug and the wood. At the rear, the breech-plug of the barrel slotted into a cutting in the stock. The breech was locked into position with the help of a tang which protruded back from the top of the plug and was screwed down near its extremity.

Two of the barrels were recessed along their right vertical faces at the breech to provide seating for the priming pans. At the front of these recesses were the touch holes through which ignition was communicated to the charge. On one barrel the pan mechanism survived (317; fig 17). It had a rectangular trough (for the priming powder) in the bottom of which was the touch hole. The outside rear corner of the trough (in plan view) was bulbous so as to be able to take the pivot for the cover, which still survived. The purpose of the latter was to protect the powder from spillage, wind and rain. It was opened immediately prior to firing. When the writer first saw this musket in 1992 it had a lobated finger hold on one corner; this was later lost because of deterioration and frequent handling. The long vertical pivot (which has also much deteriorated since 1992) also served to take the baffle (or 'fyre-shield' to the Tudors) which protected the firer's eye from any sparks that might be thrown out by the combustion of the powder. The groove into which this screen slotted can be seen on at least three of the barrels.

Several of the barrel fragments had small recesses at the rear of their upper horizontal flats, these served to take either a back-sight or a match-guide. On the horizontal flat above the breech of barrel fragment 317 featured in figure 17, were the remains of a tube of diminishing diameter, which could either have been a match-guide or a peep-sight. As the former it would have held a slow match; the tube

17 Barrel fragment with priming pan and cover still surviving *(Chris Fitton)*

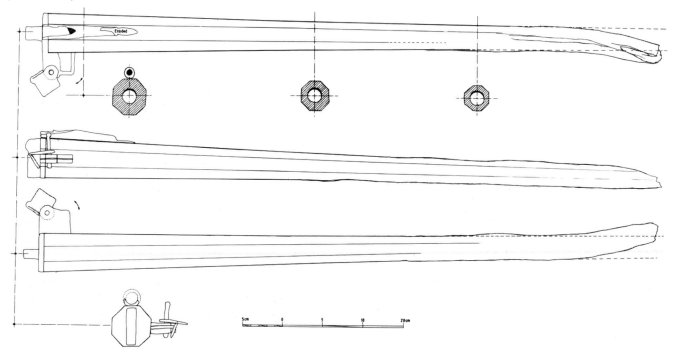

ELEVATION

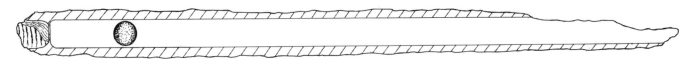

SECTION

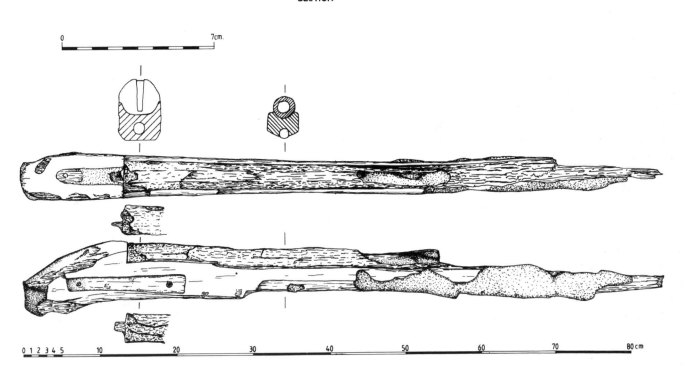

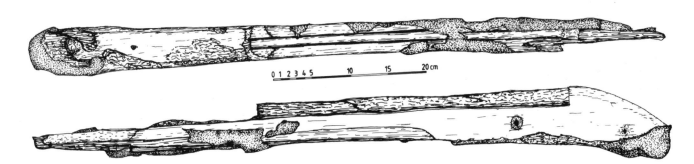

18 Barrel fragment found loaded with shot

19 Stock with part of barrel still surviving. Some concretion still adheres

would then have served to protect the match from wet weather and to prevent it from becoming entangled in the serpentine, the component which carried the burning end of the match into contact with the powder. If, however, it was a peep-sight, then the tube would have contained an iron diaphragm with a pin-hole aperture at centre. Deterioration and corrosion made certain identification impossible. Only one of the barrel fragments showed any evidence of a fore-sight.

The question arises as to whether or not the Alderney barrels were rifled, that is to say given parallel spiral grooves along the interior of their barrels which would impart a spin to the projectile, which in turn would lessen air turbulence and reduce any tendency of the shot to 'wobble' or deviate. Such effects not only greatly improved a projectile's accuracy, but also its range. It is known that barrels were being grooved spirally by 1475 and that by the end of the first quarter of the seventeenth century rifles were being made throughout Europe (Held, 1957, 36). None the less, smooth bores were the most common form of shoulder weapon through much of the sixteenth century, if for no other reason than because the rifled barrel at this time was harder and slower to load since the shot had to be tight within the bore. We would therefore expect service muskets (such as were found on the Alderney wreck) with their relatively weaker rammers, to have been smooth bores. Although deterioration forbade any certain judgements on this question, visual scrutiny of the least corroded barrel interiors supported this conclusion.

The question of bore size was also vexed by corrosion. At the time of the Alderney ship the size of musket shot was defined by how many of them, of any arbitrarily selected diameter were required to make up one avoirdupois pound. For example, pure lead balls of such a diameter that seven of them were required to make up a pound, always had a diameter of .884 inch-decimals. By 1540 the number of balls to a pound became known as the bore number, and the barrel which suited them by the same name. So, pursuing the example, balls of .844 inch-decimal diameters were for 7-bore firearms (Held, 1957, 33).

Three isolated pieces of lead shot were recovered from the wreck. They were unevenly cast, but the largest had a diameter of close to 21mm, or $^{13}/_{16}$ inches. The middle size ball had a diameter of close to 18mm ($^{11}/_{16}$ to ¾ inches) and the smallest ball had a diameter of 12mm ($^{7}/_{16}$ to ½ inches). From the above formula it can be calculated that the largest was for a 9-bore, the middle for a 14-bore, and the smallest for a 43 or 44-bore. Neither the largest nor the smallest balls fitted any of the barrels raised from the wreck, but the middle-size ball fitted the majority of the barrels which had diameters of between 18mm and 19mm. Only two of the barrels were not of this size; interestingly, one of them, which was of lighter appearance than the others, was found to be loaded (fig 18). Its ball had a diameter of 15mm which gave it a bore of 23 or 24.

Long recesses had been cut into the right sides of the stocks to take the locks (figs. 16, 19 and 20). They had an average length of 155mm, were truncated in outline with the broadest end at the front and were either empty or

20 Stock with a pronounced drop to its butt

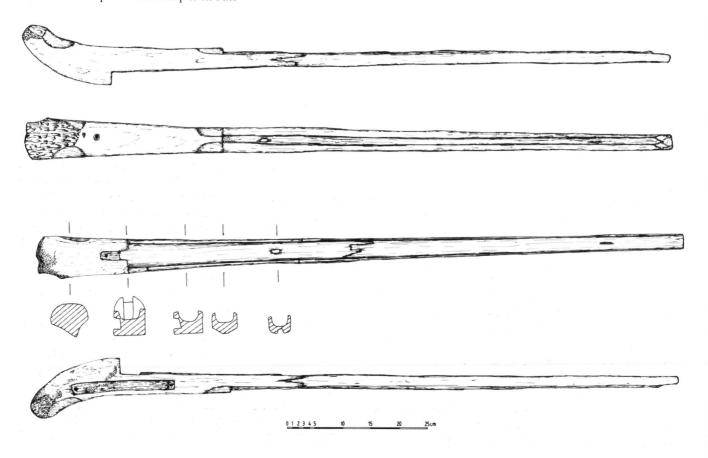

74

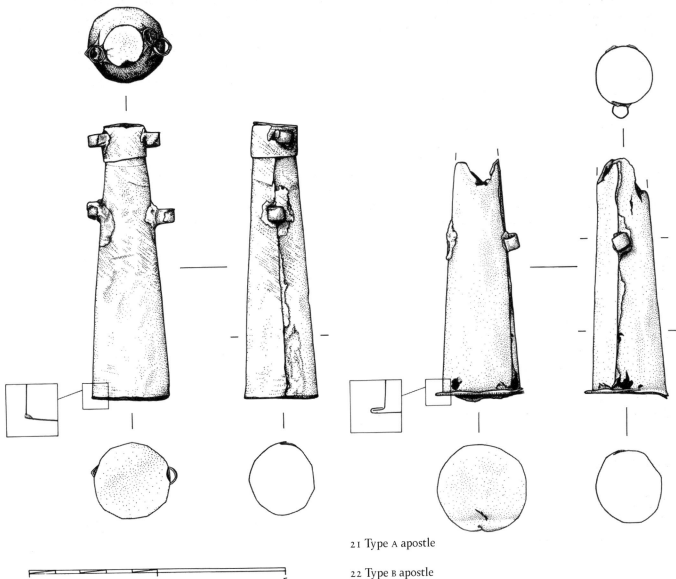

21 Type A apostle

22 Type B apostle

partially full of corrosion products; one still contained the remains of the sear and its pivot. Part of a broken leaf-spring was found which was presumed to have come from a lock mechanism.

The shape and modelling of the stock was different with each weapon. All the butts were missing, the majority having broken off at, or beside, the thumb groove. One of the stocks (3; fig 20), which was apparently older than the others, evidently had had a steeply dropped butt. It also lacked a thumb groove, but did, however, feature a broad recess on the underside to take the three outside fingers, leaving the index finger free to work the trigger bar.

On the underside of all the forestocks was a long, drilled hole (open along its length) to take the rammer. In three of the forestocks the rammer hole survived intact.

Powder containers

24 apostles, or parts of apostles, were recovered (Davenport and Burns, 1995, 33, 3; Bound, 1995, 12, 4; Bound, 1997). One was intact, 19 were semi-intact (i.e. missing caps or eyes), one consisted of only the base and three were fully covered by concretion and are known only from radiographic analyses. All were made from thin copper alloy sheets and had had their seams closed with lead-tin solder. Some contained grains of what appeared to be powder, several still smelt of gunpowder. They divided into two broad categories: type A (fig 21), without a flanged bottom (17 examples), and type B (fig 22), with a flanged bottom (2 examples). Heights (with caps) varied from 99mm to 106mm. Maximum body diameters of type A varied from 27mm to 31mm. One (496, type B) displayed stamped decoration consisting of a diagonal line of palmettes, each with nine fronds (fig 23). Midway between the palmettes were pyramidal arrangements of three small circles. Similar apostles were found on the VOC ship *Nassau* (1606) in the Straits of Malacca (see Bound, Ong and Pickford, 84-105) and wooden examples were recovered from the VOC ship *Vergulde Draeck* that sank off Western Australia in 1656 (Green, 1977, 234-5).

In addition to the apostles, two large trapezoidal wooden flasks for priming powder were recovered (figs. 24 and 25).

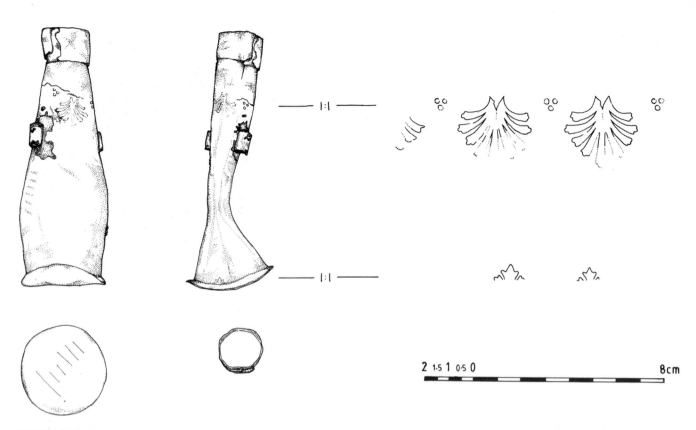

Only one (529) has so far been studied in detail. Apart from an oak panel in the base, the body was of one-piece maplewood construction. Evidence of a leather covering was also found during conservation. Its height was 182mm and its base measured 52 x 225mm.

Grenades

One intact ceramic incendiary grenade (1028) was recovered along with an additional 135 fragments which perhaps represented a minimum of between 8 and 12 further

23 *Top* Crushed apostle with stamped decoration

24 *Above left* Bryan Smith with powder flask from the wreck

25 *Above* Ian Panther of the York Archaeological Trust examines a second powder flask from the wreck which is still covered with concretion

grenades. They were all globular in form with well-defined rims over which fabric covers had been tied and tarred. Their light buff or orange clay recalled Beauvaisware. Some of the fragments had traces of the incendiary compound on their interiors, while rim fragment 1027 retained traces of fabric and a resinous, or pitch-like material which would have served as a waterproofing and sealing agent.

Bladed weapons

Remains were also recovered from a number of bladed weapons and more were seen by the author towards the north of the site. Three hilts and 16 grips were raised. The main hilt (206) consisted of no more than a concreted shell in which could be seen the cup and the voids of the lower quillon, the knuckleguard and the rear of a wedge-shaped blade with a ricasso at top.

Of particular note was a concretion that contained a sword or rapier hilt (80). It consisted of half a grip, counter-curving quillons and a protective cup and basket.

In addition there were 12 intact or fragmented grips from slashing or thrusting blades. All (with one possible exception) were of wood. The majority were four-sided with rounded edges and varied in length from 92mm to 105mm. One of the grips (86) still had part of the iron tang within the handle. At the end where the tang entered the grip it was sometimes possible to determine the section of the blade; no. 90, for example, had a void which suggested that the blade had been slightly hour-glass shaped in profile, in other words it had a 'fuller' or shallow groove down both sides, the purpose of which was to lighten the blade without weakening it.

Four pommels from the rear of sword hilts were recovered. All were holed for attachment and all were of a softish metal of a gold or brass-like appearance. Their lengths were from 12.5 to 14.0mm.

There were also four shorter grips which were likely to have been from knives or daggers. Two were wound with double-stranded, twisted, copper-alloy wire. Concretion 343 contained a wire-bound grip which had a large 29mm diameter disc at its rear, recalling the 'rondel' daggers of the 1590s.

16 pieces of sword scabbard were recovered from concretion. The remains of blades inside the scabbards suggested that the majority were double edged. One, 343, was single edged. Scabbards consisted of two wooden laths covered with leather. X-rays of one heavily concreted end-fragment revealed a chape piece.

One concretion (83) contained the void of a rapier. The blade was kite-shaped in section with the upper, shorter sides slightly concave. Lines in the concretion suggested that the weapon had been sheathed.

In 1994 parts of two swords were found concreted to the side of a breast plate and in 1995 a complete, sheathed sword was raised.

Helmets

19 intact and fragmented helmets were recovered. Three were apparently of burgonet type, seven were apparently of

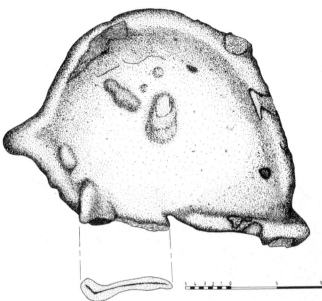

26 Project divers with helmet from wreck. Left to right: Kenny Stevens, Alan Johnson, Fred Shaw, Dave Gillingham and Mensun Bound

27 Morion helmet covered in concretion

morion type and nine were of uncertain form. Almost all were heavily concreted (figs 26 and 27). Several had been compressed out of shape. Because of the concretion precise descriptions are impossible, but it could be seen that there was much variation within the morion group. All had flaring rims and a medial rib (or comb) but some were higher, or drawn to a finer point than others At least two of the morions had cheek pieces. Around the lower body of most of the morions was a row of copper-alloy rivets with rosette heads. Two helmet fragments of uncertain type (271 and 239) contained perforated leather straps. The burgonets could be distinguished by their high combs. None had survived intact.

Body armour

The body armour consisted mainly of peascod-type breast-plates and back-plates. The breast-plates were of a scalloped shape and had a somewhat inflated appearance; some, if not

28 *Above* Breast-plate on the sea-bed with piece of star-shot in the foreground (*Tim Dingemans*)

29 *Right* A selection of pottery from the wreck (*Paolo Scremin*)

most, had a vertical medial ridge. The lower edges and arm notches were usually characterized by a short flaring lip (the latter being shorter than the former). 14 intact, semi-intact and fragmented pieces of body armour survived. All were fully concreted. Two intact breast-plates (489 and 490) were found stored one within the other. Two back-plates were also recovered. There were also many concreted fragments which could not be attributed to any specific item of armour.

In 1994, a heavily concreted breast-plate (560; fig 28) was recovered from the site. When first seen by the writer it was sitting in a semi-upright position in the sand giving the impression that it had just been exposed by the mutating sands; now, however, there is good reason to suspect that it had been disturbed from *situ* by an earlier dive. Concreted to its lower sides were two sword and scabbard fragments. Radiographic scrutiny also revealed an apostle (579) and two pieces of bone. The site, it must be remembered, is littered with animal bones and sword fragments and, at the time of writing, there was no archaeological proof to show that the swords had been hanging from the plate, or that the bones were of human origin. In other words, there is nothing to prove that the plate was being worn when it sank.

Pottery, metalware, and cutlery
The pottery (fig 29) was covered by Davenport and Burns in *The Archaeology of Ships of War* (1995, 36-40). Since then, however, there has been an opportunity for a further count of the ceramic remains.

In addition to the bellarmine pieces featured by Davenport and Burns (1995, 38, 9-11) there were some 23 fragments from similar stoneware jars. One group of fragments (1064) featured a quartered coat of arms with four lions rampant, the letter A above the shield and the numbers 8 and 6 on either side (Davenport and Burns, 1995, 38, 12). Three of the fragments, or groups of fragments (1065, 1066 and 1078), displayed parts of floral roundels. One group of fragments (1068) contained a mask that was missing its upper forehead and lower beard.

Some 51 tin-glazed albarelli fragments were counted. Most, if not all, were from the Low Countries. They had the typical pink/ochre porous fabric and featured the usual range of motifs (dots, horizontals, zig-zags, chevrons, lozenges, leaves and palmettes) in blue, yellow, red and orange against a white background (Davenport and Burns, 1995, 38, 13-16).

Some 26 fragments appeared to be from pipkins (some of the smaller pieces were not so easy to interpret). They were from the Low Countries and Northern France and had a pink or buff fabric with a green, yellow or reddish glaze on their interiors.

Some 53 fragments represented various forms, fabrics and decorative devices that can perhaps be linked to the Low Countries. An additional 60 fragments resisted any certain identification, but included what appeared to be Beauvais

stoneware and other fabrics that were very likely of French origin. One or two pieces recalled the Rhineland. Some fragments clearly came from chafing-dishes and at least two pieces were probably from tiles.

A one 'ear' pewter porringer (516; fig 30) and flask (502; fig 31) have been well described elsewhere (Bound, 1995, 13, 14; Davenport and Burns, 1995, 335, 8 and 7). Mention should also be made of another flask top (371) and a pewter bottle top (150) which has been referred to by non-specialists as a candle snuffer. Six metal fragments came from iron cooking pots. Four pewter spoons were also recovered, only one of which (491; fig 32; Davenport and Burns, 1995, 36, 10-11) was completely intact; it was 155mm long and had a round floral touch-mark and a plain wedge-shaped terminal.

Miscellaneous artefacts
Artefacts which do not fit any of the above categories included a pair of stirrups (494 and 495; fig 33), two tobacco pipes (236 and 237), a comb (136), a razor handle (22), some manicure items and shoe remains. Most of these have been presented in Davenport and Burns (1995) or Bound (1995).

Animal bones
A large number of animal bones litter the site. No human remains have so far been identified. 36 bones (many with clear evidence of butchery) were recovered which were sent

by the writer to the bones unit of Southampton University where they were studied by Mary Illes. Her analysis can be summarized as follows: nine cow bones, two pig bones, two sheep or goat bones, six fish bones (three of which were cod), ten cattle or horse ribs and seven small sheep or pig bones.

Identity, chronology and general nature of the wreck

It has been frequently said, that the wreck is that of the *Makeshift*, a small vessel of fairly common name, which, it seems, disappeared from the record sometime around the latter part of the sixteenth century. As far as the writer is aware there is no historical or archaeological evidence to link the *Makeshift* to the Alderney wreck.

There are, however, a number of useful points that can be made regarding the nationality, chronology, type and role of the vessel. It has been assumed by most that the vessel is of English origin, but this is a matter that requires scrutiny of a more considered nature. The proximity of Alderney to France means that more West Continental vessels than English would be passing by the island. Also, all the pottery that has so far been positively identified, is of West Continental manufacture and the name on the bottom of the porringer is certainly not of native English derivation. Nor can the floral touchmark on the spoons be automatically associated with the Tudor rose as this was a devise that was also common on Continental European

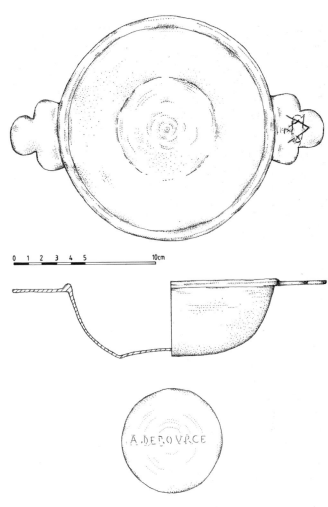

30 *Upper right* Pewter porringer with A DE POURCE (or A DE BOURCE) inscribed on its underside

31 *Below* A pewter flask with protomes to take a cord or thong

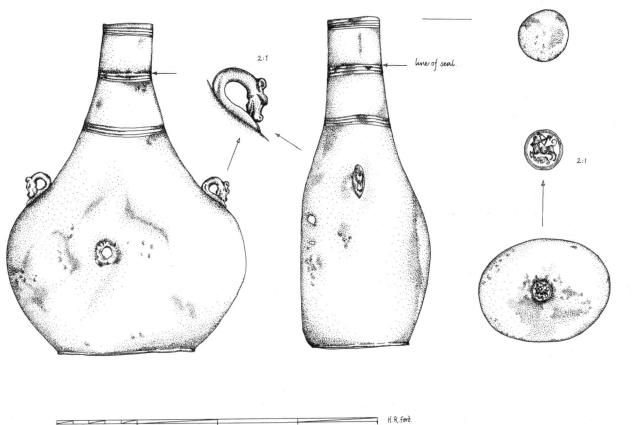

79

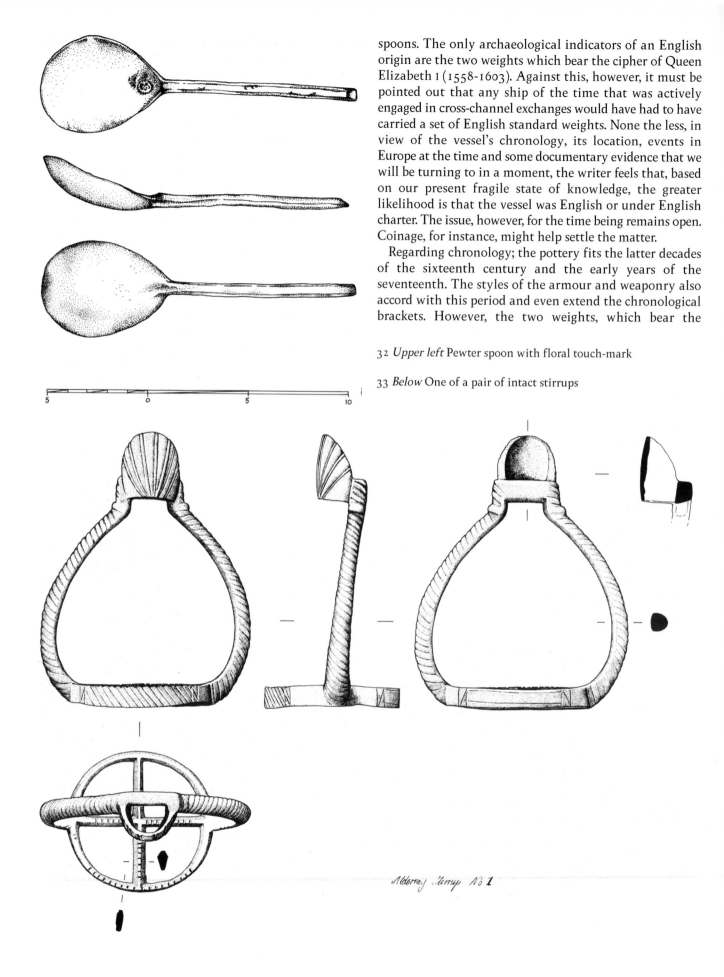

spoons. The only archaeological indicators of an English origin are the two weights which bear the cipher of Queen Elizabeth I (1558-1603). Against this, however, it must be pointed out that any ship of the time that was actively engaged in cross-channel exchanges would have had to have carried a set of English standard weights. None the less, in view of the vessel's chronology, its location, events in Europe at the time and some documentary evidence that we will be turning to in a moment, the writer feels that, based on our present fragile state of knowledge, the greater likelihood is that the vessel was English or under English charter. The issue, however, for the time being remains open. Coinage, for instance, might help settle the matter.

Regarding chronology; the pottery fits the latter decades of the sixteenth century and the early years of the seventeenth. The styles of the armour and weaponry also accord with this period and even extend the chronological brackets. However, the two weights, which bear the

32 *Upper left* Pewter spoon with floral touch-mark

33 *Below* One of a pair of intact stirrups

Alderney Stirrup Nº 1

Guildhall dagger and crowned cipher of Elizabeth I, give us a *terminus post quem* of 1588. In other words, the wreck must date between then and the early years of the seventeenth century.

What about the vessel itself and the nature of its activities? The dimensions of the timbers on the sea-bed and those raised, the size of the rudder and the measurements of her two anchors all suggest a vessel of relatively light burthen. The apparent lack of a large ballast mound (such as was found on some of the Spanish Armada wrecks of 1588 and the casualties of the battle of Cape Rachado in 1606) gives some support to this, although certainly there will be some ballast somewhere on the site.

In addition there is the evidence of her heavy ordnance. So far only six to eight cannon have been seen, even if we add a couple more to allow for guns that might be concealed by the sand, it still does not add up to an armament that might be associated with a large vessel or capital ship. The bores of the guns are perhaps a more telling factor. None of the concreted cannon seen by the writer was of a size that might suggest a culverin or demi-culverin, and the two guns which we have been able to examine were both of saker size, which, as we have already observed, is consistent with all

the shot that has so far been raised (see note 3). Surely if she was carrying any heavier artillery, cannon-balls to match would by now have been found.

Regarding the nature of her activities; the quantity of armour, muskets (but not shot), bladed weapons and grenades that have been raised and seen on the sea-bed, are quite disproportionate to the needs of a vessel of this size; thus the indications are that she was functioning as a munitions carrier. Also, there is an argument to be made that the weaponry on board is more reflective of landed warfare than that which might be associated with seaborne fighting on a vessel of the type we have just sketched.

Archive evidence

Our understanding of the wreck is helped by archive information in the Public Records Office, London, which mentions an unnamed vessel that was lost off Alderney and which not only fits the chronology but also seems to accord with the archaeological evidence described above. The research was carried out by David Parham to whom the author is indebted for sharing his findings and thoughts.

Parham's research concentrated on two letters from Sir John Norris who was commanding an English expeditionary

34 Excavation office

35 Principal holding-tank for artefacts

force in Brittany at the time (Wernham, 1984; MacCaffrey, 1992). The first letter (SP, F, 1592, vol. 78, m. 68), dated 29 November 1592; was to Elizabeth I's Chief Minister and refers to dispatches that had been sent to him after he had left England on 27 October 1592, but which had been lost off Alderney:

... Lastly I must beseech your L: to hasten her Mats resolution and answer to my former letters, whereof I have not hard nothynge but that toe packets sent from your L: sins my comying over are lost In a shypp that was cast away about Alderney ...

The second letter (SP, F, 1993, vol. 79, m. 351), dated 1st February 1593, refers to orders for musters that had not arrived and which Norris assumes were also lost on the ship which sank off Alderney.

In view of the archaeological evidence and the reliable nature of Parham's sources and the historical events to which they relate, it would seem unnecessarily perverse to ignore the possibility of a common identity between the wreck and the vessel referred to in Norris's letters.

Although Norris makes no reference to the type of vessel lost, we can perhaps assume that any ship engaged in carrying vital military dispatches in which speed was of the essence, would be fleet of movement, small of burthen and possessed of those sailing qualities that a dispatch vessel would require in order to out-manoeuvre and out-distance larger and better armed vessels of a belligerent disposition. In this regard it is significant that Parham also found a document of the Privy Council (APC., vol. 24, 10) dated 7 January 1593, authorizing the fitting out of a pinnace[5] for purposes of communication with Norris in Brittany. As Parham has pointed out (pers. comm.), it seems reasonable to assume that this pinnace was intended as a replacement for the vessel that had been lost off Alderney two months before, and that if this is so, then it is equally reasonable to suppose that the replacement would be of broadly similar type.

The loss of the vessel
The loaded cannon and musket cannot, by themselves, be taken as proof that the vessel was lost in a fire-fight situation. It was common practise during the Elizabethan period for ships to sail with their artillery loaded (Caruana, 1994, 23) and surely it is significant that the recovered cannon was found with its tampion in place. Also, at this time, fire-arms were often carried in loaded state. Furthermore, if the vessel had been lost in a fire-fight surely Norris would have alluded to it in his dispatches; indeed his very use of the words 'cast away' convey a more natural reason for her loss, such as being overwhelmed by the sea, or having her bottom lacerated on one of Alderney's many reefs. The apparent absence of personal valuables (e.g. coins) and human bones, suggest that the crew managed to escape from the stricken ship.

To conclude, the evidence, although to a certain extent circumstantial, is none the less compelling and points to a smallish, nimble, lightly armed vessel of little offensive capability that was of likely English origin (but not a Queen's ship) which was acting, at the time of her loss from natural causes in November 1592, as a dispatch carrier and military transport in support of Norris's expeditionary force in France.

36 Graham Wright with a Roman amphora recovered by Alderney fishermen from off the south of England in 1994

Acknowledgements

My foremost debt is to the Alderney Subaqua Club who not only raised the overwhelming majority of the artefacts discussed here, but who were also the backbone of the survey. I am also indebted to Rosemary Hanbury, Sherry Milan, Sue Worth, Royston Ramond, Barry Juniper, Brian and Jean Bonnard and Peter Arnold for providing accommodation and other much needed help during the preparation of this report. On scholarly matters Anne Smith gave invaluable assistance, as did Mary Illes of the Southampton Bones Unit and David Parham who generously shared with me the fruits of his research at the Public Records Office, London. Drawings by Helen Ford, Jenny Taylor, Tania Alexander, Chris Fitton and Douglas MacElvogue. Photographs by Paolo Scremin, Graham Wright and Tim Dingemans.

Notes

1 In the text artefact numbers are given in parentheses.

2 This method of recovering cannon is not recommended to other teams.

3 W. Bourne, writing shortly before the Alderney wreck in 1587 (69-70), describes three kinds of saker: those of the 'oldest sorte' having a bore of 4 inches; the saker 'ordinaire', having a bore of 3¾ inches, and 'sakers lower than ordinaire, the heygth of the mouth of the peece 3 ynches a halfe, the heygth of the shotte 3 ynches a quarter, the weyghte of the shotte of yron 4 pounds three quarters or neere 5 pound, the weyghte of the peece 1300 or 1400, the length of the peece, 8 foote, or thereaboutes'. J. Smith writing after the Alderney wreck in 1627 (70), describes the 'sacre' as having a bore of 3½ inches, a weight of 1400lbs, and an iron shot weight of 5⅓ lbs. R. Norton writing about the same time (1628, 53) describes the saker as having bore of 3½, 3¾ and 4 inches with weights of 1400, 1500 and 1600lbs (respect.), iron shot weights of 5, 5¼ and 5½ lbs (respect.) and a length of 9ft. Adrian Caruana (1994, 9), quoting Cyprian Lucar's *Art of Shooting* (1588), records the saker as having a 3½ inch bore, a shot diameter of 3¼ inches, a shot weight of 5¼ lbs and a service charge of 4lbs.

4 For reasons of space and to avoid a tedious discussion on nomenclature, I have, in this report, disregarded the words 'caliver', 'arquebus' and 'harquebus' as well as their various derivatives, in favour of the more general term 'musket' which, I think, all but the most obdurate purist will accept as covering all shoulder-arms of all calibres of both match-lock and wheel-lock type.

5 A two-master of about 30-50 tons.

References

Blackmore, H.L., 1976, *The Armouries of the Tower of London*, 1 Ordnance, HMSO London.

Bound, M., 1994, Preparing for the field: the intellectual dimension as well as some practical considerations, *Deguwa Rundbrief*, 7, 24-31

Bound, M., 1995, An Elizabethan shipwreck off Alderney, *Minerva*, 6, 2, 11-14

Bound, M., 1997, A late Elizabethan wreck off Alderney in the Channel Islands, *Underwater Archaeology*, proceedings of the 1997 Society for Historical Archaeology Conference, D. Lakey (ed.), Corpus Christi, Texas

Bourne, W., 1578, *The Art of Shooting Great Ordnance*, London.

Caruana, A.B., 1994, *The History of English Sea Ordnance*, 1523-1875, vol. 1, Jean Boudriot Publications

Davenport, T. and Burns, R., 1995, A sixteenth century wreck off the island of Alderney, *The Archaeology of Ships of War*, Mensun Bound (ed.), Anthony Nelson, 30-40

Dingemans, T., 1996, An Elizabethan-era wreck in the Channel Islands, *Sea History*, 78, 10-12

Green, J.N., 1977, *The VOC jacht Vergulde Draeck, wrecked Western Australia 1656*, BAR Supplementary Series 36(i), Oxford

Held, R., 1957, *The Age of Firearms: A pictorial history*, London

Lucar, C., 1588, *The Art of Shooting*, London

MacCaffrey, W.T., 1992, *Elizabeth I War and Politics 1588-1603*, Princeton Univ. Press

Norton, R., 1628, *The Gunner, shewing the whole Practise of Artillerie*, London

Smith, J., 1627, *A Sea Grammer: With the plaine exposition of Smith's accidence for young sea-men*, London

Wernham, R.B., 1984, *After the Armada, Elizabethan England and the struggle for Western Europe, 1588-1595*, Oxford Univ. Press

Mensun Bound (Oxford University MARE)
Ong Soo Hin (Transea Sdn, Bhn)
Nigel Pickford

1998

The Dutch East Indiaman *Nassau*, lost at the Battle of Cape Rachado, Straits of Malacca, 1606

Background

In 1497 Vasco da Gama made the first voyage to India and returned with a cargo of spices. The Portuguese quickly followed this success with the establishment of a chain of fortified trading posts around the Indian Ocean and beyond (Sofala 1505, Mozambique 1507, Goa 1510, Malacca 1511, Hormuz 1515). Using these strategically placed bases they were able to dominate the spice trade during the sixteenth century, but by the end of the century, the Dutch were penetrating these lucrative markets with growing success. In order to secure and expand their Asian interests, the various Dutch chambers of commerce joined together in 1602 to form the Vereenigde Oost-Indische Compagnie (VOC), the United East India Company. Within a short time the VOC were planning the capture of the booming Portuguese possession of Malacca. Situated on the Malay peninsular midway along the Straits of Malacca, this fortress was the hub of the spice trade. From here the Portuguese controlled the Far Eastern trades (Bound, 1997).

The voyage to Malacca

At 10.00 hours on 12th May 1605, seven ships of the Amsterdam chamber set sail from the Marsdiep Roads, south of Texel Island, under the command of the distinguished Dutch admiral, Cornelius Matelief (fig 1; Matelife, 1608). On 14th May they anchored near Fort Rammekens to await two ships of the Zeeland Chamber, *Amsterdam* and *Kleine Zon* which had made their way from Middelburg through the Wielingen. They arrived on the 24th May. Two further ships were expected, the *Erasmus* and *Geunieerde Provincien* (United Provinces) but the sailing season for the East was already well advanced, so it was decided to leave without them. The fleet comprised:

	Last[1]	Tons	Men on board
Oranje (Orange) flag ship	350	700	148
Nassau (fig 2)	160	320	85
Middelburg	300	600	124
Witte Leeuw (White Lion)	270	540	104
Zwarte Leeuw (Black Lion)	300	600	127
Mauritius	350	700	144
Grote Zon (Great Sun)	270	540	156
Amsterdam	350	700	179
Kleine Zon (Small Sun)	110	220	67

1 Title-page of Matelief's published account of his expedition to Malacca

The fleet passed Madeira on 23rd June 1605. Their first port of call was the Isle of May in the Cape Verde Islands where they anchored on 4th July to take on fresh water, wild goats meat, hens, fish and salt. On 18th July, prior to their departure, Matelief, in the *Oranje*, opened his secret instructions from the Heren Seventien, the ruling body of the VOC, formed from the directors of the various chambers. These instructions contained details of the proposed attack on the Portuguese fort at Malacca. At this stage, however, he communicated his orders only to his most trusted officers. The fleet sailed from the Cape Verde Islands on 19th July and followed a southerly course along the west coast of Africa.

They reached the Portuguese possession of Annabon on 7th September 1605, here they stopped because of advancing scurvy within the fleet and the need for additional ballast in some of the ships. They set sail again on 15th September 1605. On 21st November they rounded the Cape of Good Hope, or Cape d'Aiguilles, and on 1st January 1606, reached

AN
Historicall and true

discourse, of a voyage made by the
Admirall Cornelis Matelife *the*
yonger, into the East Indies, who departed
out of Holland, in May 1605.

With the besieging of *Malacca*,
and the battaile by him fought at Sea against the
*Portugales in the Indies, with other
discourses.*

Translated out of the Dutch, according
to the coppie printed at
Rotterdam.

Imprinted at London for *William Barret*, and are to be
sold at his shop in Paules Church-yard, at
the signe of the greene Dragon, 1608.

2 The VOC ship *Nassau* sank in flames during the Battle of Cape Rachado (*drawing Teh Soo Ghee*)

Mauritius. By 22nd March, they saw the Cape of Acheh (Cape Acheen) on the north coast of Sumatra but were unable to approach because of difficult winds. By the 28th March they were anchored in a bay on the south-west of Nicobar Island where they found fresh water of which they were in great need, and traded with the natives for chickens and coconuts.

On 3rd April 1606, a general council of the fleet was held and on the 4th they set sail for Malacca. It was at this point that Matelief informed the men of his instructions to attack and capture Malacca. Immediately there was serious unrest. The crews argued that they had been enlisted as sailors, not as soldiers to fight on land. Matelief showed them his commission from the States General and spoke of the honour that they would achieve by their action. It seems, however, that what probably had more sway was Matelief's promise that they would share in any booty obtained from the capture. He also promised a general pardon to all offenders and released those members of the crew who were in irons. For the time being the men were pacified and the voyage continued.

By 29th April 1606, the fleet was within the Straits of Malacca. Matelief had taken almost a year to reach his destination. As he drew near to Malacca, He seized three ships from Kedah carrying sarongs. On discovering their ownership he ordered their return as he wished to establish friendly relations with the King of Kedah, seeing him as a potential ally against the Portuguese. He kept a fourth Kedah vessel and paid for its contents, which consisted of rice, arrack and chickens. These provisions were distributed amongst the fleet, each ship receiving 3½ tons of rice.

As Matelief moved into Malacca on 30th April 1606, he surprised four ships at anchor close to the town's walls. The vessels were of a medium size, one of 400 tons, one of 200 tons and two of 160 tons. Armed chaloupes and canots were immediately despatched to attack and burn them. The four ships were destroyed but on the *Mauritius* three men were killed and nineteen injured by an exploding firebomb.

The siege of Malacca

Immediately upon Matelief's arrival in Malacca a dispatch boat was sent to the King of Johor to inform him of the Dutch presence and to solicit his support during the attack upon Malacca. It is clear that the groundwork for this alliance between the Dutch and the Malays had already been settled beforehand. The Dutch held a council of war to decide whether to attack straight away or to await assistance from Johor. Matelief was in favour of the former but conceded to the majority who preferred to await the arrival of Malay support.

The first Malay contingent arrived on 17th May 1606, and included the Malay leader Radja Sabrang or Raja Zabarang (now known as Raja Seberang) together with 300 Malays in galleys and fustas. On Raja Seberang's arrival he presented Matelief with a diamond studded keris whilst the Dutch presented the Malays with an inlaid double-barrelled pistol, two conventional pistols, a sword and various other armaments.

There followed some hard bargaining between Matelief and Raja Seberang after which a treaty was agreed concerning the siege of Malacca and the division of spoils and responsibilities.

Despite the arrival of a further 400 Malays, Matelief decided against a frontal assault on Malacca, his preferred method being to starve it into submission. By 4th June 1606, it appears that he had successfully managed to encircle the town.

On 14th June the *Geunieerde Provincien* and the *Erasmus*, the ships of the Meuse that Matelief had awaited in vain more than a year before, finally arrived with 145 fresh men and an invaluable supply of gunpowder.

The Portuguese made several spirited attacks from their stronghold. A certain Gaspar de Conseca made a foray with only four men. Costa de Andria made another attack with forty men, some of them Javanese. During the first of these a Dutch sentinel was killed and dismembered; his mutilated parts being displayed upon the walls. Matelief, in reply, demanded that the perpetrator of this atrocity be punished or he would execute his Portuguese prisoners. Andre Furtado, the Portuguese Captain of the garrison, refused saying that the more prisoners Matelief hanged, the more fiercely his own men would be encouraged to fight. Matelief responded by hanging in sight of the city walls one of the Portuguese prisoners, a luckless fellow called Domingus Ionsalvo. He was selected by lottery. On another occasion the Portuguese master gunner, a Dutchman, was accused of treachery for having deliberately burst a number of their cannon; he also was hanged. These incidents reflect the increasing savagery of the conflict.

3 Map of the Straits of Malacca showing the Bambek Shoal and the location of the *Nassau (Chris Fitton)*

The battle of Cape Rachado (fig 3)

By August it was becoming increasingly apparent that the town could not hold out for much longer. Every day 35-40 people were dying and the stench had become terrible.

On 14th August 1606, a much superior Portuguese fleet of thirty or more vessels (including oared galleys) under the command of the Viceroy of Goa, Don Martin d'Alphonso de Castro, was sighted by the look-out ship *Kleine Zon*. Matelief, who had been contemplating a final attack, immediately reversed his decision and gave the order to re-embark their guns and munitions. By 16th August the entire Dutch fleet was heading north towards Cape Rachado (fig 4).

The agreed tactic, as laid down by the directors of the VOC, was to avoid being boarded and to combat the Portuguese with their large cannon. Matelief came within range of the Portuguese fleet that same evening and shots were exchanged. By nightfall both sides had anchored; the wind was from the south and the Dutch were to windward of the Portuguese.

The precise nature and order of the following day's events vary from writer to writer but, in broad outline, they are all agreed that the next morning the Portuguese, with the wind in their favour, were the first to be under way. The *Nassau* (fig 5) was caught at anchor and was boarded by the *Santa Cruz*. Matelief in the *Oranje* went to her assistance, but

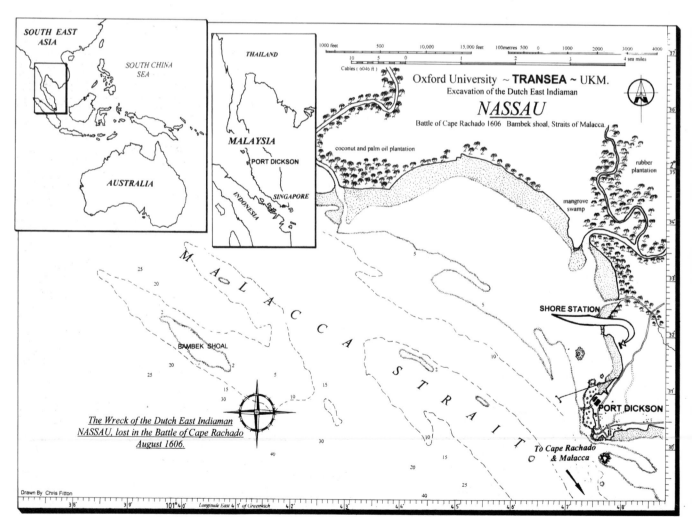

collided with the *Middelburg*. The Portuguese, seizing the opportunity, pounced on the entangled Dutch. The *Sao Salvador*, captained by Alvaro de Carvalho, then attacked the *Middelburg* and the galleon of Dom Henrique de Noronha engaged the *Oranje*. The galleon of Dom Duarte de Guerra also took on the *Oranje* and the *Mauritius* in turn attacked Dom Duarte de Guerra's galleon (fig 6).

At this point Matelief in the *Oranje* put out an anchor (presumably to try to disengage himself from the other ships by letting the current carry them away from him) but its cable was burnt (Jacques L'Hermite, 1623-26, mentions the entire bowsprit of the *Oranje* coming away and falling into the sea). A second anchor was cast which held. The galleon of Dom Duarte de Guerra, the *Middelburg* and the *Sao Salvador* drifted away grappled together and on fire. All three eventually sank - still grappled together. The *Oranje*

had meanwhile been grappled by the galleon of Dom Henrique de Noronha, who, according to Matelief's account (Matelief, 1608), surrendered to Matelief but he was unable to take possession of the ship as it was carried off on the current and so escaped being made a prize. Versions of this event vary considerably from historian to historian.

Meanwhile, the *Santa Cruz* had been joined in its attack on the *Nassau* by the *Conceicao*. They were unable to take the *Nassau* and so set her on fire. The flames would also have consumed the *Conceicao* had the galleys not pulled her away. The *Mauritius*[2] and the *Zwarte Leeuw* attempted to attack the *Conceicao* but were unable to engage because of an absence of favourable wind. According to Boxer in *The Affair of the Madre Deus* (1928-29), the *Nassau* burnt to the water line before sinking. Crommelin mentions the *Nassau* exploding at the stern.

4 Sixteenth century engraving of the Battle of Cape Rachado, fought beside the Bambek Shoal in the Straits of Malacca, 1606 *(Museum of the Book, Holland)*

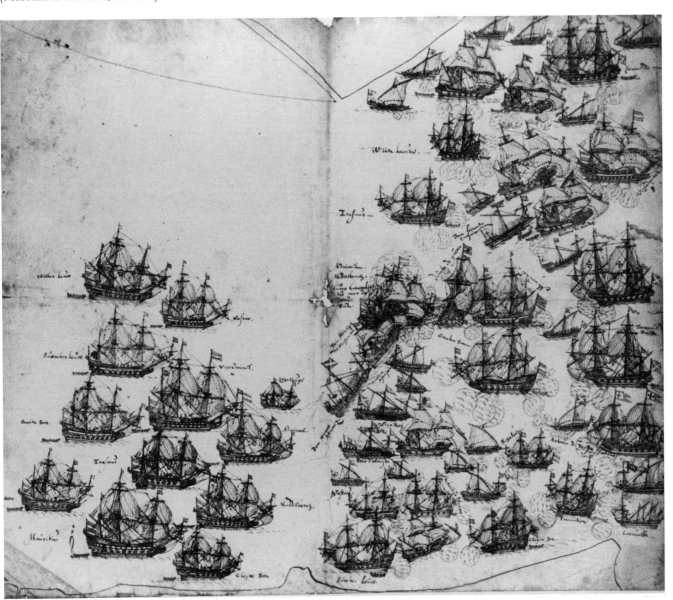

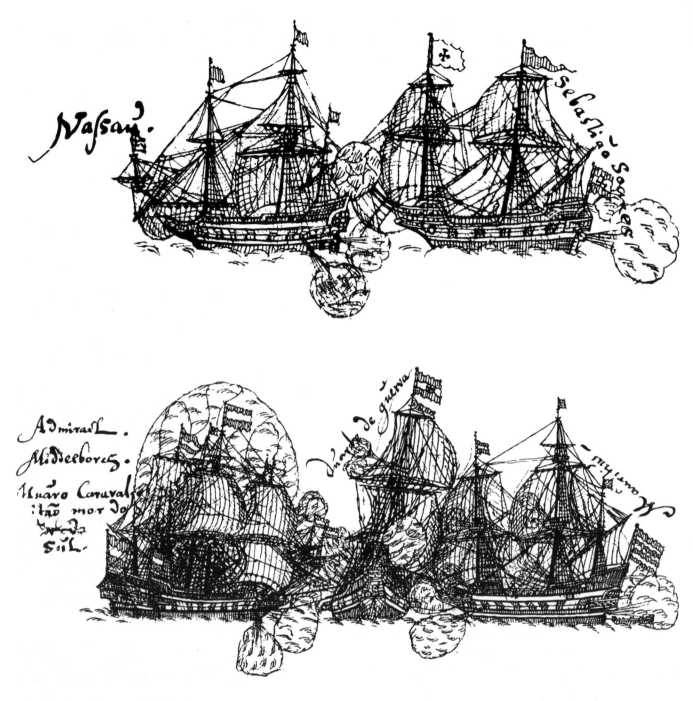

Nassau.

Sebastião Soares

Admiraël.
Middelborch.
Aluaro Carauvel...
...tão mor do...
...sil.

D'uarte de guerra

5 During the early part of the battle the *Nassau* was caught at anchor by the Portuguese. The fighting which followed was at point-blank range. After attempts to board the *Nassau* failed the Portuguese set her ablaze *(Teh Soo Ghee)*

6 After becoming entangled with the *Oranje*, the *Middelburg* was attacked on one side by the *Sao Salvador* and on the other by *Dom Duarte de Guerra's Galleon*, the latter was in turn attacked by the *Mauritius*. Grappled together and on fire the *Middelburg*, *Sao Salvador* and *Dom Duarte de Guerra's Galleon* sank. They survive as three mounds, still together, on the bottom of the Straits. In the picture, an enlargement taken from figure 4, we see the *Middelburg* and *Sao Salvador* on the left, *Dom Duarte de Guerra's Galleon* in the centre and the *Mauritius* attacking from the right *(Teh Soo Ghee)*

The next day, 19th August, both sides took stock and repaired their damage. Raja Seberang visited the Dutch in his vessel. Skirmishing continued until 21st August when Matelief, short of ammunition, decided to disengage and withdraw his fleet. The Portuguese launched a final surprise attack on the morning of the 24th, but the Dutch evaded them and on 25th August set sail for Johor arriving at the mouth of the Johor River on 13th September.

Losses

Accounts regarding the loss of life on the *Nassau* vary considerably. Matelief states that most of the *Nassau's* men were saved. Commelin (1646) remarks that all the crew were saved except six men who were killed during the fight.

Jacques L'Hermite (1923-26) refers to the loss of the master Gysbert Jakobs[3], the under-merchant Ryck Evertsz and the assistant master, unnamed, and mentions that several others on board were killed. L'Hermite states elsewhere that only 49 or 50 survived. Boxer (1928-29) states that the *Nassau* lost her captain, mate and 20 crew.

Matelief refers to the *Middelburg* as having had 18 of its men hurt and some others taken prisoner that were later released. Jacques L'Hermite suggests that most of the men on the *Middelburg* saved themselves in the 'chaloupe' but that the sick and wounded all perished. He further states that 93 out of 121 were saved. Commelin (1646) notes that the greater part of the crew saved themselves.

Valentyn (1885) mentions that from the *Sao Salvador*, Alvaro Carvalho and forty to fifty of his crew were killed while trying to save themselves in one of the *Middelburg*'s boats. Matelief mentions that most of the men on Dom Duarte de Guerra's galleon died.

The battle at Malacca

On 11th October Matelief learned from the King of Johor that the Portuguese in Malacca had split their fleet; seven ships had been sent to the Nicobars. Matelief sailed for Malacca where he found seven of the Portuguese ships, two of which were disabled.

The Portuguese drew up their ships in a line against the Isle of Naos with all their cannons on one side. Because he was short of gunpowder Matelief wanted to avoid a firefight, instead he decided to send the *Oranje*, *Grote Zon* and *Geunieerde Provincien* in an attempt to board the enemy.

They singled out the *Sao Nicolao*, under Captain D. Fernando Mascarenhas, at the northern end of the Portuguese line. She was the second most powerful ship in the Portuguese fleet (22 cannons and 160 soldiers). To reach her the three Dutch ships had to pass along the entire Portuguese line and sustain heavy fire, which, to save gunpowder, they did not return.

The *Oranje* grappled the *Sao Nicolao* from its port side and Matelief ordered his 40 musketeers to lay down fire to prevent the enemy from cutting themselves free. The *Grote Zon* grappled the *Sao Nicolao*'s starboard side while the *Geunieerde Provincien* took her bow to bow. The *Sao Nicolao*'s was held on the spot by her anchor and a cable to the next ship, the *Nossa Senhora de Conceicao* commanded by the Viceroy. Both cables were severed by the Dutch and all four ships were carried out to sea on the current. The rest of the Portuguese fleet hoisted sail and gave chase. This was exactly what Matelief had wanted, as it meant that their strong defensive position had been broken.

The *Sao Nicolao* was taken with massive loss of life. Matelief left orders for the vessel to be burned, but this was not done and, as a result, with the help of galleys, the *Sao Nicolao* was later able to escape.

Meanwhile the *Amsterdam*, *Mauritius* and *Zwarte Leeuw* attacked the *Todos Os Santos* and another vessel, possibly the *Sao Simao*. The Dutch managed to set fire to the former

so that she blew up and 'not so much as a cat or dog was saved'. The *Mauritius*, *Erasmus* and *Oranje* then attacked, and after a prolonged struggle, took the *Santa Cruz* (which had fought against the *Nassau* at the battle of Cape Rachado). The Dutch took off her 8 bronze cannons (11 bronze and 4 iron according to Commelin) and then set her on fire. The following day the *Oranje* attacked and took the *Sao Simao*. Fourteen bronze and two iron cannons were taken before she was burned.

The Dutch then withdrew for several days before returning to Malacca on 28th October. When the Viceroy saw the returning Dutch fleet he instructed that his remaining ships (i.e. *Nossa Senhora de Conceicao*, *Santo Antonio*, *Sao Nicolao* and Dom Paulo's ship) be destroyed by fire in order that they not fall into Dutch hands.

After his success at Malacca Matelief sailed north to Kedah where he destroyed a Portuguese ship and two smaller Portuguese vessels that were in the Kedah River. There followed an indecisive action against the Portuguese at Pulo Bouton after which Matelief abandoned hostilities and, to beat the monsoon, sailed for the Moluccas. After the Moluccas he went on to China via the Philippines. By this time his fleet consisted of only the *Oranje*, *Mauritius*, *Erasmus* and the yacht *Eendracht*. Chased from China by the Portuguese, Matelief then split up his remaining ships to find cargoes for the return voyage to Holland. Matelief (still on the *Oranje*) finally sailed for Europe on 28th January 1608.

Assessment

Although the Battle of Cape Rachado was indecisive the battle in front of Malacca was a triumph for the Dutch. The events of August to October 1606 can be seen as a turning point in the affairs of South-East Asia. Before the Battle of Cape Rachado the Portuguese dominated the region and its trades, but after these events their fortunes (although not immediately evident) went into decline while those of the Dutch were ascendant.

Discovery of the wrecks

In December 1992, a licence was granted by the Federal Government of Malaysia to the marine salvage and engineering company Transea Sdn Bhd (Managing Director

7 The survey of the Bambek Shoal was conducted from the 140ft *Osam Dragon* (S.H. Ong)

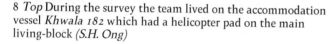

8 *Top* During the survey the team lived on the accommodation vessel *Khwala 182* which had a helicopter pad on the main living-block *(S.H. Ong)*

9 *Above* Jerry Caba working on the remote-sensing equipment that was used during the survey of the Bambek Shoal *(M. Bound)*

10 *Above right* VOC bronze cannon (dated 1604) recovered from the mound of the *Nassau* during the survey. Muzzle and part of chase missing *(Teh Soo Ghee)*

11 *Right* Detail of the cannon in figure 10 *(M. Bound)*

12 *Opposite top left* Bronze mortar, or petard, from the *Nassau*

13 *Opposite lower left* Guns recovered from the battle-wrecks on the deck of the *Osam Dragon*. The one on the left is featured in figs. 10 and 11. The three on the right (from either the *Sao Salvador* or *Dom Duarte de Guerra's Galleon*) were all by the Portuguese gunsmith Pedro Dias Bocarro. One of the Portuguese cannon had a Dutch cannon-ball embedded in its barrel

Ong Soo Hin) to search for the wreck of the British merchant ship *Caroline* that had been lost on the Bambek Shoal in the Straits of Malacca (near modern Port Dickson) in 1816.

A search-and-survey was conducted in three phases over a period of five months from June to October 1993. The vessels used during these campaigns were the 140ft supply vessel *Osam Dragon* (fig 7) and the 180ft accommodation vessel *Khwala 182* (fig 8); the principal search tools were a magnetometer, a sidescan sonar and a DGPS position-fixing system (fig 9). Numerous targets were investigated including a mound of horseshoes jettisoned from the sailing ship *General Kyd* which ran upon the Bambek Shoal in the nineteenth century. The *Caroline* was never found, but the four wrecks from the Battle of Cape Rachado were.

14 *Top right* Detail of the gun in the centre of figure 13 showing an armillary sphere, the Portuguese coat of arms and the maker's name P:DIAS *(Pedro Dias Boccaro)*

15 *Lower right* An armed guard of three to six men from either the Marine Police or the Malaysian Royal Navy were on board the *Abex* at all times to provide protection

The first wreck to be located was the *Nassau* at a depth of 90ft (27.5m). She survived as a mound of cannon, anchors, timbers, ballast and compacted mud. A bronze cannon from the Dutch East India Company (VOC) was recovered (fig 10). It was found to be missing its muzzle and much of the chase, but across the first reinforce was the relief of a ship (fig 11) and the words:

DE * VEREENICHDE * OOST
INDISCE * COMPANGHIE * TOT
AMSTELREDAM * ANNO * 1604

(United East India Company of Amsterdam year 1604)

Later, a small bronze mortar (fig 12)[4], some musket shot and two iron cannon balls were raised.

About 1200m from the *Nassau*, three more wreck mounds were found at a depth of 120ft (36.5m). These were evidently the VOC ship *Middelburg* and the Portuguese vessels *Sao Salvador* and *Dom Duarte de Guerra's Galleon* which had gone down grappled to one another and on fire. The three mounds were still alongside each other on the sea-bed; clearly they had remained tied together as they sank.

Several bronze cannon were recovered (fig 13), all of which had been made by the well-known Portuguese cannon maker Pedro Dias Bocarro who, in the sixteenth century, had his foundry at Goa (Braid, 1992, 64). One of the cannon (fig 14) was decorated in a particularly lavish manner with the name P:DIAS in relief lettering at the back of the chase and the year 1589 in a panel behind the trunnions. A smaller gun was marked P.DIZB, and another, which was badly twisted from the impact of a Dutch iron cannon-ball (the remains of which were embedded within

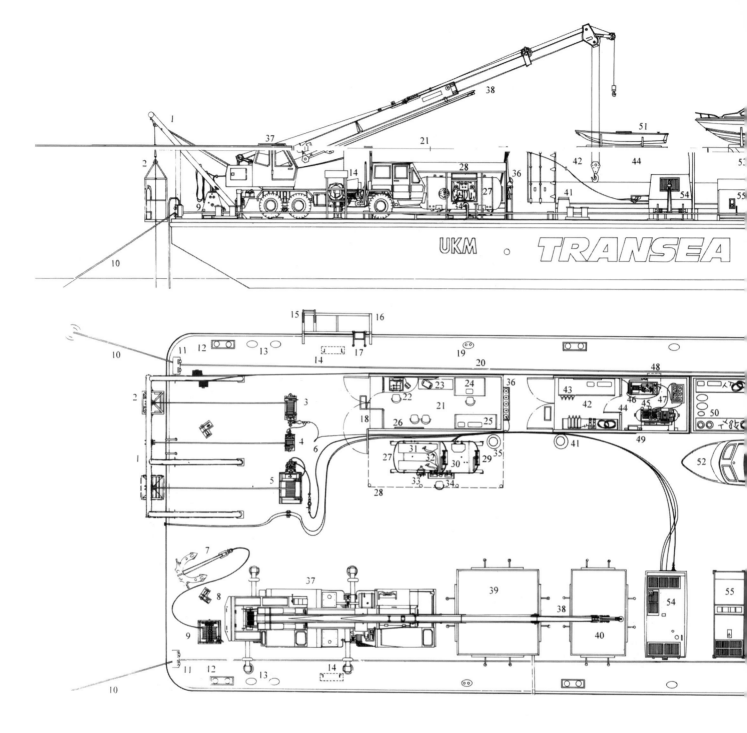

UKM · *TRANSEA*

16 Design of the *Abex* by Ong Soo Hin and Mensun Bound. Port side elevation and deck plan. Length 180ft. Port of registry Singapore *(drawing by Teh Soo Ghee)*

1. A-frame for deployment of divers and the recovery of heavy artefacts and airlift baskets
2. 'Stage' or elevator for carrying divers to and from the sea-bed. Fitted with two emergency air bottles
3. 3-ton air tugger and block for lowering and raising the stage
4. 2-ton air tugger and block
5. 5-ton air tugger and block
6. Tugger air hoses
7. Auxiliary anchor
8. Towing pad-eyes (2)
9. Stand-by mooring winch
10. 4-point mooring system. Consisted of winch-wire leading to pennant buoys and 6-ton anchors each with 90ft of chain
11. Fairleads (4)

12. Bollards (8)
13. Void-tank manhole covers (14)
14. Navigation Lights (2)
15. Ladder from deck to SCUBA platform
16. Platform for SCUBA divers
17. Ladder from SCUBA platform to water
18. Standby diver's station
19. Diesel bunker
20. Fuel pump
21. 20ft diver-control station
22. 2-diver air supply panel and 2-diver, two-way, hard-wire communications system
23. Audio-visual monitor
24. Desk area for people working on dive logs and technical documentation
25. Shelving for underwater stills and video cameras

26. White-board
27. 54 inch twin-lock deck decompression chamber (DDC)
28. DDC awning
29. DDC entrance to outer lock
30. Outer lock
31. Inner lock
32. Oxygen breathing apparatus
33. Medical lock
34. Control panel
35. Disinfectant bath for divers entering chamber
36. Oxygen bottle bank
37. 15-ton crane
38. Boom of crane
39. 12 x 12ft holding tank for large concreted objects such as iron cannon
40. Small holding tank for artefacts
41. 44 gal plastic disinfectant drums for rinsing diving equipment
42. Diving equipment and changing container (10ft)
43. SCUBA bottle storage

44. Pump room (10ft)
45. K-14 high pressure air compressor with electric motor
46. 80 CM low pressure air compressor with electric motor
47. HP bottle pod
48. Extractor fan
49. Filtration system
50. Heavy work bench
51. Emergency boat
52. Stand-by boat and cradle (deployed by crane)
53. Bosun's workshop (20ft) and storage container for heavy equipment, tools, rope, materials, etc.
54. 600 CFM low pressure air compressor for airlifts, tuggers, etc.
55. Day generator 195 KVA
56. Night generator 125 KVA
57. Hydraulic oil tank for anchor winches
58. Anchor winch engine
59. Port anchor winch
60. Heavy work table
61. Hydraulic hose ramp

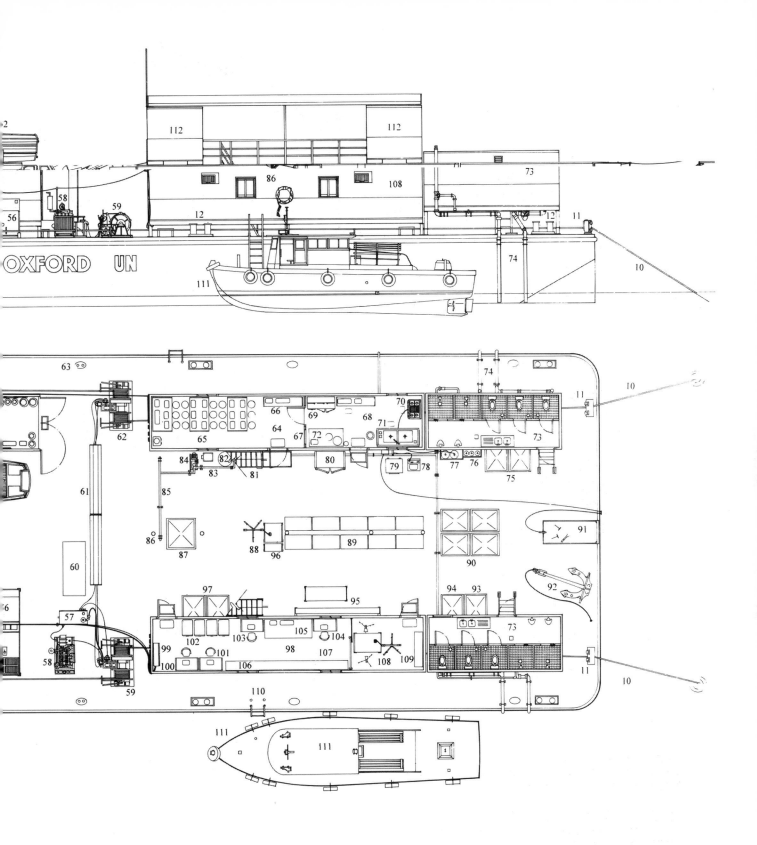

72. Serving table
73. 20ft ablution containers with toilets, shower stalls and wash facilities
74. Overboard discharge from ablution container
75. Desalination tanks for large miscellaneous artefacts
76. Acetylene gas bottle rack
77. Cooking gas bottle rack
78. Washing machine
79. Freezer
80. Fridge and freezer
81. Stair to two 40ft accommodation units

84. Potwater pump
85. Potwater pipes
86. Flag mast and night diving lights
87. Desalination tanks for timber remains
88. Outdoor photographic studio
89. Artefact storage racks
90. Storage tanks for iron concretions
91. Airlift discharge sorting table and sluicing system
92. Auxiliary anchor
93. Desalination tanks for bricks
94. Desalination tanks for coarseware ceramics

archaeological valuables
97. Desalination tank for bones and general organics
98. Archaeological work unit. Briefing and operations room
99. Control panel for all shipboard electrical functions
100. Barge master and Chief Diver's desk
101. Recorder's desk
102. Desks for Finds Officer and assistants
103. Surveyor's desk
104. Director's desk

106. Chart and plan table
107. Briefing area
108. Photographic studio
109. Photographer's desk
110. Shuttle boat mooring area; ladder
111. Shuttle boat for the carriage of food and supplies and for transport of the away-team to and from the shore station and the shore accommodation facilities
112. Two 40ft bunk rooms for archaeologists, divers, crew, galley personnel, police and naval guard detachments

a

b

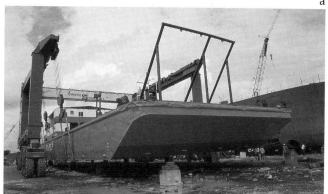

c

d

17 *Abex* in the shipyard at Singapore a) before work began
b) work nearing completion c) suspended from a 600-ton
travel-lift in preparation for launching d) on station in the
Straits of Malacca by the Bambek Shoal

the metal at the bend in the barrel), was marked PDB. All
these guns, together with the VOC cannon from the *Nassau*
were given to the Malaysian authorities at Port Dickson.

The historical importance of these wrecks was beyond
question and on 12th July 1995, the Government of Malaysia,
with the support of the National Museum (Jabatan Muzium
dan Antikuiti), granted a licence to Transea to carry out an
excavation of the *Nassau*. The excavation would be funded by
the government and nothing would be sold. The only
conditions imposed by the National Museum were that the
excavation be conducted to international standards, that it had
museum and academic involvement and that the excavation be
directed by a professional maritime archaeologist with a proper
archaeological staff. On this understanding the Director of
Transea arranged the participation of the National University
of Malaysia (UKM) and the University of Oxford in the form
of its maritime archaeological unit, Oxford University MARE.

Work on the *Nassau* began in August 1995 and ended in
December of the same year. The overall administration of
the project was the responsibility of Ong Soo Hin and his
staff at the Transea headquarters in Petaling Jaya outside
Kuala Lumpur. The excavation director was Mensun Bound
of Oxford University. The archaeological staff came from
the National Museum of Malaysia, UKM and Oxford
University MARE. The crew and dive team were recruited
from Malaysia, Singapore, Indonesia, Thailand and Europe.

18 The excavation director and chief-diver step from the stage.
Tenders had two and a half minutes to remove their gear and re-
pressurize them in the decompression chamber. Divers carried
video cameras and lights on their helmets

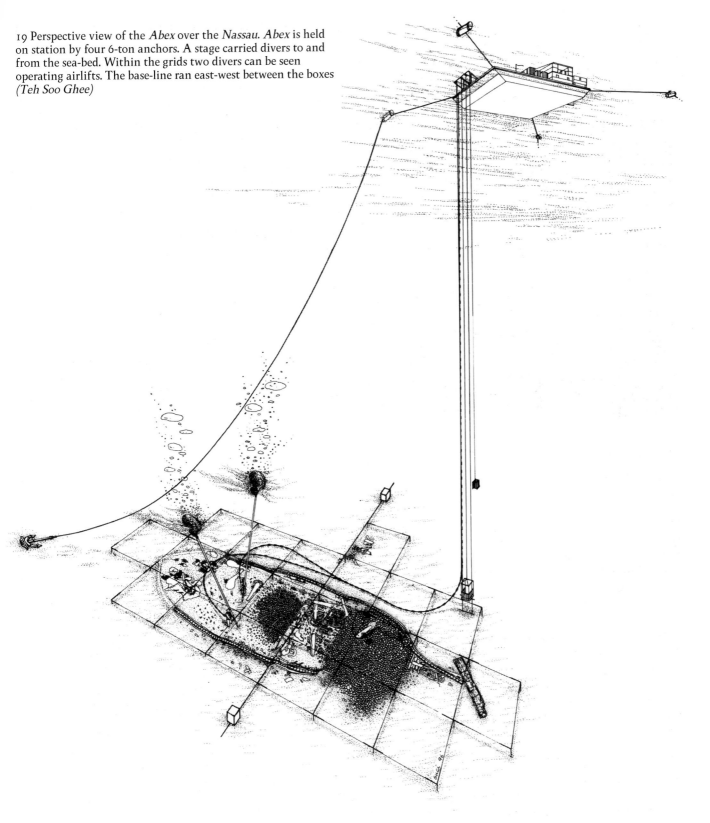

19 Perspective view of the *Abex* over the *Nassau*. *Abex* is held on station by four 6-ton anchors. A stage carried divers to and from the sea-bed. Within the grids two divers can be seen operating airlifts. The base-line ran east-west between the boxes (*Teh Soo Ghee*)

An armed guard of three to six men from either the Marine Police or the Malaysian Royal Navy were on board at all times to provide protection (fig 15).

The *Abex*

The vessel used by the team for the excavation was a 180ft x 50ft flat-top barge (Abex) that was completely structured, equipped and rigged for the project in Singapore (fig 17). It is believed that this is the first time a vessel of this size has ever been designed specifically for the purpose of maritime archaeology (fig 16). It functioned to beyond expectation and its design is recommended to any future team in the happy position of being able to afford a surface vessel of this size.

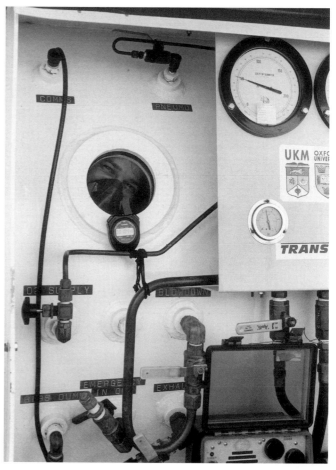

20 Diver working on cannon 2

21 Dive-supervisor (Nigel Kerr) in hard-wire communication with the divers. He could also follow their activities through video cameras (attached to the helmets) that relayed to monitors stationed beside the communication console

22 A diver on oxygen peers from a port in the recompression chamber

23 Grid being lowered to the wreck

All dive-related activities were focused at the vessel's wedge-shaped bow where an A-frame was constructed for heavy lifting and the deployment of a stage, a kind of underwater elevator for transporting divers to and from the sea-bed (fig 18). 6-ton, 3-ton and 2-ton air-operated winches and a 15-ton crane were also installed across the bow. The dive-command station and deck decompression chamber (DDC) were situated behind the A-frame. Compressor units, air storage pods and the bosun's locker were placed along the starboard side, while along the port side were sited the artefact holding tanks, generators and emergency boats. Galley, messing and recreational facilities were installed starboard, aft of midships, while on the opposite side were placed the 40ft long archaeology unit and photographic studio. Ablution facilities were located on both quarters and the accommodation blocks were sited athwart the archaeological and food-services units.

Abex was held on station by a 4-point mooring arrangement that consisted of four 6-ton anchors each with 90ft of chain

which, in turn, connected to wire rope that passed through pennant buoys (fig 19). Winches at midships tightened or loosened the anchor lines in order to achieve precise position-adjustment over the wreck.

Diving and conditions

Survey, photographic and general inspection dives were made on scuba equipment while long working-dives were made with hard-hat head-gear (Superlite 17B helmets) that were air-supplied from the surface via umbilicals (fig 20). A complete air-spread for 'Sur DO_2'-type diving was installed on *Abex* in Singapore. Divers were in hard-wire communication with the command-station and their activities were monitored

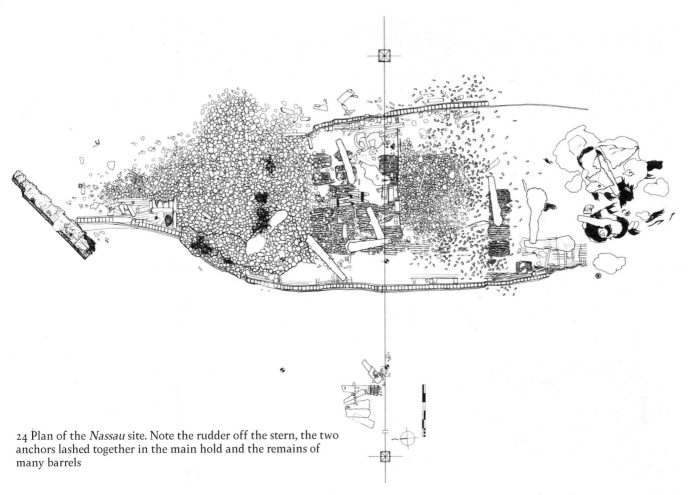

24 Plan of the *Nassau* site. Note the rudder off the stern, the two anchors lashed together in the main hold and the remains of many barrels

through video cameras attached to the tops of their helmets (fig 21).

Maximum bottom time for divers at 90ft (27.5m) on the Sur DO$_2$ system was 130 minutes. Decompression took place within the oxygen-supplied deck decompression chamber (fig 22). On leaving the water divers had less than three minutes to be stripped of their gear and enter the outer lock of the DDC. Average DDC decompression time was 69 minutes.

Although the depth of the *Nassau* was within safe diving depth, conditions complicated all in-water operations; currents were extremely strong and, except during neaps, visibility was near to zero. Lights, attached to the divers' helmets and energized from the surface, were essential. During neaps visibility increased to 5 or 6m; it was at these times that the underwater photographs featured in this chapter were taken. Towards the latter part of the excavation operations were hampered by the north-east monsoon, and frequent flash-storms, known as 'sumatras', which could bring wind-gusts of up to 40 knots. The heavy monsoon rains also expanded local riverine discharge which further added to the turbidity of the water.

The wreck

A 29.40m east-west baseline was installed across the site along what was thought, at the time, to be the main axis of the ship. This line, with its ends firmly held in place by large iron boxes filled with stud-link chain, was the primary datum-reference for the grid system, the first units of which were set in place towards the end of the pre-disturbance survey. Grids were cut and welded on the deck of *Abex* and lowered to the sea-bed by the 15-ton crane (fig 23). Each grid measured 6 x 6m and comprised nine squares each of 2 x 2m.

The orientation of the hull was not east-west as originally thought, but rather north-south (fig 24). Because of concretion and the general disintegration of the bow area, it was impossible to establish the vessel's keel length, but the indications are that it was about 33-35m. Only the lower hull remained; it listed to port and appeared to survive to only a little higher than the turn of the bilge. Although the edges of the hull were exposed on both sides, no attempt was made to reveal and study the lower timberwork. This was because of lack of time, poor visibility and a reluctance to expose any more of the hull than necessary to biological attack. Virtually nothing is known of the vessel's lower assembly or general form. Frames were close-set and had an average section of 250 x 320mm. The hull was double planked (each layer 60-80mm thick) and at several places ceiling could be seen (60-80mm thick). Most, if not all, of the exterior hull below the water-line was lead sheathed and at the stern, around the post and below the tuck, she had been partially coppered. Numerous void concretions confirmed that she had been iron fastened and treenails were also seen.

The after ballast mound was found to have spilled to well beyond the port side. Neither the after nor forward sides of the pile were well defined. The after side of the forward

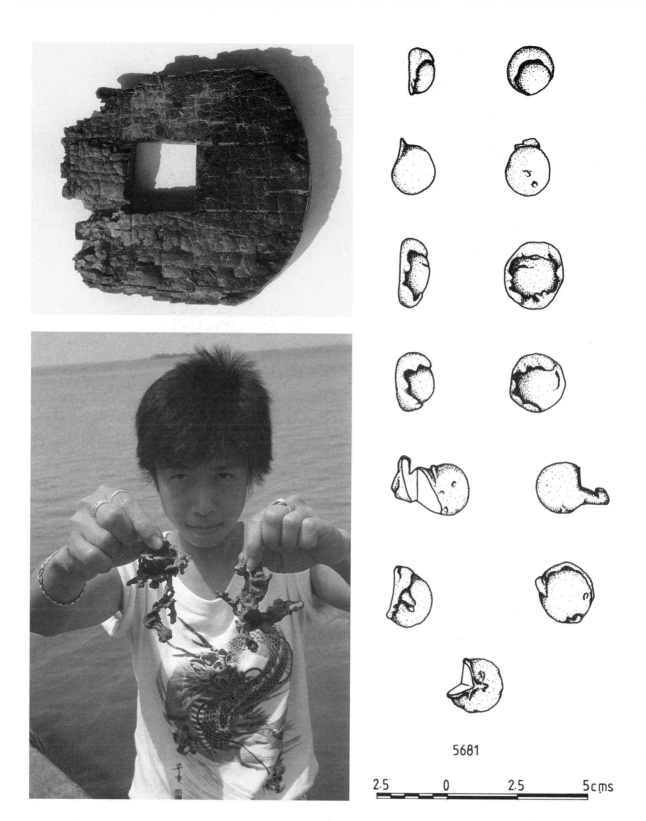

5681

2.5   0   2.5   5 cms

25 *Top* Evidence of the fire that consumed the *Nassau* came from charred wood that was found all over the site

26 *Above* Li Lin Cheah holding two of the many pieces of melted bronze that were recovered

27 *Above right* Portuguese musket balls that had been flattened or otherwise distorted by impact with the *Nassau* (*Lim Beng Keat*)

ballast pile, however, was clearly demarcated by a planked retaining wall that had become bowed by the weight of rock.

The structure of the port quarter was missing from the sternpost to the after ballast mound. The evident violence that had occurred at this point, and the artefact spreads off the stern, would seem to confirm accounts of an explosion in the powder magazine which would very likely have been situated in this part of the vessel.

28 *Above* left Musket balls recovered during a single dive being cleaned on the sluicing table at the stern of *Abex*

29 *Left* An accreted lump of musket balls in the stern of the wreck. Note the timbers to the right and the copper alloy apostle (powder canister for musket) in the foreground

30 *Below* left Coiled rope in the bow

31 *Top* Pulley wheel

32 *Above* Pulley wheel (identical to that in fig 31), melted by the blaze that consumed the *Nassau*

Throughout the site ample evidence was found of the fire that had consumed the ship. This took the form of burnt wood (fig 25), charred rope and melted metal (fig 26). Impacted musket shot (fig 27) and a broken stone cannonball testified to the fire-fight that had taken place.

Ship's fittings and equipment consisted of two large anchors that had been lashed together and stored in the main hold between the two ballast piles. Large quantities of heavy cordage (some still coiled) and lines of more moderate diameter were found in the bow area (fig 30) along with two pulley wheels one of which had been badly melted (figs. 31 and 32). The various remains of navigational instruments all came from off the stern.

The hold area between the ballast piles was lined across its bottom with at least twenty barrels (fig 24). Parts of a further

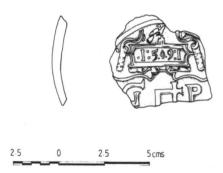

three were situated along the starboard side of the forward pile and the remains of at least seven more were found to the south of the pile. A large number of butchered meat bones from the midships hold confirmed the contents of at least some of the barrels in that area. Fish bones and coconut remains (fig 33) gave further insight into the diet on board.

Ceramic remains were found throughout the ship but by far the greatest concentration came from the main hold where tin-glazed Rhenish stonewares, alborelli and zalfpotten (figs. 34 and 35) were stored. The latter were small open-bodied pots that may have contained ointments, or similar, for medicinal

33 *Top left* Coconut recovered from the wreck

34 *Centre* Necks from bellarmine jars

35 *Top right* Bellarmine jar and zalfpotten

36 *Lower* Fragment from a North European stone-ware jar bearing the date 1591 *(Lim Beng Keat)*

37 *Lower right* Lim Beng Keat reconstructing broken pots from the ship's galley. The tubs all contain artefacts

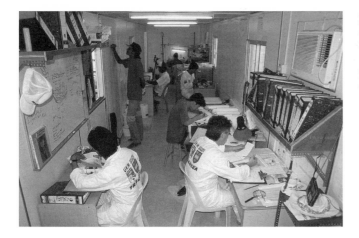

38 *Left* The archaeological operations unit on board the *Abex*. Finds officer and recorder in foreground, draughtsmen in middle-distance, photographers in background

39 *Below* VOC cannon dated 1604. Cascabel, muzzle and part of chase missing. Handles melted *(Teh Soo Ghee)*

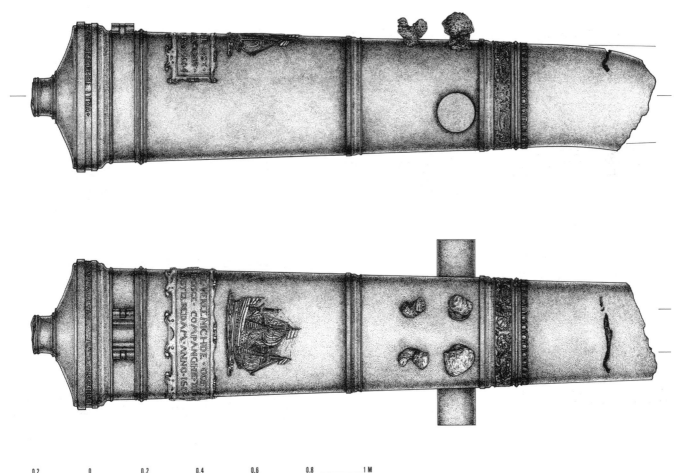

| 0.2 | 0 | 0.2 | 0.4 | 0.6 | 0.8 | 1 M |

use. Seventy-six intact or fragmented examples were recovered. A smaller number were also found on the VOC ship *Batavia* that was wrecked off Western Australia in 1629 (Green, 1989, 99). Two of the Rhenish fragments were dated 1591 (fig 36).

In addition to the tablewares there were a number of coarseware fragments from storage pots or martaban jars. These were all of South-East Asian origin and can be divided into two broad groups; those with flaring rims, well-defined necks, high shoulders and four horizontal strap handles, and those with rounded lips, short sloping necks and four horizontal lug handles.

A large number of scattered bricks were recovered from the forward half of the vessel.

Ordnance

From the evidence so far, the *Nassau* was carrying a minimum of sixteen cannon, all but two of which were recovered. Four were of bronze, the remainder were of iron. Of the four bronze pieces, three were VOC cannon of similar design, the fourth was so badly abraded that its coat of arms has not yet been identified.

Of the three bronze VOC guns, one has already been mentioned above (see figs. 10 and 11). It was missing its

muzzle and part of the chase and was decorated with the relief of a ship and the panelled relief-wording 'East India Company of Amsterdam, year 1604'. The second VOC gun (figs 39, 40 and 41) was similarly damaged, sported like artwork and, apart from some orthographical differences, the same inscription and year. The third VOC gun was badly fragmented, but from the pieces recovered, it appears to have resembled closely the other two in size and design. It is worth noting that at least two of these guns were made just a year or less before the fleet sailed, so that it is possible they were ordered with the siege of Malacca in mind.

Three of the iron guns were stripped of concretion. One was identified as a culverin. All were found to be badly cracked (Bound, 1997, 31).

The question arises as to why the *Nassau*'s cannon were in such bad condition. Our present thinking is that the iron

40 *Top* Tracing of ship on cannon in figure 39 (*Teh Soo Ghee*)

41 *Above* Conservator from National Museum of Malaysia (Mat Nasir Baba) cleaning the cannon in figures 39 and 40 with vibro-tools

42 *Top right* Under the supervision of the *Abex*'s bosun, Mustafa (right), concretion is removed from iron cannon number 42

43 *Lower right* Iron cannon number 45 comes up

guns cracked from the quenching of the red-hot metal as the burning vessel sank, while the bronze guns, by contrast, began to melt before the sinking. The latter came apart at the chase because, in their softened state they could no longer sustain the weight of that part of the barrel which was not supported by the carriage (figs 46 and 47). Two of the guns droop towards the break (figs 10 and 39), as does a bronze cannon in the Tower of London (Blackmore, 1976, 121) and

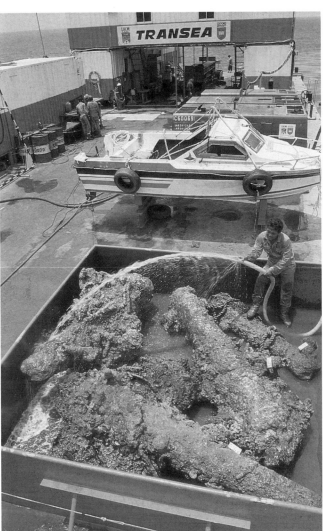

44 *Top left* Iron cannon 8 is raised

45 *Top right* Iron cannon in the main holding-tank on board *Abex*

46 *Left* Muzzle, muzzle frieze and part of chase. Believed to be the forward end of the bronze VOC gun featured in figures 10 and 11

47 *Above* Drawing of the muzzle frieze on the cannon fragment in fig 46 *(Lim Beng Keat)*

another in the Maritime Museum, Lisbon, both of which were damaged by fire.

Only thirteen pieces of iron shot were found, which suggests that the vessel was out of ammunition. A fragmented stone shot was also recovered; it is presumed that this was fired at the *Nassau* by one of the Portuguese vessels, most likely the *Santa Cruz*.

One of the more important items to have come from the *Nassau* was the bronze petard, featured in figure 12. Similar examples came from the *Mauritius* which fought alongside the *Nassau* at Cape Rachado and was later lost off Africa (L'Hour & Long, 1989, 185; see note 2).

A priming wire with a trefoil handle was also excavated.

Coinage

According to a document in the VOC archives (no. 461), the *Nassau* set sail from the Low Countries with 30,000 Spanish reales. During the course of the excavation 3,607 coins were recovered[5]. The majority were covered in corrosion products (fig 48), but a significant number (from off the stern) were in a good state of preservation and could easily be read (fig 49). 176 of these were taken as a study sample. The majority were 'pieces of eight' but there were also coins of 4 and 2 real denominations. Five mints were represented in the sample: Potosi (29%) and Mexico (20.5%) in the New World, and Seville (12.5%), Toledo (3.4%) and Segovia (1.1%) in the Old; the mint mark on 33.5% of the hoard was illegible.

All of the samples except two were cobs. That is to say, pieces cut from flat strips of silver which were then trimmed into blanks and hammer-struck between dies. Each coin produced in this manner was unique. Two of the coins, both from Segovia (dated 1586 and 1598; fig 50), were produced by a new machine-method that was introduced to Spain from Germany in 1585. This consisted of two rollers bearing the obverse and reverse dies. A sheet of silver was passed between the rollers and the impressed planchets were then punched out.

The majority of the coins dated to between 1580 and 1598, that is to say the reign of Philip II, or Philip the Great of Spain (1556-1598). Those that are legible, bear the following legend (or a variant):

PHILIPPVS. D. G. HISPANIARVM. ET. INDIARVM. REX.
(Philip by the Grace of God King of Spain and the Indies)

48 *Top left* In the blackness under water many of the Spanish silver coins went up the airlift. They were afterwards recovered from the airlift exhaust-bag that was sifted at the end of every dive on the sluicing table. Museum staff Amat Ali and Sanim Ahmad at left and right, shuttle-boat skipper, Ramlan Din Jantan, in centre

49 *Above* Pieces of eight and lesser denominations from the 30,000 Spanish reales that the *Nassau* was carrying. So far, over three and a half thousand coins have been recovered

50 *Top right* All but two of the reales were cobs, that is to say, coins cut from a bar, roughly trimmed and then hammer-struck between dies. In 1585 Philip II imported from Germany to Segovia equipment and technicians to mint coins by a new machine-process. Two of the new coins (dated 1586 and 1598) were found. As can be seen in fig 49, the results were much superior. Segovia had been a mint town since Roman times, hence its mint mark, the Roman aquaduct that can be seen beside the shield. The aquaduct survives at Segovia to this day

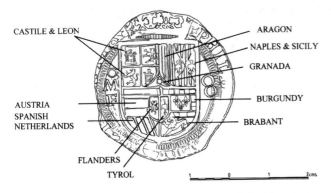

CASTILE & LEON
ARAGON
NAPLES & SICILY
GRANADA
BURGUNDY
AUSTRIA
SPANISH
NETHERLANDS
BRABANT
FLANDERS
TYROL

51 The Hapsburg shield on the obverse of one of the *Nassau* pieces of eight. The various arms represent the provinces considered by Philip II to be under the Spanish crown (*Lim Beng Keat*)

The obverse features the arms of the House of Hapsburg which was introduced on to the coinage by Philip II, and which contains the arms of the various provinces which he considered to be under the Spanish crown (fig 51). The reverse displays the Jerusalem Cross, the castles and lions within its quarters representing the kingdoms of Castile and Leon which were united by the marriage of Isabella and Ferdinand in the fifteenth century.

Conclusion

In broad terms the *Nassau* is important because she is the oldest Dutch East Indiaman to be examined by archaeologists[6] and because she participated in events that shaped the course of South-East Asia and influenced the balance of power within Europe. The excavation of the *Nassau* was the largest and most expensive maritime archaeological project that the world has seen in recent years. Certainly there is much more work to be done on this wreck but, at time of writing, no decision had been taken regarding if and when this should happen.

Acknowledgements

There is not space here to mention by name the many people who made this project possible, but gratitude must be expressed to the Minister and staff of the Ministry of Culture, Arts and Tourism, the Director General and staff of the National Museum of Malaysia (Jabatan Muzium dan Antikuiti), the Vice-chancellor and staff of the National Museum of Malaysia (Universiti Kebangsaan Malaysia), the State Government of Negeri Sembilan, the board of Transea and the Management Committee of Oxford University MARE. The project is also indebted to the Malaysian Royal Navy (Tentera Laut Di-Raja Malaysia) and the Marine Police (Polis Marin) who provided full-time armed protection for the project. Patrick Lizé helped with research. Drawings by Teh Soo Ghee, Lim Beng Keat, Helen Ford and Chris Fitton. Photographs by Mensun Bound, Mah Wai Pheng, Sanim Ahmad, Derek Park, Ong Soo Hin and Tim Dingemans.

Notes

1 A last was an estimation of a vessel's carrying capacity and was calculated by multiplying the hull length by its breadth by its depth and then dividing by 20.

2 The *Mauritius* was lost in 1609 off Gabon. She was excavated in 1986 by a French team lead by Luc Long and Michel l'Hour (L'Hour, Long and Rieth, 1989; L'Hour and Long, 1990). Another vessel that participated in the battle and which was later excavated was the *Witte Leuwe*; she was lost on St Helena in 1613 and was discovered by Robert Stenuit in 1976 (Van de Pijl-Ketel, 1982).

3 The various sources give four different names for the captain of the *Nassau*: Walter Carels (Macleod, 1927), Abraham Mathijsz (Brujin, 1980), Wouter Jacobsz (de Jonge, 1898) and Gybert Jacobs (L'Hermite, 1623-26).

4 It is interesting to note that bronze mortars were also found on the *Mauritius* (L'Hour, Long and Rieth, 1989).

5 Not a precise number as it was impossible to make an exact count of some of the coins that were concreted together into lumps.

6 The wrecks of 37 Dutch East Indiamen have now been found.

References

Blackmore, B.L., 1976, *The Armouries of the Tower of London: 1 ordnance*, London

Bound, M., 1997, The Dutch East Indiaman Nassau, *Minerva International Review of Ancient Art and Archaeology*, 8, 5, 28-32

Boxer, C.R., 1928-29, The Affair of the Madre Deus, *Transactions of the Japan Society*, XXVI

Braid, D., 1992, Ordnance and empire: Portugal in the fifteenth and sixteenth centuries, *Journal of the Ordnance Society*, 4, 55-66

Bruin, J.R., Gaastia, F.S. and Schoffer, I. (eds.), 1980, *Dutch-Asiatic shipping in the 17th and 18th centuries*, Gravenhage

Commelin, Izaak, 1646, *Nederlandsche Oost Indische Compagnie*, 3 vols., Amsterdam

de Jonge, J.K.J., 1898, *De Opkomst van het Nederlandsch Gezag in Oost-Indie, 1595-1610*, 3 vols., The Hague

Green, J.N., 1989, *The loss of the Verenigde Oostindische Compagnie Retourship Batavia, Western Australia 1629*, BAR supplementary series 489, Oxford

L'Hermite, J., 1623-26, Journal, *L'Hermite en de V.A.G. Huygen Schapenham*

L'Hour, M., Long, L. and Rieth, E., 1989, *Le Mauritius: La Mémoire Englouhe*, Paris

L'Hour, M. and Long, L., 1990, The Wreck of the Mauritius, 1609, *International Journal of Nautical Archaeology*, 19, 1, 63-73

Macleod, N., 1927, *De Oost-Indische Compagnie ... in Azie (1602-1650)*, 2 vols., Rijswijck

Matelief, Cornelis, 1608, *An historical and true discourse, of a voyage made by the Admiral Cornelis Matlief the Younger, into the East Indies who departed out of Holland, in May 1605. With the besieging of Malacca, and the battaile by him fought at sea against the Portugales in the Indies, with other discourses*, translated out of the Dutch, according to the coppie printed at Rotterdam, William Barret, London

Valentyn, Francois, 1885, Account of Malacca, *Journal of the Malay Branch of the Royal Asiatic Society*, 15: 132-138 and 1985, 16: 289 - 300

van der Pijl-Ketal, C.L., 1982, *The ceramic load of the Witte Leeuw (1613)*, Rijksmuseum, Amsterdam

Bengt Grisell (Royal Institute of Technology, Sweden)

Riksnyckeln (The Key of the Realm), Sweden, 1628

This is actually the beginning of the *Vasa* story, the great warship of King Gustav II Adolf that was found in Stockholm harbour by Anders Franzen in August 1956, and raised from its murky resting place of 333 years in 1961.

The discovery of the *Riksnyckeln* goes back to May 1920, when a local fisherman, Erik A Nordstrom, by chance found her remains on the north-east side of Viksten Island in the southern part of the Stockholm archipelago. In 1954 Anders Franzen persuaded the fisherman to tell him the story.

"One Sunday morning in mid May, 1920, I went fishing together with my assistant, Peter Sundell and Birger Hammarlund, the son of the principal civic administrator in Nynäshamn. Our destination was Gunnarsten where we intended to bob for cod and look for gull eggs. Having arrived at the tiny island of Flatskar, the other two went ashore to look for eggs. I stayed in the boat and moored off aft using a small grapnel anchor.

When my friends came back we took up the small anchor and went to Viksten to bob for cod. There we used the same anchor and line as at Flatskar. After about an hour of good fishing we decided to go home. We began hauling up the anchor, but could not feel any resistance; it had come untied. We went back to Nynäshamn without it.

About a week later we were back at Viksten with another friend, Axel Flodberg, a fisherman, who later became captain of a small steamship in Stockholm. This time we had two boats. We made a sweep with a line between the boats and managed to snag the lost anchor which we were able to raise to the surface, but just as I was about to grab hold it went back to the bottom. We than made another sweep but the line became fouled on something. To mark the spot we left 25 fathoms of manilla rope with a cork buoy on the end. There was at that time a ship called the *Sigrid* anchored at Kastbadan, a small rocky islet on the other side of Viksten a thousand meters away. They were salvaging metal from the small steamer *Gaud* which had gone aground there in 1915. As I was acquainted with both the diver, Sjo, and the master of the salvage vessel (they had been depositing their salvaged junk on my property at Bedaro), I asked them to help. They promised that if I came back one evening after work, they would help me recover the lost anchor. Diver Sjo demanded 35 kronor (about £3) and one litre of cognac for the job. Some days later we were net fishing off Malsten Island and because of the beautiful weather, we headed afterwards for Kastbadan. By the time we had reached the *Sigrid* they had finished for the day. Diver Sjo was still in his heavy diving suit. He had been working hard all day and was not keen to go down again. But after telling him that I had the cognac with me, he changed his mind. Diver Sjo took the bottle of unopened cognac and locked it in his cabin.

Diver Sjo had a relative of his with him as an assistant. We took their boat in tow and went to Viksten. Once there we found that my nice rope had gone (I suppose someone needed it), but I had taken marks for the spot. We anchored and Diver Sjo went down. Peter and I turned the airpump; Sjo's relative handled the airhose and the signal line. There was no other communication link. In less than five minutes Diver Sjo signalled that he wanted to come up. Back on deck he told us that he had found a wreck from the birth of Christ. He had descended between four bronze cannons. He went down a second time and on his return he recovered my anchor. We returned to *Sigrid*. It had all taken about one and a half hours. Diver Sjo asked for 10 kronor, which I gave him. We then went back to Malsten and took up our nets. About a day later they raised the cannons and one anchor. I then heard from customs officials, that the cannons were valued at 100,000 kronor (£7,000)."

Nordstrom continued his account by saying the he felt himself entitled to a finders reward and therefore sought legal advice. In the end he was informed that the find had been declared an abandoned, derelict vessel rather than an historic wreck site, and that therefore the State would not be giving a finders reward: instead it would only be paying for the salvage value of the guns.

Unfortunately the owner of the *Sigrid* salvage vessel had already registered the claim as his, and so it was he who eventually collected the salvage payment of 60,000 kronor ($4,000). For the rest of his life Nordstrom was greatly embittered by this experience. The owner of the *Sigrid*, on the other hand, had developed a taste for historic wrecks (particularly those with guns) and went on to salvage (with the use of explosives) the remains of the *Riksapplet* (The Orb of the Realm) which had sunk in 1676 near Dalaro, a short distance to the SE of Stockholm.

The discovery of the *Riksnyckeln* and the recovery of the guns caused much excitement and speculation at the time. During the six months following the find the *Sigrid* group salvaged seven bronze guns, six of which were 12 pounders (five Swedish, one Polish) and one 6 pounder (Polish). Today all the guns are on display in the Swedish Maritime Museum in Stockholm. One of the guns was inscribed with the name of Johan Weihers, which led some to think that the Polish guns had been captured by the Swedes during their storming of Kulm, where Weiher's residential palace was situated. Others felt that they had been taken by Charles Gustav X, or Charles XII, during the Polish Wars.

The mystery was solved by Professor Nils Ahnlund, at that time the foremost authority on Swedish 17th century history. In an article in the newspaper *Svenska Dagbladet* of 20 July 1920, he wrote:

'On the 10th September, 1628, news reached Stockholm that the ship *Riksnyckeln* had been wrecked off the island of Viksten. She had been thrown against a cliff during a severe storm and had broken up and sunk with all her beautiful guns. Nineteen men had followed her down; only the captain and a few seamen had survived in a small boat to deliver the bad news to the capital. An inquiry was held to establish the cause of the loss. Several references to the inquiry report survive in the National Archive, but the document itself seems to be missing. Some of the references date the loss to Friday, 5th September, others give Saturday, 6th September, 1628. Perhaps it happened during the night of these dates.

The *Riksnyckeln* was a royal warship, one of the pride of the fleet. It is known that during the winter of 1616 timber was collected for a big ship. It is believed that this ship was the *Riksnyckeln*, one of the very first men of war to be built for Gustav II Adolf. She was a ship of 250 laster (the *Vasa* was 400 laster) and was also called *Stora Nyckeln* (the Big Key). Her construction began at Ridö, but was completed at Vastervik in 1617. According to a list from 1628, she carried ten 12-pound and four 6-pound copper cannons, four 6-pound and four 3-pound iron cannons, and four larger assault cannons. Another contemporary list gives a somewhat smaller number of cannons. On a voyage to Prussia it is recorded that she carried 203 men, of whom 120 were soldiers and the rest seamen.

The ship saw 11 years of service in the Polish War before she was wrecked. At the time she was on her way home from Danzig, together with two smaller ships that afterwards arrived safely in

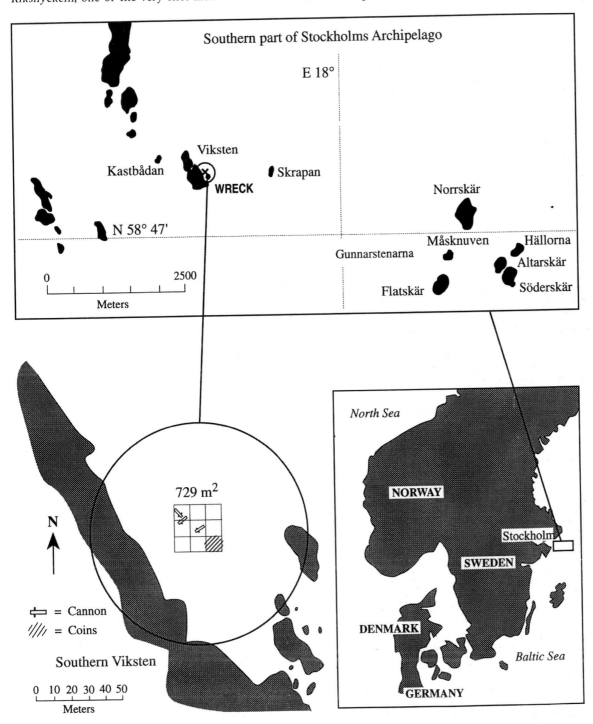

1 Southern part of the Stockholm Archipelago showing the location of the *Riksnyckeln*

Stockholm. Her remains did not appear to lie very deep. The government therefore decided to make an attempt to salvage her valuable ordnance. They managed to raise four of the guns, the rest could be felt at a depth of 4.5 fathoms, but the severe autumn storms ended their attempts for that year. I have not found anything to say that they went back. Nearly 300 years would pass before the *Riksnyckeln*'s cannons would return to Swedish soil.'

Thirty-four years after the above article Anders Franzen by chance met Professor Nils Ahnlund at the Historical Military Record Office in Stockholm. Anders, who was researching the *Riksnyckeln* at the time, naturally took the opportunity to ask the Professor if he knew anything more about the *Riksnyckeln*. Ahnlund told Franzen that he should not waste his time on the *Riksnyckeln*, but instead should try to locate the warship *Vasa* that was lying in Stockholm Strom with all her treasures. During the course of his research into the *Riksnyckeln* in 1920, Ahnlund had come across many documents relating to the *Vasa* which had sunk in Stockholm Harbour at the start of her maiden voyage on Sunday 10 August 1628. Ahnlund did not know

that, some years after her loss, most of the guns were salvaged from the *Vasa*. So Franzen gave up his work on the *Riksnyckeln* and in 1954 started to look for the *Vasa*. By the summer of 1956 he was convinced that he had found her at the depth of 100ft. In 1961 she was raised; the rest of the story is well known and need not be repeated here.

Following the excitement of 1920, the *Riksnyckeln* was again forgotten. Interest in her did not again arise until the early 1950s, when sports diving was introduced to Sweden. During the early 1960s she was much plundered. The success of the *Vasa* had its drawback in that it was as much an inspiration to treasure hunters as it was to archaeological divers. At that time there was no legal protection for submerged sites of historical interest in Sweden; it was not until 1968 that wrecks without an owner, and older than a hundred years since wrecked, became protected by law.

In 1967 I began investigating the fate of *Riksnyckeln*. During a visit to the National Maritime Museum in Stockholm, I was told that there was nothing left to find on the site. I contacted Anders Franzen by telephone. By that time he was no longer involved with the *Vasa*. He was not very interested in my questions regarding the *Riksnyckeln*. He told me that he had located the wreck and had made a sketch of the landmarks, and that this document was to be found at the National Maritime Museum. With this map it was easy to locate the site of the wreck, but upon diving we (i.e. myself and my friend Sten Ahnlberg) found that little had survived. We saw a few bricks and far from the island, in 50 m depth, we came across heavy timbers. It was evident that the place where she had sunk was exposed to both heavy winds and seas. Furthermore, she had come to rest at the relatively shallow depth of 11 m. Taking these factors into consideration, it was easy to understand how the wreck had been destroyed over the preceding 300 years.

After checking the archives we noted that there were discrepancies in the number of guns. We became certain that there were more hidden within the seabed. We decided to conduct a precise exploration of the bottom using a metal detector. We made an appointment with the Director of the National Maritime Museum and asked him to support our idea. This was not a success so we turned to the Central Board of National Antiquities and they responded more favourably.

As my collaborator, Sten Ahnlberg, was an electrical engineer and I was an engineer in precision mechanics, we decided to build our own underwater metal detector. We constructed several different models, each an improvement on the last. This was the first time, to my knowledge, that an underwater metal detector had been used on a wrecksite in Sweden, which is remarkable when one considers that the first detector was constructed in 1876 and used by Alexander Graham Bell in 1881 in an attempt to locate the assassin's bullet within the body of President Garfield.

The detectors of our devising produced mixed results, so we decided to purchase an Elsec underwater detector from the workshops of Prof. Hall at Oxford. With that instrument, and a rope grid system, we found three bronze cannons, about 1,750 copper coins, lead bullets, cannon balls, etc.

Two of the cannons were of Swedish origin. They had been cast in 1560 and 1617. Because they were loaded and closed at the muzzle it is safe to assume that they belonged to the ship. The third cannon had been cast in Danzig in 1525 and was particularly beautiful. We also recovered pieces of an exploded cannon which had been a sister of the Danzig piece. The text on the Danzig cannon read: BOSE GRIETE BIN ICK ONVORDRATEN XII SOVSTEREN TO DANSSICK WORDEN GEGATEN ANNO 1525 P W (I am Evil Grete, inexhaustible. XII sisters were cast in Danzig in 1525). The text on the fragmented barrel, although it is in a different style of script, identifies it as one of the sister cannons.

All the findings from the *Riksnyckeln* were put in storage, except for one of the guns that is now on show in the *Vasa* museum. The 1750 copper coins that we found with the metal detector were studied by the Director of the National Numismatical Collection. He drew some interesting

conclusions regarding their distribution and some informative comparisons were made with the coins of the same period from the *Vasa*, but of course they did not tell us anything we did not already know about the wreck itself.

My work on the *Riksnyckeln* led to a most fruitful working relationship with Anders Franzen. At the time when we raised the first cannon, the landowner of the area, who had taken a personal interest in the work and had been very helpful to us, invited a number of people to watch the recovery; one of them was Anders Franzen. After that Franzen worked with us. The crowning success of our collaboration was our discovery of the *Kronan* outside Oland in 1980, after a search of fourteen days.

In 1994 we will return to the *Riksnyckeln* and resurvey the site with a more sensitive metal detector, and we will do the same at the former site of the *Vasa* which has not been investigated closely since the vessel's recovery in 1961. Sadly my collaborator and friend since childhood, Sten Ahlberg will not be with me; he died on 5 September 1993. Nor will Anders Franzen; he died on 8 December the same year.

Colin Martin: (Scottish Institute of Maritime Studies, University of St Andrews, Fife, Scotland)

Dartmouth: the archaeology and structural analysis of a small seventeenth century English warship

Dartmouth was a small warship lost in the Sound of Mull off the west coast of Scotland in 1690. We are fortunate in possessing what is almost certainly a sketch of this vessel by Van de Velde the Younger, now in the National Maritime Museum (fig 1) (Robinson, 1958: 164 and 362). She was built at Portsmouth as a fifth-rate by Sir John Tippets in 1655 (Anon., 1689). Her keel length of 80ft and beam of 25ft (24.4m and 7.62m) made her (by contemporary formulae) a 266-tonner, which accommodated up to 135 men and 32 iron guns of nine-, six- and three-pound calibres, disposed along her main and upper decks (McBride, 1976). These maximum figures varied according to her employment. She was an early member of a small, lightweight class of warship, loosely called frigates, which were designed for patrol and reconnaissance work. Danish and other continental influences have been noted in their evolution (Martin, 1978).

Dartmouth's long service career was varied if rarely spectacular. She played a minor role in several general engagements with the Dutch, and undertook anti-piracy work in the Mediterranean and Caribbean (Tanner, 1894 and 1899). In April 1666, in company with two other ships, she captured three Dutch merchantmen off the Irish coast, and a few days later assisted in the destruction of a Flushing privateer (Lecky, 1913: 168-70). A notable incident occurred in 1686, when the Spanish garrison at Porto Rico (Spain then being a friendly power) attempted to detain the ship. What followed gave rise to a lengthy piece of doggerel, a manuscript version of which is preserved in the Pepys collection at Cambridge under the title '*The Treachery of the Spaniards of Porto Rico to the "Dartmouth" frigot and her company*' (Firth, 1907: 92-5). A few lines from its opening and close will suffice:

> *When the "Dartmouth" frigot lay of the town*
> *That's called Porto Rico, of some renown*
> *The captain sent thither to know if he cou'd*
> *Come peaceably in for water and wood ...*
> and
> *Thus fireing, and fireing, we held a good space,*
> *And gave 'em the go by to their disgrace;*
> *Three hours or more continu'd the fight,*
> *With fire and smoke, and a very calm night*
> *And tho' within pistol shott we were*
> *Yet nevertheless we got well clear*
> *Without much hurt or any fear*
> *And to tell you the tale we are now come here.*

1 A fifth-rate warship, probably Dartmouth sketched by Van de Velde the Younger in the 1670s
(*Photograph by courtesy of the National Maritime Museum*)

The ship's greatest moments came in the naval war which followed the dynastic settlement of 1688. In 1689 *Dartmouth* participated in the Bantry Bay action, and later that year she engaged the batteries at the entrance to the River Foyle to allow the victualling squadron to break through the boom across the river mouth and so achieve the celebrated relief of Londonderry (Powley, 1972).

In Van de Velde's sketch, apparently executed in the 1670s, *Dartmouth* is shown without masts or guns, and with no bell hanging in the belfry over the fo'castle. This

This was the cable that broke as the ship lay at anchor in the sound of Mull on 9 October, sheltering from a south-westerly gale. She had been on her way to discipline the recalcitrant Maclean of Duart, whose castle lay at the south-eastern tip of the island. Thrown on her beam-ends, and running stern-first, she was driven across the Sound to be wrecked on the small island of Rudha an Ridre. There were, so far as we know, only six survivors (Martin, 1978: 31-3).

Some contemporary salvage was carried out, and the site of the wreck was remembered locally until the mid-

2 Section through the coherent structure at R4. (see fig 4 for location of this section). Abraded surfaces are shown hatched

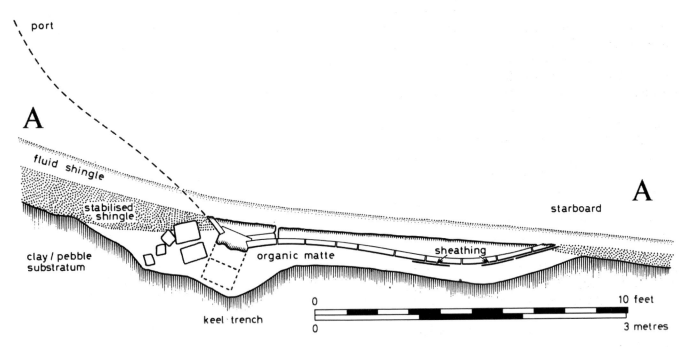

depiction was almost certainly made when the ship was refitting at Sheerness in 1678, during which - amongst other extensive structural repairs and modifications - her keel and three runs of planking on either side were replaced (PRO ADM 106/3118). The same date appears on the bell recovered from her wreck in 1973, suggesting that this item was replaced during the refit, although no documentary confirmation of this has yet come to light (Adnams, 1974: 271-2).

By 1690 *Dartmouth* was an old ship nearing the end of her useful life. Based at Carrickfergus and Greenock under the command of Captain Edward Pottinger, she was engaged in patrol activity off northern Ireland and western Scotland, carrying the writ of King William to his less enthusiastic subjects (Hopkins, 1986: 234-5; 248-9). The ship was long overdue a major refit, or final scrapping: her hull was worm-eaten and leaky, her rigging badly worn. Only a few weeks before she was wrecked Pottinger (who, together with his crew, had not been paid for several months) wrote despairingly of his ship's many defects, adding that 'our best bower cable with often anchoring, is so extremely worn as not to be trusted' (PRO ADM 106/339).

nineteenth century. Thereafter it was forgotten until 1973, when the ship's remains were discovered by members of the Bristol Undersea Archaeology Group who, in association with the Scottish Institute of Maritime Studies, excavated them over the following two seasons (Adnams, 1974; Holman, 1975; McBride, 1976; P. Martin, 1977; Martin, 1978). All the recoveries, including substantial elements of hull structure, are now in the National Museums of Scotland, which partly sponsored the project.

The aim of this paper is to summarise the structural evidence recorded during and after the excavation, and published some time ago in the *International Journal of Nautical Archaeology* (Martin, 1978). Some revision of the interpretations then put forward are presented here. Before considering this evidence, however, a few general observations are necessary. The excavation strategy was to isolate and uncover the ship's surviving articulated structure, and then move towards the periphery of the site in an attempt to understand the processes of break-up, destruction, dispersal, and deposition which the wreck's various elements underwent. An overburden of mobile sand and shingle up to 1m deep was removed from above and around the surviving structure, revealing a flat raft-like area of eroded timbers some 14m long and 5m wide These incorporated oak frames, ceiling and outer planking of elm, fir sheathing and an elm keel.

In the section presented in fig 2 it is evident that the keel is heeled over at an angle of 23 degrees. Its upper surfaces are intact and unabraded but its lower part appears to have been worn away. The extent of the missing part can be reconstructed from documentary sources. Accounts of the ship's re-keeling in 1678 show that the keel itself was 13 inches square (0.33m), and that an 8-inch (0.20) false keel was added below that (PRO ADM 106/3118). These dimensions closely match those of a shingle-filled trench cut into the hard substrate below the keel, indicating that the keel was responsible for creating it. In the process most of its lower substance was worn away. This suggests in turn that, during the wrecking process, this section of the ship rocked from side to side on the fulcrum provided by its

3 HMS *Dartmouth* general plan of wreck site

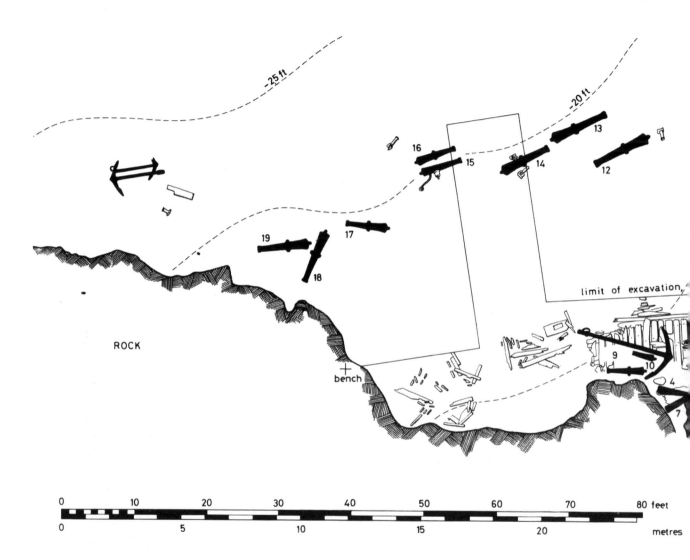

keel, thus causing it to dig deeply into the hard and abrasive clay/pebble substratum. Abrasion is not, however, evident on the outer planking, upon which some of the relatively fragile sandwich of fir and tarred hair sheathing has survived intact. It may be supposed that this planking, cushioned by water resistance, and with no direct weight forcing it into contact with the sea floor as the hull rocked to and fro, would have fanned the shingle in such a way as to form the hollow bed into which it eventually stabilised.

In the process a thick matte of wood splinters from the abraded keel, together with other organic material from the fabric and contents of the ship, became incorporated beneath and around the stabilised hull remains. The keel trench, moreover, acted as a gravity-trap for a substantial deposit of metal and ceramic objects. This suggests that the ship broke up in a continuous and fairly rapid sequence, allowing structural components and other objects which fell from the disintegrating upper parts of the vessel to gather at the bottom of the keel trench before it became stabilised

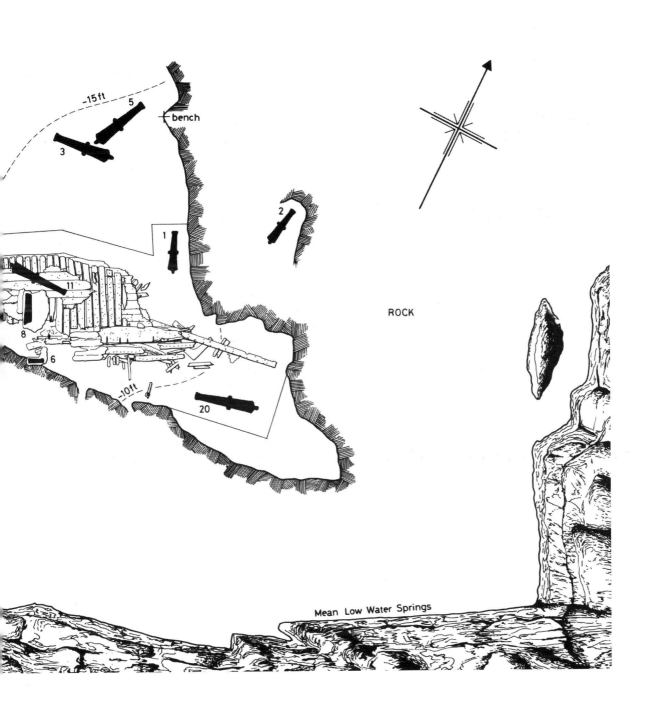

with shingle. Once the wreck elements had stabilised, the mobile sands and gravels of the seabed reasserted themselves to a depth varying from 0.6m to 0.15m or less. The moving top levels of this material have caused considerable abrasion to the upper parts of the articulated structure, grinding it to a flat conformity with the seabed profile. This process, slow but inexorable, might have been expected to continue until the structure was entirely destroyed.

Now that the nature of these processes has been established, the wreck site may be considered as a whole (fig 3). The articulated structure lies at the head of a V-shaped gully, the shallow apex of which comes close to the shore where it reaches a depth of less than 3m below Low Water. Within this gully the sea floor slopes gently seawards for some 60m where, beyond the furthest extremity of identified wreckage, it reaches the 25ft (7.5m) contour. The structural remains lie close to the southern end of the gully, and the 6m run of surviving keel stops where a spur of rock intrudes upon its axis. At this point, across which the keel

probably lay at about its midships point, the ship presumably broke her back, aided no doubt by the pile-driving effect of the mainmast. Westward of this spur no articulated remains of the ship's other end were encountered, although a considerable number of dislocated timbers, associated artefacts, and organic debris were present.

Some 9m north-west of the projected keel axis, running not quite parallel with it, a linear deposition of iron guns closely follows the 6m (20ft) contour for some 18m. At the western end of this line near two anchors lying head to tail as though lashed together and stowed when lost, several sheet-lead Roman numerals were found. These may be identified as draught-marks. Both observations suggest that this point lies close to one of the wreck's extremities. The line of guns itself is complemented by a number of lead scupper-liners, which can be associated with the side of the ship at main deck level. About half-way along this line, in the vicinity of guns 15 and 16, was a deposit of bricks, tiles, and general cooking debris, evidently associated with the

4 HMS *Dartmouth* main structural complex, 1976

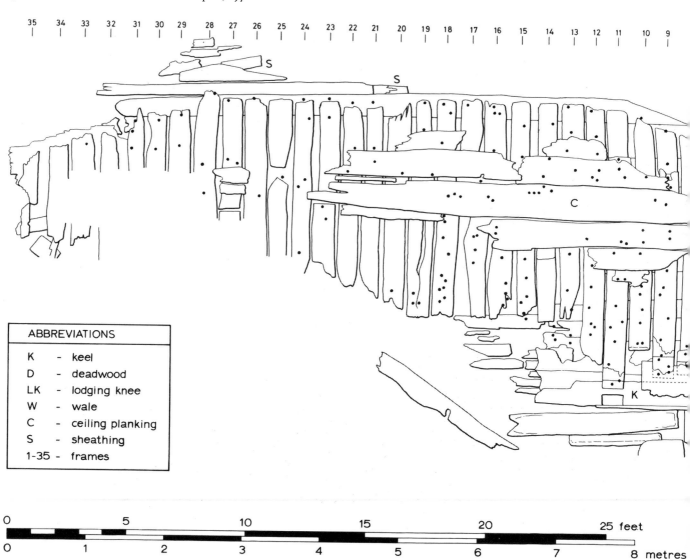

ABBREVIATIONS		
K	-	keel
D	-	deadwood
LK	-	lodging knee
W	-	wale
C	-	ceiling planking
S	-	sheathing
1-35	-	frames

galley structure. The ship's bell, which would originally have hung from the belfry immediately above the galley, was concreted to the side of gun 15.

To examine the relationship between the projected keel axis and the axis represented by the line of guns and scupper-liners a lateral trench was opened between the two. The artefact distribution noted in this trench is shown in fig 5. Its pattern is noteworthy. Between the two axes there is a remarkable paucity of objects of any kind until a point about 2m from the line of guns. Beyond this, and up to the line, objects from the ship are crowded beside and within a solid band of concretion which ends abruptly at the line itself. The impression is given of a cascade of loose objects sliding across a sloping deck until checked by the ship's side, represented by the line of guns and scupper-liners. There they will have been held long enough to become stabilised as a matrix of concretion before the containing structure, which must have stood largely proud of the seabed, disintegrated or rotted away.

The sequence of the ship's break-up can now be postulated with some confidence. One extremity was wedged into the shoreward end of the gully, where it collapsed and stabilised independently of the other half, from which it had separated at about midships. The seaward end then half-rolled down the slope to lie on its side along a slightly different alignment, matching the seabed contour. There it deposited its contents, which stabilised in the manner described. Within these parameters, therefore, it is possible with moderate confidence to restore individual finds (particularly inorganic finds) to their original locations within the ship. Before this can be done, however, it must be determined which end of the wreck represents the bow, and which the stern.

The orientation of the site was demonstrated by the late Keith Muckelroy with an elegant spacial analysis of finds categories and distributions which, by showing the arithmetic mean centres of selected groups, clearly showed that the wreck's stern lay at its inshore end (Muckelroy,

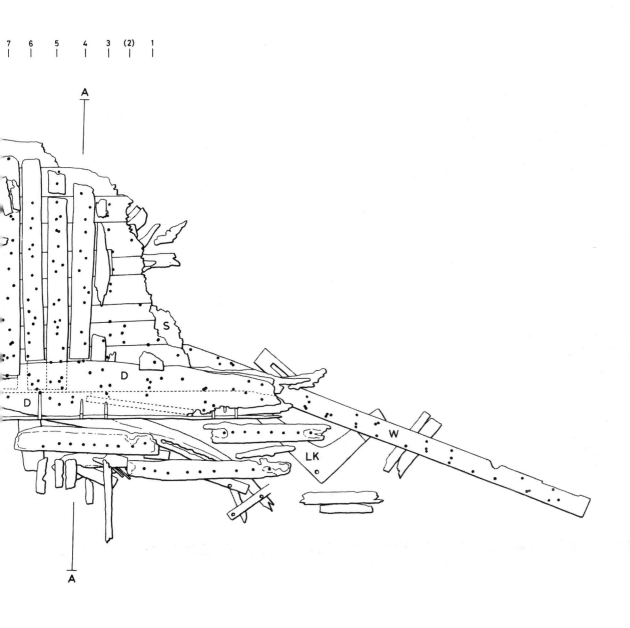

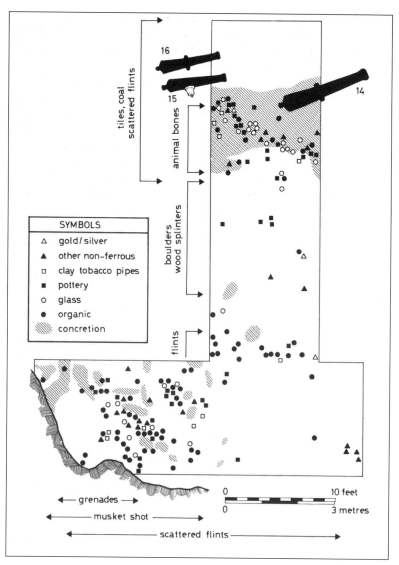

SYMBOLS

△ gold / silver
▲ other non-ferrous
□ clay tobacco pipes
■ pottery
○ glass
● organic
▨ concretion

tiles, coal
scattered flints

animal bones

boulders
wood splinters

flints

16
15
14

0 ——— 10 feet
0 ——— 3 metres

← grenades →
← musket shot →
← scattered flints →

5 *Left* Artefact distributions in the lateral and transverse trenches at the forward end of the site (see Figure 3 for location details)

6 *Below left* Exploded reconstruction of the keel scarf

7 *Below* Hypothetical resolution of *Dartmouth's* after lines, based on a projection of the faired sections of frames R5 to R12 and comparison with the Keltridge draughts

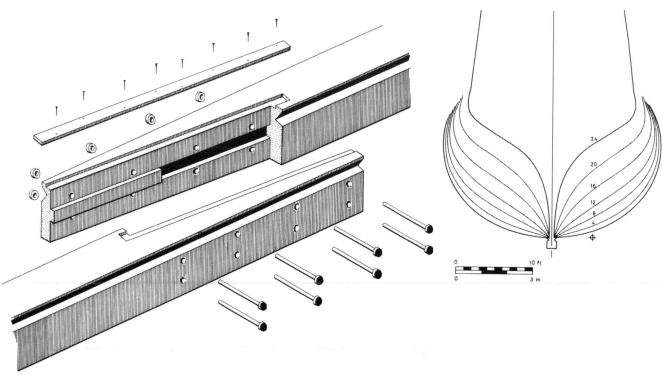

0 ——— 10 ft
0 ——— 3 m

24
20
16
12
8
4

1978: 190-1). The most conclusive indicator was a group of leaded mica pieces, cut in rhomboidal or triangular shapes. Reference to the Van de Velde representation of *Dartmouth* shows that these objects are to be associated uniquely with the glazing of the ship's stern cabin and gallery lights (Martin, 1978: 33-4).

Once the ship's orientation was known an attempt was made to fit the surviving structural remains into the framework of the hull (fig 4). To achieve this a longitudinal point of reference was required - ideally one of the keel's extremities. Unfortunately neither had survived. However the identification of what is probably the aftermost scarf joint of the keel, indicated in fig 5 by the capping piece which runs obliquely across its top surface provided a significant clue.

The dismantled joint is reconstructed in fig 6. It was noted that the scarf faces of the joint overlap by 4ft 3in (1.30m). This dimension is exactly half the 8ft 6in (2.59m) excess over the ship's registered keel length noted in Captain Castle's account for the new keel fitted in 1678. The implication is that the two scarf joints were allowed for, suggesting a three-piece keel. If equal lengths are postulated - and analogies suggest they should be - each segment will have been 29ft 6in (9m) long, a figure close to the maximum length in

which mature elm 13in (0.33m) square can be obtained. If these assumptions are correct, then the centre of the surviving scarf joint can be fixed at 28ft 8in (9.64m) forward of the after end of the keel.

With this fixed point established the frame sections provide the basis for a tentative reconstruction of the ship's after lines, which confirm the fine run of her hull (fig 7). This was to be expected in such a vessel, designed specifically for speed and good sailing qualities: what was less expected was the apparently unconventional nature of her construction. The frames are arranged in pairs, with overlapping chocked joints, although the neighbouring frames are not themselves jointed transversely. This shows, in turn, that the hull planking cannot have been built on a pre-erected skeleton of frames, but that the two elements were introduced turn and about, working upwards from the keel. This conclusion contradicts the generally accepted view on constructional techniques of the period, which are themselves based in the main on contemporary statements by theorists rather than practising shipwrights (McKee, 1976). Many of the latter were illiterate, or nearly so. John Evelyn, after attending the launch of the 1200-ton First Rate *Charles* at Deptford in 1668, noted in his diary that she was 'built by old Shish, a plain honest carpenter, master-

8 *Below left* Outside strake plan R1-R13

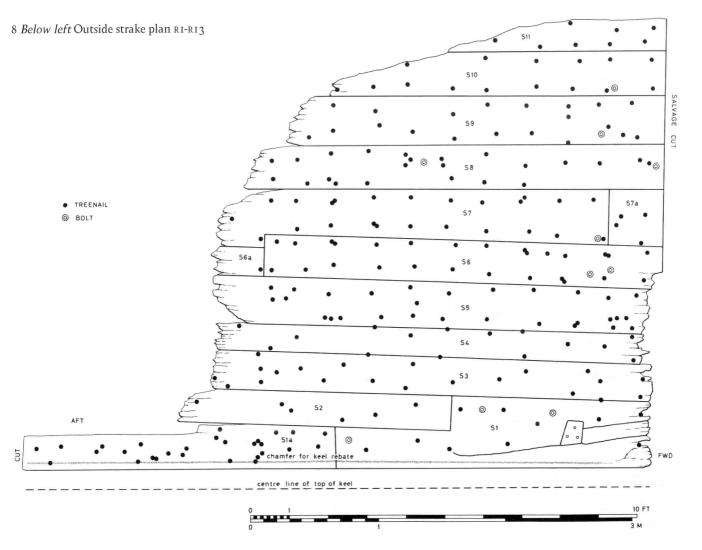

builder in this dock, but one who can give very little account of his art by discourse, and is hardly capable of reading, yet of great ability in his calling' (Martin, 1987: 230). Such men worked by rule of thumb, and in the round: their achievements are recorded not on paper but in the timbers of the ships they built.

Another unconventional feature evident in *Dartmouth*'s structure is that the frames do not span the keel, but end just short of it, where they are clamped in place by a massive elm timber. This may be seen as a deliberate measure to reduce the number of sharply-curved grown timbers required by the structure, although more probably it is connected with the replacement of the ship's keel and lower three runs of planking in 1678. If these components were rotten the central sections of the frames were probably affected too, and what we may see here is an ingenious technique whereby these portions were chopped out and replaced sequentially without the longitudinal integrity of the structure being lost in the process.

An examination of the outer strakes raises further points of interest (fig 8). The fastenings, as to be expected, closely follow the locations of the frames within the hull, with two trenails normally being applied to each joint. Viewed longitudinally, however, the trenails seem haphazardly placed, with no attempt to align them in neat rows. This was probably quite deliberate intended to avoid setting up lines of weakness along the grain of the planks. The secondary use of trenails is also notable. These sometimes impinge on existing ones, and were presumably intended to tighten up primary fastenings which had worked loose. Extensive secondary fastenings on the garboard plank S1a suggest that major problems had been experienced at this crucial point. Another interesting feature is the thin strake S4, in which the trenails are placed so close to the edges that some cut through the join between it and its neighbouring strake. If S2, which is a stealer, is discounted, the idiosyncratic S4 will be the strake which bridges the gap between the original planking and the three lower strakes replaced in 1678.

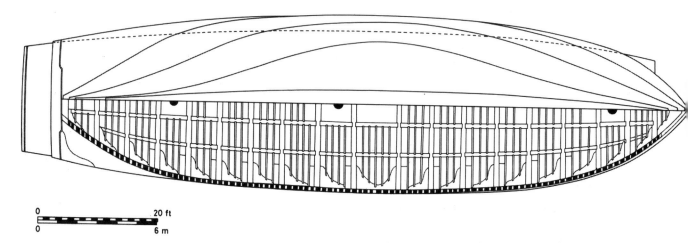

0 _____ 20 ft
0 _____ 6 m

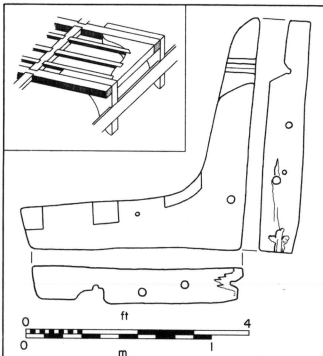

0 _____ ft _____ 4
0 _____ m _____

9 *Above* Deck-plan of a fifth-rate, after Keltridge (1684)

10 *Left* Plan and external elevations of an oak lodging knee, with a reconstruction demonstrating its function within the 5-foot modular structure of the hull

Finally, there is evidence to indicate a level of standardisation in the components and their spacing within the hull. The frames, although varying somewhat in their individual widths, all sit on centre-lines precisely one foot (0.30m) apart. A lodging knee which probably derives from the port after-quarter of the main deck indicates that the structure of that deck was based on 5ft (1.5m) modules - a dimension reflected in contemporary ship-plans, notably the Keltridge draughts of 1684 (figs 9 and 10). Archaeology has thus shown that there are similarities as well as differences to be observed when comparing sources of evidence for seventeenth century shipbuilding - all the more reason, it may be emphasised in conclusion, for seeking to integrate every available source when conducting investigations of this kind.

References

Adnams, J., 1974, The *Dartmouth*, a British frigate wrecked off Mull, 1690. *Int. J. Naut. Archaeol.*, 3,2: 269-74.

Anon., 1689, *Gloria Britannia* (*The Royal Navy of England*): reprinted by Derrick, C., 1806, *Memoirs of the rise and progress of the Royal Navy*. London.

Firth, C.H., 1907, *Naval songs and ballads* (Navy Records Society).

Holman, R.G., 1975, the *Dartmouth*, a British frigate wrecked off Mull, 1690. 2. Culinary and related items. *Int. J. Naut. Archaeol.*, 4,2: 253-65.

Hopkins, P., 1986, *Glencoe and the end of the Highland war*. Edinburgh.

Lecky, H.S., 1913, *The King's ships*. Vol. II. London.

McBride, P., 1976, The *Dartmouth*, a British frigate wrecked off Mull, 1690. 3. The guns. *Int. J. Naut. Archaeol.*, 5,3: 189-200.

McKee, E., 1976, Identification of timbers from old ships of north-west European origin. *Int. J. Naut. Archaeol.*, 5,3: 3-12.

Martin, C.J.M., 1978 The *Dartmouth*, a British frigate wrecked off Mull, 1690. 5. The ship. *Int. J. Naut. Archaeol.*, 7,1: 29-58.

Martin, C.J.M., 1987, Ships of the line, *in* P. Throckmorton (ed.), *History from the sea: shipwrecks and archaeology*, 148-51 and 230 (notes).

Martin, P.F. de C., 1977, The *Dartmouth*, a British frigate wrecked off Mull, 1690. 4. The clay pipes. *Int. J. Naut. Archaeol.*, 6,3: 219-23.

Mull, 1690. 4. The clay pipes. *Int. J. Naut. Archaeol.*, 6,3: 219-23.

Muckelroy, K., 1978, *Maritime archaeology*. Cambridge.

Powley, E.B., 1972, *The naval side of King William's war*. London.

Robinson, M.S., 1958, *The Van de Velde drawings. A catalogue of drawings in the National Maritime Museum*. Cambridge.

Tanner, J.R., 1894 and 1899, *A descriptive catalogue of the naval manuscripts in the Pepysian Library at Magdalene College, Cambridge*. Vols. II and III (Navy Records Society).

Bryan Smith (Oxford University MARE)

The Search for HMS *Resolution* (1667-1703)

Biography

The *Resolution* (figs 1 and 2) was a 70 gun, third-rate man-of-war of about 900 tons. She was built at Harwich by the famous naval architect, Anthony Deane, between 1665 and 1667. Some believe her to be Deane's most successful ship. Her service under the Crown was varied and interesting. In 1669-70 she was with Sir Thomas Allin as part of a futile campaign against the Barbary corsairs in the Mediterranean. Then, in 1672, she took part in the unsuccessful attack on the Dutch Smyrne convoy which opened the Third Dutch War. In June of that year she captured at least 23 Dutch merchant ships while cruising off Yarmouth. Later in the war she was active in the Battle of Solebay, the First and Second Battles of Schooneveld and the Battle of Texel. In 1691 she was present at the Battle of Barfleur and La Hogue. In 1693 she was in the West Indies where she was Rear Admiral Wheeler's flagship in the attack on Martinique. In May 1694, in company with the *Monmouth*, she drove ashore and burnt a French frigate and 35 merchant ships. In 1697-98 she had an extensive refit and rebuild at Chatham. The poor quality of these repairs created a scandal which resulted in changes to the system of rebuilding. In 1702 she was again in the West Indies and on her return was lost in the Great Storm of 1703.

The Great Storm of 1703

The Great Storm of 1703 was one of the worst on record in British Waters. Twelve vessels were lost, including the *Stirling Castle* that also features in this volume. A brief description of its ferocity and consequences is given by John Campbell in his *Lives of British Admirals* (1779, 392-393):

The Storm began on the 26th of November, 1703, at about eleven in the evening; the wind being west-south-west, and continued

1 Queen's ship *Resolution* by Van de Velde the Younger
(*courtesy National Maritime Museum Picture Library, London*)

with dreadful flashes of lightning, till about seven the next morning. The water flowed to a great height in Westminster Hall; and London Bridge was in a manner stopt up with wrecks. The mischief done in London was computed at not less than a million; and the city of Bristol suffered upwards of one hundred and fifty thousand pounds. But the greatest loss fell upon our navy, of which there perished no less than thirteen ships, and upwards of fifteen hundred seamen were drowned; among whom was Basil Beaumont, Esq. rear-admiral of the blue; who had been employed all that year in observing the Dunkirk squadron, and had by his great care and conduct preserved our merchant-ships from falling into the hands of the French privateers... These losses, how much soever they might affect us at home, served in some measure to raise our reputation abroad, for orders were immediately issued for building more ships than were destroyed[1].

The loss of *Resolution*

As a result of the failure of her anchor cables, the *Resolution* was driven on the shoals several times, causing such stress to her seams that the ingress of water became unmanageable. In a badly damaged and sinking state her Captain, Thomas Liell, deliberately beached her in Pevensey (or Pemsey) Bay thus saving the lives of all on board. The unfolding drama is clearly described by the captain in the ship's log which survives in the Public Records Office, London (PRO ADM 106/581 159535):

2 Stern and larboard side of Queen's ship *Resolution* by Van de Velde the Younger (*courtesy National Maritime Museum Picture Library, London*)

25/11/03
This day have had hard gales with thick weather and driving rain this morning set our course and in taking in our topsails they both split we unbent at 8 this morning made the Bill of Portland at 3 after noon made Dunoze being very thick and hazy we bore up for St Helens at the anchor in 7 fathoms the Port Bower cable parting we let go the small lower which brought up the Ship then lowered yards and topmast and spliced the second cable of the port bower to the small bower veard away wind from WSW to S by E.

26/11/03
This morning got up the topmast and bent the topsails, but it blowing so hard we could not purches our anchor, so we lowed the topmast again and veard away, Bembridge point bearing WSW 3 miles, at 12 at night the small bower cable parted, Immediately we let go the sheet and stream anchors which no sooner had brought up the ship but they parted[2], then we losed our sprit sail which blew out of the boltropes and likewise the foresail and Main sail blow out of the boltropes.

27/11/03
About two this morning the ship struck and then drove into 5 and 6 fathom of water and struck again and then drove into deeper water which she did four times before we was clear of the shoals, the ship proved so very leaky that all our men could hardly keep her above water with both pumps and bailing at fore main and after hatchways at six this morning brought to a spritsail to the foreyard and hoisted it as high as the topmast would admit, the winds being at W by S. Shorham bearing N by E about 3 Leagues at 12 this day the water increasing on us in the hold and all our men tired with pumping and bailing the water being up to the orlop beams we were obliged to put the ship a Shore near Pemsey to save our lives

Tho: Liell

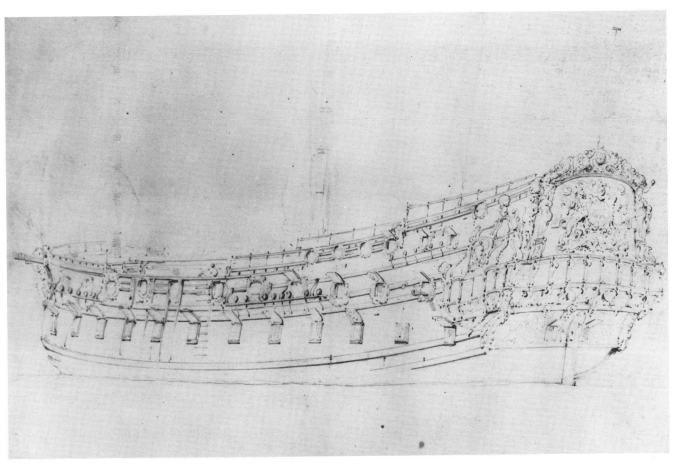

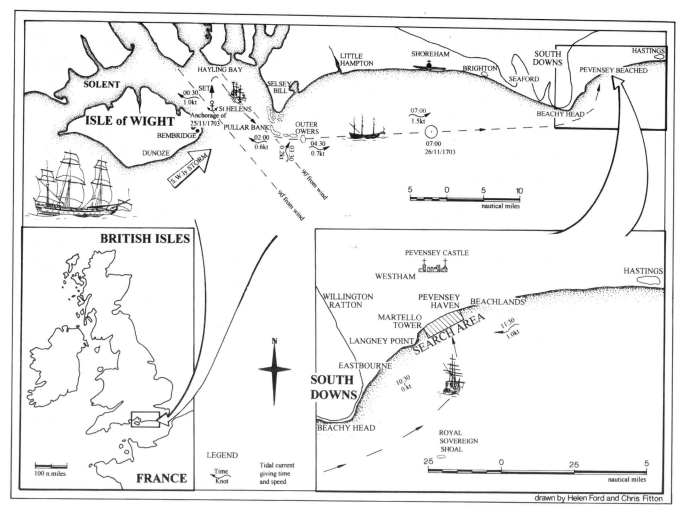

3 South East England showing the final route of *Resolution* during the Great Storm *(Helen Ford and Chris Fitton)*

A broadly similar account was given by the first lieutenant in a document dated 18/1/04 which obviously referred to the events of the 26 and 27 of November of the preceding year (National Maritime Museum ADM/L/E/91).

Strong gales thick Weather. Something past 12 last night our small bower parted and Wee emmediately lett goe our Sheet anchor and Stream anchor, which hardly brought the Shipp up though We reanded all the Sheet Cable out to 1 1/2 fath att 3/4 past 12 they both parted and our ship rolling with her head to the Swd and it being the Ebb tide Wee loosed the Spritsaile which with the strength of the wind blowed from the yard as did afterwards the foresaile and Mainsaile at 2 this morning our Ship struck upon the Owers att least 6 or 7 times We had then Depth of Water between 3 1/2 and 5 fath And after 4 our water deepened to 12 and 14 fath Wee then keeping our pumps going and baling in the Hatchways. att 7 this morning itt being day and proveing less wind we saw the land then bent a Spritsaile with both reefes in the Capps the Water then being up to the Orlopp and It still Increasing We thought it Convenient for the Safety of our lives to Run her ashore Which Wee did about Noon between Beachy and Hastings off of Pemsey Town In Sussex Where the Water Ebbing from the Ship Itt pleased God We Saved our Lives.

The position of HMS *Resolution*

Throughout the journey from Bembridge to Pevensey (fig 3), some 56.3 nautical miles, there are only four recorded positions for the *Resolution* and most of these are of doubtful accuracy. The first, the anchorage, in St Hellen's Road (Bembridge Point bearing WSW, about 3 miles from land; OLS 1, 17, 18, 19) should be reasonably dependable. When her anchors parted the tide was ebbing and the wind blowing a gale from the SW (OLS 18). It was the middle of the night and there would have been a delay before the crew was able to impose some measure of control over her motion and then get underway (OLS 17, 18, 21) by which time she would have set into Hayling Bay. The tidal current was then setting to the west at about a knot, keeping her off the reef, but the wind would have been the main factor. The sails then blew out (OLS 17, 18, 21), however, I would suggest they lasted long enough for the ship to clear the westward edges of Pullar Bank. She probably scraped along the southern edge and touched the eastern end (the Outer Owers) but if she had gone over the main part of the bank, I suspect she would have been totally wrecked. There is a discrepancy in the officers statements (OLS 17, 18, 19); three of them say she hit at 0200, but the Master states that it occurred between 0200 and 0400 (OLS 21) which seems more plausible. The tide turned about 0330 first driving her to the north then to the east. If this is the case, then, between 0030 and 0400, she made about 3.5 knots, which I believe would have put her, by 0400, as far out as the Outer Owers. This lines up with her next known position, off Shoreham, at 0700 (OLS 17) which puts her on course to pass between 1 and 2 miles off Beachy Head. The officers do not say how they recognized Shoreham or how they obtained their distance from this place (3 leagues, or, 9 miles). Their bearing at this point was N by E (011°) but they do not say if it was 'magnetic' or 'true'. Having hit the shoals several times (OLS 17, 18, 19, 21) she was by that time leaking badly. At daybreak on 27 November a sail was set and after the 0700 position they made up for Beachy Head (OLS 18), some 18 miles to the east. After passing Beachy Head and with the water inside the vessel rising over the orlop deck, Captain Liell ordered the vessel to be beached. The distance from Beachy Head, which she would have rounded at about 0930, to Pevensey is about 7.6 nautical miles which she could have covered easily even allowing from the tidal current to change from flood to ebb at about 11.00.

The problem is to determine exactly where she was grounded. Possibly the most accurate position is that given by the master who wrote '. . . she was put ashore against Pemsey at 1130' (OLS 21). The first lieutenant agreed (OLS 18). Later, in a letter to the Admiralty, the Captain gives the position between Willingdon and Pemsey. None of them mention Pevensey Haven or the Castle at Pevensey. The former had been surveyed in 1698 and though silted up was probably still visible; the latter has been a prominent landmark since Norman times.

Several maps of the period have been studied to see whether the beach has changed. There are three reliable reference points, the churches at Westham and Pevensey and the Castle between them. The present O/S map puts the beach at about 1500 metres (0.93 miles) from the castle. So do the plans of the Haven surveyed by a Navy/Trinity House team in 1698 (on which the two churches and castle are also situated with reasonable accuracy). A map by William Booth in the PRO (MR915), dated 1764, sites the Castle about 0.65 geometrical miles (probably nautical miles) from the beach. It also shows Langney Point which appears to be about three-quarters of a mile farther seaward than on the present day O/S map. In addition it shows the entrance (breakwaters?) to the Haven extending a quarter of a mile out to sea. It is, however, likely that these features have been distorted, but the western part of the map which shows Selsey and gives soundings about the Owers, appears to be quite accurate. Other maps of the period do not show Langney Point so far out. Greenville Collins' *Great Britain Coasting Pilot* of 1693, shows the point as it is today, as does *Samson's (of Paris) Atlas* of 1692 and a French chart by Bellin of 1763. *Norden's* map of 1610 and *Speed's* of 1666 show the Point well out into the Channel. So does *Budgen's* of 1724, Herman Moll's of the same year, and Overton and Bowels' of 1740, but none of them, including Booth's, put the Castle and two churches in their correct positions.

The ordnance survey map of 1813 shows Langney (called Langley) Point and the beach to Pevensey (old Pemsey, now Pevensey Bay), as they are today. The beach today extends

4 *Resolution* (foreground) holding station in a gale
(Van de Velde the Younger; courtesy National Maritime Museum Picture Library, London)

from the bottom of a ridge of pebbles (about 6 metres high) to about 250m seaward at low water spring tides; it is constantly changing, especially during periods of strong winds. It shoals slowly at an irregular rate of about 5m in 350m. The Haven is now called Salt Haven and its exit to the sea is enclosed by three culverts under the Pebble Ridge; the end of the western culvert is marked by a beacon.

The ship was beached an hour after high water, one day before spring tide. She must have been low in the sea with internal water up to the orlop beams. The volume, of the hull, below the orlop beams was 778 tons by calculation (Simpson's rules) using Dean's drawings. She would have been carrying about 100 tons of ballast and some stores in this space. So, allowing 650 tons for the excess water, her draught would be increased by about 5ft. Her normal draught, from Deane, was 14½ ft forward and 17¼ ft aft, giving a mean of 15⅞ ft. Adding the sinkage, this would give her a mean draught of 20⅞ ft and a maximum draught aft of 22¼ ft, i.e. 6.97m. Using the Shoreham tide diagram, which is similar to that of Pevensey, with a range of 6.61m and a factor of 0.92, gives a height above low water of 6.08m and a height above datum of 7.12m, at the time that she grounded. Assuming these figures are roughly correct, the *Resolution* probably took the beach just above the low water level. The Captain's letter to the Admiralty[3] suggests that the vessel was accessible at low tide. For these reasons the search has been confined to an area of beach 1 1/2 nautical miles from the modern town of Pevensey Bay.

Unfortunately the Officer's dispositions at the Court Martial (OLS 17, 18, 19, 20, 21, 22, 23) do not tell where the ship went ashore, nor do letters to the Admiralty from the Captain or the Customs Officer at Hastings, William Boswell, who was appointed to assist Captain Liell.

The question also arises regarding what was left and for what we should be searching. Most of the loose stores were taken off. A contractor (OLS 28) appears to suggest that he careened her in order to salvage the masts and yards. This seems to contradict a letter from Boswell to the Admiralty (OLS 13) in which he wrote that the French burnt the ship down to the ballast. It also seems that the guns were not salvaged because the same contractor requested permission (and payment) to dig them out of the sand into which they were fretted. There are, however, no surviving records permitting him to do so. Boswell also talks about selling off the ironwork, by which he appears to mean the rudder fastenings and the like (OLS 13). Liell and Boswell tried to arrange for vessels to come from Hastings to load stores and guns, but they refused to go around the coast because of the danger posed by French privateers (OLS 3).

So what we are seeking is a mound of ballast with up to 70 guns around it, buried under the sand of Pevensey beach, somewhere between Beachlands and Martello Tower No. 65, a shoreline distance of about 3,000 metres with a width of about 450 metres.

The search for the *Resolution*[4]

Our first attempts to find the *Resolution* (in early 1989) involved no more than haphazard beach-walking with a hand-held metal detector. We found small items of ferrous metal close to the surface, but these were mainly pieces of scaffold pole, probably from World War II defences. The metal detector had a penetrating depth of about three feet.

In June of the same year we made a dive off the car park at Pevensey Bay. Nothing of significance was seen, but it did prove that, because of the poor visibility and high-energy nature of the sea at this point, it would be impossible to cover the area underwater in a systematic and methodical manner. On 10 August 1989 we were loaned a proton magnetometer for one month. Its meter, which measured to nanoteslas, was set on an average reading; any fluctuations as the result of magnetic anomalies were displayed on a digital panel. This instrument proved to be very accurate. To systematize its use we divided the beach into search zones. This was done by establishing transits with lines of poles orientated to accord with the Royal Sovereign Light Tower, which was visible most days on a bearing of 144 degrees magnetic.

Although our efforts have so far failed we have continued our archive work as well as our searches of the inter-tidal zone and foreshore. When conditions allowed, we have also pursued our survey of the seabed. A ship of this size cannot disappear without trace and we feel certain that if we are persistent in our endeavours we will eventually find the final resting place of the *Resolution*.

Notes

1 For further information on the Great Storm see Cates and Chamberlain in the chapter on the *Stirling Castle* in this volume.

2 The equipment list shows that the ship would have been carrying six anchors. We know, however, that the cables were in poor condition (probably because she had not received new stores since returning from the West Indies), so it is possible that she lost one, or more of her anchors before anchoring in St Helen's Roads.

3 PRO ADM 1/2034; verso: '... it being past high water & the water in the Ships hold up to the Orlup beams and the men quite tired: we ware Obliged to put the Ship a shore between this place and Pemsey: to Save our lives, and the Guns and Stores etc, the gunes will be all saved, but the tides fall out so late at night & early in the Morning that we have no daylight to git anything on Shore, and the Cuntry people is for what they can Pilfer and Steale, not with standing all care Possiable is taking to prevent them, all our Powder is Dammaged for that rome was full of water in a Small time after the Ship Struck. it Eabs dry without the Ship at low water so I am in hopes to Save most of her Stores if it continue feyre Wather &the Ship Sett well. I tackle all care I can to keep our men together to Save what we can, but vary few of them gives the Attendance altho I muster them two or three times a day, and tell that those men that doe not Endeavour to Save what they can of her Majts Stores will be made R. I humbly desier his Royall Highness Direction in this afayr.

I am yor Honrs most

Humble Sarvt

The Liell

4 The team consists of Mike Laycock, Mike Woolstenhume, Ernest Perry, Alaric Smith, Jason Smith, Ann Smith and Bryan Smith.

References

Campbell, J, 1779, *Lives of the British Admirals*, Vol. III, London.

Dean, J, 1670, *Doctrine of Naval Architecture*, London.

Michael Cates & Diane Chamberlain (East Kent Maritime Trust)
with postscript by D.R.J. Perkins (Trust for Thanet Archaeology)

Stirling Castle, 1703

Historical background

After the Third Dutch War in 1674, the British Navy was reduced to a skeletal fleet of which many were so old or in need of repair that Samuel Pepys, First Secretary to the Admiralty, persistently lobbied Parliament to embark on a shipbuilding programme. He finally succeeded in 1677 when almost £600,000 was authorized for 30 Great Ships of the Line (one first rate, nine second rates, twenty third rates) to be built and completed within a two year period. *Stirling Castle* was one of the third rates built in 1679 by John Shish at Deptford.[1]

Two contemporary sources give valuable information on the history of the fighting ships during the Restoration Period (the reign of King Charles II 1660 to 1685). First, there is the artistic record left by the marine painters of the time, in particular the two Dutch artists, Willem Van de Velde the Elder (1610-1693) and his son Willem Van de Velde the Younger (1633-1707) who were noted for the accurate depiction of detail in their paintings and drawings of ships and sea battles (fig 1). Second, there is the administrative and personal archive of Pepys (1633-1703) who was instrumental in reforming and restructuring the Navy amid the political turmoil of the period. He was appointed Clerk of the Acts in the re-established Navy Board of 1660 and worked tirelessly and methodically to acquaint himself with shipbuilding methods, dockyard operations and financial management. He recorded everything he saw in his diaries. Pepys left the Board in 1673 to become First Secretary of the Admiralty, a position he held until 1679 and again between 1684 and 1689. Pepys gained the full confidence of Charles II and had great influence in developing the Navy into a powerful, functional, efficient service.

1 The launching of *Stirling Castle* in 1679 from a drawing by Van de Velde *(National Maritime Museum).*

2 Restored model of HMS *Grafton* on display at the US Naval Academy in Annapolis *(W. Utley)*

There was great rivalry between the navies of England, Holland and France to gain supremacy of the seas. In terms of construction, no country had significant advantage over the other, all the ships were of similar size and design, each country stealing the best ideas from the other and, when possible, improving and refining them. For the British Programme of 1677, the designs of masts, spars, rigging, fittings and armament were standardized. This would not only reduce costs but simplify maintenance since most non-structural components then became interchangeable between second and third rates during refits or rebuilding. Motivation and progress came from Pepys who, as a Fellow of the Royal Society (later its President), came into contact with the leading scientific personalities of the time and therefore had access to expert advice in developing a more integrated and efficient system of naval architecture combined with ordnance requirements. Charles II declared that the restrictions imposed by the Parliamentary Act which authorized the construction of the 30 Great Ships, should not be allowed to interfere with the design of the

ships and ordered the Navy Board to prepare estimates and dimensions. Responsibility for this fell to Sir John Tippets, appointed as Surveyor of the Navy in 1672 and Sir Anthony Deane, given the post of Controller of the Victualling Accounts in 1673.

Design, construction, tactics and armament

Contemporary draught plans of third rate vessels of the Programme can be found in the collection of the National Maritime Museum at Greenwich. One such vessel is the *Grafton* illustrated here in fig 2.[2] Average specifications for a third rate in the 1677 Programme were 1,008 tons, 150ft length along the gun deck, 39ft 8ins external beam and 17ft depth in hold. The *Stirling Castle*, by contrast, was 1,114 tons, had a length of 151ft 2ins along the gun deck (133ft 11ins along the keel), a breadth of 40ft 4ins and a hold depth of 17ft 3ins.

Many qualities were required in the design and construction of a sailing warship. Great strength and ample storage facilities were two major considerations, but performance was also of crucial concern. The ship had to be easily manoeuvrable and be able to carry extensive sail without causing excessive heeling. Also, it had to be capable of supporting a heavy weapons system without compromising buoyancy or stability.

With the repair programme already underway, the building of the new ships caused many problems, not least among them being the demands for timber, manpower and space at dockyard facilities. Warships were made almost entirely of wood with timbers fastened by wooden treenails, supplemented where necessary with iron bolts. The ships' main structures were made of good quality English oak with less expensive 'east country timber' from Scandinavia and the Baltic being used for planking and decks. Masts and spars were of fir, pine or spruce, some of which came from as far away as New England.

Because of maintenance needs the space available on slipways for new vessels was much restricted. The Admiralty directed that ships were to be launched as soon as they could float and be completed elsewhere so that other keels could be laid to keep the programme on schedule. Traditional practice had been to complete the ship entirely, except for masts and rigging, before launching. Extra dockyard workers were acquired through press warrants issued for compulsory service.

Construction was the responsibility of the dockyard's master shipwright who needed to be expert in all the many facets associated with the trade, from naval architecture, draughting and ship carpentry to matters of supply and organization. English shipwrights were recognized as the best in the world; their training came through lengthy apprenticeships often passed from father to son producing many generations of famous shipbuilders, as in the case of the Shish family. Jonas Shish was master shipwright at Deptford, later his son John held the same position; his other sons were Thomas, master shipwright at Woolwich and Jonas who became a private shipbuilder. Shipwrights were seen as eccentrics and various descriptions of them are recorded.[3]

Until this period warships sailed into battle independently engaging an enemy vessel in single combat. When fleets became more tightly controlled by admirals (about the time of the Second Dutch War, 1665-1667) and squadrons were formed, the line ahead formation became the established method of attack. As the guns could only be discharged through the gunports their arc of fire was determined by the direction of the ship; this limitation meant that the line of battle was the most potent configuration when engaging an enemy. Those warships capable of carrying enough armament to be an effective part of the line were known as 'ships of the line'.[4]

From the mid to late 17th century, when the standardization of naval designs in shipbuilding was beginning to take effect, warships were 'rated' according to the number of guns they carried. Six rates were introduced: a first rate carried from 100 guns, second rates from 84 guns, third rates from 70 guns, fourth rates 50 guns, fifth rates 32-50 guns and sixth rates up to 32 guns. The first, second and third rate vessels were regarded as powerful enough for the line of battle while the fourth, fifth

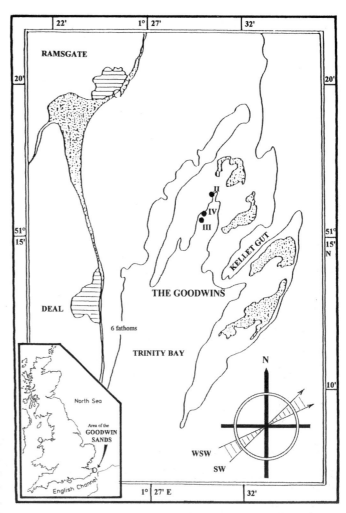

3 The Goodwins approximately as they are today with the positions of wreck sites II (*Stirling Castle*), III (*Northumberland*) and IV (*Mary*). Also the wind direction of the Great Storm

and sixth rates functioned as support vessels. Ordnance for third rates, such as the *Stirling Castle*, typically consisted of 26 demi-cannon on the lower deck, 26 twelve-pounders on the upper deck, 10 light sakers on the quarter-deck, 4 light sakers on the forecastle and 4 three-pounders on the poop deck.

Biography

Stirling Castle (figs 1 and 2) was among the third rates listed in the Revolution Fleet of 1688. She was part of the Red Squadron, under the Captaincy of Anthony Hastings, in the Anglo-Dutch Fleet which fought off Beachy Head in 1690. Under Captain Benjamin Walters *Stirling Castle* fought as part of the Blue Squadron at Barfleur in 1692. During 1699 *Stirling Castle* was rebuilt and in 1701 refitted. In 1702 she was part of a fleet of thirty English ships of the line that joined twenty Dutch ships of the line for the Expedition to Cadiz. Her final assignment was to the Mediterranean in 1703, the details of which have been described by Laird Clowes (1898):

'A great fleet, composed both of Dutch and of English men-of-war, sailed for the Mediterranean on July 1st, under Sir Clowdisley Shovell, with orders to assist the revolted Cévennois, in the south of France; to do what might be possible towards restoring Sicily and Naples to the House of Habsburg; to endeavour to enlist the Algerines, Tunisians, and Tripolitans against France; to settle certain difficulties which had arisen at Leghorn; to convoy the trade; and, generally, to injure the cause of the enemy to the utmost. Sir Clowdisley, whose presence in the Mediterranean had the effect of inducing the French fleet to lie quietly in Toulon harbour, carried out his instructions to the best of his ability; but, having been directed to return to England before the beginning of the winter, he could not remain long enough to confer any permanent benefit upon the cause of the Allies. The expedition was an ill-designed one, and that it accomplished so little was due entirely to the home government, and not at all to Shovell. His cruisers made several prizes . . . On the other hand, owing to the careless manner in which the ships had been victualled, there was a lamentable loss of life on board the fleet during its absence from England. It arrived in the Downs on November 17th, 1703.'

The Downs and the Goodwin Sands (fig 3)

The Downs, much used by the navy as a convoy assembly area and anchorage for ships operating in the southern North Sea during war time, are situated between the Goodwin Sands and the coast. They are sheltered from the west by the mainland and from the east by the Goodwin Sands. The latter are situated east of Deal and cover an area between 10 and 11 miles long and 4 miles across. At low tide up to 7 feet of the Sands can be exposed while at high water

they are submerged to an average depth of 12 feet. In broad terms the Goodwins can be said to consist of two 'islands' or banks, with a dip in between that is known as the Kellet Gut.[5] The entire complex is in a constant state of slow, anti-clockwise rotation. Located in one of the busiest shipping lanes in the world, these mutating shallow banks have claimed many vessels; their reputation as a 'Shippe swalower' is world renowned.[6]

The Great Storm of 1703 (fig 4)

While most of the fleet were still at anchor in the Downs there occurred the most violent storm ever recorded. Contemporary accounts of the devastation were reported by Daniel Defoe and by Josiah Burchett, the Secretary to the Admiralty at the time.

From 'The Storm' by Daniel Defoe (1660-1731) published 1704[7]:

'On the Wednesday morning before, being the 24th November, it was fair weather, and blew hard; but not so as to give any apprehensions, till about four o'clock in the afternoon the wind increased, and with squalls of rain and terrible gusts blew very furiously.

. . . the wind continued with unusual violence all the next day and night; and had not the great storm followed so soon, this had passed for a great wind . . . On Friday morning, it continued to

4 Picture depicting the Great Storm of 1703
(East Kent Maritime Trust)

blow exceeding hard, but not so as that it gave any apprehensions of danger within doors; towards night it increased: and about ten o'clock, our barometers informed us that the night would be very tempestuous; the Mercury sank lower than ever I had observed it on any occasion whatsoever ...

A list of such of her Majesty's ships, with their Commander's names, as were cast away by the violent storm on Friday night, the 26th November, 1703 ... *Sterling Castle*, third rate: 70 guns; 349 men; John Johnson, Com; lost on Goodwin Sands. Third lieutenant, chaplain, cook, chyrurgeon's mate; four marine captains, and 62 men saved.

... and soon after a large man of war came driving down upon us, all her masts gone, and in a dreadful condition. We were in the utmost despair at this sight, for we saw no avoiding her coming thwart our haiser: she drove at last so near us, that I was just gowing to order the mate to cut away, when it pleas'd God the ship sheer'd contrary to our expectation to windward, and the man of war, which we found to be the *Sterling Castle*, drove clear of us, not two ships lengths to leeward.

It was a sight full of terrible particulars, to see a ship of eighty guns and about six hundred men in that dismal case; she had cut away all her masts, the men were all in the confusions of death and despair; she had neither anchor, nor cable, nor boat to help her; the sea breaking over her in a terrible manner, that sometimes she seem'd all under water; and they knew, as well as we that saw her, that they drove by the tempest directly for the Goodwin, where they could expect nothing but destruction. The cries of the men, and the firing their guns, one by one, every half minute for help, terrified us in such a manner, that I think we were half dead with the horror of it.'

From the account of Josiah Burchett, Secretary to the Admiralty:

'These ships and those which rode fast at the Gunfleet, miraculously escaped, but it fared not so well with the Men of War and Merchant Ships in the Downs. Of the former there were lost on the Goodwin Sands the *Mary*, a ship of 60 Guns, and the *Northumberland*, *Restauration* and *Sterling Castle*, each of 70; nor were there more than Eighty Men saved of the whole number which belonged to them. Rear-Admiral Beaumont, whose Flag was flying in the *Mary*, perished amongst the rest ... It was a miserable sight to behold many of the Ships in the Downs; for as they were almost torn in Pieces by the Violence of the Wind, so was it not possible to give them any help from the Shore, even when they were in the greatest Extremity, and continually firing guns for relief; besides the wind was at W.S.W. and they could not carry a knot of sail to enable them to cling to the shore, so that many of them perished on the Goodwin Sands, and of about one hundred and sixty sail, of all sorts, which were in the Downs the day before, not more than seventy were seen the next morning, and many of them were only floating bottoms, for all their masts had gone by the board; but several of the merchant ships and vessels missing were afterwards heard of in Holland, Norway, or the ports of this kingdom.'

The devastation, both on land and sea, was immense and the losses to the Navy were the worst ever recorded within so brief a period. Twelve vessels[8] were lost and over 1,500 seamen drowned. In addition other naval vessels were driven ashore and more were dismasted or otherwise seriously damaged. Prompt salvage efforts successfully restored many to service in a short time.

Location and excavation of *Stirling Castle*

During the summer of 1979, the newly formed Underwater Research Group of the Isle of Thanet Archaeological Unit, acting on information from a local trawler skipper, investigated a report that a wooden wreck had appeared on the Goodwin Sands. Initial exploration of the site, which was designated Wreck Site II/1979, revealed a large British man-of-war and material recovered pointed to a late 17th century or early 18th century date. The only naval vessels known to have been lost in the vicinity during that period were the victims of the Great Storm.

The position of the wreck is latitude 51° 16' 30" north, longitude 01° 30' 27" east. The hull, which lists to starboard is aligned east-west with the bows to the west. The starboard side was found to be completely buried in the steeply shelving sand in which the vessel was firmly embedded. The masts were gone and she had lost her forecastle, quarterdeck and poop. The bowsprit and beakhead had become detached and were in the sand below the bows. The stern windows and some of the hull fabric about the sternpost was missing. A considerable amount of debris was seen around the wreck but the hull was almost complete and the orlop and gun decks were in good condition (fig 5).

The poor visibility and uneven structure made the taking of precise measurements difficult but a datum line (divided into 15ft lengths) was established running, as near as possible, from stem to sternpost. This gave an approximate length of 180ft. Offset measurements taken from the line gave a maximum beam of 60ft. These dimensions were in excess of a first rate vessel but, if one allowed for distortion as a result of the severe hogging and ruptures within the hull, then the measurements were a better reflection of a

5 One of the pewter dishes showing the initials I I which helped to identify the *Stirling Castle* (*East Kent Maritime Trust*)

6 *Above* Artists impression (by David Perkins) of the *Stirling Castle* as she was at the time of discovery and as she would appear in perfect conditions of visibility. Based on sketches and back-on-deck reports from divers. Research later carried out by Perkins showed that the bow was too vertical
(*courtesy Thanet Archaeological Society*)

7 *Right* Varying visibility does not always allow for easy identification of objects such as the cordage shown here
(*East Kent Maritime Trust*)

vessel of approximately 160 feet by 45 feet, which is nearer the size of a third rate of the period. There were three third rates lost in this area, the *Stirling Castle*, the *Northumberland* and the *Restoration*. All three were vessels of the 1677 Programme and therefore very similar.

Artefacts and material from the main deck and elsewhere were raised in an attempt to identify the vessel. The best indicators came from sets of initials found on pewter, brass, lead and wood objects with I I (fig 6) and I B recurring. The captain of the *Stirling Castle* was John Johnson with James Beverly as first officer (in the 1700s J was often written as I). Although this could be coincidence the odds are highly in favour of this wreck being the remains of *Stirling Castle*.

Conditions for diving on the Goodwin Sands are always arduous and very restricted with visibility ranging from just a few inches to several feet (fig 7). For these reasons only 180 hours of diving were possible during the first year, 1979.

There were 6 divers in the group, all experienced amateurs and an archaeological advisor. Once the archaeological importance of the wreck had been established the Archaeological Unit were able to obtain a licence from the Runciman Committee for permission to dive and raise artefacts. The vessel was purchased from the Navy for £100. Application was made for a Protection Order from the Advisory Committee on Historic Wreck Sites and this was granted. Activities in 1979 were limited to routine survey and the recovery of artefacts which might help with the identification of the wreck or were considered to be at risk from either the action of the sea or theft.

8 *Top* Dark green 'Onion' bottle with moulded glass seal; one of the first artefacts raised from the vessel *(East Kent Maritime Trust)*

9 *Above* 'William Stonas 1700' seal on the neck of an Onion bottle *(East Kent Maritime Trust)*

10 *Above right* Almost complete dark blue Delft tile with traditional Dutch scene, recovered from the galley area, height 13.3 cm *(East Kent Maritime Trust)*

11 *Right* The only complete Bellarmine jug among the ceramic items lifted, height 18 cm *(East Kent Maritime Trust)*

The finds

Many objects were raised from Wreck Site II/1979 some of which required intensive laboratory conservation. In 1984, with limited resources, the collection was transferred, without formal documentation, to the newly established

12 *Left* Dark blue and grey glazed pot decorated with small raised flowers, complete with cork stopper, height 19 cm *(East Kent Maritime Trust)*

13 *Below left* Large block and sheave *(East Kent Maritime Trust)*

14 *Above* Small pulley *in situ* on the seabed before being raised *(W. Utley)*

15 *Below* Various pewterware items showing their state of encrustation when lifted *(East Kent Maritime Trust)*

Maritime Museum at Royal Harbour, Ramsgate where the majority of the finds are now on permanent display (some items are held by the National Maritime Museum at Greenwich).

Among the very first finds raised were a large number of dark green 'onion' bottles (fig 8), some still full and corked. One of these bottles had a 'seal' of moulded glass at the base of the neck stating 'William Stonas 1700' (fig 9). A variety of smoked glass and green tinged bottles were also found.

Pieces of sheet glass approximately ⅜ inch thick (probably the remains of the stern windows) were located at the after end of the ship. Fragments of large dishes, ewers and jugs were also recovered. Other ceramic items included a broken Delft tile (fig 10), Chinese porcelain cups, one complete and several broken Bellarmine jugs (fig 11), and a blue glazed westerwald ware jug (fig 12) complete with cork in excellent condition.

Limited conservation facilities meant that only a minimum of small wooden items were retrieved; these all came from the debris on the main deck and included two fids bound with lead, a large bowl and a number of wooden buttons, fir cones, nutmegs and cups made from coconut shells or gourds. Sample deadeyes, tail blocks, double blocks and pulleys (figs 13 and 14) were all found in good condition and raised.

The recovered pewterware (fig 15) included plates, spoons (fig 17), bowls, tankards (fig 18), chamber pots and a porringer with a decorative handle. Some of these sported the owners' initials, which, as we have seen, helped identify the wreck.

Most of the lead items raised were bar, or plumb-shaped weights, but a square inkwell (fig 16), a pounce pot and a dish inscribed JB 1700 were also recovered.

There were many interesting brass objects particularly small-sword or hanger hilts. Hanger hilts decorated with lion heads and cockatrices (fig 18) were of a type that was in general use in England during the late 17th and early 18th centuries. The design is apparently that referred to in Board of Ordnance records as 'brass-hilted hangers for mattrosses'[9]. The three small-sword hilts were also characteristic of the period. The first, a type without a knucklebow and richly plated with gold, had lost its grip and pommel. The second, manufactured by the lost wax process, was decorated with ornately fretted frames and classical scenes; marks left by a binding of steel wire were just visible on the wooden grip (fig 20). The third, of English origin, was characterized by an angular pommel and moulded decoration. Other brass items

16 *Left* Square inkwell with four holes for holding the quills
(East Kent Maritime Trust)

17 *Top* Two of the pewter spoons found with other domestic items such as small pewter plates and wooden bowls, length 19.7 cm *(East Kent Maritime Trust)*

18 *Above* A small pewter tankard with hinged lid, probably belonged to one of the officers *(East Kent Maritime Trust)*

included candle snuffers with their table holders (fig 21), the bowl of a hanging lamp and its sconce, and a candlestick (fig 22) which still had a metacarpal bone attached when found. Amongst the personal items recovered were a number of buttons (some of pewter and others of sheet brass) engraved with either a flower motif or covered in silk, a purse with the initials I or JB on the inside of the frame, a range of small shoe buckles and a small key.

Several barrels and a complete stock from a brass barrelled musketoon were recovered. The barrels were stamped with the Board of Ordnance mark, a crowned Tudor rose and variously with the crowned cyphers of Charles II, James I and William III. These cumbersome weapons would have been used with a support. A number of wooden stocks from flintlock muskets were also found; their iron barrels had disintegrated but in some cases the highly corroded remains of the breech, the breech plug and lock mechanism still survived. The non-ferrous fittings, such as butt plates, ramrod thimbles and sling buckles, were all found separately. The base of a stand for six muskets was discovered near the

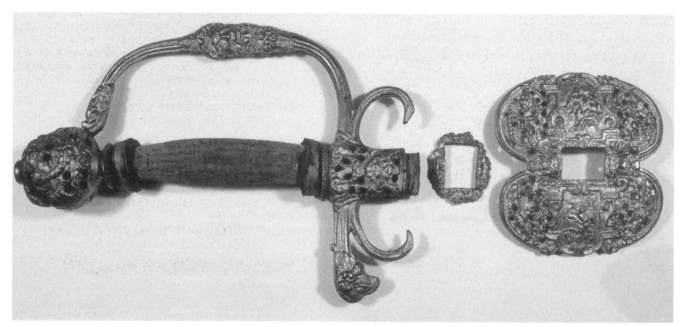

19 *Above right* This brass sword-hilt with its particularly distinctive decoration (c1690) was among the first specific naval patterns, length 13 cm *(East Kent Maritime Trust)*

20 *Above* The intricate castings on this sword-hilt were made by the lost wax process, length overall 25.5 cm *(East Kent Maritime Trust)*

21 *Right* Brass candle snuffers and table holder typical of the period *(East Kent Maritime Museum)*

22 *Opposite top left* Brass candlestick discovered with a metacarpal bone still attached, height 12.2 cm *(East Kent Maritime Museum)*

23 *Opposite centre* One of the cannon that was not lifted *(W. Utley)*

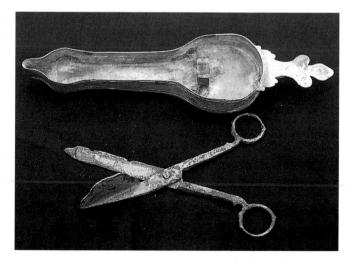

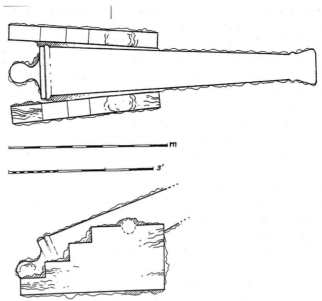

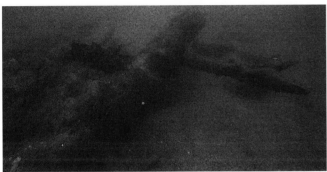

24 *Above* For conservation reasons, no iron guns have been permanently raised from the *Stirling Castle*. A cannon which had retained its carriage was however brought to the surface. This gun, a nine-pounder, was hauled clear of the water on a steel strop secured to the trawl beam of the diving tender. A measured drawing was made by the supervising archaeologist and a diver. While the gun was heavily concreted, patches of bare wood and metal at strategic points allowed this drawing to be made. The carriage had no trucks or axles, and no traces of recoil and relieving tackles or their attachment points
(drawing by Dave Perkins; courtesy Thanet Archaeological Society)

25 *Below* An ornate bronze 6-pounder gun cast by Assuerus Koster in Amsterdam in 1642 and bearing this information as a breach inscription. On initial examination it was found to have the remains of a wooden tampion in the muzzle; the gun is apparently still shotted
(drawing by Dave Perkins; courtesy Thanet Archaeological Society)

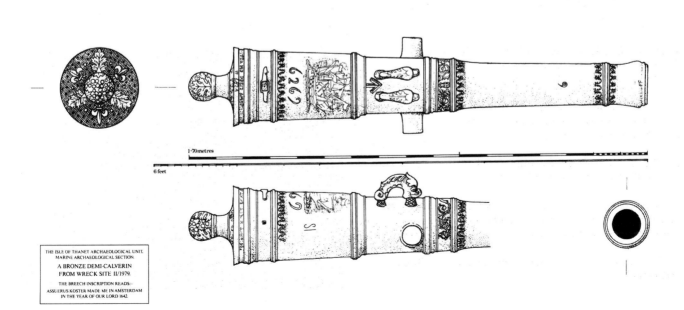

Breech Inscription ⌐ 2cm

ASWERVS KOSTER ME FECIT AMSTELREDAMI ANNO 642

1·70 metres

6 feet

THE ISLE OF THANET ARCHAEOLOGICAL UNIT,
MARINE ARCHAEOLOGICAL SECTION.

A BRONZE DEMI-CALVERIN
FROM WRECK SITE II/1979.

THE BREECH INSCRIPTION READS:-
ASSUERUS KOSTER MADE ME IN AMSTERDAM
IN THE YEAR OF OUR LORD 1642.

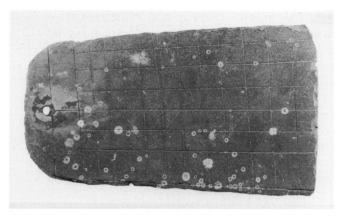

28 & 29 Samples of the navigation slates which were found among the debris in an area between the main deck and quarterdeck, length 22 cm *(East Kent Maritime Trust)*

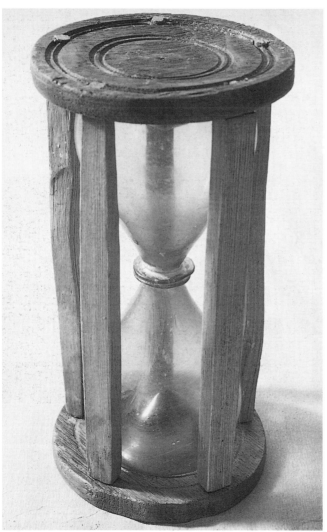

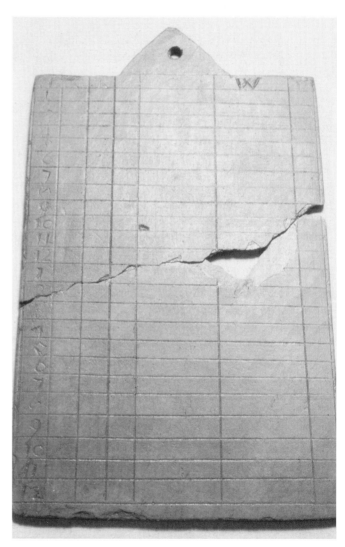

26 *Top* Samples of the brass dividers from the wreck are similar to those used today *(East Kent Maritime Trust)*

27 *Above* Sand-glass comprising disc ends, four side bars and a pair of bottles. Such glasses were the only means of accurately measuring time on board ship before the introduction of the chronometer later in the 18th century

stocks. The lead shot recovered was the subject of a paper by D.R.J. Perkins in the International Journal of Nautical Archaeology and Underwater Exploration (1983).

None of the heavily concreted iron guns (figs 23 and 24) were recovered because of the nature of their conservation requirements. Rough measurements of the cannons and solid shot were taken to give some indication of the ship's armament; from this it was found that the vessel's fire-power was consistent with a third rate. The bronze six-pounder Drake of Dutch manufacture recovered (fig 25), is stamped with the British Board of Ordnance broad arrow and the figure 6269 is its number from the English Survey of late 1695, which place the gun on the quarterdeck of *Stirling Castle*. Other marks give its weight in Amsterdam pounds (682A) and calibre (6). The decorative ship is the Coat of Arms of the Verenigde Oostindische Compagnie. Also found was a shot gauge marked D C for demi-culverin.

Among the navigational and drawing instruments recovered were nine pairs of brass dividers without their steel points (fig 26), an accumulation of sand-glasses in kit form (which made up into five sizes giving different

and a Gunter's scale (fig 32) (a device used for computing the magnetic variation, comprising a 2 foot rule graduated with the trigonometric functions on one side and their logarithms on the other; named for its 17th century inventor).

The ship's copper kettle (figs 33 and 34) with brass fittings was recovered along with representative samples of the fire-bricks, tiles (fig 35) and hearth stones from where it would have been sited within the galley.

The ship's bell (figs 36, 37 and 38) has no name, just the date 1701 and the Board of Ordnance arrow. This is significant as it is consistent with the practice mentioned earlier of standardizing fittings and materials.[10]

The personal belongings included leather book covers (fig 30), leather pouches, shoes and a case containing razors and a bone object. Bone finds consisted of a toothbrush, a comb (fig 39), knife and fork handles and tobacco pipes

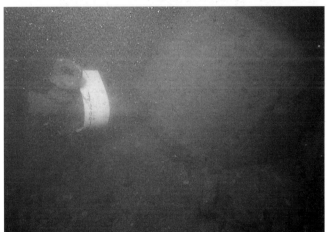

durations) (fig 27) and six navigators' slates (two with remarks concerning wind direction and force still visible) (figs 28 and 29). From the remains of a sea-chest on the forward end of the gun-deck came a small microscope (fig 30), a br oken cross-staff (fig 31) (the device for measuring latitude by holding the instrument at arm's length and pointing directly at the sun),

30 *Above left* Leather book covers and a small microscope. The latter unscrewed at the middle *(East Kent Maritime Trust)*

31 *Left* The cross staff, used for determining latitude by observing the sun's meridian altitude. On display at the National Maritime Museum Greenwich *(East Kent Maritime Trust)*

32 *Top* 'Gunter's Scale, called by navigators simply the gunter, is a large plain scale, generally two feet long and about an inch and a half broad, with artificial lines delineated on it, of great use in solving questions in trigonometry, navigation etc.' (from the Encyclopaedia Britannica Vol II, 1771). On display at the National Maritime Museum, Greenwich *(East Kent Maritime Trust)*

33 *Above* The ship's copper kettle where it was found and labelled before being raised *(East Kent Maritime Trust)*

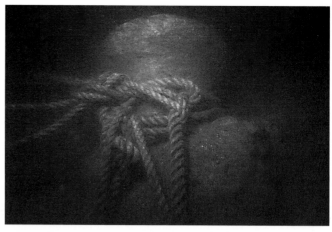

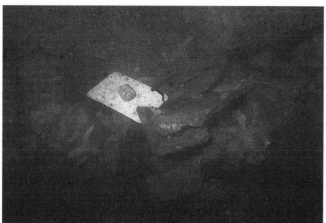

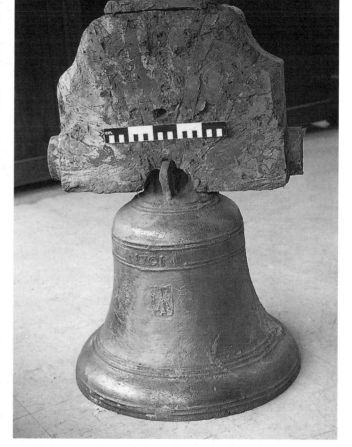

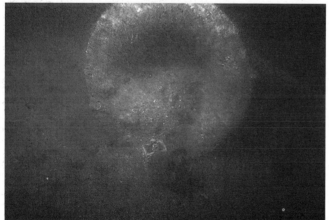

34 *Top* The kettle being lifted on to the trawler that was used for recovering artefacts during the summer of 1979. The owner of this trawler was the first to signal the appearance of a wooden wreck on the Goodwins (*East Kent Maritime Trust*)

35 *Centre* Samples of the tiles located in the galley area on the main deck. The cooking pot would have been mounted on stone slabs surrounded by the tiles in a brick hearth (*East Kent Maritime Trust*)

36 *Bottom* The deeply encrusted ship's bell when first found. In the front is a slab-built lead container with bored lugs, possibly for suspension. Of uncertain use, it has been suggested that it may have functioned as an adjustable weight (*East Kent Maritime Trust*)

37 *Top* The bell ready for lifting to the surface (*East Kent Maritime Trust*)

38 *Above* Cleared of encrustations the bell revealed the date 1701 and the Board of Ordnance arrow (*East Kent Maritime Trust*)

(fig 40). Fabric artefacts included fragments of clothing and a roll of canvas in a case.

A number of skulls and other bones were seen within the wreck, but these were left untouched as a mark of respect and memorial to those seamen who perished in the Great Storm.

At the start of the 1980 season the divers descended at the appropriate co-ordinates only to find that the Goodwin

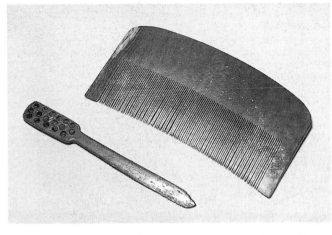

39 *Left* The personal possessions of the crew included this comb and a toothbrush. The latter pre-dates the period of its accepted invention *(East Kent Maritime Trust)*

40 *Above* One of several broken tobacco pipes, length 25.5 cm *(East Kent Maritime Trust)*

41 *Below* The oldest known dockyard model of a third rate. It dates to 1650 and is very similar to the *Mary (W. Utley)*

Sands had reclaimed *Stirling Castle*; once again she was buried within the seabed.

The group, however, investigated reports of other wooden wrecks and succeeded in locating two other casualties of the Great Storm, the third rate *Northumberland* (wreck site III) almost certainly identified from artefacts, and either the third rate *Restoration* or fourth rate *Mary* (wreck site IV), the identity of this latter wreck has not been confirmed but the indications are that it is the *Mary* (fig 41).

During the 1981 season it was decided not to raise any more items because of conservation needs and costs. The entire time was spent searching for the fourth man-of-war that is known to have been lost in the Great Storm. To this day it has not been found.

Although annual checks are made and licences to dive on the wrecks have been continually granted, the Goodwin Sands have not released any of the vessels for the last few years.

42 Members of the dive team examining artefacts from the wreck *(courtesy D.R.J. Perkins)*

A post-excavation postscript

D.R.J. Perkins (Director, Trust for Thanet Archaeology)
During the location and investigation phase of work on the *Stirling Castle* (1979-80) some two hundred items were raised to help with the identification and evaluation of the site. Of these only a small percentage (large objects and those with visual appeal) were cleaned and conserved during the period, the objects being variously treated by the National Maritime Museum, the Thanet Archaeological Society (TAS) and professional conservators employed by TAS. The bulk of the finds (most were heavily concreted) were kept at the TAS laboratory, being stored in holding tanks or allowed to slowly air-dry as appropriate. Although no funding could be found for further treatment, TAS and later the Trust for Thanet Archaeology undertook responsibility for the finds, and commenced a necessarily protracted programme of conservation and research under the direction of the writer.

The objects conserved, drawn and researched over the last fifteen years have ranged from a silver tankard and Marines' leather cartridge boxes, to a wooden crate of grapeshot rounds, and 'case' gin bottles with pewter snap-cap tops. Some analytical work on materials such as glass

and metal alloys from such objects as the ship's bell have been carried out by neutron activation analysis and X-ray fluorescence. Bearing in mind the important 'time-capsule' nature of this assemblage, publication has always been intended. The possibility of this taking the form of one of the Kent Archaeological Society's monograph series has been discussed.

Notes

1 Deptford, on the south bank of the River Thames, was one of the earliest true naval dockyards of England, where ships were laid down, built and repaired. It became a naval dockyard in the reign of Henry VII (1485-1509). Considerable improvements were made during the last years of Henry VIII's reign (1509-1547) and by the Restoration it was the most important of English naval dockyards. The headquarters of the Victualling Board was also at Deptford where extensive warehousing stored the requirements for the naval service. The shipbuilding and repair work of the Deptford yard transferred to Chatham and Sheerness dockyards in 1869 with the site being converted to the Royal Victualling Yard for the manufacture and storage of naval requirements of all kinds, until the Royal Navy ceased to occupy the area in 1965.

2 *Grafton* was a third rate built in 1679 at Woolwich Dockyard by Thomas Shish.

3 Jonas Shish, master shipwright at Deptford was described by diarist John Evelyn as a 'plaine honest Carpenter (master builder of this Dock) yet one that can give very little account of his art by discourse, as hardly capable to read, yet of greate abilitie in his calling: They ben Ship - Carpenters in this Yard above 100 yeares', he also reported 'it was the custome of this good man, to rise in the night, and to pray kneeling in his owne Coffin: which many yeares he had lying by him'.

Pepys says of John Shish, when he was master shipwright at Deptford, 'old Shish's son, as illiterate as he ... low spirited, of little appearance or authority ... little frugality ... his father a great drinker and since killed with it'.

4 A battle was fought with a fleet sub-divided into three squadrons each consisting of a number of warships under the control of an admiral. The admiral's squadron had a red flag and commanded from the centre, the vice-admiral had a white flag and operated from the van or front position, the rear-admiral, carried a blue flag and formed the rear. As fleets grew in size, three admirals were allocated to each squadron, a full admiral in command with a vice-admiral as his second and a rear admiral as third in command. Squadrons were ranked in the order Red, White and Blue with the Admiral of the Red in command of the whole fleet. This practice was discontinued in 1864.

5 This feature of the Sands, which almost completely severs the South Goodwins from the north, cutting right across the widest part, was found in the survey made by HMS *Kellet* in 1926. Previous surveys in 1865 and 1896 showed no sign of it, although the channels appear in surveys made in 1795 and 1844 (Cloet, 1954).

6 The Kent Topographer William Lambarde in *Perambulation of Kent* (1570) quotes Hector Boethius the Scottish Historiographer '... this place, being sometime maineland and of the possession of Earle Godwine, was then violently overwhelmed with light sand, wherewith it not onlie remaineth covered ever since, but it has become withal a most dreadful gulfe and shippe swalower, sometime passable by foote, and sometime laide under water so that it may bee said either sea, or land, or neither or both'

7 'The Storm' a compilation of contemporary comments gathered from observers of the Great Storm of November 1703.

8

Ships	Guns	Men lost
Vanguard	90	
Restoration	70	391
Stirling Castle	70	206
Resolution	70	
Northumberland	70	220
Mary	60	269
Newcastle	50	193
Reserve	50	175
Vigo Prize	50	
Mortar		
Eagle	18	
Canterbury		
		1519

9 A mattross was a contemporary term for a sailor

10 The bell raised from Wreck Site III is very similar to that of the *Stirling Castle* with no name, just the date 1701 and an arrow

References

Cloet, R.L., 1954, Hydrographic Analysis of the Goodwin Sands and the Brake Bank, *Geographical Journal*, CXX, part 2

Defoe, D., 1704, *The Storm*, London

Laird Clowes, W., 1898, *The Royal Navy A History From the Earliest Time to the Present*, London

Lambarde, W., 1570, *Perambulation of Kent*

Perkins, D.R.J., 1983 An analysis of lead musket shot from the wreck of an early 18th century man-of-war. *International Journal of Nautical Archaeology*, 12, 4: 339-342

Jørgen Christoffersen (Curator, National Museum, Denmark)

The warship *Dannebroge*

Around four o'clock on Saturday October 4 1710, the Danish ninety-gunner *Dannebroge* went down with almost all hands after a short but fierce engagement with the Swedish fleet in Køge Bay. Amongst those who perished was the ship's captain, Ivar Huitfeldt, who, by sacrificing his ship and his crew in order to obstruct the manoeuvring of the Swedish fleet, became celebrated as one of the nation's naval heroes.

The background to these events, as with most previous wars between Denmark and Sweden, lay in the important strategic issue of access to the Baltic. In various alliances with Holland, England and Russia, sea battles were often decisive in determining the outcome of these wars, which - at least for a time - gave the victor control over the 'key' to the Baltic.

In the second half of the seventeenth century Sweden was the unchallenged superpower in the Baltic, with a large fleet that, after a victory over the Danish fleet in 1644, guaranteed the security of Swedish military operations on the Continent. Denmark had also lost large areas of territory on the east side of the Øresund, and thus forfeited control over that narrow channel. In 1676 and 1677, however, a combined Danish-Dutch fleet succeeded in breaking the Swedish supremacy at sea through a series of decisive strikes around Öland and Køge Bay. In these attacks, several ships were sunk which today have become famous wrecks, most notably the largest warship of its time, *Stora Kronan*, off the coast of Öland.

About fifty years later, in 1710, during the Great Scandinavian War, the Danish and Swedish fleets, with altogether some fifty warships carrying 3,000 cannon and 20,000 men, were to do battle for the last time, once again in Køge Bay.

On this occasion, the Danes were allied with the Russians, who had promised to provide 6,000 men for an attempt to conquer Sweden. Late in the summer of 1710 these auxiliary troops were to be collected from Danzig, and the Danes assembled a transport fleet of about a hundred craft, thirty of which were warships. In its voyage across the Baltic, this fleet ran into several storms, and had suffered significant losses when it reached the island Bornholm. At the same time, typhus broke out amongst the crews. The enterprise was abandoned and, on October 1, the fleet returned to Køge Bay for repairs and to discharge several thousand sick hands. The *Dannebroge* put ashore a quarter of its crews, 156 men, which were replaced by about 50 fresh hands.

1 I. Huitfeldt's memorial, Copenhagen. The statue and other bronze ornaments are cast from salvaged guns from the *Dannebroge*. Five of the best preserved guns are situated at the base of the column

All the while, the Swedish fleet, under Admiral Wachtmeister, had been hunting the Danes - now, at last, they found them. The Swedes approached under full sail, and on the night before October 4, surreptitiously dropped anchor in a bay just south of the Danish fleet.

At dawn the next day, the Swedes sought to take the Danish fleet by surprise at anchor in Køge Bay, a plan that nearly succeeded.

The man in charge of the Danish fleet, Admiral Gyldenløve, had called a council of his captains on the flagship that same morning. After a couple of hours the meeting was interrupted by the report of Swedish sails on the horizon. Immediately all ships were signalled to cut their cables and prepare for battle, while the captains were rowed back to their ships. Accounts tell of how bunks, chests, livestock and everything else that could not be stowed away instantly, was simply flung overboard.

The *Dannebroge* was situated on the southern flank, closest to the Swedish fleet which came racing into the bay with 23 warships on a strong wind. The *Dannebroge* and two other Danish ships quickly set sail and turned into the wind in order to cut off the Swedes (fig 2).

The 70-year-old Swedish admiral was a cautious man, and although he had every advantage on his side (i.e. the benefit of surprise, position and speed on the wind) he wasted the unique opportunity of crushing the Danish fleet by turning parallel to the three Danish ships that had set out. This gave the Danish fleet vital time to get under sail and tack up in the lee of the Danish vanguard.

The leading Danish ships engaged the Swedes roughly in the middle of the bay. In particular the *Dannebroge*, under Ivar Huitfeldt, went about and sailed down the Swedish line firing several broadsides.

In return the *Dannebroge* itself came under fire from virtually all of the Swedish ships. Eventually a fire broke out on the port side of her quarter-deck, probably as a result of wadding that had been blown back into the mizzen channel. Instead of retreating in order to extinguish the fire, Huitfeldt dropped anchor and continued the battle acting as a torch to block the Swedish advance. Three more salvoes were fired from the *Dannebroge* before her masts, one by one, fell overboard. Those crewmen who were able, tried to escape the fire by retreating to the bowsprit, but soon the flames reached here also. Shortly after the fire reached the powder room deep within the hull and, with two enormous explosions, the ship sank. At this point the battle ended; thanks to the holding and delaying actions of the *Dannebroge* and her companions, a potentially disastrous action for the Danish fleet had been avoided, very few ships had been able to engage one another.

The Swedish fleet did not leave the battle without loss; two of their ships ran aground off the island of Amager and were burnt by their own crews.

Only nine of the *Dannebroge*'s crew of about 550 were saved. Amongst those who perished was Huitfeldt himself, his body washed ashore and was later buried in his home village of Hurum in Norway.

A number of contemporary sources for the events of that day have survived in the form of ships' logs and reports. These disagree on several points and have thus led to some lively discussion in later literature An especially vivid account is preserved in the diary of the Norwegian seaman Trosner, which he illustrated with a series of drawing (fig 3). In addition to these there is a drawing of the action by another eyewitness sea lieutenant Bendstrup which shows, amongst other things, the bows of the *Dannebroge* still on the surface of the water after the explosion (fig 11). Clearly the ship had not burnt right down to the waterline (as indeed later investigations would demonstrate). The investigations further confirms that this was not the last time explosions and violence damaged this venerable man-of-war.

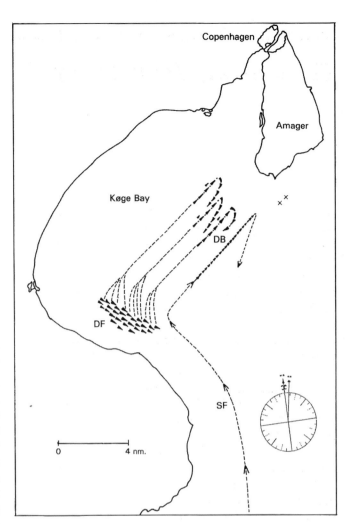

2 Sketch map of Køge Bay 1710
DB: The *Dannebroge*
DF: The Danish Fleet
SF: The Swedish Fleet
XX: Two grounded Swedish ships

In 1985, the wreck was rediscovered, and over the next three years the Danish Naval Museum, in collaboration with amateur divers, investigated both the wreck itself and a large area of the surrounding seabed. By this means, some details of the construction and interior of the ship were revealed, and information acquired that helped illuminate the vessel's dramatic final hours as well as some of the subsequent salvage work (both legal and illegal) that took place on her.

The *Dannebroge* was named after a distinguished Danish heraldic order, the insignia of which adorned the stern. She is of particular interest, because, amongst other things, she was the first ship to come from a naval shipyard that was newly founded in 1692. Furthermore, she was built to one of the oldest surviving sets of Danish construction plans (fig 4). The hull measured 164ft in length, 42ft 6 inches across and had a draught of 20ft 6 inches. She was one of the largest ships in the Danish navy with a crew of 600 and was constructed with two full-length gun decks carrying a total

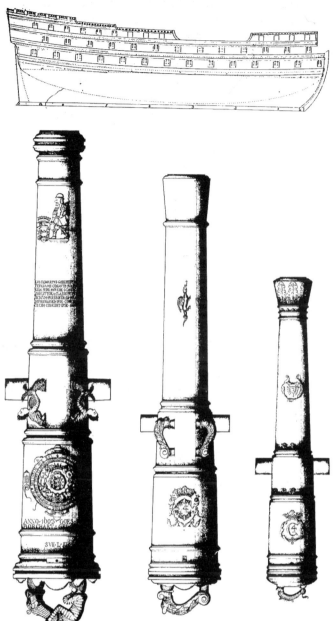

3 *Left* A page from the diary of ableseaman Trosner

4 *Top* One of the constructional drawings of the *Dannebroge*, 1692

5 *Above* 14-pounder "Old King", 8-pounder "Dragon", 4-pounder "Clipped Nettle"

of 94 iron cannon. Iron cannons, however, were quickly superseded, and the last relevant list (the 1710 navy inventory) describes an armament of 78 metal (bronze) cannon: twenty-six 24-pounders; twenty-two 14-pounders; twenty 8-pounders; ten 4-pounders; twenty 8-pounders; ten 4-pounders, and four 14-pounder iron howitzers. The details of calibres given here are rather drab in comparison with the names that the cannon were otherwise known by at the time, such as 'Little clipped nettles' (4-pounders), 'Shield-toads' or 'Dragons' (8-pounders), and not least 'Old Kings' (14-pounders). All of these names refer to relief motifs on their muzzles (fig 5). We do not know how many different types there really were on board, but several of them were already rare, and others would have been antiques by the time the ship was lost. In terms of the history of armament, the *Dannebroge* thus constitutes an exceptionally interesting object.

It was not, however, antiquarian interests that motivated the first salvage operations on the wreck, but rather the fact that the cannon were of considerable value either re-used or melted down. Early in the spring of 1711, salvage began under the direction of one Scoutbynacht, a man who himself had participated in the battle of the previous year. With the help of the primitive diving bell and techniques of the day, it proved possible to save a number of cannon and twelve tons of cannon fragments which were recast as smaller guns. The exact number of pieces recovered is unclear; nearly all the cannon had blown up or were unusable as a result of the enormous heat and abrupt cooling when the ship burnt, exploded and sank.

In 1873, the wreck was rediscovered, and the salvage company Svitzer, which was one of the first companies with professional divers, recommended the search for valuables, primarily cannon, of which thirteen examples were raised in the years 1873-75, together with one large anchor and a pewter plate. It did not prove a lucrative enterprise as it was necessary to use large amounts of dynamite; also for several years the company was involved in disputes with the Danish government over the value of the guns.

These cannon, however, did achieve a position of honour and value again, as half of them were used in monuments to Huitfeldt that were raised both at the harbour of Copenhagen (fig 1) and at Hurum church in Norway, where the hero lies buried. The other half were deposited in the collection of the Royal Danish Arsenal Museum. A further monument was raised in the form of the salvaged anchor at the naval station of Holmen in Copenhagen. In all, in the years 1711-1875, some 52 tons of material are reported to have been recovered from the wreck, which is about half of the total weight of cannon on the ship. The fact that the vessel had carried guns of antiquarian value was published shortly after the finding of 1873, and it is not improbable that illegal salvage operations have taken place since then. During the investigations of 1986-88, which have covered a much larger area, only four large cannon fragments (total weight, about 2.5 tons) have been found. Some pieces could, however, still be hidden deep in the sand. Three 14-pounder 'Old Kings' fragments were found together with a small signal cannon inside the wreck area, and about 200m west of the site a large part of a 24-pounder lay completely on its own on the seabed. This cannon too is a historical rarity, one of only eleven examples that were cast by Franciscus Röen in Glückstadt; unfortunately it is broken at the same point in the muzzle as the others. The explosion of 1710 cannot have thrown this piece, which weights some 2 tons,

6 Block for the main halyard at the surface 1987

so far from the ship. It was probably lost from a barge under tow during the initial salvage work of 1711-14.

With such a large site, it soon became clear that only a very extensive and expensive project would result in complete excavation. The museum therefore decided to concentrate on mapping the wreck itself and the surrounding area with visible objects, cutting a trial trench through the best preserved section of the bows and around the stern, and salvaging those object which, apart from being a temptation to weaker souls, might be exhibited to illustrate the conditions on board a man-of-war. The selection of objects included typical items of rigging, such as blocks, sheaves and deadeyes; also raised was the enormous, 125cm long block for the main halyard (fig 6).

In addition there were examples of various grenades, lead balls for hand guns, gun carriage wheels and so on. From the galley came examples of pots and pans, bottles, crockery and cutlery. Larger pieces of contorted copper foil may be remains of the equipment for distilling fresh from salt water that had been experimentally installed on the ship. The personal effects of the crew were represented by a wide range of items; simple belt buckles of the seamen, officers' fine shoe buckles, silver buttons, sword holders, pins, seal dies and signet rings. An especially fine object was a combined pocket sundial and compass. More mundane was the discovery of the ship's doctor's pewter bottles used as piggy banks for silver coin. Beneath the protective layer of

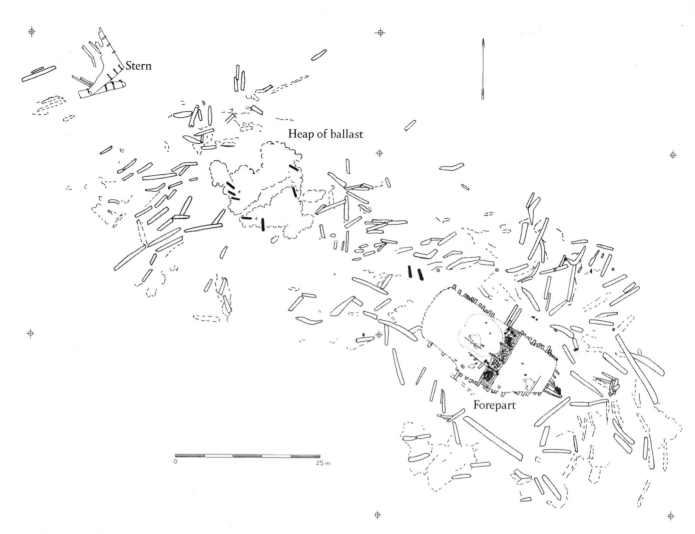

Stern

Heap of ballast

Forepart

0   25 m

7: *Above* Map of wreck area

8: *Right* The bows

sand, organic material in the form of textiles, shoes and a broad silk ribbon, as well as the remains of animals and the men themselves, proved to be quite well preserved.

Fig 7 gives us a plan of the site where pieces of wreckage are visible above the sand; it covers about 3,000sq.m. The investigations have shown that inside this area, deep in the sand, are preserved considerable quantities of timber and metal. It is also probable that pieces of wreckage are to be found beyond the mapped zone which is now a protected area.

The investigations have shed light on other matters, in particular on the end of the ship. The evidence suggests that the explosions in the powder room broke the vessel amidships. Stone and old iron cannon used as ballast fell to the seabed from the hole that appeared. The front of the ship (about 25m) was lifted so far up and forward in the water by the force of the explosion that it sank in seven fathoms (just as stated by contemporary sources),25m to the south-east, with a slight leaning to the stern. The rear of the ship, which was much more burnt than the bows, was found on the seabed in a completely disintegrated state. A large quantity of powder appears to have been stored in the after

part of the vessel and this may have contributed to its destruction. The stern itself, with some of the keel, had broken away, and lies horizontally, together with the rudder, 90m behind the bows.

Fig 9 shows the preserved section of the upright timbers, keel and rudder indicating something of the dimensions and the forces from the explosion. The front of the ship was preserved to a height of only 2m, with a 3m high piece of the actual bow assembly (fig 8).

Around the bows were seen a quantity of heavier structural timbers, these consisted of deck beams, knees and

9 *Below* Keel, stern and rudder at the wrecksite

10 *Bottom right* Silver Rigsdaler

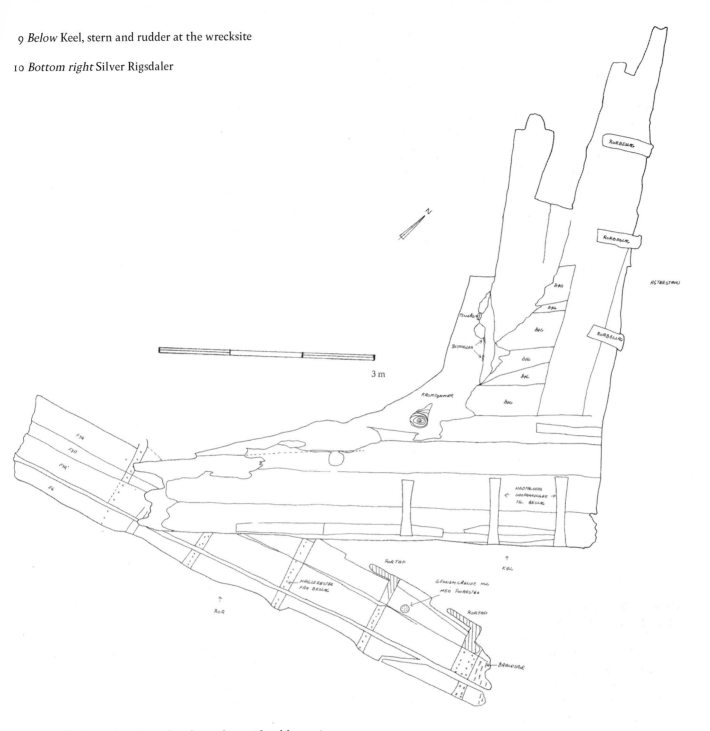

frames. The investigations also showed considerable sections of the sides and decks of the ship lying hidden in the sand right beside the wreck.

In addition to the artefacts noted, intact sections of the brick-walled galley and hundreds of bricks were found spread over the bows on top of the wreck. A diving report of 1873 describes the appearance of the ship before dynamiting, which when integrated with our own observations of more than a century later, indicates that the bows went down with the main deck intact, perhaps also the upper deck, as indicated in Bendstrup's drawing (fig 11).

In the course of the 163 years preceding 1873, the planks that had been fixed with iron nails above the water fell off and the decks collapsed. The distribution pattern of objects

11 Sea Lieutenant Bendstrup's drawing of the battle of Køge Bay 1710, showing *Dannebroge* exploded

and timbers that were found in the fore part of the wreck area is overwhelmingly the product of Svitzer's dynamiting which was primarily intended to move the deck beams and other timbers out of the way in order to gain access to the cannon deeper within the ship. These explosions scattered the bricks from the galley, which, together with other artefacts and bones, sank down and settled on the ballast and in between the objects in the bottom of the ship. Four rooms were discovered in this area; they were partitioned off and organized to a sufficient degree to suggest a storage deck. In the outermost rooms on both the port and starboard sides there were stacks of gun carriage wheels, and in the two inner rooms on either side of the keel were cannonballs and spare parts for the rigging.

When Svitzer began his dynamiting, much of the walled galley with its pots, pans and cauldrons, even with remains of the national dish, dried peas, was still preserved. Also in the galley area were found around 500 silver coins together with the remains of the pouches in which they were contained.

It is assumed that the money was put here as a place of temporary safety from the conflagration astern. There were probably more coins, but there is still a large gap between this and the silver hoard of 160,000 *Rigsdaler* (for which divers have searched) which is believed to have existed on the strength of the information that the paymaster of the fleet was on board the *Dannebroge*. This sum, however, was meant to cover the expenses of the whole fleet, which had already suffered a number of losses. A whole month before the battle of Køge Bay, the paymaster complained in a letter that the cash store was empty. The excavated coins therefore most likely represent the ship's own money, and as such, do not in fact amount to very much. Together with the coins in the galley were found the bones of two boys of seven and sixteen years of age whom it is presumed were seeking refuge from the fire. Physical anthropological studies of their remains concluded that they were very probably brothers.

The loss of the *Dannebroge* had important consequences, in the form of revised rules for the conscription of men for the fleet. Groups of men from particular areas and towns had been concentrated on for *Dannebroge*, and her loss meant, for instance, that Kerteminde, a small town on Fyn, lost most of its population of productive craftsman at a stroke. This left many widows and children, who had great difficulties in obtaining public support.

Mensun Bound and Patrick Gosset

The *Dragon*, 1712

One naval wreck that has long eluded maritime archaeologists is the *Dragon*, a vessel with a long and distinguished history which went down upon the infamous Casquets beside Alderney in the Channel Islands on 16th March 1712 (fig 3). She has been the object of many searches since the 1960s,[1] but it was not until the mid 1980s that she was found by a dive group from the Northampton area of England working from research that had been given to them by Patrick Gosset.

1 *Below* Early print of the lighthouse on the main rock of the Casquets. In 1723, three coal fires within lanterns were established on the rock. In 1790 the three towers seen here were built and the fires were replaced by oil lamps. The towers were named St Peter, St Thomas and Donjon (or St John)

2 *Bottom* Les Casquets lighthouse in the early 1990s. In 1877 the three lights were replaced by one in the newly heightened north-western tower. The other two were shortened. In 1972 a helicopter pad was built on the eastern tower. The lighthouse was automated in 1990 *(courtesy Brian Green, Guernsey Press)*

On the map, various labels are visible:

68 Yards
E. b N and W. b S.

40 Yards
N W and S E.

54 Yards
N.N.E. and S.S.W.

These 3 Lights are placed on ye Westermost part of the Casketts & bear from each other as above, when live are in one they will be of an equal height.

The Caskets

Loquetiere le Biblet Lesquets
Petite a la Fourche l'Etacq au Guillinots la Fourquie
la Noire Roque

Ortacq

Vincent
la Grande Ansisq

This Figure represents the Dragon Man of War which with several Merchant Ships and many mens lives was lost in March 1713 which induced the Author (for the publick good) to make this Survey there never having been any of this kind before been [illeg.] of these dangerous places

A South View of the Casketts as they appear at half Ebb

A Representation of the use of the Instrument call'd the Marine Surveyor

3 *Below* 1727 map by H. D. Saumares showing the Casquets and the sinking of the *Dragon*. Inscription reads: The Figure represents the *Dragon* Man of War which with several merchant ships and many men's lives was lost in March 1713 which induced the author (for the publick good) to make this survey there never having been any of this kind before been (illeg.) of these dangerous places *(courtesy National Maritime Museum Picture Library, London)*

Construction and biography[2]

The *Dragon* (the fifth naval vessel of that name) was the first Royal Navy ship to be built at Chatham. Launched in 1647, she was a 414 ton, 96ft long, 38-gun ship with a crew of 220. Later she was enlarged so that her tonnage approximately doubled.

In February 1653, while under the command of Captain John Seaman, she took part in the Battle of Portland, a running fight up the Channel against a Dutch convoy of some 200 vessels and its escort of approximately 85 warships under Admiral Tromp. The English were victorious and the Dutch lost about 55 ships (the exact number varies in the accounts); the English lost one vessel and had two or three captured which were afterwards retaken.

Later the same year the *Dragon* was one of the Rear, or Blue Squadron, that fought against the Dutch off North Foreland. The Dutch were badly beaten, eleven prizes were taken and some eight more were sunk or blown up (again accounts vary). No English ships were lost.

The *Dragon* afterwards took part in the action off

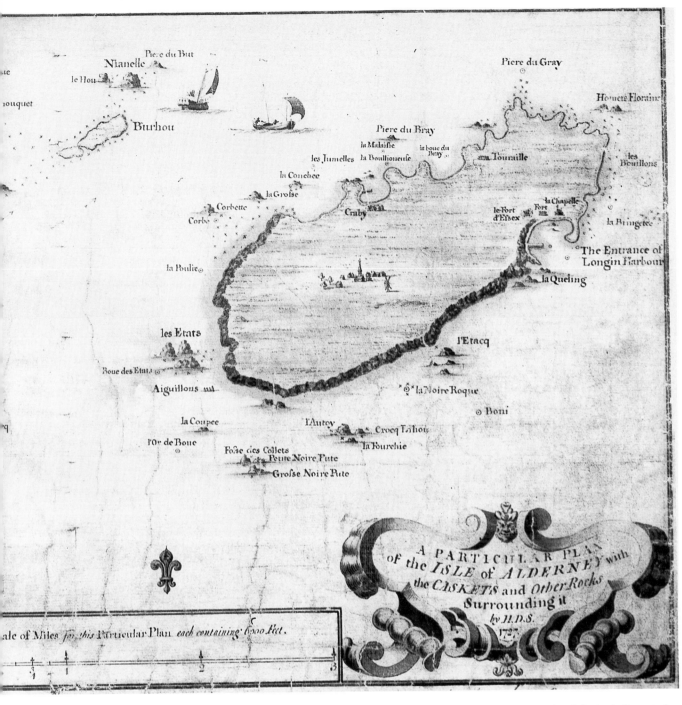

A PARTICULAR PLAN of the ISLE of ALDERNEY with the CASKETS and Other Rocks Surrounding it by H.D.S. 1727

Scale of Miles for this Particular Plan each containing 6300 Feet.

Katwijk and the Battle of Scheveningen, in which Captain Seaman of the *Dragon* and the famous Dutch Admiral Tromp were both killed. About 26 Dutch and 3 English vessels were lost. By the treaty of 5th April 1654, the Dutch had to strike their flag and lower their topsails to any English warship in sight. This was a source of great irritation to the Dutch and in 1657 the Dutch Admiral Obdam, while escorting a convoy of 30 sail, refused to salute the *Dragon* and another ship. Obdam was forced to comply when the *Dragon* and its companion threatened to engage.

In June 1665, the *Dragon* was one of the victorious English fleet that fought the Dutch in the Battle of Lowestoft during which 14 ships were captured and 14 destroyed. The English had one ship taken. In May 1671, the

Dragon played a prominent part in Admiral Spragge's attack on Algerine corsairs in Bugia Bay in which the entire Algerine squadron of 10 ships was destroyed. In September 1672, while guarding a convoy off Berry Head, she was attacked by two Dutch privateers. One was sunk and the other was driven off.

In 1690 the *Dragon* underwent a rebuild at Deptford. In May 1694, she was one of the six ships which drove the famous French seaman René Duguay-Trouin among the Scilly Isles and captured his ship. Duguay-Trouin was taken to Plymouth under charge of firing on an English ship while flying English colours. The French admiral, however, managed to escape and, with four companions, sailed to Brittany in a small boat. On 23rd October 1702, the Captain of the *Dragon*, Robert Hollyman was killed while engaging a French man-of-war off Spain. In 1710 the *Dragon* led a squadron of six ships in an attack against Port Royal in the Bay of Fundy, Canada. The French governor capitulated and Port Royal was renamed Annapolis Royal.

The loss of the *Dragon*

On 16th March 1712, the *Dragon*, under Captain George Martin, was lost on the Casquets while on convoy escort duties (figs 1 and 2). The convoy, which was in two parts, was due to rendezvous south of the rocks. The details of what happened can be found in the records of the court martial (PRO ADM1 5269) that took place on board HMS *Dreadnought* in the Downs on 8th May 1712. Sir Edward Whitaker Knt., Vice Admiral of the White Squadron, presided.

The various accounts of what happened on Saturday, 15th March are all broadly similar. Events preceding the disaster are described by the *Dragon*'s Master Gunner, Joseph Lopdell:[3]

'... being in Guernsey Road at 9 in the morning the wind sprung up At S; imediatly made the signal to unmoor soon after the Capt went ashore in order to get the trade ready, at one in the afternoon we weighed and stood off and on waiting for the fleet a bout three the Capt came a board and said he would go through the Greate Russel which was what the Pilott did not (design?) ...' (fig 4)

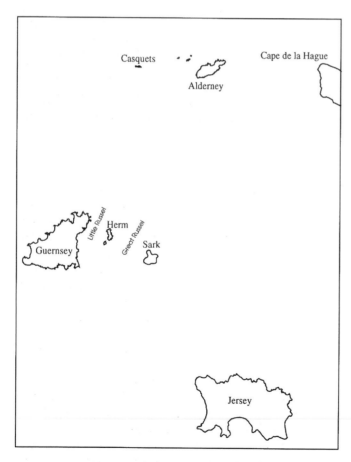

4 Channel Islands, showing the Great and Little Russels and the position of the Casquets in relation to Alderney and Guernsey

The deposition given by a certain Mr P. Bravell is slightly more fulsome:

'At 9 in the morn ye wind sprung up at S. made ye signall to unmoor at ye same time ye Capt went a shore with both boats in order to geet ye merchant ships out of (peer?) at his goeing a shore he left orders with me that as soon as ye pilot should come off and weigh (illeg.) We weighed and stood off and on (illeg.) at which (illeg.) ye ships being goat all out ye Capt came on board and asked ye Pilot which way he desired to goe he said through ye (Little?) Russall but ye Capt said he would go through ye Great Russall where up on ye pilot ordered to geet ye fore tack on ... ard (?) ...'

What happened next is best told by D. E. Pullam, the *Dragon*'s First Mate:

'... being ye near 5 o'clock we made ye signal and bore away through ye Great Russell: setting the Courses, Topsails and Staysails, having fairweather and a fresh gail, at S or S by W, at ½ past 5 by ye pilotes order hall'd ye mainsail up to gett ye sheet anchor on ye gunnell: and at ye pilots order me to go down and tell ye Capt that if he pleased he would shorten saile for ye fleet; being a great ways astern, which I did: ye Capt calling out of ye gallery winder to take in ye mizen topsaile, haul down ye stacells, and bunt ye mainsaile which was done: the Pilote ordering to steer right for ye casquetts, which wee saw very plain, then bearing N: dist. about 8 or 9 miles, to avoyde some sunking rocks (as he said) lay to ye Westward ...'

By this time the captain had gone below leaving the Mate in charge and the pilot on the poop to steer the ship. With them was the purser, David Woodmeston, who, in his own words

'... staid on the deck till it was dark dureing which time he heard Capt Martin severall times from the Starboard gallery window speake to the Pillott; and enquire how the Casquetts bore and told him that when he thought himself clear of them, to shorten sailes for the fleet as it came dark ye weather came dirty ...'

Soon after 8pm the Mate was relieved by the Second Mate, William Wright, who came on deck to find the vessel

'... steering N, 09 wind about SW (illeg.) forsail and two topsails soth, ye mainsail bunted and mizon topsail fished, about ½ past 6 we halled our foresail up, and a little after lowered our main topsail by ye pylots order, at 7 I set ye Casquett and it bore 11 degrees dist abt 5 mile by my judgemt. The Pylot ordered us to steer NW by (illeg.) wee did, and abt ½ past 7 the Capt asked the pylot (in my hearing) how ye Casquetts bore, who made answer abt NE by N, he further asked him whether he might not hand the main topsail to stay for ye fleet (being there a good distance asterne) the pylot made answer, yes, and ordered it to be taken in and soon after the foretopsail to be lowered halfe mast we then steering between NW & NW by N the wind at the SW dark weather, at 8 I hove the logg, and our ship run 4 knotts ...;

Just before 8pm the Captain summoned Bravell and asked if he had 'all things ready in case of meeting an enemy'. Bravell left the cabin to return again at 8 where he found the captain 'looking out of ye starboard gallery and talking with the pilot on the poop'.

'... while I was with ye Capt a man came and told me that they did beleve that they saw land right ahead whereupon I went up on deck and saw ye rocks very plaine; we then ordered to loose the topsails and (illeg.) ye fore saile which was soon dun and presently after we (illeg.) a stayes in ye mean time she was a stayes a merchant vessel fell on board us on ye larboard bow and struck us . . . '

The collision with the merchant vessel was clearly the principal contributing factor to the loss of the *Dragon*. The purser, who by this time had gone below, returned to deck as soon as all hands were called and found that the mainsail of the 'small vessel' on the weather bow had become entangled in the *Dragon*'s anchor flukes, in which position she was held 'some time'.

The most authoritative account of the collision and the events that followed is probably that of the Mate who had again taken the watch soon after 8pm:

'. . . in less ye a quarter of an hour after I took ye deck the Midshipman from the forecastle called aft, and told me he saw rocks under the lee bow, which I did ye same, and gave orders for the sails to be sett, and imediately acquainted ye Capt of ye same, being in his cabben, who followed me up and gave orders for to tack ye ship, but she mist staying by reson of a bark that fell on board us, upon ye larboard bow, I being at ye forebraces, heard them call from ye Quarter deck to cutt away the anchors, which I repeted, but be fore it could be don, having a strong tide of flood, we struck against ye rocks, and down came ye bowspreet, and foremast, but ye tide forsd us inbetween two large rocks, where she bildgd and stuck fast; all this I will declare on oath.'

The drama of the event is also well conveyed in a contrasting account given by the Master Gunner:

'I continued below till I heard a cry on deck then run up I see ye Casquetts and breakers under our Lee bough, we hauled up awind making sail (having but little a broad), endeavoured to tack but missed stays, I believe occasioned a bark which fell on our weather bough. I heard the word given to cutt away the anchors, we endeavoured it but before it could be performed we struck on ye Casquetts and carried away the Bow-spit head and (illeg.) mast, and soon after another sea forced us in between two large rocks where she bealged and stuck fast.'

The Second Mate's deposition ends with a description of how they got ashore:

'. . . soon after I was relieved by the Chief mate, about half past 8 I hoared a noise upon deck, I made what haste I could, I saw the Casquetts to leeward Ship put in stays but a small vessel falling aboard ye weather bow occasioned our misstaying, having trimmed our sails endeavoured to stay againe but instead having not room to weare our ship fell off & run (illeg.), against ye rocks where our bowsprit and foremast came by ye board, our maintopsails. (Illeg.) aback, wee fell in betwixt two rocks at once cut away our mainmast and mizen our ship being bilged, and let go our anchors to keep her ashore, where at low tide wee got on shore.'

The foregoing accounts are all in close agreement (perhaps suspiciously close), but a letter from two anonymous 'well wishers of our Queen and Country' tell an entirely different story:

March ye 25th 1712

My Lords,

In justice to our Queen and country we think ourselves obliged to give your Hons. acount how carlesly ignorantly and unadvisedly Her Majesty's ship ye Dragon was lately lost on ye Casquetts to ye admiration of all ye hearers we speek nothing out of dislike to any of our officers on our own account but besides our own losses; are greefed that ye Goverment should loose such a ship out of ye weaknes and carelesness of all ye comanding officers who not three minutes before ye ship struck was drinking and dancing to excess with several females which was we judge a great inducement to ye lose: ther being no officer on deck but ye Masters Mate we hope your Hons. will not be angry to reecive this account which is the truth from ye well wishers of our Queen & Country: at the same time are your Lordships most dutifull and obedint servant

B.F.

S.C.

Without the identity of its authors, the letter was regarded as inadmissible evidence and thus had little influence upon the court which, in the end, delivered the following judgement:

Enquiry was made by the Court into the occasion of the loss of Her Majesty's late shipp the *Dragon*, of which Cap George Martin was commander which was bilgd on the Casquetts near the Islands of Guernsey on the 16th of March 1711/12 at which time one Peter Cock was pilott onboard her; and on information from an unknown hand dated the 25th of March 1712 signed - B.F. & S.C. relating to the behaviour of the Captaine and officers of the said shipp. And after having strictly examind the evidence upon oath it appeared by the course they steered and the baring of the Casquetts when last seen and the run the said shipp made from that time to the time of her being lost it would in all probability have carried them clear. It is therefore the opinion of the Court that the irregular setting of the current was the sole occasion of the loss of the said shipp, and no objection being made by the pylott or any other person against the Captaine or any of the other officers of their not having done their dutys, nor any person or persons appearing to make good the allegations in the letter signed B.F. & S.C. notwithstanding publick notice had been given of the Tryal. The Court considering the whole have acquitted Capt Martin and the rest of the officers as also Peter Cock the Pylott as to the loss of Her Majesty's ship the *Dragon* and they are hereby accordingly acquitted.

Discovery of the wreck

Around 1985 a diving group from Northampton, who were planning to visit the Casquets, were asked by the naval historian Patrick Gosset if they would conduct a search for the *Dragon* based on his research in the Public Records Office (some of which is featured above). The wreck was located exactly where Gosset had thought it to be. A small amount of material was recovered and subsequent visits were made to the site by the same group. Gosset himself visited the wreck in 1992 while part of another team (the Maritime Archaeology Group) that was searching for the *Victory*. He reported the site to the Receiver of Wrecks on Alderney and the following year took a diver from the Alderney harbour authority to the site.

The remains of the wreck are situated in the narrow gap between the two large rocks described in the court martial papers (fig 5). They act very like a weir when the current is running. It would seem that the *Dragon* wedged herself into this gap before breaking up. As she came apart wreckage spread both north and south of the weir. On the north side of the site the reef falls steeply into deep water where there

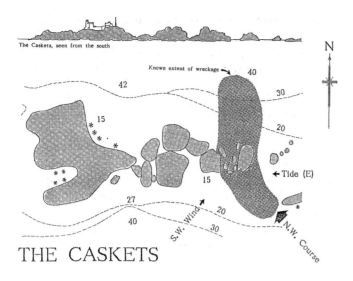

The Caskets, seen from the south

Known extent of wreckage →

40
42
30
15
20
15
27
20
40
30

← Tide (E)

S.W. Wind

N.W. Course

N

THE CASKETS

5 Plan of the *Dragon* site *(Mark Arnold)*

6 Sounding lead, length 272mm *(Mark Arnold)*

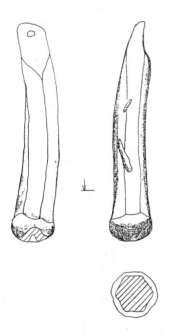

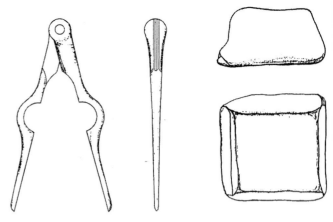

7 *Above left* Navigational dividers, height 101mm *(Mark Arnold)*

8 *Above right* Lead ingot, 27 x 53 x 56mm *(Mark Arnold)*

9 Latten spoon with trifid handle. Detail shows Dublin plate mark from inside of bowl. Length 181mm. Traces of silver plating survive *(Mark Arnold)*

10 Latten spoon with letters IW on back of handle. Length 212mm *(Mark Arnold)*

11 A fork, Length 183mm *(Mark Arnold)*

is an undulating gravel bottom. At this point there is at least one cannon at a depth of 100ft or more. The northern half of the site is in a gully, which at its top, has a depth of only about 10ft, deepening (and widening) to about 45ft before dropping off into deeper water. The bottom, prior to the drop-off, is characterized by iron concretion and cannon balls. The tide runs through the gap with great force so that it is best dived at slack water.

The southern half of the site is well covered by kelp and being generally shallow is more prone to tidal surges, making diving difficult at most stages of the tide. Much of the sea-bed here is also covered by concretion. It would seem that the greater part of the hull ended up in this area. Most of the artefacts featured below came from this part of the site.

At least two iron cannon are situated to the south of the Little Casquet. If indeed these pieces came from the *Dragon*, then it would seem that she struck this area first before bumping eastwards along the reef and wedging into the gap.

Finds

Finds from the wreck include a sounding lead (fig 6), two pairs of dividers (fig 7), a small lead ingot (fig 8), two spoons (figs 9 and 10), a fork (fig 11), a book clasp (fig 12), a brass candlestick (ht. approx. 6in) and two sword hilts (figs. 13 and 14), one of which is intact and has woven silver thread about the grip.

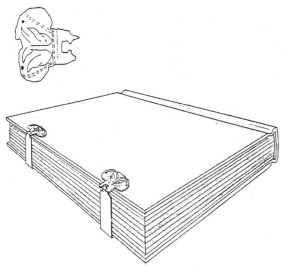

The remains of several shoes and buckles were of particular interest. The shoes (now in Northampton Central Museum) were typical men's foot-wear of the period with overlapping straps fastened by a buckle, which was transferable from one pair to another.[4] Several buckles were recovered, all were of bronze and had probably been burnished to give a golden colour. One of the buckles, 1¼ x 1⅗ in., was oblong with rounded corners and a swelling at the centre of its top and bottom to take the central bar. A second buckle (fig 15), 1⅛ x 1⅜ in., was of similar form with decorative sides. A third example, thinner than the others, was incomplete and may, or may not, have been a shoe buckle.

Of considerable significance was a pewter pot with a hinged lid (missing) (fig 16) and a pewter plate (fig 17) inscribed with the letters D.W. on the upper side of the rim;

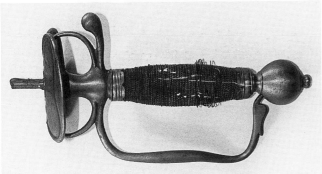

12 *Top* A book clasp *(Mark Arnold)*

13 *Above* Sword hilt, length 190mm *(W. Gosset)*

14 *Below* Part of a sword hilt *(W. Gosset)*

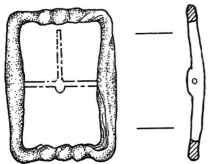

15 *Lower left* Buckle, 1:1 *(Mark Arnold)*

16 *Above* Pewter drinking vessel. Height 76mm; base diam. 57mm *(W. Gosset)*

undoubtedly these were the initials of the ship's purser, David Woodmeston. Also on the upper side of the rim were three oblong hallmarks; the first has been injured by wear, the second has a leopard's face, while the third contains what appears to be a mortar and pestle. On the underside of

17 Pewter plate inscribed with the initials of the ship's purser, David Woodmeston (see detail). Also, the restored touchmarks from the underside of the plate: John Kirton of London. Rim diam. 9 ¼ in. Base diam. 6 ⅞ ins (*W. Gosset*)

the plate are the touchmarks of John Kirton of London who was given leave to strike on 2 June 1702.

Ordnance

At least seven iron cannon were seen in the wreck area.[5] Of these one was raised in 1994 by the Alderney diving club and is now on the island in unconserved state. Once its

18 Iron cannon from the *Dragon (Brian Bonnard)*

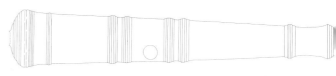

19 Same iron cannon as in figure 18

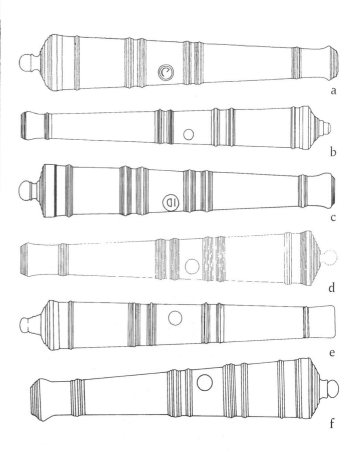

20 Findbankers (not to scale): a. Royal Armouries Collection, England, late 17th century b. *Batavia*, 1629 c. *Vergulde Draeck*, 1656 d. *Kennemerland*, 1662 e. From a vessel lost in the Zyderzee in 1672 f. *Mauritius*, 1609 f. from a vessel lost in the Zyderzee in 1672 (*T. Alexander*)

concretion was removed it could be seen to be of 'findbanker' (or finbanker') type (figs 18 and 19). Its cascable was missing and the trunnions were damaged; gouge marks on the barrel suggest that this might have been the result of over-zealous hammer and chisel work while removing the concretion.[6]

Findbankers are iron guns characterized by pronounced barrel rings that have more fillets supporting the astragal than normal (Blackmore, 1976, 150). However, as Green has pointed out (1989, 45), there is considerable confusion over the term findbanker. The Danes for instance, clearly recognized a much broader range of forms, as evinced by a typology reproduced by Green (1989, 53, fig 31) from a Danish manuscript of c. 1770 entitled *Søtøjhusbogen: Tegninger af Sö-Etatens Skyts i Aaret 1771*.

Findbankers were made in Sweden, Holland, England, Germany and elsewhere. The name appears to derive from Finsong, one of the Swedish foundries that was producing them in the seventeenth century. Their main customers were the Dutch who, traditionally, had specialized in the manufacture of bronze cannon. Up until the 1620s the Dutch had imported most of their iron guns from the Weald in England, but political difficulties then forced them to turn to Sweden for the bulk of their heavy iron ordnance (Blackmore, 1976, 150; Green, 1989, 45).

The *Dragon*'s findbanker is of standard form, but the situation regarding its origin is confused. An 18-pounder of broadly similar design in the collection of the Royal Armouries (fig 20a) is described as late seventeenth century Swedish (Blackmore, 1976, 150), but drawings of the type in the *Søtøjhusbogen* manuscript mentioned above, label the form as Dutch. In this latter regard mention should be made of a 1660 survey of the *Dragon* in the Public Records Office, London, which records that her 8-pounders were captured Dutch guns. Some of her 12-pounders are likely to be of similar origin.

Findbankers of comparable form to that from the *Dragon* have come from several wrecks: the *Banda* which sank in 1615 (Dumas, 1981, 89); the *Trial*, 1622 (Green, 1986, 203, fig 7); the *Batavia*, 1629 (fig 20b; Green, 1989, 45, particularly nos. 5 and 8); the *Vergulde Draeck*, 1656 (fig 20c; Green 1977, 271); the *Nordstiernan* and *Pollux*, 1658 (Tojhusmuseum, Copenhagen); the *Kennemerland*, 1664 (fig 20d; Price and Muckelroy, 1974, 262, fig 4); the Mullion Cove wreck, 1667 (?), (McBride *et al.*, 1975, 247); the wreck of a patrol vessel in the Zuyderzee, 1672 (fig 20e, Puype, 1990, 14), and the *Enigheden*, 1679 (Tojhusmuseum, Copenhagen). 6-pounder and 12-pounder findbankers are also illustrated by Petersen (1969, pl. 42, nos. 1, 2 and 5). Brown (1995, 115) mentions 'a sort of proto-findbanker' on the *Mauritius*, 1609 (fig, 20f; L'Hour, *et al.*, 1989, 114-115).

Conclusion

Built in 1647 just after the end of the Civil War, the *Dragon* was one of the ships of the Commonwealth's 'new model' Navy. During her long life she fought through the Dutch Wars of the Restoration and before, and into the wars with France that mark the accession of William and Mary and the beginning of the classic age of fighting sail. In her time she saw the Navy grow - in part, thanks to Pepys - from a small ineffectual fleet, heavily dependant upon merchant ships, into a large, purpose-built, professional fighting force that stretched around the world. In addition to the interesting historical period through which she served, there were her battle honours; if combat is the ultimate test of a warship, then the *Dragon* was a vessel of proven metal. It is to be lamented that this important wreck has never been examined in a full and proper archaeological manner. Although she was lost in one of the most difficult corners imaginable, it would, none the less, be a benefit to learning to have the site surveyed and perhaps also excavated.

21 A wreck that has long evaded maritime archaeologists is HMS *Victory*, a first-rate ship which went down in the vicinity of the Casquets and Alderney during the night of 4th October 1744. Although wreckage was washed ashore at the time, the site itself has never been found despite numerous searches. The *Victory* was armed entirely with brass guns. Painting by Peter Monogamy, 1681-1749
(courtesy National Maritime Museum Picture Library)

Acknowledgements

The authors are grateful to the members of the Northampton BSAC dive group that found the wreck and in particular to Mark Arnold and Jim Tyson who kindly supplied the information on the artefacts they found.

Notes

1 For instance, in 1993 the first author was the archaeological director of a Naval Air Command Sub-aqua Club (NACSAC) expedition led by Lieutenant Commander I.G. Milne that tried unsuccessfully to find the *Dragon*.

2 Most of the details concerning the activities of the *Dragon* have been taken from Lecky, 1913.

3 The original orthography and syntax have been retained in all the extracts.

4 Ms J.M. Swann (Keeper of the Shoe Collection at the Northampton Central Museum) writes: '(Buckles) as designed in 1660 (were) to be transferable, from one pair of shoes to another, and not permanently attached like the buckles to which we are now accustomed. Consequently, people could have quantities of buckles if they were ostentatious, or only one pair if they couldn't afford more. Particularly after the 1720s, buckles became the only fashion feature of men's shoes, and old-fashioned buckles were then traded in for the latest style. As a consequence, most of the surviving buckles belong to the later years of the craze, the 1770s-1780s. Very little survives from the pre-1720s, partly because the size of buckles and the straps to support them grew steadily from then on.'

5. The authors have not been able to substantiate frequently repeated reports of two bronze cannon that were taken from the site around 1991-92 and sold on the French market.

6. Surviving length of cannon 2.67m. Mouth full of concretion thus preventing a precise measurement of the bore; approximately 100mm. Surface condition poor and the profiles of the mouldings lack definition; this is reflected in the drawing of figure 19. Muzzle/chase mouldings consist of two raised astragals with recessed band at centre and broad flanking oggee-curved fillets. The double mouldings either side of the trunnions appear to be similar with a raised flat astragal at centre and oggee-curved flanking fillets. Possible traces of a device at the upper forward end of the first reinforce. Vent astragal rounded with oggee-curved flanking fillets. Plain vent hole 40mm behind rear vent fillet. Base appears to consist of two raised ovolos with a recessed band at centre. Breech mouldings badly worn.

References

Blackmore, H.L., 1976, *The Armouries of the Tower of London*, I Ordnance, HMSO, London

Brown, R.R., 1995, Arming the East Indiamen, *The Archaeology of Ships of War, International Maritime Archaeology Series*, Vol. 1, Mensun Bound (ed.), 114-119

Dumas, J., 1981, *Fortune de mer a l'Ile Maurice*, Paris

Green, J.N., 1977, *The Jacht Vergulde Draeck, 1656*, vol. 1, BAR Supplementary Series 36 (i), Oxford.Green, J.N., 1986, The Survey and identification of the English East India Company ship *Trial* (1622), *International Journal of Nautical Archaeology*, 15, 3, 203

Green, J.N., 1989, *The loss of the Verenigde Oostindische Compagnie retourship* Batavia, *Western Australia 1629*, BAR International Series, 489, Oxford

Lecky, H.S., 1913, *The King's Ships*, vol. 11, London, 258-260. L'Hour, M., Long, L., and Rieth, E., 1989, *Le Mauritius, La Mémoire engloutie*, Grenoble

McBride, P., Larn R. and Davis, R., 1975, A mid-17th century merchant ship found near Mullion Cove: 3rd interim report on the *Santo Christo de Castello, 1667, International Journal of Nautical Archaeology*, 4, 2, 237-252

Peterson, M., 1969, *History Under the Sea*, Smithsonian Institution Pr., Washington

Price, R. and Muckelroy, K., 1974, The second season of work on the *Kennemerland* site, 1973, *International Journal of Nautical Archaeology*, 3, 2, 257-268

Puype, J.P., 1990, Guns and their handling at sea in the 17th century; a Dutch point of view, *Journal of the Ordnance Society*, Vol. II, 11-23

Svein Molaug (Director Emeritus, Norsk Sjøfartsmuseum)

The excavation of the Norwegian frigate *Lossen*, 1717

By 1717 the Great Nordic War of 1700-1721 had reached a critical stage. The Danish-Norwegian admiral Peter Wessel Tordenskiold had fallen into disgrace with the monarch, and this situation had weakened the kingdom's naval strength. Swedish privateers used this weakness to their advantage, becoming ever more active and aggressive. Convoy protection was crucial to ensure direct communication by sea between Norway and Denmark; a vital link for both countries.

In December 1717, 65 transport vessels and merchant ships had gathered at Stavern, Norway, to sail in convoy to Frederikshavn in Denmark. Several naval ships were assigned to protect them during the crossing. The frigate *Lossen* was one of them.

Before noon, on 22 December, the convoy weighed anchor and headed for Kattegat. The wind was NNE and the weather was clear. Towards evening the wind changed to the SW and built rapidly into a violent storm. The convoy was scattered during the night; several vessels were lost, while others headed for ports in Norway.

On the morning of December 23, *Lossen* was 21 nautical miles WSW of Marstrand on the Swedish coast. It was the worst winter storm for many years; the following night was equally terrible with a very heavy sea raging. The captain steered northwards in an attempt to reach the protection of the Oslofjord. At dawn on December 24, an effort was made to lighten the front of the vessel by throwing the forward guns overboard, but the deck was repeatedly swamped by the sea which made access to the foredeck impossible. At noon the wind, with undiminished force, changed to the west. *Lossen* was now nearing an extremely dangerous lee shore. When an effort was made to veer the vessel around, she was struck by a heavy wave which drove her over on her beam-ends, a position she held for about half an hour.

By 8.30 pm her master, Commander Bruun, could see the first breakers and also make out the weak shimmer of the Store Færder beacon, which marked the western entrance of Oslofjord. Having proceeded two nautical miles farther into the darkness, *Lossen* struck violently, head-on against a cliff on the north-west side of Hvaler, smashing her stem. The masts went overboard, and *Lossen* sank in five fathoms of water (fig 2).

There were 109 people on board, including six Swedish prisoners-of-war. Only 54 survived. No burials related to the shipwreck are recorded in the Hvaler church book. Those who perished were buried at the edge of a bog near the site of the disaster.

1 There is no known picture of the frigate *Lossen*; she was too small and insignificant to have received any attention from the painters of naval glory. She was, however, both in size and rigging, much like *Løvendahls Galley* featured above *(Norsk Sjøfartsmuseum, Oslo)*

The frigate Lossen - a brief description

The classification of Danish-Norwegian naval vessels was determined by their armament and not by their place in line formations. Ships carrying more than fifty guns were designated as 'orlogsskip' (capital ships), while those which had fewer guns, but with the same full three-masted rig, were usually classified as frigates. *Lossen*'s armament consisted of 18 six-pound and 6 three-pound guns.

Lossen was laid down at Fredrikstad, Norway, in 1684, and built under the supervision of Harman Thiessen, a Dutch shipwright. She had a length of 28.7 metres and a beam of 7.5 metres. Her name 'Lossen' is a Nordic synonym for the animal lynx.

She was completed and ready for naval service in 1686. During the following years, she performed various duties, including the transportation of Norwegian conscripted

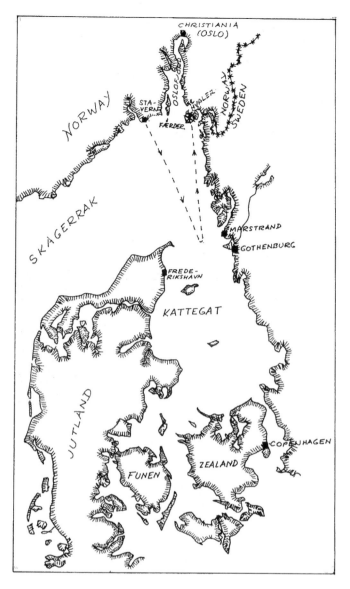

2 Map of Scandinavia showing the final voyage of the frigate *Lossen*

naval ratings to Denmark. She was also frequently used as a convoy escort and took part in several engagements.

The Lossen excavation

Wind force, spread of canvas and the time period between her last determined position and the moment of impact, were revealed through careful study of the inquiry reports following the disaster. In 1963, these clues led to the discovery of the wreck at Stolen, a small bay about a mile south of Papperhavn on Vesterøy, Hvaler, a group of islands on the eastern side of the Oslofjord entrance. Guns were observed, and further investigations revealed ship's timbers in the mud.

The shallow depth of 10 metres and the protection and preservation of the wreck through considerable silting, made this a good site for excavation. It should be observed that underwater archaeology was, at that time, a new discipline in Norway and that the *Lossen* excavation was thus a pioneering project. The undertaking was therefore organized as an experimental operation, with emphasis on the testing of methods suitable for conditions in Norway. An equally important concern was the training of personnel. Most of the 46 excavations and extensive investigations which have since been carried out in the district under the jurisdiction of the Norwegian Maritime Museum, have, in some way, derived and benefited from this first experience.

The development of a method for underwater documentation in poor visibility conditions, was of particular importance. The so-called three-point measuring system was thus developed. This system is based on a combination of three basic fixed points and a calculation programme, which makes it possible to define any point in three dimensions. The method was later elaborated in many other countries through the use of electronic probes and computer-controlled drawing programmes, e.g. the SHARPS System, from Applied Sonic Corporation (Andersen, 1969; Christensen, 1969).

The excavation of the *Lossen* took place in 1967-68 and 1974. The main aim was to carry out a survey of the functional and social aspects of life on board a relatively small man-of-war from the early 18th century.

Hull and rigging

Most of the lower hull, to just below the waterline, had been protected by silt. That above had been destroyed by natural erosion, wave action and worm attack. A large and surprisingly varied number of artefacts still survived within the hull; many were found in their original contexts. The following is a brief description of the foremost categories of finds (for further details, see Molaug, 1983; in Norwegian).

Enough survived of the vessel's bottom to determine its construction. The hull was compactly framed; its inner lining consisted of 13 inches x 2 3/4 inches oak planks. Double frames ran across the inner lining, about six feet apart. The mainmast was stepped slightly aft of midships, about 14 metres from the stern, while the mizzen-mast stood about 6 metres from the stern.

Beneath the lowest continuous deck was the space for cordage, provisions, etc. Five chests were found far aft,

3 *Above* View from the south illustrating the excavation as it was in 1968. Two airlifts were used. The row of guns at left shows that the frigate slewed violently to port as she sank. On the right, stone and iron ballast, fused together, protrudes from the sea-bed. Most of the bow was crushed when she struck the cliffs. The 'three-point' measuring system (centre) was used for the first time on this excavation. Some experiments with underwater stereo photography were also conducted (right foreground) *(Drawing: Ole A. Krogness and Erik Karlsen)*

4 *Left* One of the sketches made on the site during excavation. This particular drawing shows an area with bottles, pipe stems and small jars in between debris from seamen's chests. Jar 669 has been fixed into the three dimensional measuring system by the co-ordinates X=1116, Y=790, Z=740 *(Drawing: Erik Karlsen)*

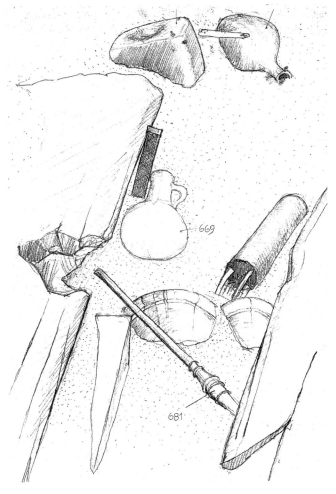

perhaps indicating where those who were permitted to bring their chests on board had their living quarters.

One transverse bulkhead was situated between the mainmast and the mizzen-mast, while another, farther aft, separated the captain's cabin from the officers' quarters.

The stern had 8 x 12cm lead-framed window panes, stiffened with metal cross-rods.

Although most of the rigging went overboard when *Lossen* struck, several interesting objects from aloft were found. Some of them were spare parts, while others were in use when the vessel sank. There were 36 single blocks, some of them with the blockmaker's stamp, as well as sheaves, deadeyes of various sizes and belaying pins. Additionally, there was an interesting selection of krennels, cleats, rollers, trucks and parrel-trucks.

Cordage of various dimensions was raised; this included balls of twine, coils of rope and remnants of the huge anchor

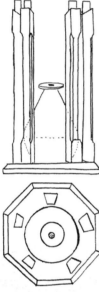

5 Navigational instruments. From left: pocket compass, slide rule (Gunter-scale), pocket monocular, pocket sundial and compass, half-hour sand-glass and brass dividers
(courtesy Norsk Sjøfartsmuseum, Oslo)

6 A wasp-waisted, half-hour sand-glass

cable. Much of the cordage had been treated at the ends, and there was a rich variety of various knots and sennits.

Other fittings and equipment

A rudder and a tiller marked "No. 55" probably belonged to one of the boats which *Lossen* carried. A bailer was recovered and also a wooden spade, the latter was presumably used to shovel snow. A rather unusual find was two wooden firepumps, 67cm long, intact with rods.

Some rectangular wooden timbers (about 30cm x 23cm) were found in pairs, separated by two layers of coarse fabric. They had nail holes in each corner, but there was no trace of nails in the fabric.

Some frame-shaped wooden items may have been what Röding (1794-98, 603) describes as "Flügelschere", or vane-stocks, used to spread the vane or pennant. Sizes varied considerably: the three smallest had a beam of 15cm, two of medium size measured 44cm and the two largest were of 100cm. Since all were found in an incomplete condition, their actual lengths were difficult to determine.

A chest with eight compartments for spikes and iron nails of various sizes was also, no doubt, part of the ship's equipment.

Navigational instruments (Fig 5)

It was quite a surprise to learn that the Jacob's staff was still in use during the early 18th century. The staff from *Lossen* was 70cm long and 17 x 17mm in section. It had three cross-pieces, the innermost of which had a bone plate. It could also be used as a backstaff. Apart from astronomical observations, the staff was also convenient for angular measurements when distances from ship to shore, and perhaps also to artillery targets, had to be determined.

Two slide rules (fig 7) were so well preserved that it was still possible to read the figures and letters. The larger rule (32.4cm) was a Gunter rule, its bottom line served for multiplication and division. The smaller rule, 17.4cm long, was inscribed with the following numbers:

618

753

294

Regardless of how these figures are added - vertically, horizontally or diagonally - the sum is always 15. Their purpose is unclear.

Other navigational instruments included dividers (fig 5), a log, a log glass, a sounding-lead and a slate-board for arithmetic calculations and tallying.

It was no great surprise to find a pocket sun-dial and two pocket compasses (fig 5). Contemporary records tell of how a pocket compass came in very handy on one occasion when the ship's compass had been shot to pieces during an encounter. Much less expected was the discovery of a pocket telescope, 12cm long and 2.3cm in diameter.

Three sand-glasses were brought up (figs 5 and 7), each of 30 minutes duration. Sand-glasses were used to indicate the length of each watch. A four hour watch lasted eight glasses.

Armament

Lossen was armed with 18 six-pound and 6 three-pound guns. All the guns which were found were of cast iron, now heavily corroded. The vents had been covered with lead sheets, shaped to fit the contours of the breech. The plates were tied to the guns, as demonstrated by fastening holes on either side. Several ramrod heads were also raised.

There was a surprisingly small number of cannon balls, but the calibre of those recovered corresponded to the calibre of the guns. A cannon ball and a bar-shot were located on a piece of iron concretion, 39cm long. The balls on the dumb-bell-shaped bar-shot had a diameter of 12.5cm. Grape-shot was also found.

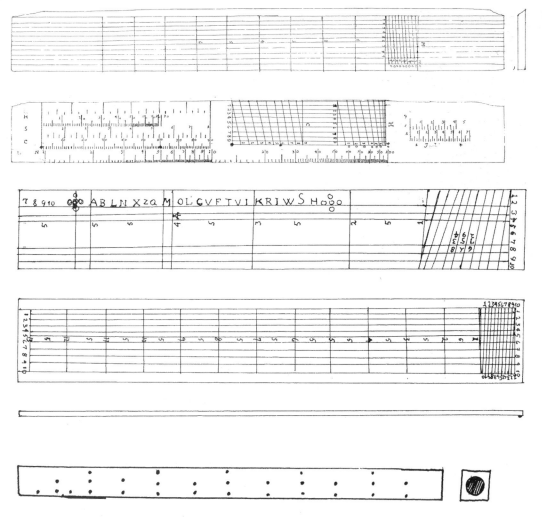

7 *Above* Drawing of the Gunter-scale on the ruler from *Lossen*. Two slide rules were found on board

8 *Right* Examples of the types of shot found on board. Left: grape-shot (partly reconstructed with new canvas and twine). Right: bar-shot, diam. 12.5cm. Front: grenade, diam. 9cm, and lead musket shot, some with casting knots. *Lossen* carried 6 three-pound and 18 six-pound guns
(Pål Abrahamsen/The Norwegian Maritime Museum)

Other finds included pistol shot, fragments from both shoulder and hand guns, and a number of grenades of 9cm diameter, each with a hole to take the fuse.

Galley equipment
A pile of bricks were found forward of the mainmast. Charring proved that these were from the vessel's stove. Split sticks of beech-wood and an iron box with two compartments, recalling a tinder-box, were found nearby. The discovery of a 9cm long piece of tinder confirms the assumption that fires were lit with old-fashioned methods.

Since no large earthenware cooking-pots were found, one can assume that the food was usually prepared in copper and iron vessels. A copper pot without any supporting legs was raised (ht. 36cm, diam. 33cm). Near the rim had been inscribed "Neptunus Veig 1 L x 1/2 x Ao 1685". "Veig" (weight) may indicate that the pot was used when provisions were distributed. "Neptunus" was the name of another naval vessel that had recently been decommissioned.

Rather unexpected was the discovery of a copper coffee pot, a luxury restricted to the officers since coffee had not yet become a common household drink.

Two steelyard arms of different type, and several counterweights, helped to bring alive the working atmosphere of the ship's galley.

Small earthenware objects (side-handle pots and jars) were also discovered.

Provisions

Dietary regulations had been set down in official lists by the navy. Shipboard fare on Danish-Norwegian warships in the 17th/18th century included beef, mutton, pork, dried fish, porridge, butter and liquor. The finds from *Lossen* have thrown further light on provisions and food preparation on board.

Meat was kept in barrels and was served on stave-made, round trays with outward-sloping sides. A barrel made of beech contained butter. Beech is scarce in Norway but common in Denmark, so one may assume that the butter was Danish. A butter spade explains how the butter was scooped out of the barrel. A ladle and a small scooper, both of wood, were also recovered.

Analyses of bone remnants by the Bergen Zoological Museum showed that 200 of the bones came from fish and 1,400 from mammals. Of the latter, 230 were from sheep and 200 from pigs. The total absence of dorsal vertebrae from pigs indicates that pork chops were not a part of the ship's fare.

Barrels and other cooper's products (fig 9)

Staves from 100 barrel lids and 120 barrels and kegs were located. The length of the staves varied from 141 to 220cm. Some of the barrels had been inscribed with the year of make and the name LAASEN. The dating and identity of *Lossen* was thus confirmed.

Water on board was usually stored in casks, each taking 926.5 litres. One of the recovered lids probably came from such a barrel. Barrels and kegs displayed the cooper's name as well as other marks. One lid was decorated with a six-leaf rose within two concentric circles. The symbol may have served a prophylactic purpose, to prevent the contents from becoming spoiled or turning rancid.

White cooperage is represented by mess trays and wooden pots.

Bottles, glasses, tankards and small jars (fig 10)

The consumption of wine must have been considerable, as testified by the large number of glass bottles of various

9 *Right* Wooden vessels of all kinds and shapes were found on the wreck. From the left: small wooden bucket, a miniature keg (14 x 10cm) and a crozed can. Wooden spoons were crafted on board, and probably also many of the handles from knives and cutlery (foreground)
(Pål Abrahamsen/The Norwegian Maritime Museum)

10 *Above* A number of small brandy jars were found inside the seamen's chests (right). The simple wooden beakers in front of them contrast with the more opulent crystal cups and Chinese porcelain of the officers (centre and left)
(Pål Abrahamsen/The Norwegian Maritime Museum)

shapes and sizes. Bottles of green glass had a verdigris-like coating, created by seasonal variations in sea-water temperature. A test was made at an early stage to determine whether these 'growth rings' could be used as a dating method, but the results were inconclusive.

Smaller bottles and flasks were presumably used for perfume and medicine.

There were also a number of wine and liquor glasses, shaped in contemporary styles. Some of them sported nicely cut ornamentation.

Four small earthenware jars, each with a single lug-handle, may have been used for liquor rations (ht. 11cm; diam. 8cm). Their capacity of about half a pint is approximately the same as the prescribed brandy ration.

Several tankards, of both wood and earthenware, testify to liberal beer consumption on board. An unusual item to be found on a ship was a wooden "stave-bottle", of a type that was commonly used in rural Norway for several centuries.

Cutlery

The sailor's eating utensils consisted of knives, spoons and fingers. A large and varied amount of knife handles made of wood and bone were raised. All the blades had been lost to corrosion. A considerable number of wooden and metal spoons of various shapes and sizes were also recovered (fig 9).

A few pewter and stoneware plates were found; these were probably for the use of officers. The same applies to a couple of Chinese teacups with matching plates (fig 10). The presumed coffee-pot mentioned earlier may indicate that they were also used as coffee cups.

Some small boxes made from wooden off-cuts may have contained butter. One of them had a cross inscribed on the lid, perhaps this was intended as a protective device against evil spirits or thieves. Butter boxes of this kind were quite common in rural Norway.

Finally, mention should be made of ten small turned wooden vessels with lids. Their heights varied from 6 to 8cm. They may have been used as spice pots.

Clothing

Contemporary drawings show that ordinary sailors wore a shirt, knee-trousers, jacket, stockings, shoes and a hat, but the wide range of buttons from the wreck indicates that subordinates did not wear uniforms.

The 925 buttons varied greatly in material and decoration: wood, bone, brass, pewter and silver. A wooden box was brought up which contained silver buttons wrapped in twine for protection against rubbing caused by the rolling of the vessel (fig 12).

There were 57 intact shoe and belt buckles. These were made of brass or pewter and were of many and varied shapes.

The shoes were sometimes fashion-made by professional shoemakers, but more often they were of coarse make, probably produced on board. This assumption was confirmed by the discovery of shoe lasts and awls.

The knife has always been a part of the sailor's basic equipment. Handles for knives and daggers were found in

considerable quantity (fig 10). Many of them were quite elaborately decorated. Some scabbards were also located.

Containers for equipment

Although subordinates were not permitted to bring their own chests on board, they would, none the less, have required storage space for personal belongings. A number of barrels contained a variety of such items, indicating that these containers were shared by several people. Some chests were found far aft, an indication that they belonged to the officers or the specialist craftsmen on board.

Hygiene

The crew slept in hammocks. During day-time, these hammocks were rolled up and stowed in special nettings along the rails on deck; at night they were slung beneath the orlop deck. Their cord fastenings passed through a bow-shaped wooden piece at either end of the hammock. One such piece had wear marks on the upper side, probably because the hammock was too short for the sleeper when fully stretched out.

Cleanliness was important to create an atmosphere of well-being on board. A couple of brooms and some brushes were found. The brooms were used for sweeping, while the brushes were used for the scrubbing and washing of clothes.

There were a number of combs made of horn and bone. Some had a double row of closely-set teeth, indicating that lice were a shipboard affliction. A shaving knife and a hand-mirror may have belonged to the ship's barber.

Tobacco pipes and snuff-boxes (fig 11)

Tobacco was widely used on board. Smoking was only permitted on the top deck forward of the mainmast, and the pipe head had to be hooded. 83 clay pipes with their heads intact were brought up from *Lossen*. Maker's marks confirm that most of them were of Dutch origin. Clay pipes are brittle and break easily, and some stems had been repaired. Wooden cases were used to protect the pipes; some of the 11 found were beautifully decorated with carvings. Two wooden pipes were also discovered. One had a long stem of 25cm; its decorated head had been red-lacquered.

Two snuff-boxes made of horn and birchwood and a brass tobacco-box were also recovered. The latter, decorated with a sailing ship, carried the name AMSTERDAM.

Tools

Sail-maker's tools included three bodkins, a mallet and a small, barrel-shaped wooden item which may have been used to make fishing-nets. With regard to woodworking tools, an axe handle and an auger were found, plus a cross-iron for cooperage.

Three wooden yardsticks bore interesting witness to the measurement methods of three centuries ago.

The sailors had to mend their clothes themselves. It was no surprise to find small wooden needle-boxes and spools.

Games

There was a large number of dice (fig 11), one of which was roulette-shaped. Rounded and square gaming-pieces of wood

11 *Right* Some of the most interesting items found on board *Lossen* were the pipe cases made of wood (background). A long-stemmed, decorated wooden pipe is displayed in the middle. On the left, snuffboxes made of brass and wood. Foreground right: wooden gaming pieces and three bone dice
(Pål Abrahamsen/The Norwegian Maritime Museum)

12 *Above* Writing box and contents. From right: slate pencils, nutmeg, stick of sealing wax, signet engraved with letters AB, a collection of small 'crowbars' and pins from a game known as "scratch nose". On the left: small wooden box in which were found silver buttons wrapped in twine. Front: some of the 57 metal buckles found
(Pål Abrahamsen/The Norwegian Maritime Museum)

were also found, some were inscribed with crosses or stripes. These pieces may have been used for games in which no special game-board was needed, the necessary grid system being chalked onto a slate (concerning the 'scratch nose' game, see the paragraph below on writing materials).

Books

Some paper fragments were found, but they were in such an advanced state of decay that conservation was impossible. Pieces of wood with remnants of thin leather may have been book covers, while four tiny brass clasps may have come from hymn books.

Leisure activities

Wages were modest, so any opportunity to earn something extra was eagerly sought. Twenty-four half-finished wooden spoons were found, indicating that they were produced on board during spare time, to be sold ashore when finished. An elaborately carved child's rattle is hardly the first object one would expect to find on a warship.

Carved decorations on boxes, pipe cases, etc., are of great cultural historical value, since such objects when sold ashore may have influenced local decorative art.

Writing material

Writing materials included ink pots, pencils, slate pencils, chalk pieces and signets.

Two writing boxes were found; one of which was probably the most intriguing item to have come from the vessel (fig 11). It measured 22.4 x 15.6 x 7.3cm., and was partitioned into one large rectangular and three small square spaces. It was a thrilling moment when the lid was opened and its contents were revealed.

One space was used for sand which was sprinkled on wet ink to make it dry faster. Another space was intended for the inkpot, but instead it contained three slate pencils, half a glass bead, a collar button, a stick of black sealing wax, three buttons without eyes and 11 small cleaved shafts. In the middle space, covered with a lid, were 11 ordinary buttons, two double buttons and a straight pin. The contents of the box revealed its owner as a person not much bothered by a sense of order.

This impression was further confirmed when the contents of the rectangular partition were analysed: four slate pencils, one red and one black stick of sealing wax each with the maker's mark, and five more cleaved shafts. There was also a whole nutmeg and half of another that had been rasped at one end. Nutmeg rasp was sometimes used to improve the taste of sour wine. The same space also contained a fragment from a silver chain. Most surprising, however, were 392 straight pins.

The cleaved shafts were cleft at one end only, thus giving them the appearance of miniature crowbars. The form of the cleft was ideal for gripping a pin. The pins and shafts were perhaps used to play the so-called "scratch nose" game, in which the pins are placed in a heap on a table and the players try to extract one needle at a time without disturbing the others. The player with the least number of needles is the loser, and must be scratched on his nose with a shaft as punishment.

On the lid of the writing box were painted the letters AB in a retrograde beneath a coronet-shaped flower stand which could be taken for a baronet's crown. Was the owner a snob as well as a messy person?

The discovery of this box added a strong human dimension to the knowledge we had gained from the excavation. The records from *Lossen* revealed that the initials were those of lieutenant Anders Bose, one of the victims of the disaster.

References

Andersen, J., 1969, A new technique for archaeological field measuring. *Norwegian Archaeological Review*, Vol 2: 68-75

Christensen, A.E., 1969, The significance and practical value of the 3-point method, *Norwegian Archaeological Review*, Vol 2: 76-77

Molaug, S. and Scheen, R., 1983, *Fregatten Lossen, et kulturhistorisk skattkammer*, Norsk Sjøfartsmuseum monograph series no. 43

Röding, J.H., 1794-98, *Allgemeine Schiffswörkerbuch* Vol I

John M Bingeman

Invincible (1744-1758)

The following paper concerns the historical importance of the French built *Invincible* and the new knowledge acquired as a result of her ten year excavation.

Historical importance

There are varying opinions on the relative merits of English and French shipbuilding. It is fair to say that both shipbuilding industries had their strengths and that they both regularly cribbed ideas from the other. In the 1740s there was conflict in Britain between the Admiralty and Navy Board because of the shortcomings of our warships, and how their design might be improved. The passing of the 1745 Establishment did little to rectify the situation and dissension remained between the two authorities. Because of their differing views, the Establishment was rigorously enforced by the Navy Board and any divergence had to receive Privy Council approval. This had not been the case previously, when a certain amount of licence could be taken by Master Shipwrights.

Over the Channel, the French constructors, uninhibited by the constraints of any Establishment, were free to use new scientific knowledge to improve ship design. In the 1740s, the idea to build a new design of 74 gun ships was conceived; the first was the *Terrible*, built at Brest by Francis Coulon, and a further two were laid down at Rochefort. The second, designed by Morineau, was called *l'Invincible*, and launched on 21 October 1744. Her service with the French Navy was short. After a successful deployment to the West Indies, she fought off single handed a superior English Force of the *Plymouth* (60), *Strafford* (50) and *Lyme* (24). No mean feat against the English who were, on this occasion, convincingly out-gunned by *Invincible*. She returned safely to France with her convoy of eighty-one ships.

A year later, she was off again in support of an East India convoy. Unfortunately for the French, she was captured near Cape Finisterre when fighting off a much superior Force of 14 Ships of the Line under Admiral Lord Anson. While being towed back to Portsmouth, Anson sent his carpenter onboard to measure her, after commenting that she was "a prodigious fine ship, and vastly large". Back at home, and presumably on the instigation of Anson, the Admiralty tried to circumvent the 1745 Establishment, which had 'no mention of a ship of two and a half decks to carry 74 guns', and ordered two ships to her design. Both were cancelled for lack of funds when the war ended a few months later.

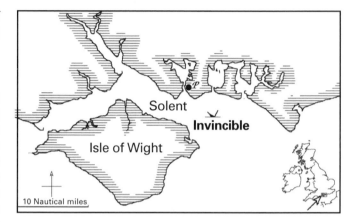

1 *Invincible* (1758) Wreck Site

However, *Invincible*'s method of steering with a rudder angle indicator prompted the Admiralty to issue a directive on 22 January 1747/8:

"*Invincible* a model showing in what manner she is fitted in regard to steering her, to send one to each yard and to cause all His Majesty's Ships to be fitted in that manner for the future."

An example of the indicator can be seen today in *Victory*.

No similar class of ship has existed previously, and after her capture, the authorities had not known how to 'rate' her, since she was larger than the second rates but only carried 74 guns. Her shortfall in guns was compensated for by her 32 pounders being six feet above the waterline; the English first and second rates' guns were only three to four feet above the waterline, preventing the use of their heaviest guns in all but the calmest of seas. Admirals, particularly Anson, were immediately convinced that this was the future 'way ahead' for English warship design. This was why *Invincible*'s capture was so important; it introduced 74s that were to be the backbone of the Fleet for nearly a century.

Presumably as a result of French influence, the English started building their first 74s in the early 1750s. It is worth noting that they were slightly smaller than the French models. They were not entirely successful and led to the Admiralty Board's decision on the 21 May 1757 to build the *Triumph* at Woolwich and the *Valiant* at Chatham, using *Invincible* as the model. To quote an extract from the letter of authority (Public Records Office 1757):

". . . and experience having shown that His Majesty's Ship the *Invincible* is in every respect, the very best ship of her Class, and

168

answers all purposes that can be desired of a Ship of War, We do therefore hereby desire & direct you to cause the two beforementioned Ships to be built by the Draught of the *Invincible*, and in every respect, of the same Scantlings notwithstanding any former Orders to the contrary;"

When Captain Rodney was sailing the new 74 gun ship *Dublin*, he complained that the rudder was too large and that the poop-deck lifted under the press of canvas (Spinney, 1969: 132-9). This illustrates the lack of technical understanding in English shipbuilding; clearly the English did not appreciate that by half copying the French they were introducing problems. Taking the rudder for example, the English ships had a 12 to 16 degree stern post and when they fitted the same size rudder to a French near vertical stern post, the English rudder was too effective and twice broke *Dublin*'s rudder head. The belief that English ships were stronger than their French counterparts is questionable, since *Invincible*'s deck did not lift under full sail. The fact that the majority of *Invincible*'s hanging knees were made of iron may have given her that extra strength. The design of French iron knees is of interest. After cleaning the corrosion from a main gun deck rising knee, we found a nut at its lower extremity which presumably had served as a tightening device during service (fig 2).

At first glance the French and English draughts seem similar; on examination, however, it is evident that the French designs have a fuller bow and slimmer stern; in other words a better hull for speed. According to Captain Bentley's sailing report dated 13 November 1752 (Public Records Office, 1752:SR), *Invincible* was capable of 13 knots; while contemporary British ships recorded speeds of no more than 11 knots. Benjamin Slade, the Surveyor at Plymouth and kinsman of Sir Thomas Slade, had been aware of the difference when writing to Anson about the recently captured 24 gun French privateer *Tiger*:

"I am strongly of opinion the present draughts of the 24 gunships are too full aft, and that the *Tiger* is as much the contrary, ..." (Staffordshire Records Office, 1747:LP)

In 1747, there had been complaints from sea officers about the poor sailing qualities of the new 24 gun ships designed by the Naval Surveyor, Sir Jacob Ackworth. The Admiralty Board decided to order two new 24 gun ships outside the Establishment. Since Anson and Benjamin Slade had already been discussing their shortcomings, it was no coincidence that it was Slade who was ordered to build a ship, in all respects a copy of the *Tiger*, with the greatest possible expedition. This can perhaps be seen as the precedent that, ten years later, allowed the Admiralty to swallow its pride and order two copies of the *Invincible*.

The building of *Valiant* at Chatham was recently commemorated by Chatham Historic Dockyard Trust setting up the £4M exhibition "Wooden Walls"; the gallery depicts *Valiant*'s building and exhibits *Invincible*'s artefacts. It is visual confirmation of *Invincible*'s importance in our Naval history.

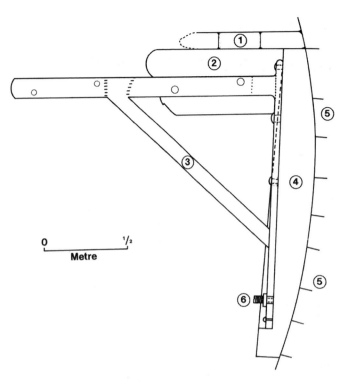

2 Iron knees were extensively used in the French built *Invincible*. The knee attached to LG-5 (5th deck beam on Lower Gun Deck) after the 20mm pine panelling had been removed.

1 - Three sections of deck planking
2 - Eroded deck beam
3 - Iron knee
4 - Oak pad piece
5 - Line of Ship's side inner planking
6 - Tightening screw

To some, it may be near heresy to suggest that French technology influenced English shipbuilding; however, it now seems that not only shipbuilding but also English gun design was influenced by the French!

In December 1755, the Office of Ordnance ordered *Invincible*'s thirty 18 pounders to be exchanged for 24 pounders (Priddy's Hard, 1755:IL). This order to fit heavier ordnance would at first sight seem foolhardy since it increased top weight and in action would cause extra strain to the ship's side. In fact, neither of these risks were taken.

The *London Magazine* of June 1747, reported that the French 64 gun ship *Mars* was captured with documents relating to experiments in which lighter guns with smaller charges were used to fire large shot. The French found that with smaller charges: "A bullet, which can just pass through a piece of timber, and loses almost all its motion thereby, has a better chance of rendering and fracturing it, than if it passed through it with a much greater velocity". The advantages were many; lighter guns were easier to operate and smaller charges not only saved powder but kept the guns cooler and quieter, "and at the same time more effectually injuring the Vessels of the Enemy" (*London Magazine* 1747: 258-9). The *Mars*'s documents, with Anson's blessing, were followed up by Mr Benjamin Robins,

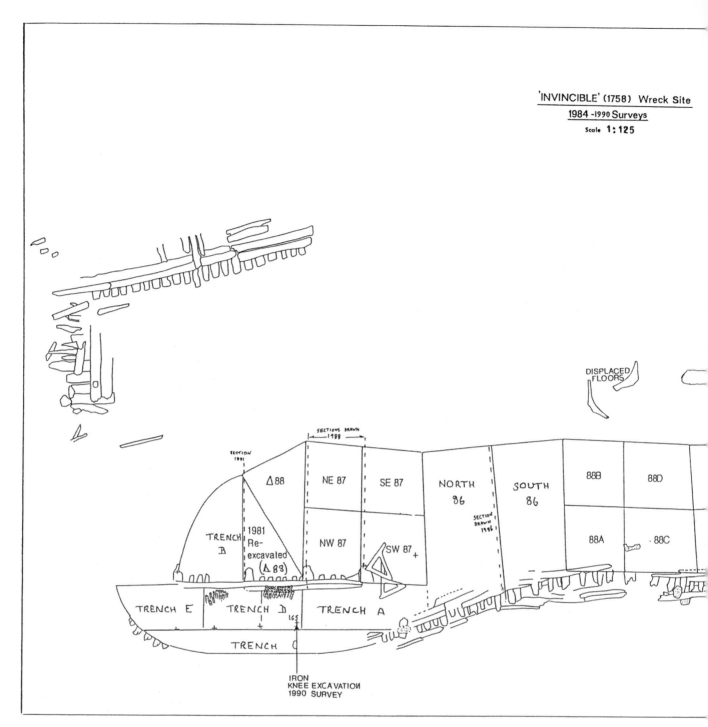

3 *Invincible's* pre-disturbance survey showing excavation trenches

a member of the Royal Society, who had been working on similar theories. The next we hear about these new guns was in the *Gentleman's Magazine* for August 1755, (XXV:376H): "Lord Anson and other Lords of the Admiralty have been down to Woolwich to see a proof of some new invented guns that are but half the ordinary weight and will do as much execution."

It seems likely that the Admiralty would request the Board of Ordnance to order the new light weight 24 pounders for trial in *Invincible*, since she was not subject to the constraining regulations of the Establishment. *Invincible's* ordnance stores list refers to "Quoins for quoining guns of the

new pattern" (National Maritime Museum, 1748/55:RUSI) and an Office of Ordnance letter about *Invincible* refers to giving, "...directions for the New 24 Pounder Carriages..." (Priddy's Hard, 1755:IL).

Invincible was also one of 13 ships selected to try out new cannon locks to speed up the rate of fire (Public Records Office, 1755:OL). The order gave instructions for the quarterdeck 9 pounders to be fitted with locks. Shortly after she ran aground six of these guns were thrown overboard "in order to bring her on an even keel" (Public Records Office, 1758a:IL). To the south of the wreck's present position there are magnetometer readings which optimistically might be

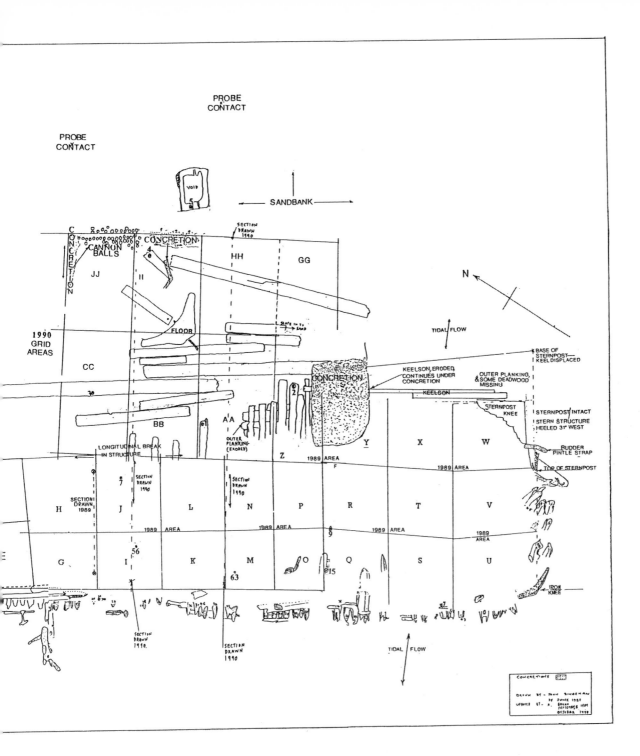

the quarterdeck guns complete with locks. One of *Pomone*'s (built 1805) 18 pounders on the Needles Site, Isle of Wight, still had a lock when recovered 171 years later. The trial of the locks required flints, and this would explain the finding on the *Invincible* site of over 2,000 such items which were too large for musket locks (Bingeman, 1989:41).

The driving force behind the many developments taking place at this time was Lord Anson, who has been given little credit by Naval Historians for his outstanding contribution. His four year circumnavigation of the world gave him a unique experience of ships, sea warfare and the knowledge to assess the worth of new ideas. I hope the newly formed

Anson Society can correct the lack of appreciation for this remarkable Admiral. As we have seen, it was Anson who captured *Invincible*, and it was he who had the understanding and foresight to ensure that the superior features of this vessel were incorporated into the ship designs of our own navy.

Excavating the Invincible

The initial pre-disturbance survey was carried out in May 1980. The methods used were rudimentary rope jackstays secured to iron stakes hammered into the sands surrounding what was correctly identified as the coherent hull structure.

4 His Majesty's ship *Invincible*, of 74 guns, one of six French Men of War taken the 3rd May 1747 by the British Fleet

This survey was carried out as an Adventure Training activity by a group of mainly young Naval sailors untrained in archaeology. Comparing it to a second survey carried out later by professional and experienced amateur archaeologists, it turned out to be surprisingly accurate.

Using the sailors' pre-disturbance survey, application was made to the Advisory Committee on Historic Wreck Sites for a protection order. The statutory instrument was issued on the 30 September 1980, the 22nd site to be protected under the 1973 Act. Interestingly, it was only the second site to be marked by a Government navigational buoy, the *Mary Rose* being the first. We were able to use the *Rose* buoy as a precedent when negotiating with the Department of Trade.

The Project team in 1980 consisted of Arthur Mack, the fisherman who found the wreck, John Broomhead, a local diver, and myself, the Chairman and Diving Officer of the Portsmouth RN Sub-Aqua Club whose members worked the site. The Project went through the usual domestic dramas: insufficient funds; poor quality volunteer work; an attempt by Portsmouth Museum to take over the Project on their terms, followed by the City Council's withdrawal of

conservation facilities which meant setting up our own conservation laboratory. Today, thirteen years on, the three of us are back where we started with no outside funding. We are proud of what we have achieved, and Arthur Mack and I continue our researches and work on the written archive.

The excavations of the coherent hull structure were carried out between 1981 and 1990 when the whole structure was emptied of artefacts. The plan (fig 4) shows the three metre square trenches that were dug using airlifts and how the rate of progress varied considerably over the years. During the three years following the Project's re-financing in September 1987, the majority of the excavations took place with four full-time paid divers as the core team.

When we started, the name of the wreck was unknown; it was only later when we had identified her, that we were able to compare our findings with the historical records. The transcript of the Court Martial held onboard the *Royal George* (Public Records Office, 1758b:CM), describes how the 1,800 ton *Invincible* with a 23 foot draught had flooded to a depth of 12 feet, and dug a 'grave' in the sandbank. The depth at this point is 18 feet today. After a severe pounding over three days, she was driven over on her port side beam ends by gale force winds. On the 8 May, a report to the Admiralty (National Maritime Museum, 1758:IL) discounts any possibility of salvage since, "the ship greatly twisted, waving and cambered", and was severely 'hogged' being six feet down by both the bow and stern. The upper works and starboard side broke up over the intervening 230 years and are now scattered to the NE. The excavations so far have been within the coherent hull, that is to say, the part of the structure still remaining in the original 'grave'. The grave now holds the bow down to the keel, the stern with part of the keel, and the connecting port side midship section down to the first futtock. Both the bow and stern sections feature two gunports. The rest of the ship's main gun deck, which had been bent upwards as a result of the 'hogging', could be among the untouched timbers lying to the NE. These findings are all consistent with the 8 May report by the Portsmouth Officers' to the Admiralty.

During the re-survey of the site, major hull structures were used as fixed points to triangulate the position of the timbers relative to each other. Artificial datum points were established where necessary for the sake of control and accuracy. During the 1983 and 1984 season a survey was carried out on the detached timbers lying to the NE. This area remains largely unexplored and could provide an area for worthwhile excavation in the future.

Artefacts of particular interest

The remarkably pristine condition of the wooden artefacts after 230 years underwater, surprises many. This can be attributed to the artefacts being sealed in an oxygen free environment, and to the shallowness of the site which means the low pressure reduces the saltwater penetration of the wood's cellular structure.

Many thousands of artefacts have been recovered; the following have been selected because of their general interest and historical/archaeological importance:

Rigging

A varied collection of rigging has been recovered: a massive two hundred weight "top block" identified by a carved wooden label marked 'TB', would have been used for hoisting the main yard; an unusual 'rack block', 58 inches long, containing five single blocks carved from the same piece of elm, marked appropriately "XXXXXVIII" and used for the control of the spritsails under the bowsprit; also a large collection of mushroom, fiddle, clew garnet, euphroe, heart, clump and snatch blocks of varying shapes and sizes. These latter items make the *Invincible* assemblage one of the most complete collections of mid-eighteenth century rigging blocks in existence. Many sizes of rope were excavated including parts of a 23 inch main hawser, sections of both 12 and 9 inch heavily tarred cable laid hawsers, as well as many smaller sizes of rope in complete bales, down to coils of one inch. Many of the boatswain's tools, such as fids and serving mallets were recovered, and two extremely messy barrels of odoriferous Swedish tar will never be forgotten by

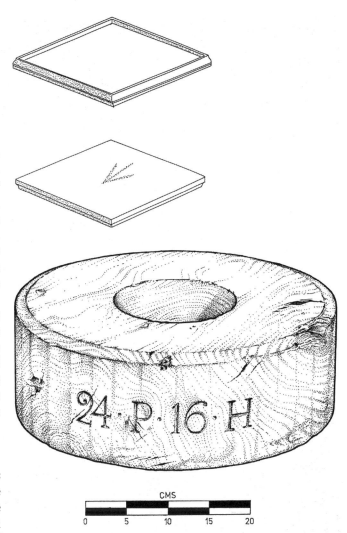

5 *Top* Square oak plate or platter, width 23 cm

6 *Below* 24lb gun carriage truck cut from a single piece of elm. See text for the significance of the markings

the divers who, unknowingly, covered themselves with the dreadful stuff. No wonder sailors were called 'Jack Tars'!

Navigation

Sand-glasses to record 14 and 28 seconds were used in conjunction with a log line to determine the ship's speed. A 'log chip' that I found was much smaller than expected and had a lead strip along the curved edge. In fact we found two leads and only one wooden chip, the first lead's holes did not match the holes in the chip but I was delighted when the second lead strip's holes matched the chip's holes perfectly. The chip is on display without the lead strip at Chatham, which is a pity since it is an extremely rare artefact.

Sounding leads in two sizes, 14 and 21lbs, were recovered; these are stamped with numerous broad arrows. Practically all the artefacts recovered have broad arrows, from leather shoes to a pewter spoon. Often the broad arrow is just roughly scratched on to the artefact and can be quite large, as seen on the blade of a shod shovel or on the side of a leather bucket. On rigging blocks they are much neater, usually stamped, or in the case of powder barrels burnt on, which seems surprising considering the risks involved.

Domestic

Some of the square oaken plates, or platters, had large broad arrows scratched underneath (fig 5). They measured 12 x 12 inches (256mm) and had a fiddle or lip to the edge. The plates caught the imagination of the public as they may explain the origin of the expression 'a square meal'.

Ordnance, accessories and related items

Fifty complete powder barrels were recovered. These were banded with hazel (much weakened) and copper which had reacted with the gunpowder to form a brittle copper oxide band of no mechanical strength. I am hopeful that the Curator of the rotunda may one day be able to identify the various markings burnt into the barrel ends.

From the forward Magazine came two bronze adzes and two brass 'setters' to remove the bands from the powder barrels. In Glascock's Officers' Manual, it states that 'setters' should be made of wood, but this was not the case with those recovered from *Invincible*.

Tampions, in spools of sixes, recovered from the Gunner's Store suggest that tampions were expendable. The practice may have been to remove the tampion with the first round to save time when preparing the gun for action.

'Cases of wood for Cartridges' were used to carry the charges from the magazine to the guns. Apart from plaster replicas in a ceiling at Boscawen's home at Hatchlands near Guildford, I know of no other surviving examples. Perhaps this is not surprising, since the cases were made of poplar and had the consistency of *papier mâché* when raised. Our Conservation Officer, Simon Aked, found them extremely difficult to stabilize.

Naval gunnery equipment was supposedly inter-changeable between all warships, and there is considerable correspondence from the 'Office of Ordnance' instructing "the carriages to be lowered to fit *Invincible*'s ports". A large quoin marked "INVINCIBLE 32.P" had a 'divot' on each side to make handling easier, and since it has a ship's name, it is assumed to be non-standard to match the modified carriages. Another smaller quoin was wedge shaped with a burnt broadarrow mark and bears no ship's name. A similar style quoin with the four distinctive 'divots' marked "SAN JOSEPH 32P" came from another captured ship, the *San Josef*, a Spanish 112 gun ship taken by Nelson in 1797 and now on display on the Island of Tresco, Isles of Scilly, in the Valhalla Exhibition.

Carriage trucks are made from solid pieces of elm and not fabricated like most reproduction wheels. Interestingly, they appear to have been cut using an adze with small neat chip marks. Some of the trucks found in a forward store were marked on the outside rim. One example is stamped "24 P 16 H", meaning: 24 pounder, 16 inch diameter, and 'H' for hind or rear gun carriage wheel (fig 6). A front wheel is marked 'F' for fore.

Many of the gunnery artefacts come in three sizes for the 9, 24 and 32 calibre guns. Examples are: rammer heads, tampions, sponge bodies, gun wads, gun carriage stools (fig 7), and cartridge cases. Aprons of lead have been recovered in two sizes.

Hand grenades ready for use were found in a lead lined box. Fuse markings must warrant a study in themselves. An unused fuse with a solid base, confirms the method of tamping down the fuse substance before cutting off the stem at an appropriate length to match the delay required. The procedure was standardised in 1752 (Caruana, 1979:23). Our grenade fuses had flannel and canvas cappings, while Caruana describes caps of cured paper first, with a second layer of brown paper. It is interesting to note the different sealing arrangements found on Naval grenades compared to those used by the Army.

A fourteen foot slow match, coiled and covered in dark red fearnought, had a 'feed hole' on its circumference to allow the match to be pulled out as it burnt (fig 8). While such items were known to exist, none had ever been found.

Clothing and personal belongings

The large number of leather shoes come in at least six different styles. Some have a DC marking standing for 'deceased clothing', showing that they had been sold to raise money for a widow or mother. The purpose of the DC mark is to prove that it has been a legitimate transfer of property. Today, we have the same mark but it is more tactfully known as 'declared clothing'. A pair of wooden shoe formers used in the manufacture of shoes, suggests that there was a cobbler onboard, who not only repaired shoes but also made them. Many of the shoes had been repaired and without exception, the heels had been secured with wooden nails. A lady's patten has also been recovered; this raises the question whether women were travelling on the Expedition to Canada, *Invincible*'s destination at the time of loss.

Prior to the *Invincible*'s excavation the dating of Army buttons was thought to be precise. Unfortunately, the Regiment of Foot numbered buttons predated accepted dates for their introduction. I am not sure where we stand with Button Experts, many of whom do not accept that buttons from the 6, 13, 14, 24, 30, 39, 43, 57, 59, 64 regiments, and some others, could have been in use as early as 1758. Another button with a single 'H' makes one wonder if this belonged to one of Lord Howe's servants or even to Major Sir William Howe himself, who was known to have been travelling to North America with the Expedition; the Howe family signet ring was found in the same area of the wreck.

Miscellaneous

Over 160 of the 180 besom brushes that were carried for 'breaming' have been recovered (fig 9). The practice of breaming, or burning off the growth when careening a ship, was essential despite the risks involved. The besom brushes were found closely packed together in a store just aft of the Gunner's Store on the port side.

7 Gun carriage stool for a 9 pounder with an 8½ foot barrel

8 A slow match within a maroon coloured double lined fearnought pouch. The LH sketch illustrates how the match pulls out from the centre while passing through its own coil

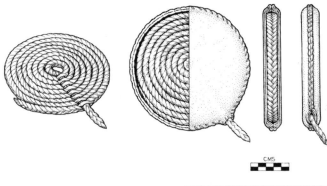

9 One of the 160 besom brushes recovered; they were used for 'breaming', length 69 cm

Miniature Barrels measuring 225 to 250mm long, with end diameters of 40mm increasing to around 52mm in the centre, are just one of many identification puzzles (fig 10). The most likely explanation seems to be a 'writing kit'. Fine sand in the barrels was perhaps used as a blotting medium; and a black gooey substance, found at one end turned out to be 97% carbon and iron with a trace of gallic acid, the ingredients of ink. A 1764 London shop sign for Joseph Pitcher advertised the trade of a 'colourman or oilman'; the signboard displayed a 'Good Woman' (a beautifully painted lady in a long dress without a head) with barrels resembling *Invincible*'s miniature barrels hanging on either side (Heal, 1947:55). It is possible that writing and painting materials were packaged in similar barrels. The only other known miniature barrel was found in a Navigator's chest in the *Stirling Castle* wrecked on the Goodwin Sands in 1703.

Achievements

Chatham Historic Dockyard Exhibition "Wooden Walls" is our premier display and since 1981, the Project has had a window exhibit at the Royal Naval Museum on the walkway to the Museum's Main Entrance. Over the years we have had loan exhibitions in Anson's ancestral home Shugborough, the Boscawen home at Hatchlands, Weymouth Museum, and abroad in Canada and Germany, to name just a few.

In 1983 we funded a £4,500 'travelling exhibition' which was displayed at Portsmouth, Chichester District Museum, and on HMS *Unicorn* at Dundee, but despite writing to over 150 museums, it failed to catch on and did not justify the considerable cost and effort involved. When running a Project like *Invincible*, it is the human resources that limit what can be done. Five out of six of us were holding down full time jobs, and only the Project's Conservation Officer was full time. When working on an exhibition, it takes all the effort away from diving, and conservation has to mark time. The diving was in fact less of a problem, as two to three weeks each year was more than sufficient to swamp the conservation laboratory for a further year.

We made a first class choice in funding Brian Lavery to write the definitive book (Lavery, 1988). The cost was around £20K and by printing a thousand each of soft and hard back copies we expected to break even after selling three-quarters. The first interim report appeared in the *International Journal of Nautical Archaeology* (Bingeman, 1985). Much of the content of this paper will make the basis of the second interim report.

Probably the most successful fund raiser was our mobile exhibition bus. It contained four glass cabinets to display artefacts, with a sales counter behind the driver's seat. To make it successful, it needed one of the divers to talk visitors through the various display cases, as their enthusiasm for the Project created a good sales climate. The shop sold musket shot, old rope, timber pieces of uncertain purpose, and a host of souvenirs, such as 'T' shirts, Biros, pencils, etc. Attempts to man the Bus with volunteers was financially disappointing; they lacked that important personal touch.

Countless lectures have been given and I have bookings into 1994. We prefer not to charge a fee, but rather to invite a donation for the Project's funds. If appropriate, we take advantage of the lectures to sell books, musket shot and souvenirs.

10 Miniature barrels were 'writing kits', length 23 cm

Future

The Project was funded by 'Invincible Conservations (1744-1758) Limited' which unfortunately, owing to financial pressures, has ceased to exist. The Company had a formal agreement with Chatham Historic Dockyard Trust; the Curator has confirmed that the Trust wishes to remain associated with future work on the site. The intention is that the written archive will go to Chatham, but I still have much work remaining before transfer can be completed.

In 1991, less than three-quarters of a mile from the site, a new sewage outfall came on stream which discharges 17 million gallons of sewage every 24 hours. This has obviously created a health risk to divers, so until satisfactory tests have been made to establish the degree of risk involved, diving has been suspended. The site continues to be monitored by the Licensee and the Advisory Diving Unit. To comply with European Economic Community's regulations, Southern Water Authority plans to build a sewage treatment plant in 7 or 8 years time.

Finally, there is the vexed question of selling artefacts. My background as a Naval Officer has taught me to apply common sense to all situations. The ideal would have been to have kept all the finds together; realistically, however, the quantity of identical artefacts and the financial pressures have led to a compromise. We set up an agreement with Chatham Historic Dockyard Trust for their Curator to have first pick each year of all artefacts and to take at least one of every type. The remainder are sold with a significant number going to maritime museums around the world. Some may say that we should not have started if we could not afford to keep the collection together. I doubt if the financial climate will ever improve sufficiently to achieve this ideal. Meanwhile, the seabed is gradually being lowered by dredging which removes something like 2000 tons of aggregate a day from the Eastern Solent; if this continues the site could be destroyed within 50 years.

In 1979 when the site was discovered, pillaging started immediately. By protecting it under the Designation of Wrecks Act, we saved it from further desecration. By setting up the Project, we have excavated and conserved artefacts from probably the most important Warship of the mid-18th Century yet discovered.

Acknowledgements

I would like to record my thanks to Arthur Mack for valuable research information used in this paper; to Dr Margaret Rule CBE FSA, the Project's Archaeological Director for her support and advice over many years; and to my Wife for her help with editing the paper.

References

Bingeman, J.M., 1985; *International Journal of Nautical Archaeology and Underwater Exploration* 14.3 191-210

Bingeman, J.M., 1989; Gunlocks: Their Introduction to the Navy. In Smith, R.D. (Editor) *British Naval Armaments* (Royal Armouries Conference Proceedings 1) 41-44

Caruana, A.B., 1979; *British Artillery Ammunition* (Museum Restoration Service, Bloomfield, Canada)

Gentleman's Magazine, August 1755; *Historical Chronicle*

Heal, Sir A., 1974; *The Signboards of Old London Shops* (Batsford, London)

Lavery, B., 1988; *The Royal Navy's First Invincible*, (Invincible Conservations (1744-1758) Limited, Portsmouth)

London Magazine, June 1747; *Proposal in relation to our Ship-Guns*
National Maritime Museum, 1748-55; RUSI/6

National Maritime Museum, 1758; *Admiralty 'in' Letters*, POR/D/13, 8 May

Priddy's Hard, Gosport, 1755; *Respective Officers at Portsmouth 'in' Letters* 130, 23 December

Public Records Office, 1752; *Admiralty Sailing Reports*, Adm 95/25, No 67

Public Records Office 1755; *Admiralty 'out' Letters*, Adm 2/219, 21 October

Public Records Office, 1757; *Admiralty 'out' Letters*, Adm 95/12, 21 May

Public Records Office, 1758a; *Admiralty 'in' Letters*, Adm 1/1489, 29 February

Public Records Office, 1758b; *Courts Martial*, Adm 1/5297, 6 March

Spinney, D., 1969; *Rodney* (Allen & Unwin, London)

Staffordshire Country Records, 1747; *Earl of Lichfield's Paper*, D615/P(S)1/9/22, 21 July

Javier F. Garcia Cano (Director, Albenga Foundation, Buenos Aires)

HM Sloop of war *Swift*

Introduction

HM sloop of war *Swift*, 263 tons, was built beside the Thames in 1762 and launched on 1 March 1763. She had a length of 29.4m, a beam of 7.75m, and a height of 4.03m. She carried 14 6-pounders and 12 swivel-guns and had a crew of 125. She was designed by Sir Thomas Slade (figs 1 and 2) but based, it is believed, on the lines and layout of the French vessel *Epreuve* which was taken by the British Navy in 1760 before the Seven Years War.

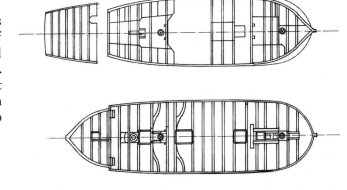

1 and 2 HM sloop of war *Swift*, built 1762. 14 guns. Designed by Sir Thomas Slade

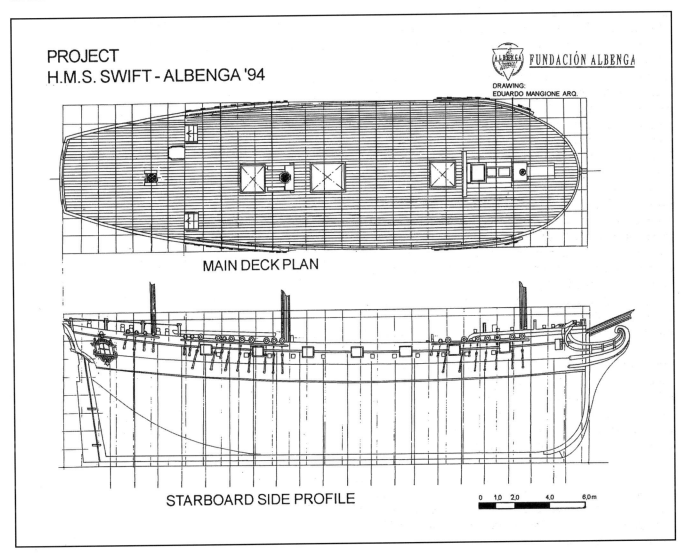

PROJECT
H.M.S. SWIFT - ALBENGA '94

FUNDACIÓN ALBENGA
DRAWING:
EDUARDO MANGIONE ARQ.

MAIN DECK PLAN

STARBOARD SIDE PROFILE

0   1,0   2,0   4,0   6,0m

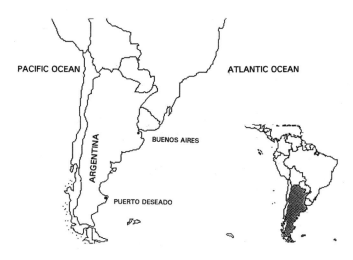

Discovery of the wreck

In March 1982, she was found by the *Comision de Busqueda y Rescate de la Corbeta Swift* (The Commission for the Search and Recovery of the Sloop *Swift*), a local group specially established for the task. In 1986 Mrs Maria Isabel Sanguinetti, the Director of the 'Mario Brozosky' Regional Museum of Puerto Deseado, contacted the Argentine Committee of the International Council on Monuments and Sites (ICOMOS) to ask for its help with work on the preservation of the wreck and its contents. They were concerned that the items which had been recovered by the team had not received any proper conservation care, and, as a result, were beginning to deteriorate. Because of the lack of national support and the absence of salt water conservation laboratories in Argentina, ICOMOS recommended to the Government of Santa Cruz Province that no more artefacts should be recovered and that no attempt should be made to raise the hull until adequate core-funding and conservation facilities were in place. ICOMOS did, however, urge that the site should be fully surveyed. The aims of such an examination would be to:

i) confirm the identification of the wreck

ii) determine the state and disposition of the remains

iii) prepare a site plan of the visible remains

iv) properly document those items that had already been raised.

Four seasons of survey work were conducted on the wreck (1986-1989) which was found to be on her keel in 9m to 15m of water in conditions of poor visibility (0.50 to 1.50m). The wreck was confirmed as the *Swift*.

The remains were found to be remarkably complete and in a relatively good state of preservation. 25m of the vessel

3 *Above left* The *Swift* was lost in 1769 at Puerto Deseado, Argentina, following a visit to Port Egmont (Saunders Island) in the Falklands

4 *Left* Puerto Deseado. The reef upon which the *Swift* sank can be clearly seen about one-third of the way down the picture

5 *Below* Map of the shore showing the reef and the disposition of the wreck

The *Swift* arrived at Port Egmont, Saunders Island, in the Falkland Islands in 1769, after which she sailed to the east coast of South America where she was caught in a sudden storm. Her captain, George Farmer, decided to head for the shelter of the River Deseado near modern day Puerto Deseado in the north of Santa Cruz Province, Argentina (fig 3). Here she hit an uncharted rock and sank (figs 4 and 5).

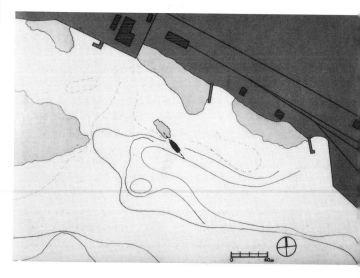

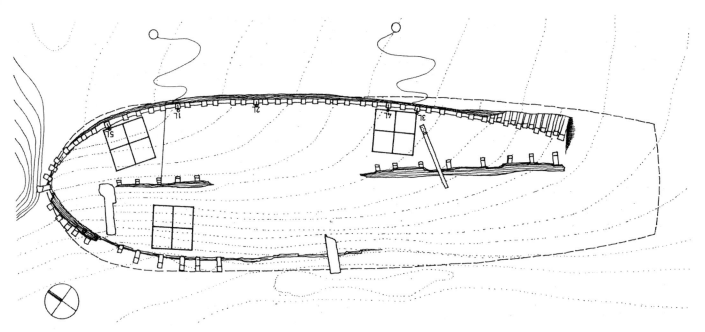

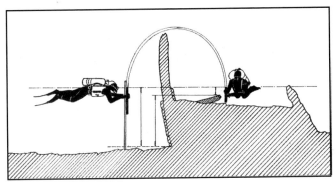

6 Plan of the site made during the 1986-89 campaigns

7 Section through the wreck showing divers establishing levels with a tube full of air

were showing above the seabed to heights of between 1.8m to 3.0m. It was judged that 7m of hull was missing from the stern, mostly from the starboard side (fig 6). Of particular note was the bow area which was well preserved because of its position next to the reef which acted to deflect the currents.

The deterioration of the stern and parts of the port side can be explained by their exposure to the currents which can run at up to 3 knots. Most of the timbers from the poop area have been well dispersed by the currents. Other parts of the vessel have fallen into the hull area.

A grid was built over the site to map and record the wreck. It was made from 100mm diam. plastic tubing and divided up into rectangles of 2m x 8m. Within this fixed framework a mobile grid of 2m x 2m was constructed, which itself was divided into 1m x 1m squares. Structure and objects were mapped from the grid system by basic triangulation. Outside the wreck area 2 metre long metal stakes were hammered into the seabed for use as datum points. Each stake was positioned in relation to known fixed points along the vessel's starboard side.

8 Sandglass recovered during the 1989 season

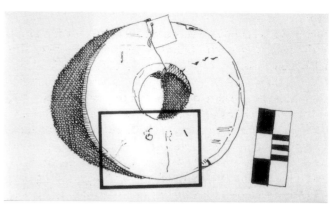

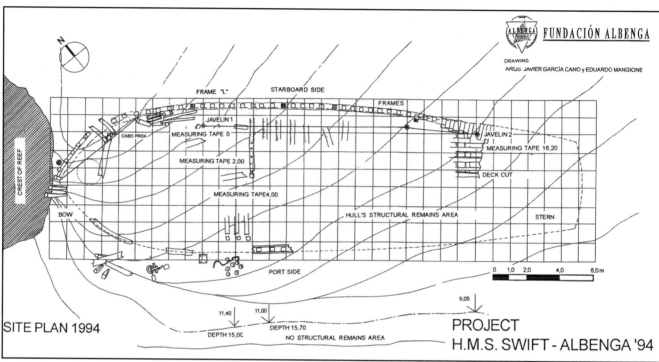

9 *Top* Truck from a gun carriage with detail showing the inscription 6P which indicates that the carriage supported a six pounder

10 *Above* Plan made during the 1994 season

11 *Below* Starboard view of wreck taken during the 1994 season

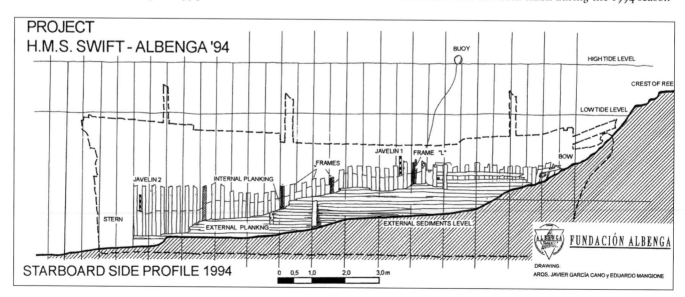

Finds

Since 1982 nearly 90 objects have been recovered, mainly by the local divers who found the wreck. Because of the lack of conservation some items were lost to deterioration. Now less than 70 survive. An important part of the ICOMOS programme has been to document fully these pieces.

Most of the time during the four seasons (1986-89) was spent preparing an accurate site plan. Some excavation took place, during the course of which a number of artefacts were recovered. These included two sand glasses (fig 8), pieces of rope, shoe fragments, ceramic bowls and plates, rigging blocks and a caulking hammer. Only objects that were at risk of being lost during the off-season were recovered. The only tools were a waterdredge and our hands. Funding came from the Government of Santa Cruz Province.

All work ended in 1989 as a result of a dramatic decline in the nation's economy. Since that time archive research has continued (both in Buenos Aires and London).

Conclusion

The *Swift* is important for the range and quality of her contents and also for the information she will give on both British and French naval design and construction. In particular she offers a rare opportunity for archaeologists and historians to study an 18th century, small burthen man-of-war. Furthermore, she is one of the best preserved submerged historic wrecks in Argentine waters, and as such will give valuable insight into the maritime activities of the Late Colonial Period of Argentine history At another level this project is important as the first scientific underwater excavation in Argentina, and will serve, it is hoped, as both a 'school' and source of inspiration to others in the country who may wish to become involved in underwater archaeology.

Notes

Since this report was written in early 1994 there has been a further season of excavation, the results of which are featured in figs 5, 10 and 11.

David C. Switzer (Plymouth State College, University System of New Hampshire)

The *Defence*

Introduction

Sometime between midnight and 1400 hours on 14 August 1779, in the fourth year of the American Revolution, HMS *Camilla* was standing off the entrance to an inlet on the then far eastern coast of the State of Massachusetts (at that time Massachusetts included what is today the State of Maine). *Camilla* had been in pursuit of an American privateer; that vessel was now trapped with no means of escape. A boat dispatched to investigate the situation returned to *Camilla* with the news that the privateer was on fire. Minutes later the sound of an explosion was heard. The privateer had been scuttled to prevent impending capture.[1]

The scuttling of the American ship was not an isolated incident; rather, it signalled the climax of a chain of events that had commenced two months earlier. Back in June, word had reached Boston that a British force had occupied the small coastal community of Majabagaduce some 170 miles to the east on the upper reaches of Penobscot Bay which indents the present day coast of Maine (fig 1).

Massachusetts responded to the news of the invasion by organizing what was to be the largest combined military and naval effort ever mounted by the Americans during the War for Independence. Known as the Penobscot Expedition, the force consisted of nearly 1,000 militia and a fleet of forty-three vessels, including three Continental Naval vessels, three state naval vessels, twelve privateers and some twenty supply and transport vessels (Mayhew, 1974).

When the armada reached its destination a siege ensued; the small British garrison, behind hastily-built fortifications, was surrounded. The final advance by the Americans never took place because of the timely arrival of a Royal Navy relief squadron. Upon the approach of the five men-of-war, including one 64-gun ship, the Americans broke off the siege and evacuated the troops. With the British in pursuit, the American fleet sailed towards the mouth of the Penobscot River. By the end of the day, the British had won a significant naval victory without the loss of a life or a ship. The victory, however, produced few prizes; of the forty-three American vessels, only two were captured. The Penobscot River by evening was illuminated by burning hulks. One of the last American vessels to be scuttled was the privateer *Defence* which had been pursued by HMS *Camilla*. A 170 ton brig or brigantine, newly launched at Beverly, Massachusetts, *Defence* was one of the last vessels to join the Penobscot Expedition on what may well have been her maiden voyage.

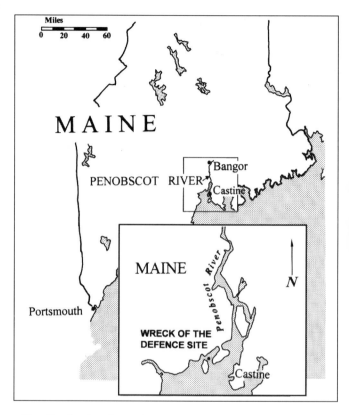

1 New England and Penobscot Bay

The remains of *Defence* were discovered in 1972 during a sonar survey of the inlet, known today as Stockton Harbor (fig 1). Across Penobscot Bay at Maine Maritime Academy in Castine (the original site of Majabagaduce), Professor Dean Mayhew had done extensive research on the aftermath of the Penobscot Expedition. It was his work that had prompted the sonar search carried out by a small group of faculty and students representing the Maritime Academy and Massachusetts Institute of Technology.

The discovery of a wreck was reported to the Maine State Museum. The team was given a permit to conduct an exploratory survey of the site. Probe excavations revealed a considerable amount of hull structure deeply buried under an overburden of silt and mud. Finds recovered from the hull were remarkably well-preserved owing to the prevailing anaerobic environment and included barrel parts, shoes, pulley blocks, grape-shot stools and two cannons.

A task force organized by the State Museum was given the duty of recovering the material culture from the hull and recording the construction details of a heretofore unseen product of an eighteenth century American shipyard. The team included the Institute of Nautical Archaeology, Maine Maritime Academy and the State Museum. Maine Maritime Academy was to serve as the base of operations and would supply logistical support and technical assistance. The Museum would be responsible for the conservation, care and display of the artefacts. The Institute of Nautical Archaeology would be responsible for the running of the excavations which began in 1975 and continued until 1981.

The site and excavation goals

The investigation of the wrecksite in 1975 revealed that as much as 40% of the vessel's structure was intact. The hull itself was found to be resting in the mud with a 15 degree list to port. In the bow, test trenches revealed numerous barrel parts. Projecting above the mud was the stump of the foremast; immediately behind it was the brick cooking stove, complete with copper cauldron. Forward of the mainmast stump could be seen the upper level of the shot locker and the adjacent bilge well (fig 2).

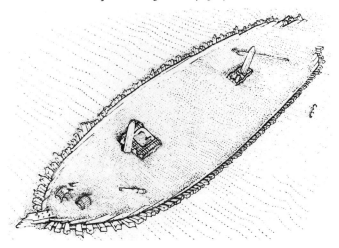

2 A view of *Defence* as it would have appeared to the Maine Maritime Academy team had there been perfect visibility (*P. Hentschal*)

3 1975 site plan (*D. Switzer*)

Coincident with test excavations, the first steps were taken to develop a site plan. Although the high tide depth of the wreck was no more than 24ft, visibility was found to be extremely limited and upon disturbance of the mud and silt, non-existent. The sea-bed surrounding the wreck proved to be featureless, barren of any outcrops that might have served as survey stations. Mapping of the site was, therefore, completed by tape-measure triangulation. When completed, the site plan (fig 3) provided the first opportunity to see the wreck in its entirety; it had a maximum beam of 22ft and extended 72ft from the stem to the point aft where the structure terminated.

The 1975 field season saw the implementation of the basic methods and operational procedures that were to be followed as the excavation progressed throughout the hull. An airlift proved to be the most effective tool for removing the natural overburden as well as the uppermost level of ballast, which comprised small rocks and pebbles (fig 4). Later, heavier ballast was raised by means of bucket lines.

During the same season, test-excavations were carried out within grids emplaced at the bow, midship and stern. When full-fledged excavation began in 1976 a more refined system of control and provenance plotting was initiated. Supported above the sea-bed by vertical uprights, a levelled grid frame of 5ft squares served as a datum plane. Within a grid square the provenance of each find was plotted and recorded in two dimensions, horizontally and vertically within a particular grid square quadrant. The former provided a plan view while the latter gave its depth within the hull below the datum plane.

The recording of specific features on a limited basis began in 1975. Efforts to photographically document structural details proved to be unreliable. Ultimately, plan view, isometric and perspective drawings of structure proved to be the best means of fully recording the hull (figs. 5, 6). Augmenting *in situ* documentation, structural items such as knees, deck beams, frames, floor timbers and ceiling were brought to the surface and drawn to scale. Following the recording process, the items were re-deposited in designated areas within the hull. Other structural items such as the foremast stump, a section of the bow including a

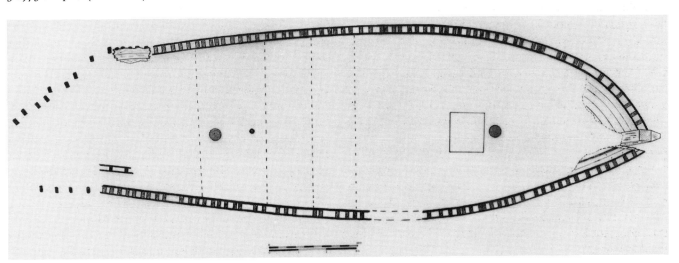

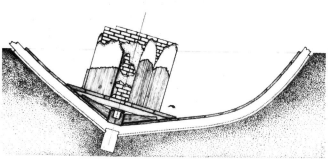

4 *Left* Airlift and sieve box *(D. Switzer)*

5 *Below* Galley cookstove and transverse section of the hull. Note the angle of deadrise *(P. Hentschal)*

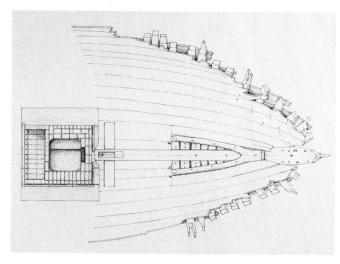

6 Plan view of bow with breasthook, cookstove and details of ceiling planking *(P. Hentschal)*

knighthead and a hawse hole, and disassembled parts of the shotlocker/bilge well, were transported to the Museum for further examination and documentation.

Beginning in 1976, and at the termination of every following season, exposed hull areas were sheathed with plastic sheets and then backfilled with loose and bagged sand.

Hull construction and design

So far archival research has provided no information as to the identity of the builder of *Defence*. Apart from her burthen tonnage (170 tons), her armament (sixteen 6-pounders), and her rig (variously described as a brig or brigantine), the historical record is silent. From the hull remains it has been possible to learn something of the basic details of her construction. In addition there is structural evidence that has prompted speculation regarding the method of construction as well as certain specific design features (for a full, detailed interpretation of the hull see Switzer, 1981 b).

The builder of *Defence* used three or four varieties of wood. The frames, stem pieces, deck beams, breasthook and deadwoods, were of white oak, as was the exterior sheathing and ceiling. The deck beams were supported by lodging and hanging knees (none of the latter were recorded) (Wyman, 1981, 90, 91), some of oak and others of hackmatack or larch. Only fragments of deck planking have been found; they were of oak, pine and fir. The one intact deck beam that was recovered revealed that the deck of *Defence* was slightly cambered. Its curve indicated that, at mid-point, the deck was approximately 2 inches higher than at the waterway (Wyman, 1981, 90). Oak and pine were utilized in the construction of inboard structures. The brick galley stove stood on a platform of heavy oak planks. Encasing the stove on three sides were 2½ inch thick 'pumpkin' pine boards, some as wide as 25 inches. Similar pine boards were used to build the shot locker and adjoining bilge-pump well located forward of the mainmast. The mast stumps were of white pine. Both had been hewn octagonally and were banded with iron just above the tenon which was stepped into the keelson. Both mast-steps were braced with oaken crutches that butted the steps on either side.

Naturally curved timber was used extensively in the construction of the hull. In addition to the knees, natural curves were found in floor timbers, futtocks and the inner and outer stem. The most striking example of the use of such timber was the breasthook, which was fashioned from an oak crotch and had been adzed on only one side to assure a close fit against the bow ceiling.

To rip planks from logs, the builder must have had access to a mechanical 'up and down' saw. Evidence of this is based on the even pattern of the vertical kerf marks found on ceiling and other planks.

Concerning the fastenings. Iron was used within the hull; ¾ inch diameter drift-bolts secured the breasthook, keelson and deadwood in place as well as the beams to their knees. Nails or spikes, varying in size from ⅜ inch to ½ inch, fastened the ceiling to the frames. Eight-sided oak trunnels of 1⅛ inch diameter secured the outer sheathing to the frames. Their heads were wedged with square or diamond shaped wedges. Trunnels used for fastening together frame floors and futtocks were also eight-sided but were unwedged.

Turning now to those aspects of the physical evidence that require speculative interpretation. Two questions have influenced the interpretation of the structure: was *Defence* a hastily constructed vessel that was perhaps considered by her owners to be an expendable investment; or, was she designed to be a fast sailing vessel? To answer these questions we combined historical archive information with our archaeologically-derived information.

American ships during the Colonial era were not notable for the excellence of their construction and durability. The majority of schooners, brigantines, and brigs built during the Revolution were cheaply made, fast sailing and expendable (Chapelle, 1935, 9-10). In the case of *Defence* a number of features suggested hasty construction (fig 6). The breasthook, perfunctorily adzed for a close fit, may be such an indicator. Another is the fact that many frames still had bark attached. The fastening of the ceiling was also informative: in the bow, the nail pattern was fairly regular, but beyond frames 6 and 7 the planking was secured by only a single nail in every third or fourth frame. Runs of planking as long as five or six feet are devoid of nails, perhaps indicative of a wartime iron shortage.

Other evidence of shortcuts, even perhaps of shoddy or unskilled workmanship, can be seen in the shot locker and bilge-well (fig 7; Switzer, 1981 a, 81). The locker and well were a narrow, rectangular assemblage which incorporated the mainmast. Divided approximately at midpoint by a partition, the forward section of the structure served as the bilge-well; one octagonally hewn pump pipe was still erect. Aft of the well was the shot locker. At its base the locker/well, was longitudinally bisected by the keelson. Upon recovery and reassembly it was found that the notches cut to receive the keelson were misaligned by an inch or two. The pine boards making up the sides were also ill-fitted and crudely sawn. Without comparative evidence it is difficult to account for what appears to be clumsy carpentry.

An example of inboard structure that exhibited more substantial and painstaking construction practices was the galley stove/hearth. Built of brick, faced with pine boards and standing 5 feet high with the hearth facing aft, the stove was an impressive feature, as was the copper cauldron which was recovered and conserved.

Other details of careful craftsmanship were evident. For example, the sharp edges on the keelson, mast step crutches

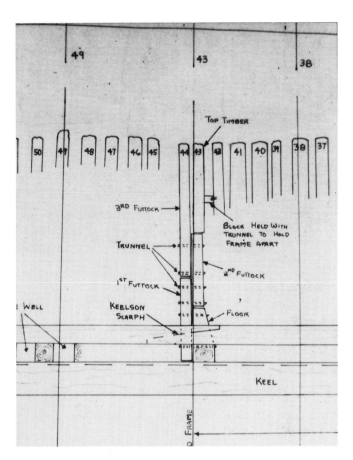

8 Mould frame details (*D. Wyman*)

and deadwood were all neatly bevelled or chamfered. One small knee and a piece of unidentified inboard structure featured a beaded trim. Fragments of what may have been carefully planed trim or finish work were also recovered.

Recently discovered documents suggest that *Defence*'s last-minute outfitting had to be hastily completed for her to be ready for duty in the Penobscot Expedition. The blend of scrupulous and less than careful attention to details may be indicators of eleventh hour preparations.

Speculation also weighs heavily when considering the design of *Defence* and the method of construction. With regard to design, comparative information can be derived from the plans of a smaller but similar American vessel of the same period. This vessel was a privateer built and captured in 1779 and later put into Royal Naval service as HMS *Swift*. Preserved at the National Maritime Museum, Greenwich, the lines of *Swift* were included in Charnock's *History of Marine Architecture* and much later were republished by Howard Chapelle (1935, 27) who described *Swift* as a 'highly developed class of ship with very good lines and moderate power'. Certain recorded features of *Defence* bear a striking similarity to those of *Swift*.

A similarity can be seen between the deadrise of *Swift* and that of *Defence* (obtained by means of recording seven transverse sections inside the hull). The midship deadrise of *Swift* was 30 degrees; that of *Defence*, measured at frames 17 through 49 averaged 25 degrees (Chapelle, 1930, 21-24). *Swift*'s bow may have been a bit sharper than that of

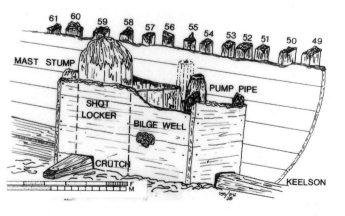

7 Shot locker/bilge well assemblage (*D. Switzer*)

Defence. The fact that the first eight frames in the bow of *Defence* were canted, as opposed to being hawse pieces, indicated that the vessel was not bluff bowed or 'apple-cheeked' (Wyman 1981, 90). Other parallels between *Swift* and *Defence* were noted. The inner angles of their stems were almost identical; mast and stove locations were proportionally alike and the moulded beam of each was similar - *Swift's* being 20ft 5 inches and that of *Defence* 22ft

1 inch. Measured between perpendiculars, *Swift's* length was 75ft. 7 inches while that of *Defence* was 78ft 7 inches. (Chapelle, 1930, 21). In tonnage *Defence* at 170 tons exceeded *Swift* by 27 tons.

The lines of both vessels, suggests that to their builders, speed had priority over hull capacity. This raises another intriguing issue. *Swift* has been described as a prototype of later Baltimore Clippers, as well as a development of the

9 Sheer and half breadth plan of the hull of the *Defence* including transverse sections (*D. Wyman*)

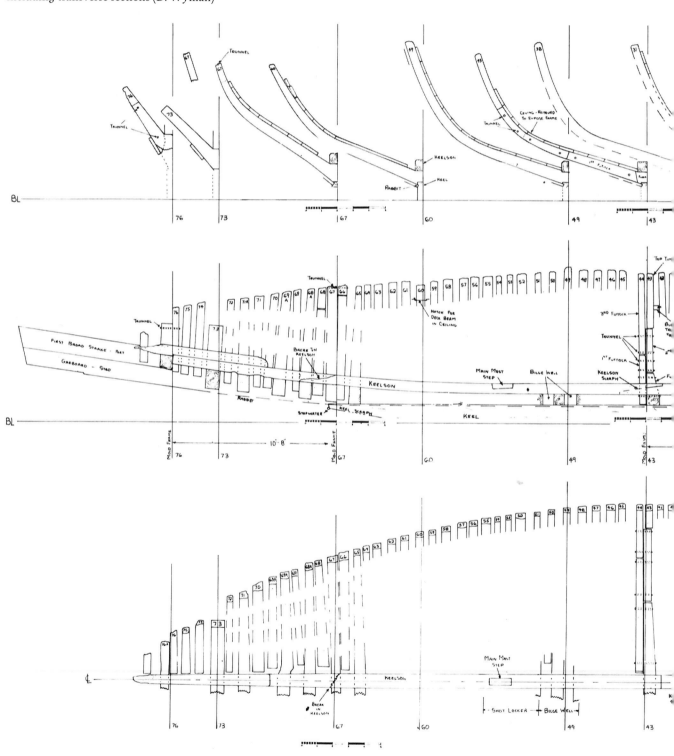

186

Chesapeake-designed or 'Virginia-built' craft, the latter being sharp, fast vessels which exhibited design traits seen in earlier Bermudian and West Indian sloops. Although built in Massachusetts, *Defence* seems to have been the outcome of the migrating design trends from the Chesapeake area (Chapelle, 1930, 34).

With regard to the techniques of construction that were employed by the builder of *Defence*, these appear to have deviated from traditional building methods, and, as already noted, there are also examples of sub-standard workmanship. After the keel was laid nine mould frames were set up; these have been identified as heavy composite (double futtock) frames (fig 8). The mould frames were spaced at irregular intervals, varying from 4ft 2 inches to 10ft 8 inches. Their irregular placement does not seem to reflect contemporary standard practice; the same can be said of the following

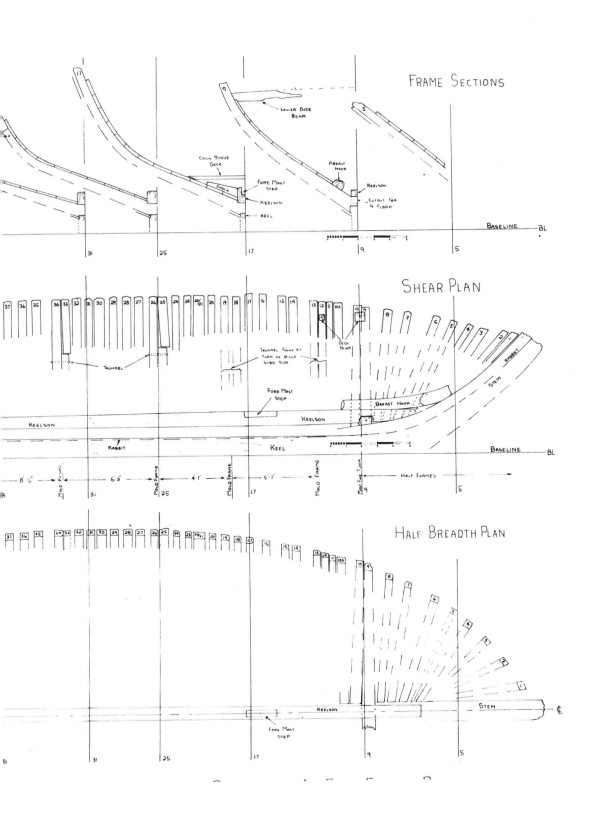

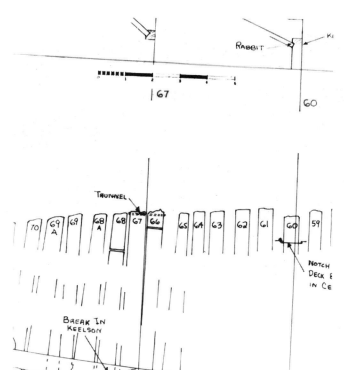

10 Keel scarph and crack in keelson *(D. Wyman)*

phases in the framing of the hull. Rather than being made up of overlapping futtocks, the frames that were situated between the mould frames, were single futtocked (Wyman 1981, 86). That is, rather than being the usual composite frame with overlapping timbers, the futtocks of these frames simply butted one another. Apparently they were secured by trunnels driven through the sheathing from the outside; the futtocks had to be installed as the sheathing was applied. Between these frames were similarly constructed frames; however, with these, the first futtock butted against a half floor which was not attached to the keel since it did not cross it in the manner of a true floor timber. In the plan (fig 9) this framing pattern can be seen in the stern between mould frames 66/67 and 76. Although not shown on the plan, the same framing sequence was observed upon removal of the ceiling in the mid-section between mould frames 25/26 and 33/34, and further forward between mould frames 12/13 and 17/18.

Once the vessel had been planked inside and out, this particular manner of framing would not have been apparent. One wonders if the owners of *Defence* knew that the builder had pursued such a framing procedure and had sanctioned it as a means of hastening construction.

Another interesting aspect of her construction, was the position of mould frame 66/67, immediately above the end

of a scarph joint on the keel (fig 10). Considering the lack of integrity that resulted from the use of single futtock frames and 'floating' floor timbers, the placement of a heavy mould frame over a scarph could be considered as another example of careless workmanship. Also interesting was the alignment of the scarph. A cut in the opposite direction would seem to have served better to maximize keel strength, particularly aft where it was less susceptible to downward stress and other forces resulting from forward motion (Switzer, 1981 c, 148).

Early inspection of the stern area suggested that it had received damage not found elsewhere in the hull. The frames were in disarray and no part of the aftermost structure could be located. This is most likely attributable to an explosion, probably in the magazine, that sent *Defence* to the bottom.

Further evidence of blast related damage was discovered during the process of documenting the sternmost framing sequence. Following completion of a plan view of the area, frames, half frames, loose planking and a piece of the deadwood were lifted to the work-float for reassembly. Two floor timbers, shaped from crotches, showed signs of damage caused by internal violence. The sharply rising arm of one had been severed; the other had been partially ruptured. Forward of these frames and opposite mould frame 63/64, a jagged crack was discovered in the keelson (Switzer, 1981 c, 148). Its direction and nature suggested an extreme downward force. Ceiling planking and intervening frames between the keelson crack and damaged floors were found to be unscathed, but beneath them the keel was missing. It had been separated from the hull at the above-mentioned scarph joint.

All this damage is consistent with what we might expect from an explosion of the magazine, which by analogy with *Swift* was situated near the stern. The presence of grenades (primed and fuzed) in areas adjacent to the keelson crack is further indication that this was the area in which the vessel's magazine was situated.

We believe that the intensity of the explosion was not great. It was, however, capable of destroying and/or separating an extensive amount of stern structure and capable, too, of exerting an outward and downward force great enough to wrench apart timbers that were lying deep under ballast. That neither the remains of the mainmast nor the shot locker showed signs of blast damage, leads to the conclusion that the source of the explosion was at a higher elevation and at a location where we might expect the magazine to have been situated. From such a location, the upward, outward, and downward effects of the blast are understandable. Perplexing, though, is the sequence of events that caused the rupture and separation of the keel while leaving the garboard and broad strake intact. It may be that this reflects further structural weaknesses resulting from the already noted questionable construction practices.

From the archaeological perspective, particularly regarding the artefacts recovered from the hull, the substandard construction techniques were a positive factor. Sturdier construction might have allowed *Defence* to float

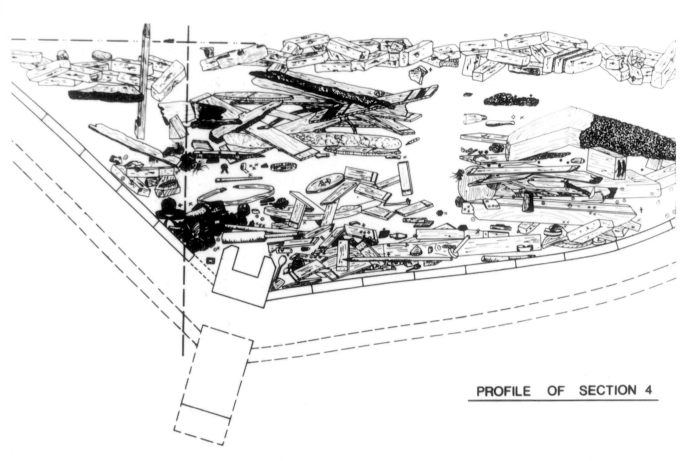

PROFILE OF SECTION 4

11 *Above* Trench contents including barrel staves, ordnance-related implements, mess kid parts, a fid, barrel withy, a knee and cookstove bricks *(C. Orr)*

12 *Right* Barrel head with barely discernible lettering E A FORD PORK 32 PIECES *(Maine State Museum)*

and burn longer, thus destroying so much more of the hull and its contents.

The artefacts

Because of the anaerobic environment, organic material was found to be extremely well-preserved (fig 11). The same may be said of the pewter, copper and brass objects. Not so with ferrous material, although as might be expected, cast iron suffered less from saline immersion than wrought iron. Iron or steel implements once associated with wooden handles, such as gimlets, augers and knife blades, were non-existent.

The artefacts recovered from the hull represented various facets of life and work at sea during the eighteenth century. Another aspect of the recovered material culture is that there were 'collections within collections'; for instance, various examples of cooperage; stylistic contrasts between pewter spoons; distinctive variations in shoemaking; different techniques of glass-making; twenty-five types of buttons and numerous examples or graffiti.

The majority of the artefacts can be divided into the following five categories: (1) food storage and distribution, (2) ordnance related, (3) apparel and personal adornment, (4) tools and instruments, and (5) fittings and equipage.

Food storage preparation, and distribution

Recalling the concept of 'collections within collections', this category or use/function grouping provided many examples, the first of which was cooperage. Within this group the most common example was the provision barrels.

189

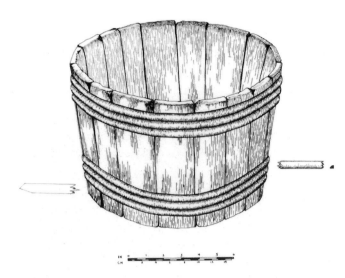

13 Mess kid used to carry food allotments from the galley *(H. Townsend)*

14 Pewter spoon with graffiti and maker's mark *(F. Harrington)*

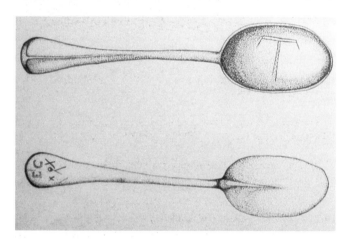

15 Carved wooden 'mess tags', length 7.5 to 10.5 cm *(Maine State Museum)*

They were made with 28 inch staves and 18 inch diameter heads and contained approximately thirty-two gallons. These wet-type barrels were bound with withies and their head pieces sealed with rushes. With the exception of one complete head (inscribed PORK 32 PIECES AEFORD) and a fragment bearing indecipherable lettering, marks or inscriptions identifying barrel contents were not found (fig 12).

Mess kids (fig 13) comprised another variety of cooperage. These were frequently roughly inscribed with graffiti that ranged from initials, or other identifying or decorative symbols, to one which bore the date 1779. Found in association with the mess kids were mugs, bowls, spoons, a trencher and a pewter plate. Like the kids the spoons also carried their owners' marks or initials. The pewter spoons had a high lead content which was reflected by tooth-wear on the bowls. These marks indicated the 'handedness' of the user; right handedness was predominant (Smith, 1986, 138-139). One spoon bore the mark of a London pewterer, SWANSON; another sported the cast initials EC, tentatively identified as Ephraim Cobb of Boston (fig 14).

Most enigmatic of the mess-related finds were small carved wooden tags (fig 15). Some had initials matching those found on mess kids; others were inscribed with Xs. At first they were taken to be tallies of some sort, or possibly gaming pieces. All were found in close proximity to the galley stove. They have been identified (by the Mariner's Museum at Newport News, Virginia) as the means by which a particular allocation of salt beef or pork was designated for a particular mess section. A string connected the tag to a junk of meat which was being boiled down in the cauldron (fig 16). At mess time, the 'captain' of a mess section went forward to the galley, identified his piece of meat by the tag and returned carrying it in a kid to divide up among his mess mates (Switzer, 1978, 44). Although their use has been recorded (Dandridge, 1911, 340-1), these tags are excellent examples of mundane items often overlooked in the literature, but which are significant in understanding at least one aspect of life at sea.

Excluding three officers, a cook, and bosun's mate, there were ninety-five men on board *Defence*. They divided into sixteen mess sections of six men each. Sixteen individual mess tags were recovered from the galley area. Other initialled mess-related finds were two stave-built tankards, one of which had a broad arrow inscribed on its base.

Ordnance-related artefacts

These included various forms of ammunition as well as equipment used in servicing the guns. Only two of the sixteen 6-pounder cannons which *Defence* is known to have been carrying were recovered. Strong magnetometer readings from outside the hull suggest the possibility that other guns lie deep in the mud. Markings on the recovered cannon give a casting date of 1778 and indicate that the casting was done at The Massachusetts State Foundry (Mayhew, 1974, 31-33).

Of the various types of ammunition found in the wreck, the most ubiquitous were wooden (ash and oak) grape-shot stools, the supports for the stacked and bagged balls which

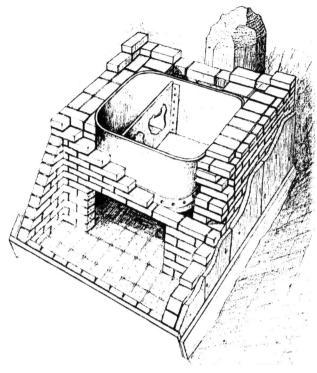

made up a stand of grape-shot. A concreted assemblage of stools comprised the uppermost level of the contents of the shot locker (fig 17).

Cannonballs, including bar shot, were frequent finds. Loose balls were found in the overburden and in concretions. One intact shot garland was raised.

A rare type of ammunition was recovered from the stern near the shot locker. It was a concretion containing a mixture of nails, bolt fragments and pieces of cast iron. Further examination of the concretion produced a small canvas bag containing scraps of iron. The association of the bag with iron debris suggests that the assemblage was langrage, ammunition used to clear decks or destroy rigging.

Gun station accessories, in the form of handspikes or heavers, a quoin, numerous tampions and carriage trucks were recovered at various in-hull locations. The quoin,

16 *Above left* Perspective view of cookstove and cauldron, width 4ft 5ins *(P. Hentschal)*

17 *Left* Stand of grape-shot conserved at the Museum laboratory, height 22.5 cm *(Maine State Museum)*

18 *Above* Lead apron or vent cover from a cannon *(Maine State Museum)*

tampions and trucks appeared to have been unused and therefore were probably from the gunner's stores. Such stores were found in a forward athwartship trench and included a rammer, a swab and cannon wadding made up of tightly rolled balls of a jute or a hemp-like substance.

The identity of the wadding was confirmed when one of the cannon was sent to a U.S. naval research laboratory for electrolysis treatment and was found to be charged and loaded with the wadding intact. Another interesting piece of gun-station equipment was a lead vent cover or apron. Although quite a few of these items have been recovered from European wrecks, they are rarities on North American sites (fig 18).

Other miscellaneous ordnance-related items included the previously mentioned grenades and numerous musket balls. Some of the latter had been incorporated in stands of grape-shot, others undoubtedly were ammunition for small-arms. Also related to small-arms were gun spalls and flints of French and English origin. With the exception of a brass pistol butt cap, no remains of small-arms were recovered.

Apparel/personal adornment
The upper surface of the ballast yielded a number of buttons and buckles. Many styles of buttons were represented. Some were professionally manufactured; others composed of

19 A variety of buckles, width 3.5 - 6 cm *(Maine State Museum)*

20 A shoe as excavated; a good example of the anaerobic conditions that prevailed *(D. Switzer)*

wood, bone, and leather appeared to have been the products of a 'home industry'. Buckles ranged from strictly utilitarian belt-types to quite ornamental shoe fasteners. The latter may be evidence of economic status and thus probably were worn by officers rather than seamen (fig 19).

The shoes were another instance of a 'collection within a collection' (fig 20). Two varieties of leather were used and two traditions of shoemaking have been identified. The English-American made shoes were interchangeable. The European type was made for a specific foot - possibly another indicator of economic status. Beneath the heel counter of the European shoe, only one of which was found, were the impressed words CUIR BRUGE. The average size of thirteen complete shoes was a man's 4 (American measure). In twenty heels there were as many as seven variations of wooden peg patterns (Smith 1986, 128).

No immediately identifiable items of clothing were preserved except for a silk ribbon, now black but originally green. A considerable amount of multifolded textile with wooden buttons was exhumed; upon touch it fell apart. Laboratory analysis revealed it to have been linen.

Tools/navigational instruments

Gimlet/auger handles, an axe handle and two shovel handles, were the extent of the hand tools recovered. It is supposed that more tools were on board but were carried ashore by crew members when they departed the ship.

Some navigation instruments were also left on board. A pair of brass dividers (missing their steel tips) was recovered in the course of sorting ballast. More unusual objects were identified as parts of a Davis quadrant or backstaff. These included a sight vane, a shadow vane and a magnifying glass. Unusual, too, was a Gunter scale. Fashioned out of boxwood, the scales engraved on it were used to solve time and distance problems by means of trigonometric functions.

It was hoped that the excavation of the midship area would yield other material reflecting life at sea, such as a sea chest or evidence relating to berthing arrangements. Sea chests were not found, although one trapezoid-shaped board with dovetail mortises has been tentatively identified as the end of a six-board chest. The only clue to berthing arrangements was what appeared to be the whipped end of a hammock support rope and a wooden hammock frame. Near the galley stove some hay was found. It has tentatively been identified as mattress stuffing. From the same area, boards forming a shelf were found placed longitudinally along the lower ceiling planking; it was surmised that the boards were the remains of a berth for the cook or an 'idler' such as the carpenter.

Ship's fittings and equipage

The inventory for this category is quite varied but lacks any iron material, the latter having long since deteriorated out of existence. For example, on a fragment of outer hull planking was an imprint from a piece of metal and a bolt hole which we believe to have been made by the lower end of a chain plate. This fragment was a surface find from outside the hull just abaft the foremast; nearby, one of only three deadeyes was recovered. The deadeye, in combination with the chain-plate imprint, points to the general location of the channels where the forward shrouds were spread and fastened.

Pulley blocks of various sizes and shapes as well as remnants of cordage provided information, albeit scant, on rigging characteristics. A number of blocks were found nested deep within the forepeak during the early investigation of the wreck; the assortment included large single and double blocks, presumably spares for the running rigging. Similar but generally smaller pulley blocks were recovered elsewhere within the hull. The size of some suggest that they may have been associated with the relieving tackle on gun carriages. Block parts were of native oak rather than of tropical woods such as *lignum vitae.*

A number of cordage remnants provide examples of the size of standing rigging as well as examples of 'marlin spike seamanship'. One deadeye was found with a portion of shroud still attached. It is impossible to be definite as to the original diameter, but based on the width and depth of the deadeye groove and the size of the strands, it would appear that the original diameter of the rope was no less than 2½ inches. Several lines or ropes of lesser diameter were also recovered, some tarred. They ranged from ½ inch to 1½ inches. Fragments of both right and left-handed laid rope were found. Fragments of braided three ply line were also recovered.

Examples of 'marlin spike seamanship' included short splices, whipping, and some spliced rope grommets of 6 inch diameter. The function of the latter is unclear. One suggestion is that they were used to secure 'triced up' hammocks.

Three wooden cleats and a portion of a fourth were found in the hull. Judging from their size, 14 inches, and their in-hull provenance, they were bulwark fittings. A small number of belaying-pins were recovered from deep within the hull. They exhibited no evidence of wear, thus suggesting that they were spares. No anchors were found, nor any hawser or cable-handling equipment such as riding bitts or a windlass. As mentioned above, a hawse hole was found in a section of detached outer hull that included a knighthead.

It is possible that the lack of finds related to fittings and equipage may be the result of no more than deterioration, but it may also be that the disintegration of the deck took some time to occur, in which case the *Defence* would have been easy prey for salvors immediately after the sinking. Considering that the water depth at very low tide is 14ft or less, her deck would have been covered by about only 4ft of water and thus accessible to an unsophisticated salvage operation. Salvage operations are known to have taken place on other sites in the area at a later date. In 1780 an American force returned to the Penobscot River and succeeded in capturing two British sloops engaged in salvaging cannon. Later in the nineteenth century a crude diving bell was utilized to recover some thirty cannons from other Penobscot Expedition wrecks (Cayford, 1976, 54, 58; Fowler, 1979, 31). Although it cannot be verified from the historical record that such activities took place on the *Defence*, it is none the less likely that the vessel has been scavenged.

Conclusion

The excavation of the *Defence* was an important contribution to American maritime/naval history. Not only did it provide a rare insight into life and work at sea during this period, but also the vessel itself was of a previously unknown style of construction, and as such represents the third hull type to have come down to us from the Colonial/Revolutionary era.

Notes

1 Admiralty Records, Captain's Logs HMS Camilla, ADM 51/157 part V, 12.

2 Evidence of a stern explosion was also evident from the scatter-patterns of glass and ceramic sherds. A fan-like pattern of blast-

thrown material proceeded aft from the shot locker and terminated 10ft aft of the galley stove. Some sherds that were found forward (particularly those from a Whieldon-ware teapot) matched fragments recovered from the stern. In addition to confirming the blast theory, the distribution pattern also provides clues as to the original height of the shot locker and the presence of bulkheads in the mid-section of the hull. For a detailed analysis see Smith, 1981. For a more detailed account of the stern and explosion related damage see Switzer, 1981, 144-150.

3 For the most complete study and interpretation of the *Defence* artefact collection, see Smith, 1986.

4 The artefacts from *Defence* have been fully recorded and are available for study by arrangement with the Maine State Museum at Augusta, Maine.

References

Cayford, J., 1976, *The Penobscot Expedition*, Orrington, Maine

Chapelle, H., 1930, *The Baltimore Clipper*, New York

Chapelle, H., 1935, *The History of American Sailing Ships*, New York

Dandridge, D., 1911, *American Prisoners of the Revolution*, Charlottesville, Virginia

Fowler, Jr., W., 1979, Disaster in Penobscot Bay, *Harvard Magazine*, July-August

Mayhew, D., 1974, The *Defence*: Search and Recovery (sic), *The International Journal of Nautical Archaeology*, III, 312-313

Smith, S., 1981, Tell Tail Provenance, *Underwater Archaeology: The Challenge Before Us*, Proceedings of the Twelfth Conference on Underwater Archaeology, G.P. Watts (Ed.), San Marino, CA, 102-105

Smith, S., 1986, *The Defence: Life at Sea as Reflected in an Archaeological Assemblage from an Eighteenth Century Privateer*, Unpublished Ph.D. Dissertation, University of Pennsylvania

Switzer, D., 1978, Provision Stowage and Galley Facilities Onboard the Revolutionary War Privateer *Defence*, *Beneath the Waters of Time*, Proceedings of the Ninth Conference on Underwater Archaeology, J.B. Arnold III (ed.), Austin, TX, 39-44

Switzer, D., 1981a, Recovery and Initial Interpretation of The Shot Locker and Bilge Pump Well From the Privateer *Defence*, *In the Realms of Gold*, Proceedings of the Tenth conference on Underwater Archaeology, W.A. Cockrell (ed.), San Marino, CA, 76-81

Switzer, D., 1981b, Nautical Archaeology in Penobscot Bay, *New Aspects of Naval History*, C.L. Symonds (ed.), Annapolis, 90-101

Switzer, D., 1981c, Interpretation of the Stern Area of the Privateer *Defence*, *Underwater Archaeology: The Challenge Before Us*, Proceedings of the Twelfth Conference on Underwater Archaeology, G.P. Watts (ed.), San Marino, CA, 144-150

Wyman, D., 1981, Developing the Plans for the Privateer *Defence*, *In the Realms of Gold*, Proceedings of the Tenth Conference on Underwater Archaeology, G.A. Watts (ed.), San Marino, CA, 85-94

Max Guérout (Excavation Director)

The wreck of the *Slava Rossii*

The wreck of the Russian warship *Slava Rossii* (Glory of Russia) was discovered off Levant Island, South of France, in 1947. When she was examined by an archaeological team in 1980 and 1981 a remarkable cache of almost seventy copper alloy icons was discovered. This paper outlines the historical background to the loss, which occurred on 3 November 1780, and then goes on to describe the nature of the site, the extent of the hull remains and the principal artefacts recovered, in particular the heavy ordnance and icons.

Historical context

In 1780 the American War of Independence was raging and France was at war with England. During this conflict a closely contested secondary diplomatic struggle was taking place between France, England and Russia. France's objective was to ensure the continual flow from Russia and the Baltic countries of the materials (wood, hemp, tar, iron, etc.) which were necessary for the construction and maintenance of her fleets (Fauchille, 1893, 57).

Vergennes, the French Minister of Foreign Affairs was attempting to loosen Catherine II's traditional links with England. His persistence was finally rewarded at the beginning of summer, 1780, when, on a Russian initiative, the Northern States signed a treaty of armed neutrality intended to allow the free navigation of neutral nations; a freedom which had previously been restricted by the English.

The treaty's principle had scarcely been accepted when Catherine II ordered the mustering of a fleet of fifteen warships which she intended would guarantee the freedom of commerce and navigation that was enshrined in the document (Fauchille, 1893, 320). She instructed her various ambassadors to prepare for the visits of Russian vessels and ordered that arrangements should be made with their host nations so that the ships would be granted 'entrance to their ports and all the help that may be necessary to them in case of accident or need to withdraw'. Versailles responded immediately with the following cautious orders to all naval commanders: 'In the event of any of the Empress of Russia's vessels entering our ports, it is the King's wish that they be received amicably. Furthermore they shall be granted all the help they should require and everything must be done to convince the Russian Empress of His Majesty's desire to express his satisfaction with the glorious and helpful diplomatic policy that she has just adopted'. In May the commanders of the fleet received the more forceful order

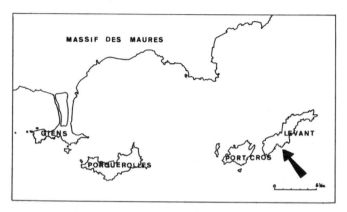

1 Arrow points to where the *Slava Rossii* was lost on Levant Island in 1780 *(drawing M. Guérout)*

that they must 'conform with the greatest exactitude to what is prescribed with respect to neutral ships, in particular, those of Russia'.

On 22 June 1780, the Russian fleet left Kronstadt for Copenhagen. They took advantage of this visit to seal the Treaty of Neutrality with the signatures of Denmark and Sweden. Russia's was added on 23 June at St Petersburg. With the treaty fully ratified, the Imperial Navy set sail in three flotillas.

The first consisted of five ships of the line and a frigate under the command of Admiral Alexander Ivanovich Kruse. Their instructions were to cruise the North Sea. The second consisted of five ships of the line and two frigates under the command of Admiral Palibin. Their instructions were to cruise the Atlantic.

The third force was instructed to sail the Mediterranean under the command of Admiral Ivan Antonovich Borisov who had previously flown his flag from the *Isidor*. The 66 gun flagship was commanded by Captain Gips. The six other vessels were the 66 gun *Asia* under Captain Spiridov; the 66 gun *America* under Captain Conconzov; the 66 gun *Slava Rossii* under Captain Ivan Abrasimovich Baskakov; the 66 gun *Tverdyi* under Captain Selmanov; the 32 gun frigate *Simeon* under Captain Golenkin and the 32 gun frigate *Patricki* under Captain Danizov.

Admiral Borisov called first at Copenhagen (2-3 July), then Texel (10-15 August), Dover (16-26 August) and Lisbon (8 September - 19 October). The flotilla passed through the Straits of Gibraltar on 21 October and headed for the port of Livorno (Leghorn), Italy. However, the long calls at port meant that it was late in the season and bad weather from the east had already arrived. The flotilla travelled along the coast of Provence intending to reach Livorno by sailing around the north of Corsica.

On 3 November, towards nine in the evening, the *Slava Rossii* lost contact with the rest of the flotilla. Baskakov estimated that he was approximately thirty miles out to sea and ordered a course towards the coast intending afterwards to head once more out to sea. The ship continued at half sail. Suddenly, at around 11 p m, to everyone's horror, a rocky coastline fringed with foam appeared before them. It was too late to change direction so Baskakov gave the order to drop anchors. The panic-stricken crew released the two davit anchors. The ship swung and was successfully halted from proceeding on its fatal course, but the surging sea and backwash were extremely strong and it was not long before the chafing ropes gave. The heavy ship broke loose and drove aground on the rocky coast of Levant Island, an island of which the Russians were completely unaware (fig 1). A cannon was fired to alert the local inhabitants who came running, but they could do nothing but stand by and watch helplessly. Contrary to all expectations the ship stopped rolling as it became wedged between two rocks. The islanders went to the mainland to summon assistance and by morning help had arrived from the town of Hyères. Of the 446 crew only 11 perished. On dry land the survivors were given all the care and attention they required. Louis Francois de Gardanne, the town consul, in particular distinguished himself through his efforts. Captain Baskakov declined the offer of transport to Toulon and so the survivors were housed at nearby Recollets and Cordeliers. The French Royal Navy rushed to their assistance and a small boat was chartered to take provisions to the men.

Admiral Bovisov arrived safely with the rest of the fleet at Livorno. His worst fears concerning the absence of the *Slava Rossii* were realized on 20 November when he finally learned of her loss. The frigate *Patricki* was sent back to pick up the survivors and any items that could be recovered from the wreck. She anchored at Hyères on 10 December.

Fate had it that the ship sank close to a rocky point (fig 2) which was red in colour and no doubt already known to fishermen as *Roucas Roux* ('Red rocks' in Provençal), although this is not documented. As the two words 'roux (red) and 'russe' (Russian) were almost perfect homonyms in Provençal, the place was henceforth known interchangeably, as *Pointe du Russe* (Russian point) or *Pointe de Roucas Roux* (Red Rock Point). To this day these names remain confused within the spoken language without anyone trying to clarify the ambiguity (Tailliez, 1980, 17).

Discovery of the wreck

In 1957 Louis Viale, a fisherman from Port-Avis on Levant Island, found several pieces of wood in his nets. When a certain Dr Delonca of St Raphael, who spent his holidays on the island, learnt of this he carried out a series of exploratory dives which resulted in the discovery of a number of cannon pointing upwards from amidst the weed. Several other pieces

of artillery were situated nearby in a similar position. Following the discovery of a pewter plate engraved with Cyrillic initials, research was undertaken in the naval archives by its curator, M.M. Forget, the naval librarian Andrew Morrazzini and a local historian, Commander Emmanuel Davin. One key item of correspondence that they uncovered, signed by Naval General Lieutenant M. de Saint Aignan, mentions *Slava Rossii* by name, although at first it had been corrupted to *Victoria Russa* and then *Esclavia Russa* by secretaries unaccustomed to Slavonic pronunciation.

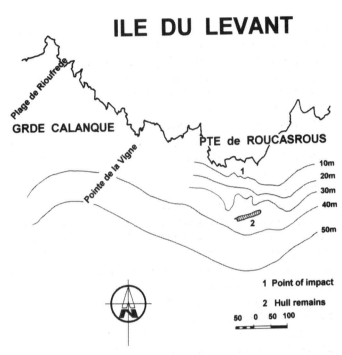

2 Detail of Levant Island showing position of wreck
(drawing M. Guérout)

Three of the cannon were raised by the well-known French excavator and naval officer, Philippe Tailliez, who at the time was working on the Roman wreck near the lighthouse at Titan. To recover the cannon Tailliez used lifting tackle from the naval transporter *Sahel*. Later, on 24 October of the same year, he returned with the *Criquet* and raised seven more. The latter were stored at the Royal Tower in Toulon. One of them was handed over to the town of St Raphael and can now be seen in the presbytery gardens.

The first attempt to excavate the site was not made until 1980. In the meantime, however, research continued. Of particular interest were a number of documents found in the Soviet naval archives in Leningrad, which not only gave the circumstances of her loss (which were recounted above), but also details regarding the vessel's technical specifications and other features.

Technical information

Peter the Great, who had been Tsar of Russia from 1682 to 1725, was so anxious to build up the Russian fleet that for a time he stayed in Holland where he learned the theory and

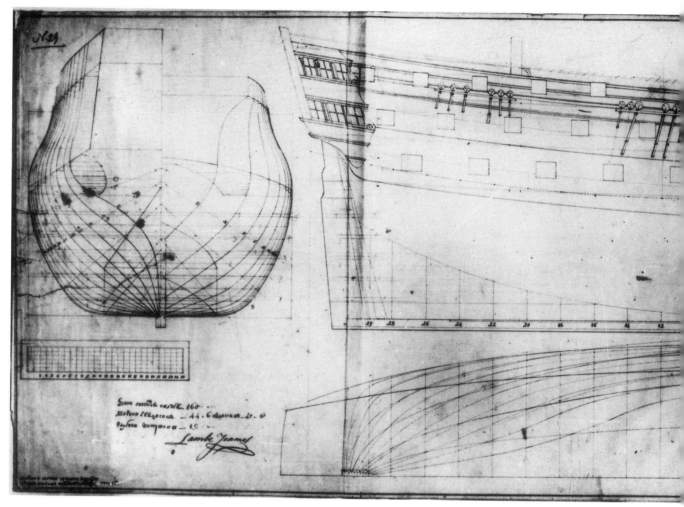

3 Plan of the *Slava Rossii* from the archives in Leningrad

practice of ship building, after which he went to Britain, to study ship deployment and methods of command at sea. Later he returned to Russia with a group of specialists drawn from various countries. These included a number of Scotsmen who were to be the master builders and captains of his ships until the Russians themselves were able to take over.

One of them was the master builder, Joseph Nay (Russian name Osip Nai; Anon., 1849, 5); it was he who, drawing on his experience of contemporary English and Dutch naval construction, conceived and built the first 66 gun ship which was to be the mainstay of the Russian navy for many years. The prototype of this long series (51 ships between 1731 and 1779) was the first *Slava Rossii*. Her construction began in Kronstadt on January 28, 1731, and she was launched on April 30, 1732. She was broken up in 1752 (Veselago, 1893).

Our *Slava Rossii* (fig 3) was built at Arkhangelsk, with slightly different proportions, by two Russian master builders, Gunion and Portnov. She was launched on May 13, 1774 (Veselago, 1893). Regarding her technical specifications and weapons systems we know the following: Hull length 52m; beam 14.49m; depth 6.17m; 66 cannons (28 36-pounders were in the first battery; 28 12-pounders were in the second battery; and 10 6-pounders were situated on the quarter deck. In addition there were three so-called *licornes*

('unicorns'), these were short, heavy-shot guns which can be seen as precursors of the better know carronades). Portable weapons consisted of 77 muskets, 40 carbines, 40 pistols and 60 sabres. Munitions: 990 cannon balls, 75 shells, 700 grenades and 3,630 pieces of fire-arm shot.

Details regarding the crew on board were obtained from Captain Baskakov's log book: 289 sailors (including 14 naval officers); 57 gunners (including 1 officer); 93 fusiliers (including 2 officers); 7 servants. This gives a complement of 446, a number that is significantly lower than the official number of 526 which appears in the Leningrad archive documents. The difference can be attributed to disembarkations as the result of illness that were made during the four and a half month voyage. A dispatch from Lisbon dated September 19 mentions that, at that time, the Russian squadron had more than 500 men in the town's hospitals. According to estimates, on departure Admiral Borisov's squadron consisted of 3,400 to 3,700 men, the sick who were disembarked therefore represented 13% to 14% of the total - a figure that broadly supports the noted discrepancy.

Excavation of the wreck

The loss of the *Slava Rossii* occurred in the south of Levant Island, slightly to the east of Riou Frède Cove. Situated as it

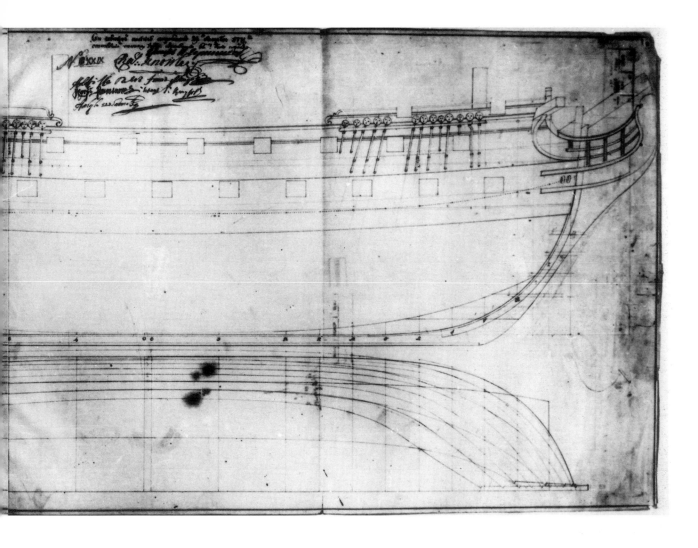

is at the foot of a steep, rocky slope covered in weed, the site is almost inaccessible from land. The slope continues down underwater, until, at 40m, it reaches a sandy plateau whereon are scattered the wreck remains.

The point of impact was near the shore; the first remains, pottery, ballast and cannon, were found concreted to the rock, below where the vessel had struck. It was here that in 1961 Frederic Dumas found a sounding lead (Dumas, 1976, 10) which he gave to the project twenty years later, at the time of the excavation.

The middle zone, between 15m and 30m below the surface, consists of a large irregular mass of fallen rocks and weed. It is an area which makes searching difficult and forbids the efficient use of an airlift. Small objects are found scattered throughout a multitude of holes and crevices, all of which are filled with sand and covered in weed.

The main part of the wreck is located between 36m and 40m below the surface on the plateau, at the foot of the rock-face (fig 4). The remains are buried beneath 30cm of sand. What is left of the hull covers an area 35m long by 5m wide. Parallel to this main deposit, on the offshore side, is a 15m long pile of concreted material which most probably represents tackle, rigging elements and spillage from the hull.

The 1980 and 1981 campaigns concentrated on the deeper part of the site. During this time 692 dives took place from the tuna boat 'Meinga'. Financing of the operation was made possible by the generosity of various sponsors including the navy.

Our first objective was to study the topography of the area and then to expose, survey and make a photogrammetric record of the hull remains which consisted of the lower timbers from one side, but not the keel (fig 5).

From the start the great attraction of the site was the considerable number of objects scattered around the hull. During the first dive on 3 August 1980, while removing sand from the hull with our hands, we revealed a metal icon, a coin and a baldric buckle. Many more such finds were made during the dives that followed, putting the wreck's identity as the *Slava Rossii* beyond doubt (fig 6).

The origin of the ship gave these objects a particular interest, both because of the exceptional nature of their presence in the Mediterranean and because very few Russian men-of-war have ever been properly examined archaeologically. To date, only two have been excavated; one was the badly broken up *Evstaffi* which went down off the Shetlands in the same year as the *Slava Rossii* (Stenuit, 1976, 221-243); the other was the 32 gun frigate *Nicholas* which

197

SLAVA ROSSII

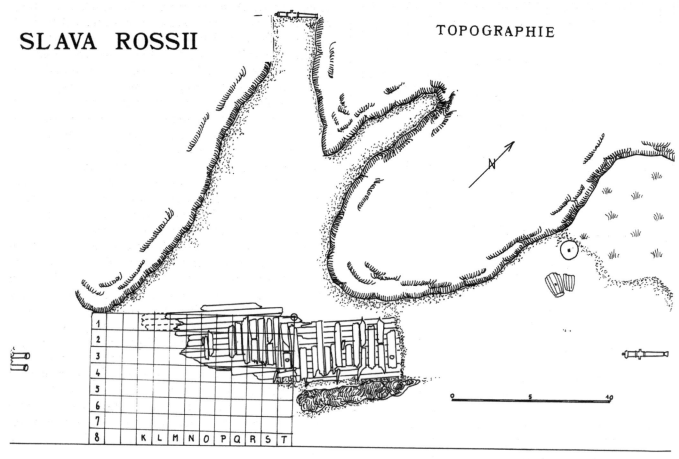

4 Topography of the site *(D.M. Guérout)*

5 Detail of the hull remains. 1. Lead scupper 2. Porthole 3.
Futtocks 4. Hull planking *(A. Carrier/CRA Sophia Antipolis)*

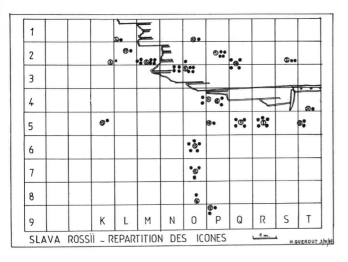

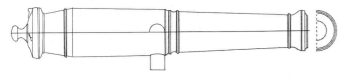

6 *Top* Distribution of the icons (D.M. Guérout)

7 *Above* Bronze gun: licorne of 1 poud (Poud, a Russian measure = 16,380kg). Overall length 3.030m (D.M. Guérout)

sank in the access channel to the port of Kotka in Finland during the Battle of Svenskund which took place on 9 July 1790, between Russian and Swedish fleets. This last ship which was found to be in an exceptionally good state of preservation, was unfortunately extensively damaged by

clearance works to improve the channel (Ericsson, 1972, 172-179). None the less, both these ships provided informative *comparanda* for our work on the *Slava Rossii.*

The finds

Most of the cannon were salvaged after the sinking; the frigate *Maria* came to collect them in February 1782. A letter written at the time by M. de Saint-Aignan to one of his ministers mentions 24 guns, but an inventory of the salvage from the Leningrad archives, also dated February 1782, records 39. It is likely that the latter document is the

more accurate. As noted, in September and October 1957, the French navy raised 10 guns. Therefore there should still be 17 on site, but to date we have only found 3. The others are probably still buried in the sand or covered in weeds.

Among the projectiles we found were round shot, chainshot, grape-shot (called 'bunches of grapes') and 'carcasses' (hollow explosive or incendiary shells filled with powder). Some accessories were found, such as a power ladle, rammer heads and wedges for backsight adjustment.

Infantry armament consisted of the remains of sabres, swords, daggers, muskets, pistols, a large number of shot of all sizes and nearly 120 gunflints. Three small 8 pound bronze mortars of the 'cohorn' type can also be included in this category (figs 8 and 9). Of particular interest was a butt-plate bearing the Imperial Crown and the monogram of Catherine II (fig 10) and two decorative plaques from powder horns, one of which was inscribed with the emblem of the Russian naval infantry (figs 11 and 12). Mention should also be made of the great many pieces of military equipment and apparel that were found; such as buckles for baldrics, belts and shoes, buttons, boots and gloves.

The shipboard equipment fittings and tackle made up a category of finds, which, if not always spectacular, certainly gave insights into the way the very young Russian navy absorbed the knowledge brought in from abroad by Peter the Great. Although it must be said that, at first sight, there are no significant differences, for an archaeologist, between the wreck of the *Slava Rossii* and other naval wrecks of the period.

Of interest also were the very great variety of everyday objects. These included Russian imitation Wedgwood crockery, Meissen and Chinese porcelain, soup terrines, salt-

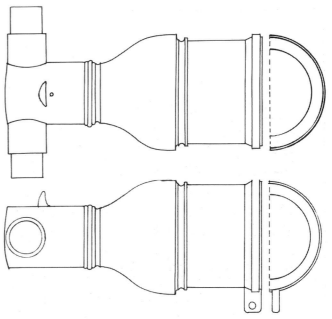

8 Bronze Cohorn (8 pounder mortar), length 32.5 cm (GRAN/M. Guérout)

9 Bronze Cohorn (8 pounder mortar), length 37.5 cm (D.M. Guérout)

included half kopecks and one, two, four and five kopeck pieces. They ranged in date from 1730 to 1779, and represented the reigns of Russian sovereigns from Anna Ivanovna to Catherine II.

Finally, let us return to the icons. Over 63 were recovered (figs 16 and 17). They were found either within the sand, or directly on top of the hull timbers within a relatively small area of the assemblage. Their condition varied considerably. During the second season (1981) we found the final two parts of a four-panel icon that we had discovered the

10 *Top left* Butt plate from a musket bearing the monogram of Catherine the Great *(GRAN/C/ Petron)*

11 *Above centre left* Remains of a powder flask decorated with a double-eagle, anchors and the coat of arms of St George (the crest of the 'marine infantry') *(GRAN/C/ Petron)*

12 *Left* Powder flask *(D.M. Guérout)*

13 *Above* Copper scent bottle decorated with a unicorn and a leopard *(GRAN/G. Martin)*

previous year. In 1981 we also found three triptychs nested together, in perfect condition, under one of the timbers. One of these (fig 18) was outstandingly beautiful. We know that the religious feeling of the Russian people was very strong, and that each sailor probably possessed his own icon to help with his prayers.

The disposition of the icons on the site raises several question. First, in what part of the vessel had they been kept? The timber remains, unfortunately, could be attributed to any specific part of the hull, however, the presence of fire-arms and bladed weapons which were traditionally kept in the stern (directly under the eyes of the officers) as well as the discovery in the same zone of some fairly refined crockery and pewterware, which can perhaps also be associated with the officers, suggested that we were in the area of the vessel's aftercastle.

cellars, plates, goblets, pewterware, engraved Bohemian glassware, forks, spoons, candlesticks, candle snuffers, bronze apothecary mortars, copper magnifying glass frames, clay pipes, dice, combs and perfume bottles (the latter, a reminder of the often unbearable smell produced by 500 men living in a confined space - fig 13).

More than 900 coins were recovered from the site. There were some rare silver denominations (such as the 20 kopeck coins and a one rouble piece bearing the effigy of Catherine II - figs 14 and 15), but most of them were copper; these

14 *Far left* Obverse of a one rouble silver coin. Bust of Catherine II (GRAN)

15 *Near left* Double-eagle. Reverse of the rouble in fig 14. Minted in 1765 (GRAN)

16 *Below* Some of the icons found on the site (GRAN/CNRS/Foliot)

We do not know very much about religious practices on the ships of the Russian Imperial Navy. We know that copper icons (rather than painted icons which were more precious and delicate) were given to travellers, particularly sailors upon departure. In fact this is why they were known as 'travelling icons'. We do not, however, know how they were used on board ship; were they kept with an individual's personal possessions, were they put together in a specially designated spot, or, iconostasis, as was the custom in homes ashore?

The idea of an iconostasis at the rear of the ship for the use of the whole of the crew (which we must remember, numbered nearly 500) seems doubtful. If this were the case we might have expected to find more in the areas. A more plausible theory is that they belonged to the ship's officer class (about 25 in all) and that each would have possessed three or four icons. It may be that the officers kept them together in an iconostasis at the stern. Further research we hope will provide answers.

Conclusion

The excavation of the *Slava Rossii* has provided insight into a little known aspect of the history of the Russian navy, that is to say, Catherine II's use of it to represent the Imperial Crown beyond the Baltic Sea. It has also provided an opportunity to explore the role of the league of neutral countries, which was encouraged by France to draw up international maritime laws, particularly concerning freedom of the seas (its first legal expression).

Finally, the discovery of this remarkable series of icons gives physical expression to the religious feelings which are known to have pervaded the Holy Russian Empire, and, in particular, it contributes to a better understanding of popular religious acts and practices within the Russian military (Pellenc-Turcat, 1993, 17). The icons are also important as they provide a chronological fixed-point within an art that, to a certain extent, has suffered from confused dating because of the blind repetition of its images.

Acknowledgements

The author and editor are indebted to Mrs Monique Meager, Kate Mallett and Dr Peter Riou for the translation of this article into English.

References

Anon., 1849, History of the Russian fleet during the reign of Peter the Great by a contemporary Englishman (1724), in *Navy Record Society*, XV, 5

Dumas, F., 1976, *Trente siècles sous la mer*, Paris

Ericsson, C.H., 1976, A sunken Russian Frigate, *Archaeology*, 25, 172-179

Fauchille, P., 1893, Une entente franco-russe pour la liberté des mers (1778-1780), in *Nouvelle Revue*, vol 80, Paris

Pellenc-Turcat, F., 1993, Les icones de la *Slava Rossii*, technologies, typologies, catalogue sommaire et comparaison, in *Travaux scientifiques du Parc de Port-Cros*, vol 15, Hyères

Stenuit, R., 1976, The wreck of the pink *Evstafii*, a transport of the Imperial Russian Navy, lost off Shetlands in 1780, in *International Journal of Nautical Archaeology and underwater Exploration*, 25, 3, 221-243

Tailliez, J., 1980, Elements de toponymie nautique provencale, in *Annales hydrographiques*, n. 775, 17

Veselago, F.F., 1893, *Liste de tous les navires de guerres russes de 1668 a 1860*, St Petersburg

17 *Above left* Bronze icon with an enamel relief of St Nicolas, patron saint of sailors *(GRAN/CNRS/Foliot)*

18 *Below* Bronze triptych representing St Nicolas in the centre and four orthodox religious scenes on the side panels *(GRAN/CNRS/Foliot)*

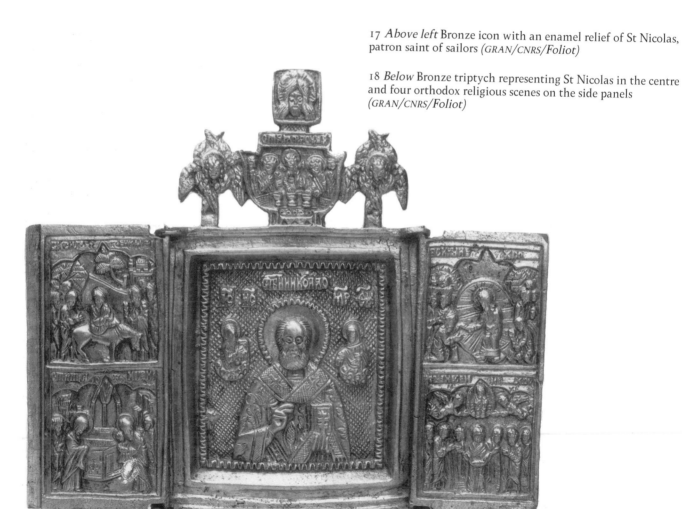

Mensun Bound (Oxford University MARE)
Brian Riggs (Turks and Caicos Museum)

HMS *Endymion*(1790), Turks and Caicos Islands

Background

In May 1992, Oxford University MARE in collaboration with the Museum of the Turks and Caicos Islands carried out a preliminary survey of a cannon wreck on a coral reef to the south of the archipelago. The work was conducted on behalf of the Department of Tourism using boats provided by the Department of Fisheries.

Attempts to determine when the wreck was first found have not been successful. It is known that the site was visited by treasure hunters in the 1980s but it was not until late 1991 when it was rediscovered by local dive school owner, Bryan Sheedy, that the wreck first came to world attention. On the charts the reef upon which the wreck is situated was named Endymion Reef, but the reason for this had long since been lost to memory. Those who had found the wreck, however, conducted a little research and discovered that a British naval frigate of this name had been lost in the area in August 1790[1].

Location and site

The Turks and Caicos are a string of low-lying islands on the Atlantic edge of the Caribbean, 80 miles north of Hispaniola and some 570 miles south east of Miami, Florida (fig 1). The Endymion Reef is at the southernmost end of the Turks Bank some 8 miles south-west of Great Sand Cay, the final isle in the chain.

The reef crests at about 3m from the surface while the wreck itself is situated within clefts and gullies on its

1 Map of Turks and Caicos Islands (*Chris Fitton*)

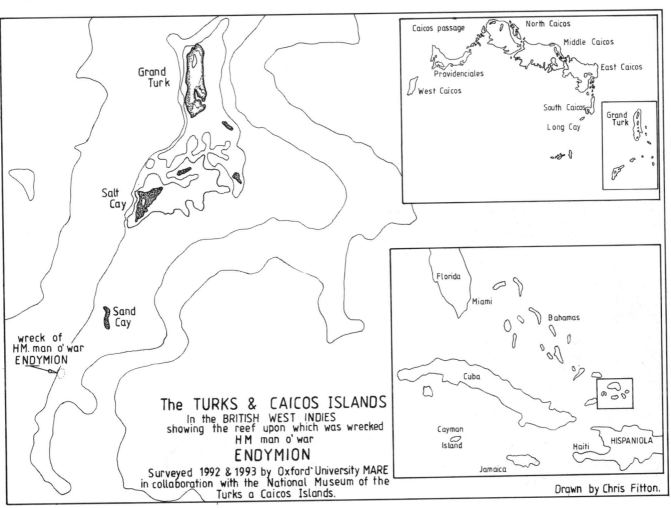

The TURKS & CAICOS ISLANDS
In the BRITISH WEST INDIES
showing the reef upon which was wrecked
HM man o' war
ENDYMION
Surveyed 1992 & 1993 by Oxford University MARE
in collaboration with the National Museum of the
Turks a Caicos Islands.

Drawn by Chris Fitton.

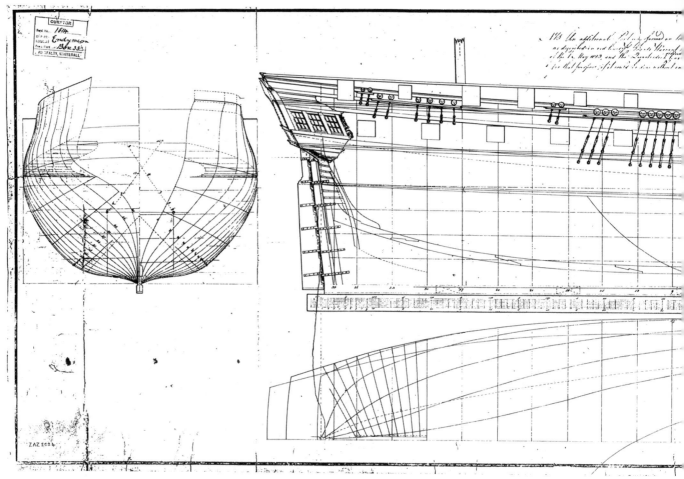

2 Architect's draughts of the *Endymion*
(*courtesy National Maritime Museum Picture Library, London*)

western side in 9 to 10.5m. The remains consist of 18 cannon, four large anchors, ballast blocks, hull sheathing and fastenings. Everything is covered by sponges, corals and other marine growth. Part of the wreck has been fully enveloped by coral.

On the other side of the coral head lies another wreck of uncertain identity but which is believed to be from the second half of the nineteenth century. Particularly prominent are her boilers and anchors. Her chain, which snakes around the coral head, can be seen in the background of fig 10.

Historical background

The *Endymion* was built at Grave Yard, Limehouse, and launched on 28th September 1779 (figs 2 and 3). She was one of the Thomas Slade's Roebuck Class[2] and had a displacement tonnage of 894, a gundeck length of 140ft, a keel length of 115ft 7in, a beam of 38ft 1in and a hold depth of 16ft 4in (Lecky, 1913, III, 1-2).

At a time when naval ships were rated according to the number of guns they carried, the *Endymion*, which had 44, was considered to be a 5th-rater, which puts her within the so-called frigate class of fighting ship. Frigates were not expected to participate in the line of battle; their superior sailing qualities meant that they were used as fleet look-outs, and, in battle, as repeating ships which relayed the admiral's

instructions to other ships that were perhaps concealed by the smoke of gunfire, or were not at the right angle to read the signals from the flagship. They were also frequently deployed as convoy escorts or on independent cruising missions.

The details of much of the *Endymion*'s life can be pieced together from her logs, muster books and other documents held by the Public Records Office and the National Maritime Museum at Greenwich (PRO ADM 51 296 - (5) - 6; ADM 36, 8190).

The *Endymion* was first commissioned in August 1779, to Captain (later Admiral) Philip Carteret. Her first venture beyond British waters began in February 1780, when she went patrolling around the Channel Islands, Normandy and Brittany in company with *Emerald, Surprise, Nimble, Hussar, Squirrel, Griffin* and *Beaver's Prize*.

On 28th May 1780, she sailed for Africa via the Cape Verde Islands, with *Beaver's Prize, Zephyr* and six merchant ships, then across the Atlantic to Barbados. After some cruising she left Barbados on 4th October 1780, as a convoy escort together with *Beaver's Prize, Vengeance, Ajax, Montagu, Egman, Amazon* and *Andromeda*. On the twelfth of the month she was caught by a storm off Martinique during which she lost her main mizzen, fore topmast, bowsprit and foreyard. On 19th October she fired on the *Marquis de Brancas* from Bordeaux. On the 30th of the

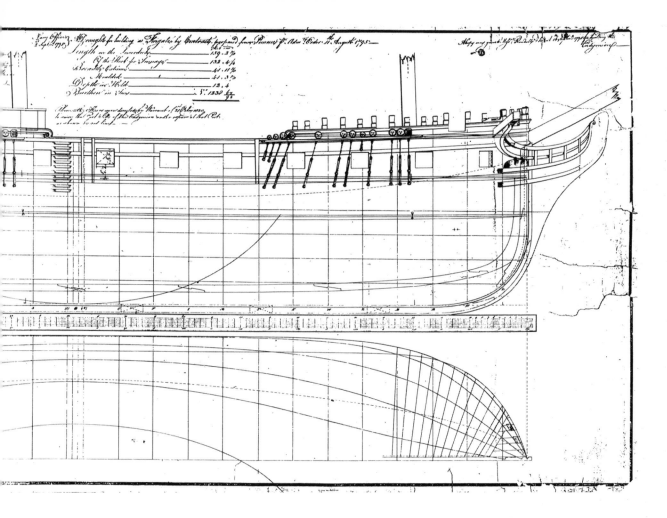

month she went to Port Royal, Jamaica, where she put prisoners ashore and repaired storm damage. On 4th November she sent her boats to Kingston to capture Dutch ships. On 17th March 1781, she left Port Royal with HMS *Trident* and a large convoy. On 4th May she took the prize *Le Marq'de la Fayette* to Boston. She finally returned to Britain (Sheerness and Chatham) on 22nd July 1781.[3]

On 31st January 1782, Captain Edward Tyrrel Smith took over her command. On 12th February she sailed with *Princess Caroline, Alarm, Andromache* and seventy merchant ships for Barbados and St Lucia arriving at the latter on 21st March 1782.

It was at this stage that the *Endymion* participated, as one of 15 British frigates, in the most famous event of her ten-year service: the Battle of the Saints, named after the group of islands in the West Indies near which it was fought on 12th April 1782 (fig 4). It was the final naval battle of the American War of Independence (1775-82) and was fought between a British fleet of thirty-six ships of the line under the command of Admiral Sir George Rodney, and a French fleet of 30 ships of the line commanded by Vice-Admiral Comte de Grasse. It was a decisive British victory, but the battle is remembered today not so much for this but rather for the introduction of new tactics. Up until this point naval battles were very much stereotype, set piece encounters in

which fleets, in line ahead formation, passed each other on opposite tacks, exchanging broadsides. By this time, however, ship design and artillery technology had reached a level whereat these great formal duels ended, more often than not, in stalemate with both sides claiming victory. The pattern changed at the Battle of the Saints when the wind opened up the French line, and Rodney drove his ships through the gap, thus separating the French rear from the van and throwing them into confusion. The new tactic was so successful that it immediately found its way into *The Fighting Instructions for the Navy*, and was, with considerable variation, used with similar success by Nelson and Collingwood at Trafalgar 23 years later. The Battle of the Saints was also a turning point in the history of naval gunnery, for this was the first serious test of the carronade (or 'smasher'), a short gun which could discharge a heavy shot over a limited distance.

The *Endymion*'s log (PRO ADM 51, 296 (7)) records how they first saw the French fleet with a large convoy on the 9th April 1782, and how, two days later, a general chase to windward was ordered. The following day, 12th April, the signal was given for the van to attack. Her log records how, after the battle, the *Endymion* had to stand by disabled French ships that had struck their colours. She later put 30 seamen and 20 marines in *La Ville de Paris* which had

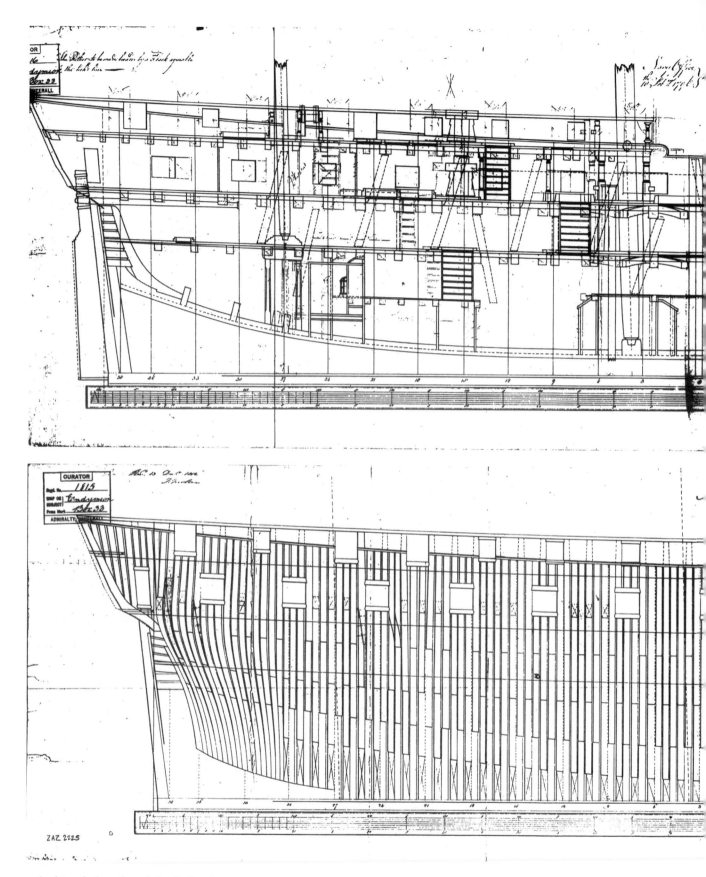

2 Architect's draughts of the *Endymion*
(courtesy National Maritime Museum Picture Library, London)

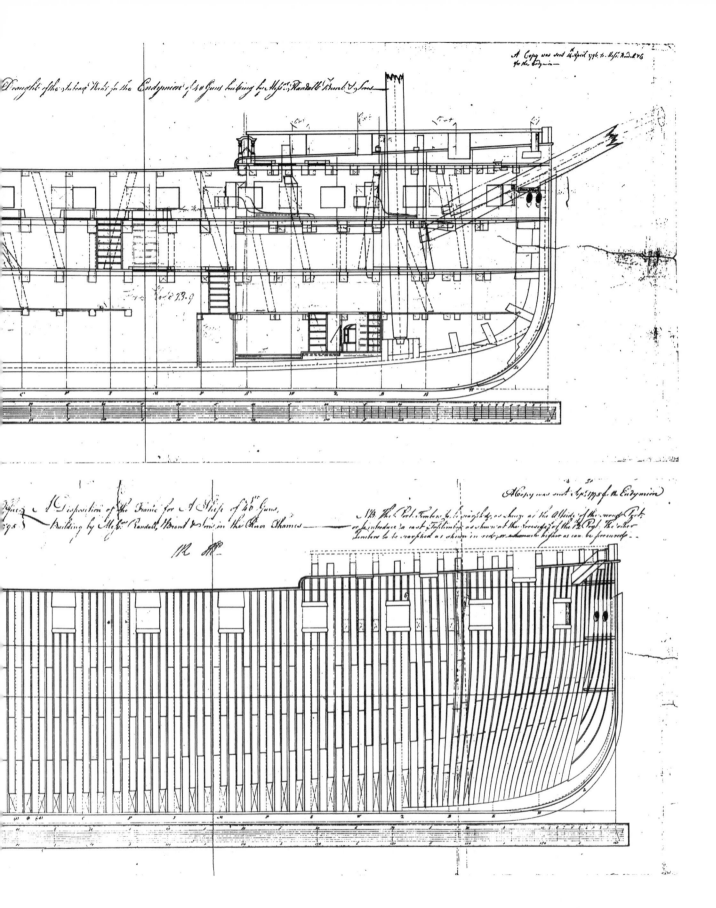

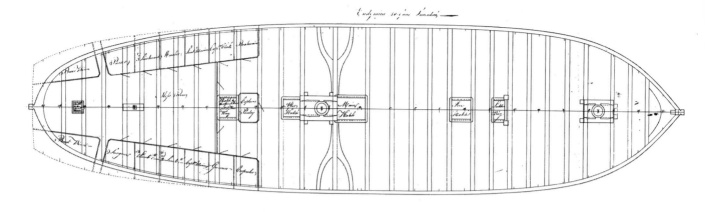

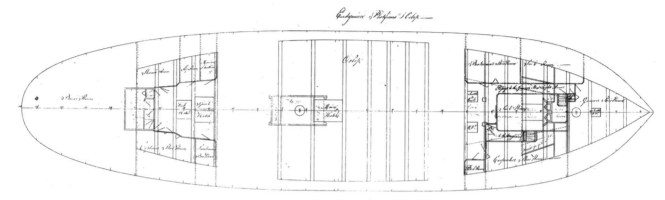

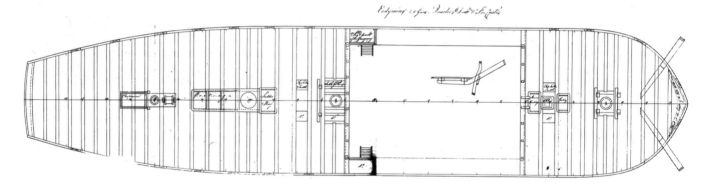

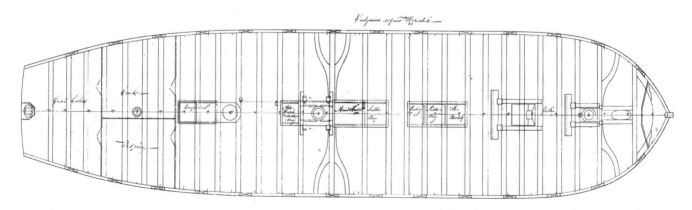

2 Architect's draughts of the *Endymion*
(*courtesy National Maritime Museum Picture Library, London*)

3 *Opposite top* 19th century model of the *Endymion*
(*courtesy Christie's of London*)

4 *Opposite bottom* **Endymion** was one of 15 British frigates at
the Battle of the Saints, April 1782 (*courtesy National Maritime
Museum Picture Library, London*)

struck to Sir Samuel Hood. On 14th April she gave chase to a number of French merchantmen without success, but two days later succeeded in taking a Danish Schooner. By 26th April the *Endymion* was back in Port Royal.

In July she sailed for America with HMS *Pigot* and in November was involved in the Blockade of Cape François. On 2nd January 1783, while on convoy duty she assisted the *Magicienne* in action against *La Sybille* (40 guns) and *Le Railleur* (16 guns) off Santo Domingo.

In October 1787, Captain Lieutenant J. Sall was put in command of *Endymion* and then in 1789, her final master, Lieutenant Dan Woodriff took command. His first mission was to transport troops from Ireland to America; he sailed from Spithead with orders dated 28th January 1789. The officers and crew consisted of (PRO, Admiralty Orders):

1 Lieutenant Commander
1 Master
1 Gunner
1 Carpenter
1 Purser
1 Surgeon
1 Master's Mate
2 Midshipmen
1 Clerk
4 Quartermasters
2 Boatswain's Mates
1 Carpenter's Mate
1 Gunner's Mate
1 Cook
1 Purser's Steward
75 Able Seamen

On reaching Nova Scotia he was instructed to sail to Jamaica for a refit. It was while on this voyage from Halifax to Port Royal, that, on 28th August 1790, the *Endymion* hit the previously unknown reef to the south-west of Great Sand Cay (then sometimes known as Sand Cay Jamaica).

Loss of the *Endymion*

Details of the loss can be found in the archive of the Public Records Office, London (ADM 5328), and in the Woodriff papers held by the National Maritime Museum at Greenwich (WDR/1/1, 2, 3, 11).

In the following, taken from a log in the National Maritime Museum collection, the original spelling and syntax have been retained:

At 8 a.m., was informed by the Master that there was 7½ fathom water, and in 5 minutes after the ship struck; attempted to keep the ship too, but she fell off in consequence of the eregularness of the ground, there being 7½ fathoms water under the main chains when the ship struck and 2 fathoms under larboard fore chains, and 3 fathoms under the mizen chains and ¼ 4 under the counter, hove all the sails aback but found it useless. Hoist out the jolly boat and sent the master to sound around the ship. Found the ship surrounded with high ridges of rocks from 2 fathoms to 8 or 9. Cleared up the sails and hoist out all the boats. Carried out the stream anchor to the ESE in 9 fathoms water. Found the ship hung by the starboard bow and starboard quarter, and struck very heavy

and that she had made 2 feet water. Rigged all the pumps and worked them but found the ship gained very fast upon the pumps. Hove in strain on the stream cable but found we could not move the ship, and she continuing to strike very heavy, and the water gaining fast in the hold insomuch that at 9 o'clock there was five feet water. Handed all the sails and tryed again to start the ship, but proved inefectual. At 10 saw a sail to the N called a counsel of all the officers who gave it as their gen. opinion that if the ship could be hove off she would go down at here anchors and that the most advisable method would be to cut away the main and mizen mast in order to ease the ship as it appeared impossible to free her of water (illeg.) cut away the main and mizen mast and cleared the wreck. At this time 7 feet water in the hold. The coal hole and magazine overflowed. Broke the people off from the pumps and began to preserve some part of the provisions. At noon the water nearly up to the orlop deck. Fresh breezes and hazey, W. ESE.

29 Aug
Fresh Breeze and (illeg.). Preserving as much as possible of the provisions and at 2 was joined by the schooner *New Hope*, James Small (or Smart) Master from Philadelphia and bound to Kingston who informed me of his surprise at the ship being on shore, not knowing of any shoal or reef in that direction and distance from Sand Key. At 3 sent the Master off in one of our boats to Turks Islands to give them information of our situation and for assistance (illeg.). Began to get the new sails and part of the best stores to hand in order to put them on board the schooner *New Hope*, the master of which promised to continue by the wreck to save the people and stores if practicable. Sent some stores and people on board the *New Hope* in the Cutter; the boat returned and the sea running so high and the ship labouring so much was impossible to send any more at this time. Got the foresail and foretopsail jib and foretopmast staysail. Middle (illeg.) staysail unbent and made up. Endeavoured to clear the wreck of the main and mizen rigging from the ship but could not by reason of the rigging having caught the rocks where by the boats got stove with the wreck. At ¼ past 10 the ship became so very laboursome and struck so hard as rendered it necessary to cut away the foremast, got the jib boom in and cut away the spritsail yard. At ½ past 10 observed the ship began to separate at the break of the forecastle deck. Cut away the two Bower anchors to ease her bows. At ¼ before 11 found the ship was going down foreward. Got all hands aft in the poop and fired all the remaining loaded guns, signal to the *New Hope* in 5 minutes after the ship was intirely under water foreward with the Boltspires (illeg.) end just out of the water with her stern considerable up. Continued to send the men on board the *New Hope* expecting the ship to part every minute. At 5 a.m. the cutter and launch returned from the *New Hope*, sent them away with more men. At 7 she returned with information that the *New Hope* could take no more. The ship underwater as far as the mainmast without a possibility of saving anything more than what had been got up on the quarter deck and poop. After observed a schooner coming down to us and spoke (to) her. Prooved to be the *Twins* (illeg.) who also gave me information that they knew nothing of the reef on which the ship lay, but that they had come down to assist us. Punnished George Campbell with 24 lashes for disobedience of orders. Sent part of the small arms on board the *New Hope*. At noon the master returned. Fresh Breezes and hazey, the wind at ESE.

The situation at this stage is depicted in a remarkable annotated sketch (fig 5) by (presumably) Woodriff himself. It shows the vessel down at the bow with its masts and rigging cut away. The remaining personnel can be seen escaping down a rope ladder into a waiting boat. The sketch also gives the wind direction and the compass bearings to Sand Key and Salt Key. A caption in the lower left corner reads:

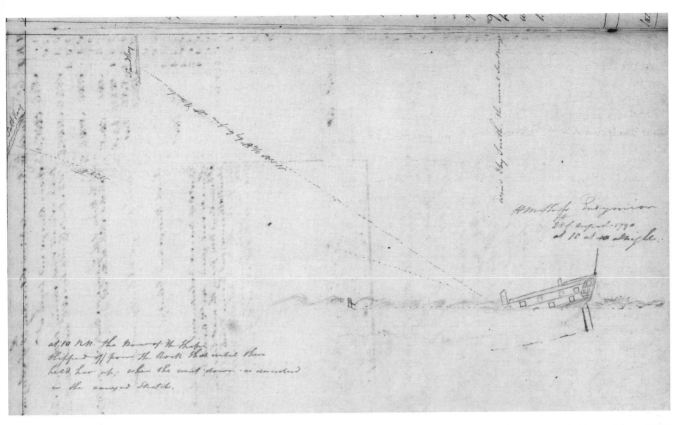

5 Sketch by Captain Woodriff, dated 28 August 1790, which shows the *Endymion* down at the bow and people abandoning her by a rope ladder from the stern into an awaiting boat. The masts and rigging have been cut away. Wind direction and bearing to Salt Key and Sand Key are given. The inscription in the lower left corner reads, 'at 10 pm the bow of the ship slipped off from the Rock that until then held her up - when she went down - as described in the annexed sketch'
(courtesy National Maritime Museum Picture Library, London)

at 10 p.m. the bow of the Ship slipped off from the Rocks which until then held her up - when she went down - as described in the annexed Sketch.

On Monday 30th August the *Endymion* was still down at the bow and the sea had reached the 'Capstern'. The schooner that had arrived the previous day was standing by, but the rocks had cut her cable and she had lost an anchor. A certain Mr Deane also appeared on the scene offering to recover whatever he could from the *Endymion* once Woodriff had quit the ship; in return for his services he would retain an appropriate proportion of the materials. At 4 p.m. Woodriff hauled down his colours. Soon after he and his crew were taken to Grand Key (Grand Turk) on the schooners *New Hope* and *Twins*.

On Grand Key sails were erected as tents for the sick and the search began for fresh water. In the days that followed 30 men and officers were sent to Jamaica on the *New Hope*, and the launch returned to the wreck to see whether it was possible to salvage any of the guns. In order to avoid a heavy bill, efforts were also made to recover the anchor that had been lost by the schooner. They were able to save one 9-pounder and its carriage but not the anchor. Discipline was

evidently breaking down for on 2nd September Will Parkinton, Ian Bond and Hess Watson were each given two dozen lashes and on the following day Josh Wilson and R. Harden received 12 lashes each for disobeying orders. On 9th September news was received of a declaration of war between the courts of Great Britain and Spain.

The Court Martial

Five weeks after the vessel's loss, on 6th October 1790, a court martial was convened on board His Majesty's ship *Blonde* in Port Royal Harbour, Jamaica, to try Woodriff, his officers and crew, and Samuel Barnett, the pilot, for the loss of the *Endymion*. Those present included William Affleck Esq. Commander of the *Blonde*, Rear Admiral of the Blue and Commander in Chief of His Majesty's ships and vessels at and about Jamaica, and captains Thomas Macnamara Russell, William Albany Otway, Davidge Gould and George Burdon. A notarized copy of the proceedings and final judgement are to be found in the Public Records Office, London (ADMI 5328) and the Woodriff papers held by the National Maritime Museum at Greenwich (WDR/1/S).

During the proceedings attention focused on whether or not the reef had been previously known. Charts of the area were brought in and scrutinized, particular attention was given to those from the most recent surveys of 1789. The reef did not feature on any of them. Woodriff and the pilot were cross-examined on their actions.[4]

Court: Lt. Woodriff, was the Ship, from the time of your Departure under the Pilot's Direction as to the Course?

Woodriff: She was; I only advised occasionally.

Court: ... When the Master informed you that the ship was in 7½ Fathom Water at 8 a.m. on the morning, what Precautions were taken to keep her off?

Woodriff: When the Master informed me there were 7½ Fathom Water, the ship then steering NNE, the Pilot, who was also on Deck and acquainted with the same; ordered the ship to be kept more away; on my informing him the Ship's Head was off to N. he ordered her to be kept up a little, at which Time the Ship struck the Ground.

* * * * *

Court to Pilot: How long have you been Pilot for the Navigation of Turks Island?

Pilot: Twelve years and better.

Court: Can you work a day's Work?

Pilot: I cannot; my Method is to navigate Vessels from the Place of my Departure.

Court to Woodriff: Had you any body at the Mast Heads?

Woodriff: We had a man at each Mast Head and I was up myself, once or twice, with the Master and Pilot.

Court to Pilot: Did you steer the same course with the *Endymion* from the Place of her Departure, that you have done in former times when Ships were under your Charge?

Pilot: I did.

Court: When you was informed by the Master that you were in 7½ Fathom Water, what was your reason for ordering the Ship's Course to be altered?

Pilot: Because I knew deep water was to leeward of the ship.

Court: How came you by that knowledge?

Pilot: By seeing the White Water, and knowing it was off the S West End of the Island. I knew by keeping away I should get off the Land and come into deeper Water, but didn't know of the shoal on which the Ship Struck.

Court to Woodriff: If you had kept your original course would you have cleared the Shoal?

Woodriff: I have every Reason to believe we should

The court returned the following verdict:

"... and having strictly enquired into the circumstances of the case on the part of the Crown, as well as heard what Lieut. Daniel Woodriff, his Officers and Crew, and the said pilot had to offer in their defence, and having very maturely and deliberately considered the whole and every part thereof, is of opinion that Lieut. Daniel Woodriff acquitted himself with great zeal and ability in his exertions to save his Majesty's Ship *Endymion*, and in his subsequent endeavour to save some part of her stores: the Court is likewise of opinion that the other officers and ship's company are blameless in the loss of his Majesty's ship *Endymion*; but that she was lost through the unavoidable ignorance of the pilot, as it has appeared from the most experienced pilots and inhabitants of Turks Island, that the Rock on which she struck was, until then, totally unknown. And Lieut. Daniel Woodriff, his officers, and ship's company and Samuel Barnett the Pilot are hereby acquitted accordingly.

James Cutforth, Judge Advocate on the Occasion.

Woodriff's later career

Woodriff went on to a distinguished career in the navy (as, indeed, did his son, also called Daniel, who first went to sea on the *Endymion* and was with his father on her final voyage). Details of Woodriff's post-*Endymion* service can be found in Marshall's *Royal Naval Biography* (1830, 540) and O'Byrne's *Naval Biographical Dictionary* (1849, 1321). Two years after the loss of the *Endymion*, Woodriff (still a lieutenant and again accompanied by his son) was in command of the *Kitty* on a voyage around the world, the primary purpose of which was to relieve the infant colony of Port Jackson in New South Wales.

In 1795, Woodriff made the rank of Commander and, in 1802, that of Captain. The same year he was appointed to the *Calcutta*, a 50-gun ship armed *en flute*. It was fitted out for the conveyance of convicts and was sent to establish a new settlement at Port Philip in Bass's Straits. Woodriff arrived there in October 1803, but found the site entirely unsuitable. He then sailed for the River Derwent on the south coast of Van Dieman's Land (Tasmania), where the settlement of Hobart was established. He returned to Spithead in July 1804, where the *Calcutta* went in for a refit so that it might again function in its full capacity as a man-of-war. With the alterations complete Woodriff and the *Calcutta* were ordered to St Helena to escort home any merchantmen that might be there awaiting naval protection. While on convoy duty back to England he fell in with a French squadron comprising one 3-decker, four 74-gun ships, three 40-gun frigates and two brigs of war. To give the convoy time to escape, Woodriff engaged the enemy and then, after a spirited engagement, surrendered. Woodriff was a prisoner of the French squadron for three months before being landed at Rochelle and then marched 600 miles, in mid-winter, to Verdun. Woodriff wrote several applications to Talleyrand to procure his release, and then around June 1807, Bonaparte ordered his return to England, for which the British released a French prisoner of like rank. At a court martial for the loss of the *Calcutta*, Woodriff was not only fully exonerated but was also commended for his action and described as 'a brave, cool and intrepid officer'. In 1808 Woodriff was appointed agent for prisoners of war at Gosport, and afterwards was posted to Jamaica as Commissioner. In 1830 he moved to the Royal Hospital at Greenwich where he died on the 24th February 1842.

The writer of this chapter, Mensun Bound, found Woodriff's resting place in the tiny cemetery beside the Royal Naval Hospital (fig 6). Unfortunately the cemetery had taken a direct hit from a bomb during World War II and Woodriff's grave was one of those that had been badly damaged if not destroyed. The gravestone, however, had not been discarded and was found inserted against the wall of the enclosure where it had become completely overgrown by bushes and dense undergrowth (fig 7). The inscription read:

Sacred to the memory of
Daniel Woodriff Esq RN CB
and one of the Captains of Greenwich Hospital
who died 24th February 1842
(in the?) eighty-sixth year of (life?)

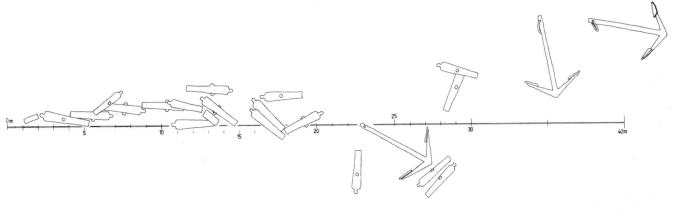

Adjacent to Woodriff's marker is the horizontal flag-stone memorial to his wife and son. Undamaged by the bomb, the inscription reads:

Sacred to the memory of
SARAH
relict of the late Capt Daniel Woodriff RN
who died 2nd January 1860 aged 90 years
Also Capt Daniel James Woodriff RN
(...) son of Capt Daniel Woodriff
who died 20th January 1860
aged 71 years
their remains are interred
in Saint Mary's catacombs
adjoining.

The wreck

The site consists of a line (just over 40m long) of 18 or 19 iron cannon (the majority of which appear to be 18-pounders; figs 8, 9 and 10) with four anchors at one end (figs 11 and 12). From their remarkably linear arrangement it would seem that the ship eventually settled with a pronounced list to port so that her guns ended up one on top of the other. A number of other features were visible; mainly rows of ballast blocks with smaller items of debris in between and hull sheathing underneath (fig 13). Particularly prominent was part of the keel structure with a row of large, upward-pointing keel bolts (fig 14).

There was only time to map the cannon and three of the anchors. The method was simply to lay a 40 metre tape along the main axis which functioned as a baseline from which off-set measurements were taken to the artefacts.

6 *Top left* The small cemetery beside the Royal Naval Hospital, Greenwich, where Woodriff and his wife and son are buried. Woodriff's grave stone was found completely concealed by the undergrowth below the railings that can be seen in the back of this photograph *(M. Bound)*

7 *Top right* Woodriff's grave stone through an opening made in the dense undergrowth. The cemetery (see fig 6) was bombed during World War II. Woodriff's grave was badly damaged by the explosion. His grave stone was afterwards set against the enclosure wall where it became overgrown by bushes and vines *(M. Bound)*.

8 *Above centre* Plan of the cannon and anchors on the reef. 1992 survey *(Oxford University MARE)*

9 *Lower right* The line of cannon can be seen below the diver *(Gianluigi Sacco/Oxford University MARE)*

letter dated 29th August 1791, in the Public Record Office's *Board of Ordnance Bill Books* of 1600-1800, concerning the costs of salvaging the *Endymion*'s guns (personal communication 13/2/93). The document is from the Lord's

10 *Left* Mapping the cannon. Anchor chain from a nineteenth century wreck on the other side of the reef can be seen wrapped around the coral head
(Gianluigi Sacco/Oxford University MARE)

11 *Below left* Anchor from the *Endymion*
(Gianluigi Sacco/Oxford University MARE)

12 *Below* Anchor from the *Endymion*
(Gianluigi Sacco/Oxford University MARE)

There was not time to double-check the measurements (as is our custom) and so the complete accuracy of the plan presented here in figure 6 cannot be guaranteed.

Certainly some of the wreck has been concealed by the coral head, and maybe also cannon, but none the less, it seems that over half the guns are missing[5]. It has been established that the site was visited by treasure hunters prior to its rediscovery in 1991, and it may be that they were responsible for the removal of some of the cannon[6], but it is more likely that the majority of the guns were recovered by salvors soon after the vessel's loss. Indeed, the ordnance specialist, Ruth Brown, has located a

Commissioner of the Admiralty and concerns a letter from the Commander-in-Chief of His Majesty's ships at Jamaica stating that the salvor was requesting half of the value of any guns raised as payment. Their Lordships, however, could see no reason why any more than the standard one-third should be paid. The outcome was not clear, but the evidence on the sea-bed seems to suggest that an agreement was reached and that the salvors were partially successful in their efforts. It may be that some of the anchors were also salvaged, for it would seem that a ship of this size would have carried more than those recorded by the team during the preliminary survey.

survey, a number of small objects were observed in the gaps between stones and some of these were removed to the safety of the Turks and Caicos Museum. These items are illustrated in figures 15 and 16. Most of the nails in these photographs were round-headed tacks for the attachment of hull sheathing.[7]

The four anchors were of admiralty pattern form typical of the middle and second half of the eighteenth century.[8] Similar anchors were also found on the wreck of HMS *Sirius* which sank the same year as the *Endymion* (see Stanbury pp 217-229, and Henderson & Stanbury, 1988, 109). A like example is also on show in the grounds of the National Maritime Museum at Greenwich; it was an isolated find from off Sheerness and is believed to be from a naval vessel.

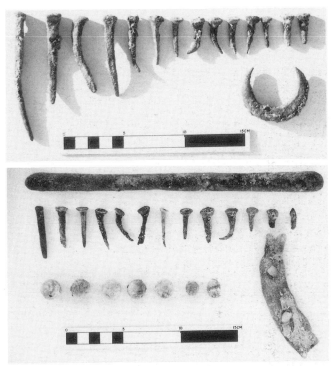

13 *Upper left* On one side of the cannon-line is a spread of ballast blocks and hull sheathing (*Gianluigi Sacco/Oxford University* MARE)

14 *Below left* Keel bolts (*Gianluigi Sacco/Oxford University* MARE)

15 *Top right* Items recovered during the 1992 survey (see note 7)

16 *Bottom* Tacks, musket balls and unidentified objects recovered during the 1992 survey (see note 7)

The finds

Particularly noticeable was the absence of the kind of ancillary material that usually accompanies a wreck of this nature. Certainly, at this depth, some material would have been swept away during periods of storm and more would have been lost in the currents (which at times during our visits were so strong that we had to pull our way along the sea-bed, stone by stone), but more than that, the site had the feel of a wreck that had been 'picked over' by souvenir hunters, so that the only small items left were things of little curiosity value. None the less, during the course of the

Merchant ships of the period, however, also carried anchors of this type; for instance the British East Indiaman *Winterton*, which sank off Madagascar in 1792 (only two years after the *Endymion*), had anchors of similar style (Stenuit, 1991, 63). The form is distinctive for its pointed crown and the sharp angle between the arm and shank, features which indicate that it was made before the manufacturing improvements of around 1800. These advances involved a strengthening of the iron used in the anchor-making process as well as the introduction of the steam hammer for welding around 1830. The main weakness in anchors of the *Endymion*-type was at the 'throat' or 'trend' (i.e. where the arms join the shank). Indeed the evidence of underwater archaeology would support this, for in the first author's experience, when broken anchors of this form have been recovered, the break has nearly always occurred at the throat. The *Endymion* anchors were all intact but were missing their stocks, which was entirely to be expected in view of the fact that they had been made of wood. Wooden stocks during this period were frequently filled with nails to inhibit the action of marine borers. Interestingly, near where the stock of one of the anchors would have been, we did indeed find, absorbed into the coral, a number of long nails and a hoop.

Recommendations

Although the site is of historical interest and of great heritage value to the Turks and Caicos Islands, it is unlikely that the excavation of the wreck would reveal much that is not already known or represent a significant step forward in historical learning. It is, however, a particularly dramatic and exciting wreck located within a shallow setting of outstanding natural splendour both from the point of view of the coral formations and the fish life. For these reasons, it is felt that the *Endymion* should be made a protected 'monument' site to which authorized diving organizations should be allowed to take visitors on a strictly 'look-but-don't-touch' basis. A site such as this, if suitable boat transport were available, would certainly attract additional recreational divers to the island, and in so doing would increase tourist revenue.

Interest aroused in the wreck because of the survey has resulted in the Endymion Reef and its surrounds being made into a National Historical Park, but none the less the threat of vandalism remains high. Certainly the distance of the site from land will discourage casual souvenir hunters and the like, but that same distance will favour the more determined looters. For this reason, if no other, a full survey of the site is much to be desired. In this way, if the worst happens and the wreck is destroyed by cumulative souvenir-picking or massive acts of vandalism, then at least it will have been fully documented.

Acknowledgements

The authors are particularly grateful to Kevin Grant, Cliff Hamilton (Director of Turks and Caicos Tourism) and Arabella Smith (Ministry of Natural Resources) for arranging the survey and securing the necessary governmental support and authorization. Brian Wood (Ministry of Natural Resources) and Chris Ninnes (Dept. of Fisheries) provided fishery patrol vessels and crew to carry the team to and from the site. In Britain Bryan Smith spent many hours carrying out much needed research in the Public Records Office. Others to whom we are indebted include Brian Sheedy, Cecil Ingham, Mitch Rolling, Gianluigi Sacco, Christina Giordano and Grethe Seim.

Notes

1 There is some confusion in the records concerning the date of her loss; some sources give June, others July.

2 One of the *Endymion*'s sister ships in the Roebuck class was the *Serapis* which was taken by John Paul Jones during the famous action with the *Bonhomme Richard* off Flamborough Head on 23 September 1779.

3 According to Rupert Jones' lists of Royal Naval vessels in the National Maritime Museum at Greenwich (483-484), she was said during this period (1780-81) to have taken the French vessel *Fauvette*, but of this we have not been able to find any further evidence. Could it be that Jones mistook *Fayette* for *Fauvette*?

4 The opinion of another pilot, John Young, was also sought. He was ill in the Port Royal Naval Hospital at the time and had to testify by letter:
"... He believes he has gone through the passage fifty times; and declares he never, till the *Endymion* struck on the Rock, or Shoal, heard of it; and now believes it was not known before that time."

5 The full complement would have been about 48.

6 At one point fresh breaks, pitting and discoloration of the coral suggested that a gun had recently been forcedly removed or displaced.

7 Fig 15: Crescent shape piece of copper alloy, 33mm from tip to tip, 11mm across at middle. Nails (numbered 1 to 14; 8 to 11 intact) from left to right: 1) length 104mm. Shank square in section, diam. of head 10mm. 2) 1.73mm; shank oblong in section, head 8 x 12mm. 3) 1.65mm; oblong in section. 4) 1.68mm; oblong in section. 5) 1.45mm; square in section. 6) 1.38mm; square in section. 7) 1.34mm. 8) 1.36mm. 9) 1.36mm. 10) 1.36mm. 11) 1.36mm. (12) 1.30mm. 13) broken, 1.24mm. 14) broken, 1.23mm
Fig 16. Copper alloy bar at top. 13 nails, numbered 15 to 27: 15) 1.43mm. 16) 1.35mm. 17) 1.32mm. 18) 1.36mm. 19) 1.33mm. 20) 1.34mm. 21) 1.33mm. 22) broken. 1.25mm. 23) broken. 1.27mm. 24) 1.34mm. 25) broken. 1.20mm. 26) broken. 1.15mm. 27) broken. 1.15mm. Seven pieces of firearm lead shot: left to right: 1 to 5) of 16mm diam. 6) diam. 11.5mm 7) distorted shot with excrescence of metal from mould on one side. Curved, perforated strip of copper alloy, broken at both ends, length 108mm, width 22-26mm, diam. of holes 8-11mm and 9-10mm. Function uncertain but recalls sprit-trees for hammocks found on the frigate *Lossen* (Molaug and Scheen, 1993, 112).

8 One anchor had a shank of 17ft, arms of 7ft 5in, flukes of 3ft 10in x 3ft 10in x 3ft and a ring of 2ft 6in diameter.

References

Henderson, G. and Stanbury, M., 1988, *The Sirius, past and present*, Collins, Sydney.

Jones, R., Unpublished list of naval ships in five bound volumes at National Maritime Museum, Greenwich.

Lecky, H.S., 1913, *The Kings' Ships*, 3 vols., London

Marshall, J., 1830, *Royal Naval Biography or Memoirs of the Services of all the Flag-Officers, Superannuated rear-Admirals, retired Captains, post-Captains and Commanders*, London.

Molaug, S. and Scheen, R., 1993, *Fregatten Lossen*, Norsk Sjofartsmuseum, Oslo.

O'Byrne, W.R., 1849, *A Naval Biographical Dictionary, comprising the life and services of every living officer in her Majesty's Navy*, London.

Stenuit, R., 1991, Il Tesoro del Winterton, *Sub*, VIII, no. 74.

Myra Stanbury (Curator, Maritime Archaeology, Western Australia Maritime Museum)

HMS *Sirius*: 'reconstructed … pygmy battle ship' or 'appropriate' 6th Rate vessel?

Introduction

HMS *Sirius* is one of Australia's most important shipwrecks, its significance derives from its leading role in the European settlement of Australia in the late eighteenth century. The *Sirius* was commissioned by the British Admiralty in 1786 to escort a fleet of eleven ships, sailing with convicts, on a voyage of more than 12,000 miles (19,312km). Leaving England on 13 May 1787, under the command of Captain Arthur Phillip, the First Fleet embarked upon a unique venture in European history. The mission was to establish a new British colony at Botany Bay on the east coast of Australia. Although European powers had been expanding their spheres of influence by creating settlements in various parts of the world, especially along major trade routes, no attempt had been made to establish a new colony across such a vast distance, or with convict labour. After a journey lasting eight months, the fleet arrived safely at Port Jackson (Sydney) in January 1788.

Despite a wealth of literature relating to the voyage of the First Fleet, few accounts give any detailed information about the ships which undertook this epic journey. Moreover, the role of HMS *Sirius*, whose history was closely associated with the taint of Australia's convict past, has tended to be overshadowed by the glory attributed to Captain James Cook's *Endeavour*.

Many contemporary and subsequent historical accounts have presented the *Sirius* in a critical light (see Frost, 1994, 5-8), giving the illusion that the ship was either a 'typical' decrepit, leaking convict hulk, or, as Irvine (1988, 40) has described her, 'a reconstructed . . . pygmy battle ship'. Implicit in these assumptions is the notion that the vessel was not an appropriate choice and was ill-suited to its role. In the broader context, such views tend to perpetuate a commonly held theory that the expedition to Botany Bay was hastily organized and poorly equipped, since it was merely a temporary expedient to relieve England's overcrowded gaols following the American War of Independence (Gillen, 1982). Alternative theories, however, view the settlement at Botany Bay as part of a well-executed strategic plan to establish and maintain a permanent British presence in Eastern and South Pacific waters (Frost, 1980, 1987a, 1994; Oldham, 1990, 153; Whitmont, 1992/93).

In 1983, it was proposed that 'the remains of the ship [*Sirius*] would be raised as a reminder to all Australians of the country's European origins and displayed as a feature of the bicentennial celebrations in 1988. This marked the beginning of the *Sirius* Project and provided an opportunity to challenge existing theoretical views using archaeological evidence. Following a feasibility study, archaeological investigations were carried out at Norfolk Island (where the vessel was lost) in 1985, 1987, 1988 and 1990.

This paper will briefly outline the history of HMS *Sirius* and discuss some of the archival and archaeological data which are being used to address one of the principal research problems identified by the *Sirius* Project, i.e. to establish whether or not the *Sirius* was:

> … an 'appropriate', reasonably equipped and maintained vessel for its role as protector and provider in the first phase of the British colonisation of Australia (Henderson, 1989a, 9).

Background and wrecking of the *Sirius*

Once the First Fleet had arrived at Botany Bay and the convicts, military personnel and stores had been off-loaded the greater part of the convoy departed; some vessels went whaling, others took on freight for the return voyage to England. The naval tender, HMS *Supply*, proceeded to Norfolk Island in the South Pacific (lat. 29° S, long. 168° E) where Lieutenant Gidley King had orders to establish a satellite colony. This left the *Sirius*, the larger of the two naval vessels, to perform the vital function of protector, provider and communications link with the outside world (Henderson, 1989b, 5).

By September 1788, the colony at Botany Bay was struggling to survive. Governor Phillip had little choice but to send the *Sirius* on another lengthy journey around Cape Horn to Cape Town, to fetch stores and medicines. After surviving heavy storms off Tasmania on the final passage home, the *Sirius* arrived at Port Jackson on 9 May 1789, to find that fresh supplies still had not arrived from Europe and that the situation at Botany Bay was critical. To reduce the demand on scarce resources, Governor Phillip decided to dispatch both the *Sirius* and *Supply* to Norfolk Island, 1,500km east of Sydney, with a substantial number of convicts and marines; after which the *Sirius* would proceed to China to buy provisions.

Departing on 5 March 1790, the two ships endured a stormy eight-day passage before reaching their destination. Bad weather made it impossible to off-load people and provisions at Sydney Bay, adjacent to the settlement, but they managed to land the marines and convicts at Cascade Bay before being forced out to sea. When the gale moderated on 19 March the two ships again approached Sydney Bay.

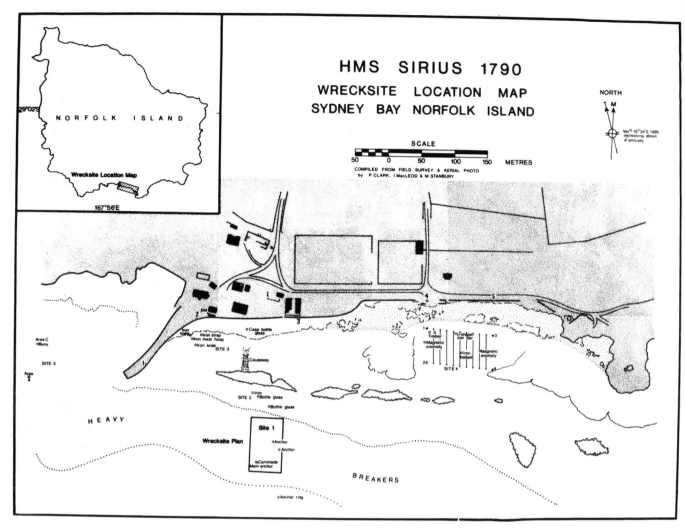

1 Location of the *Sirius* wreck site at Norfolk Island

HMS *Supply* had already completed its off-loading by the time the *Sirius* sailed into the Bay. The signal flag on shore was raised, indicating that longboats could land without danger, but by the time the *Sirius'* boats were launched and loaded with stores, Captain Hunter noticed that his ship was drifting rapidly shorewards, perilously close to a reef off the west point of Sydney Bay. Heeding a warning from Lieutenant Ball of the *Supply*, he hastily made sail.

Unfortunately, a sudden wind shift prevented the *Sirius* from tacking out to sea, in the wake of the *Supply*, and the vessels became embayed. Hunter attempted to alter course eastwards past the landing point, but the onshore wind and current made it impossible for the ship to avoid the fringing reef situated some 100m from shore. Hunter tried in vain to change tack, but it was too late. As Lieutenant Newton Fowell later described in a letter to his father dated 31 July 1790:

… She [*Sirius*] came Round but before She was paid off Sufficiently on the other Tack She was thrown a Shore by the swell on the Reef & payed Round off with her broadside on the shore in a Great Surf/ An Anchor was let go on Her first striking/in Less than 10 Minutes the Masts were all over the side, the Ship an intire [sic] Wreck (Newton Fowell, Letter 20, 31 July 1790, in Irvine, 1988, 119-20).

The process of wrecking was a slow one, the ship taking almost two years to finally break up and disappear beneath the pounding surf. During this period, everything that could be safely salvaged was removed from the vessel. The location of the wreck site has always been known; it was recorded on contemporary and subsequent charts of Sydney Bay, and throughout the nineteenth century one of the anchors remained visible on the site at low tide, serving to pinpoint the area where the ship foundered.

The *Sirius* wreck site: location and description

Norfolk Island is an isolated volcanic island rising abruptly from the Norfolk Ridge which stretches 1,770km from New Caledonia to New Zealand. The island is almost entirely surrounded by steep surf-lashed cliffs up to 91m high with water depths dropping off rapidly to 200m then to 2,000m.

The location of the *Sirius* wreck site is shown in fig 1. Five main areas of artefact deposits (Sites 1-5) have been identified, the main areas lying between 150 to 300m east of Kingston pier and extending approximately 200m south from the high, inshore reef. The latter encloses a small lagoon adjacent to Slaughter Bay (Site 4) and is separated from the outer reef platform by a deep gully (Site 2), invariably filled with white water and subject to strong along-shore currents.

The depth of water across the 200m site varies from 1.5 to 8m (north to south), the bottom falling away quickly over the last 60m offshore. Waves of up to 1.5m break at the inshore end of the wreck site at mid-tide and the breaking wave zone spreads offshore as the waves increase in height or as the tide falls (figs 2 and 3; Cresswell, 1989). There is rarely a day when no swell or break exists over the wreck site making diving conditions and visibility extremely difficult.

Especially good conditions in 1987 and 1988 enabled a detailed survey of the wreck site to be made (fig 4; Jeffery, 1989). The main concentration of archaeological material lies on top of a flat, gently sloping reef in which there are numerous gullies and holes several metres wide and up to 1m deep. The sea-bed consists of hard calcareous rock with a light covering of weed and numerous sea-urchins. While many of the artefacts were difficult to excavate in the prevailing sea conditions, numerous small objects were easily recovered from the shallow gullies.

Several thousand items have been raised from the wreck site. These include large bower anchors, two carronades, pintles and gudgeons, various small fastenings and a single copper, Spanish, two Maravedís coin bearing the head of Charles (Carlos) III of Spain, dated 1774 (Stanbury, 1994). Under the supervision of conservators from the Western Australian Maritime Museum and the Museums Association of Australia, the bulk of the material has been conserved on Norfolk Island by members of the community. They have also assisted in the fabrication of replica wooden stocks for the bower anchors and a sliding carriage for one of the carronades (Kimpton, 1992). These and other objects are displayed in the *Sirius* Museum at Norfolk Island; a selection is also on view at the Australian National Maritime Museum in Sydney.

Archival contributions to the theoretical debate

Historical records have already shed new light on many aspects of the *Sirius*' design and construction (Henderson & Stanbury, 1988). The archival evidence generally supports the thesis that the *Sirius* was a well constructed vessel with good sailing ability and more than adequate cargo carrying capacity, and that criticisms of its 'unseaworthiness' during the voyage could well have applied to any similarly built vessel of the period.

Contrary to previously held beliefs, the *Sirius* was shown to have been constructed as a Baltic trader or 'East Country' ship named *Berwick*, as opposed to an 'East Indiaman'. The 511-ton ship, built on the Thames at Rotherhithe in 1780/81, was a large vessel for the period. While still on the stocks at Christopher Watson's yard (Stanbury, 1994, 10), the *Berwick* was purchased by the British navy for a substantial price and taken to Deptford to be fitted out as an armed storeship (fig 5). Although contemporary accounts suggest that the *Berwick* was completed using 'refuse of the Yard' (King, 1787-1790, 19), historical evidence does not support

2 Diver in breaking surf on the *Sirius* wreck site
(Photo: Patrick Baker, WA Maritime Museum)

3 Underwater site conditions
(Photo: Patrick Baker, WA Maritime Museum)

this assertion. Rather, the same quality materials were used as on similar ships built at Deptford and other Royal dockyards at the time.

The *Berwick* exhibited features of both a frigate and a bark hull design. Essentially, it was a 'short, beamy, deep vessel with good cargo carrying qualities' (Henderson & Stanbury, 1988, 46), in some respects a larger version of the collier barks *Endeavour* and *Resolution* which Cook used for his South Seas voyages. Whether heavily laden with cargo or lightly ballasted, she maintained a good speed and performed well in various wind and sea conditions — as reported by Lieutenant Baynton Prideaux, the *Berwick*'s first commissioned officer (*Berwick*, 9 Jan. 1784, Ship's Sailing Qualities, ADM/95/36, Public Record Office, London), and substantiated by the *Sirius*' sailing performance during the voyage to Botany Bay (Henderson & Stanbury, 1988, 72; Oldham, 1990, 146).

After several voyages across the Atlantic and to the West Indies during 1782 to 1785, the *Berwick* was surveyed and considered suitable for further foreign service. A comprehensive re-fit was carried out and in October 1786, Admiral Howe wrote to the Navy Board directing that the

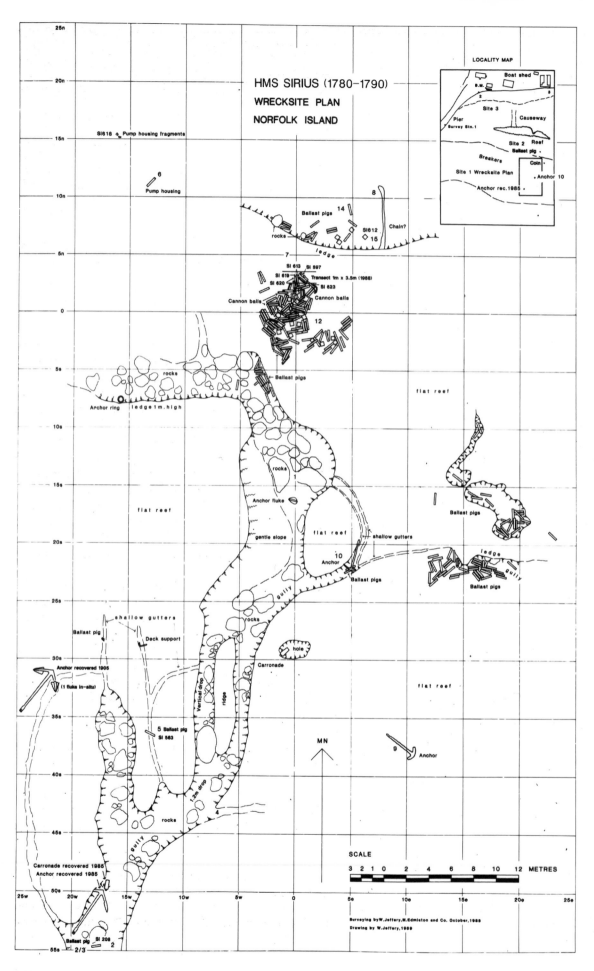

HMS SIRIUS (1780–1790)

WRECKSITE PLAN

NORFOLK ISLAND

LOCALITY MAP

Boat shed

B.M.

Site 3

Pier

Survey Stn.1

Causeway

Site 2 Reef

Ballast pig

Breakers

Coin

Site 1 Wrecksite Plan

Anchor 10

Anchor rec.1985

25n

20n

15n   SI618   Pump housing fragments

6

10n   Pump housing

8

14

Ballast pigs

rocks   SI612

15   Chain?

7   ledge

5n

SI 613   SI 597

SI 619   Transect 1m x 3.5m (1988)

SI 620   SI 623

Cannon balls   Cannon balls

0

12

5s   rocks

Ballast pigs

flat reef

Anchor ring   ledge 1m.high

10s

rocks

15s   Anchor fluke

Ballast pigs

flat reef

gentle slope   flat reef   shallow gutters

20s   10   Anchor

Ballast pigs   ledge   gully

Ballast pigs

25s   gully

rocks

shallow gutters   rocks

Ballast pig   Deck support   hole

30s   Anchor recovered 1905   Carronade

(1 fluke in-situ)   flat reef

Vertical drop   ridge

35s   5 Ballast pig   MN   9   Anchor

SI 563

40s

1.2m drop

45s   rocks   4

gully

SCALE

Carronade recovered 1985   3 2 1 0   2   4   6   8   10   12 METRES

Anchor recovered 1985

50s

25w   20w   15w   10w   5w   0   5e   10e   15e   20e   25e

Ballast pig   SI 208

2

55s   2/3

Surveying by W.Jeffery, M.Edmiston and Co. October, 1988

Drawing by W.Jeffery, 1989

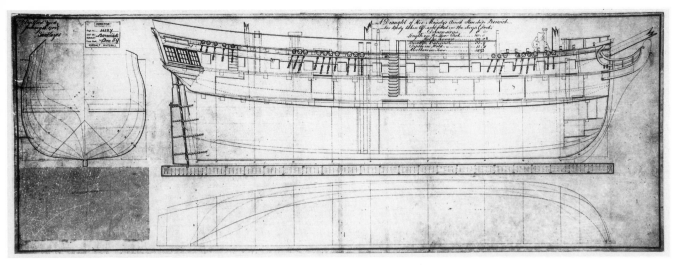

4 *Opposite* Plan of the *Sirius* wreck site (*Surveyed and drawn by W. Jeffery, 1989*)

5 *Above* Draught of His Majesty's Arm'd Storeship *Berwick*, January 1782 (*Courtesy of the National Maritime Museum, Greenwich*)

Berwick be registered as a 6th Rate by the name of *Sirius*. More work was then ordered to prepare the ship for the voyage to Botany Bay. Once again, there is no evidence to suggest that the maintenance and repair work undertaken did not comply with normal Navy standards. Nevertheless, officers on board complained about various defects — decaying gun deck planking and skirting boards, leaking upper decks, and dry rot on one of the top timbers (Henderson & Stanbury, 1988, 70-72). Many of these defects were commonplace, resulting from inadequate caulking, worm-eaten or damaged skirting boards, and so on.

Throughout the First Fleet voyage the hull stayed watertight. But on the long voyage to obtain stores, corrosion of one of the old iron bolts caused a leak (Henderson & Stanbury, 1988, 71, 74-77). The *Berwick* was originally fastened with iron bolts and, had the ship been used for the Baltic trade for which it was designed, it would probably not have been coppered (Rees, 1971-2, 89). However, once the *Berwick*'s destination to the warring American colonies and the tropical waters of the West Indies was determined, the Navy, in 1782, clearly saw advantages in coppering the ship, despite the inevitable consequences of electrolytic reaction which corroded the iron fastenings. During the overhaul of the *Berwick* in 1786, copper bolts were driven into the hull to supplement the iron fastenings (Henderson & Stanbury, 1988, 60) and spares were put on board for the voyage to Botany Bay.

Archaeologically, the study of the *Sirius* aims to identify recovered artefacts and to correlate them with particular parts of the ship and known events in her life history. It is hoped that this will also give a better appreciation and understanding of the quality of the materials used in the various phases of construction, repair and maintenance, and their durability as evidenced by their survival characteristics.

In terms of analyses, the *Sirius* may be viewed as a 'composite' or 'reconstructed' ship — that is to say an original ship which has been modified in various ways over a given time span. To evaluate the ship's 'appropriateness' by comparison with other contemporary vessels of standard design specifications, the *Sirius* needs to be considered on three different levels: the *Berwick* as a Baltic trader, akin to the north-east coast colliers, such as Cook's *Endeavour* and *Resolution* (McGowan, 1979; Jones, 1984); the *Berwick* as an armed naval storeship similar to HM Storeships *Porpoise* and *Elephant* (Syrett, 1988, 1989); and as HMS *Sirius*, a 20-gun naval 'frigate' in many ways comparable to HMS *Pandora* (Gesner, 1988, 1991; McKay & Coleman, 1992). On the one hand we are dealing with a ship originally built in a private dockyard where standards of workmanship and materials often left much to be desired, and, on the other, a ship rebuilt and refitted according to the rigours of naval rules and regulations.

With regard to broader interpretations, analyses of the artefacts in relation to the modifications or alterations may help to evaluate these changes qualitatively in terms of the advances being made in late eighteenth century shipbuilding technology, and the purposes for which these changes were made. The late eighteenth century was perhaps one of the most progressive periods in English shipbuilding, 'technological progress being made during a period in which few branches of the [British] economy showed marked technical advances, and many showed none' (Davis, 1962, 392). Yet, there are many aspects of eighteenth century ship design and construction, particularly concerning ordinary merchant ships prior to the end of the 1790s, that are not at all well known (Davis, 1962, 71). The remains of the *Sirius*, therefore, may serve to enhance our knowledge of shipbuilding techniques of this period.

What has the archaeological record revealed?

Many of the artefacts recovered from the *Sirius* are lending support to the thesis that the ship was well constructed and fitted out. Remains of a sextant and other scientific instruments are comparable to those taken by Captain James Cook on his exploratory voyages; indeed, a number of the instruments supplied to the *Sirius* were the same ones issued to Cook by the Board of Longitude (Stanbury, 1991; 1994, 58-66). This is regarded, therefore, as a positive reflection of the standard of preparation for the voyage to Botany Bay and the degree of commitment to the success of the expedition.

Other artefacts are providing evidence of the type and quality of materials used in the construction of the *Sirius*, as well as information on eighteenth century technology in general. Metal fittings and fastenings especially, have usefully demonstrated the way in which an aggressive shipwreck site degrades different materials, the corrosion performance providing a measure of the quality of the materials used to manufacture these items, and hence a measure of the seaworthiness of the *Sirius*. The following will highlight some of these findings.

Bronze spectacle plate

A bronze spectacle plate found prior to the *Sirius* Project in a gully to the west of the Kingston Pier (Site 5) is the only object which positively identifies the *Sirius* wreck site. Cast into the band is the name 'BERWICK', the name of the original ship (fig 6). During a comprehensive refit of the *Berwick* in 1786, in preparation for the First Fleet voyage, the rudder was unhung so that moulds could be taken of the pintles and gudgeons in case spares should be required. Since the copper sheathing was never removed, it is certain that the vessel had carried the same spectacle plate since it was coppered in 1782.

In the 1780s, rudder fittings were reputed to be often badly made (Anon., 8 Oct. 1782, Deptford Yard Letter Book, ADM/106/3472. PRO, London; Knight, 1973, 303). The spectacle plate thus provided one of the earliest opportunities to examine the quality and metal composition of the fittings used in the construction of the *Berwick*. From 1784, copper founders were required by the Navy Board to mark their products with their names. A similar spectacle plate found on the wreck of HMS *Pandora*, built for the Navy, was marked with broad arrows and the name of the manufacturer (Forbes), but the *Sirius* piece bears no maker's mark. Quality assessment, based on a known source of production, was therefore not possible.

Corrosion patterns on one surface of the spectacle plate were consistent with the object being intermittently buried and exposed. It also exhibited casting porosity (gas bubbles in the metal) patterns identical to rudder gudgeons and a pintle recovered from the main wreck site deposit (Site 1). Chemical analyses of metal samples from these objects were thus undertaken in order to confirm their archaeological association (Sites 1 and 5 being more than 350m apart, with known evidence of other vessels having been wrecked close to Kingston pier after the *Sirius*). The data showed that the spectacle plate, a rudder gudgeon (NI 18), and a pintle (NI 16) were probably cast from the same melt; the compositional range within the metal is consistent with the variation one

6 Bronze spectacle plate marked 'BERWICK', and rudder chains. (Photo: Patrick Baker, WA Maritime Museum. Courtesy of the Australian Bicentennial Authority)

7 Bronze rudder gudgeon NI 18 (length 60cm). (Photo: Graeme Henderson, WA Maritime Museum)

would expect to find within an individual object as the result of repeated sampling (MacLeod, 1985, 54; Stanbury, 1994, 24 ff., 103-4). Other fittings were similar in composition and possibly derive from the same source.

Gudgeons and pintles

Chemical analyses have helped to identify and correlate artefacts that ended up in different parts of the site, as well as confirming the physical associations within fragmented objects.

The *Berwick* had five sets of pintles and gudgeons. Only one complete gudgeon (NI 17) and one pintle (NI 16), however, have been recovered from the site; two broken gudgeon brackets, five arms and three pintle pins represent the additional remnants of the complement.

Two gudgeon brackets (NI 18 and NI 19) had both arms broken off at approximately the same place — a short distance beyond the point where a through bolt would have fastened the gudgeon to the stern-post. This raised issues as to whether there might be a potential area of 'weakness' to account for breakages commonly occurring about this point, and if this could be the consequence of poorly made fittings? Reconstruction of the broken rudder fittings was aimed at determining the configuration of the fastenings, and to derive further insight as to the way in which the breakages may have occurred. The apparent physical correlation between broken components, however, was not always a reliable basis for matching the parts.

The hypothetical reconstruction of the gudgeon in fig 7 was based on what initially appeared to be a good physical match; it was later proved to be incorrect by virtue of comparative chemical analyses. Bracket NI 18 and arm SI 87 were sampled either side of the break; results demonstrated a bronze or 'mixed metal' composition (89.4-89.6% copper and 6.72-6.99% tin). Arm NI 14, however, is copper and more closely resembles the composition of strap SI 397; they contain 98.55-98.8% copper and 0.11-0.26% tin (MacLeod, 1993 in Stanbury, 1994, 103). Given these results, it is now evident that the *Sirius* had rudder fittings made from two different metal compositions — 'mixed metal' or bronze, and copper. Since the specifications for the *Berwick* indicate that the braces and pintles were of 'mixed metal' (Henderson & Stanbury, 1988, 48), these findings suggest that either the original complement of fastenings did not fully comply with the specifications, or some of the original bronze braces/pintles were replaced with copper ones.

While most of the rudder fittings were well worn and distorted, one bronze gudgeon strap (SI 237) was recovered from the main wreck deposit in almost pristine condition. Two fastenings remained *in situ*, a copper alloy lag screw and a rudder nail marked with a broad arrow, indicating Royal Navy issue. They clearly demonstrate the system of alternating screws and bolts used on naval vessels in the 1780s (Lavery, 1984, 114; fig 8) and possibly relate to the refitting or repair of the *Sirius*. Based on physical and chemical analyses, the strap has been shown to fit with worn gudgeon bracket NI 19 (MacLeod, 1993 in Stanbury, 1994, 25, 103), and provides a good visual comparison of the differential corrosion that has occurred to parts of the same object.

A number of copper alloy lag screws and rudder nails marked with the broad arrow have been found on the site and are compatible in size with the fastening holes in the gudgeon and pintle straps (fig 9). They were concentrated in Areas 1 and 8 of Site 1, those from Area 8 being in a far better state of preservation. Other concentrations of fastenings in Area 8 (copper alloy clench rings, sheathing nails, etc.) suggest that the better preserved fastenings may have been spares.

Hull fastenings

Bolts of several types and dimensions have also been recovered from the *Sirius* site. So far, however, only three iron bolts have been raised from the main wreck site deposit. This indicates that either the iron fastenings have

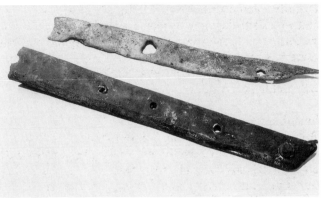

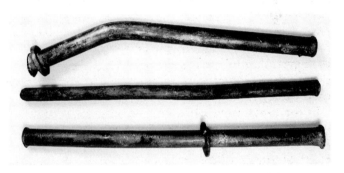

8 *Top* Lag screws marked with the broad arrow (length 12 cm max.). *(Photo: Patrick Baker, WA Maritime Museum)*

9 *Centre* Bronze rudder gudgeon/pintle straps - SI 397 (top), SI 237 (bottom). Note contrast in preservation (length 85 cm). *(Photo: Patrick Baker, WA Maritime Museum)*

10 Copper clench bolts. Top to bottom: SI 381, NI 10 and SI 301 (length 60 cm) *(Photo: Patrick Baker, WA Maritime Museum)*

disintegrated in the high energy environment, or that almost all of the original iron bolts in the hull were replaced with copper fastenings during the Sydney refit in 1789.

Several copper clench bolts stamped with multiple broad arrows are clearly identifiable as Navy issue and appear to be good quality fastenings (figs 10 and 11). The metallurgical analysis of one copper bolt recovered prior to the *Sirius* Project identified it as an impure tough-pitch copper, probably fabricated from an ingot by cold hammering (Samuels, 1983, 69; 1992).

A number of unmarked bolts from Site 5 (in the vicinity of the spectacle plate) were not so easily identified. Two

seemingly 'brass' bolts from this location were chemically analysed and provided interesting results: one was found to be a low tin bronze (SI 32C) of similar composition to the bronze rudder fittings (MacLeod, 1985, 54-55, 59), while another (SI 15) was found to be a standard 'yellow metal' composition (i.e. two parts of copper to one of zinc), typical of nineteenth century brasses (MacLeod, 1994, 270-72). Only the bolt SI 32C, therefore, is deemed to be associated with the *Sirius*. Wood attached to this bolt was identified as chestnut (*Castanae* species), probably *Castanae sativa* or European chestnut (Mills-Reid, 1985). Chestnut timber was regarded by some shipbuilders to be as good as oak and could be used for the framing of ships without loss of class (Desmond, 1919, 14). Given that the availability of timber in Britain suitable for shipbuilding was a problem in the eighteenth century, it is not improbable that chestnut was used in the construction of merchant vessels like the *Berwick*. There is no further evidence at present to confirm whether this may have been the case.

Planking/skirting nails

A quantity of nails with die heads, rectangular shanks and flat points, ranging in length from 49mm (1 15/16in) to 92mm (3 5/8in) are believed to be planking or skirting nails. During the voyage to Botany Bay, the *Sirius* carried 'spike nails of the white composition' for experimental repair of skirting boards (Bradley, 1786-1792, 38; Henderson & Stanbury, 1988, 77). At this time, the Navy dockyards were being advised that hardened Copper nails from 3½ to 2½ in for fastening the skirting above the Copper sheathing manufactured by Parys Mine Company were to be used for all future work (ADM 106/2797, 3 May 1787. PRO, London).

Once again, chemical analyses of two of these fastenings (SI 228-1 and SI 228-2; fig 12) have given interesting results. They were found to contain 91.4% and 90.0% respectively of copper and 8.16% and 8.0% respectively of tin thus classifying them as tin bronze (MacLeod, 1994, 268). The high tin content would afford them a considerable hardness and resistance to corrosion (MacLeod & Pennec, 1990). Of all the *Sirius*' bronze fittings and fastenings analysed so far, these two nails have the highest percentage of tin. In terms of actual corrosion performance, one of the nails (SI 228-2) had eleven times as much iron as the other (SI 228-1) with the effect that the mean corrosion rate of SI 228-2 was found to be double that of SI 228-1 (MacLeod, 1994, 273). The analytical results thus demonstrate the sensitivity of bronzes to impurities such as iron, which is reflected in the

11 *Top* Head of copper bolt SI 301 showing broad arrow marks (*Photo: Patrick Baker, WA Maritime Museum*)

12 *Centre* Tin bronze planking or skirting nails SI 353, SI 228-1 and SI 228-2, with copper alloy lead sheathing nail SI 64 (length 9 cm max) (*Photo: Patrick Baker, WA Maritime Museum*)

13 *Left* Reverse side of copper sheathing showing lines of corrosion possibly due to wood acids (*Photo: Patrick Baker, WA Maritime Museum*)

different corrosion rates of alloys of otherwise similar chemical composition.

Copper sheathing and sheathing nails

By the time the *Sirius* was fitted out for the voyage to Botany Bay, the Royal Navy had been experimenting for more than twenty years with the use of copper sheathing as an antifouling device for ships' bottoms (Henderson & Stanbury, 1988, 37-37, 47). The copper sheathing and over two thousand sheathing nails recovered from the *Sirius* site therefore provide useful information concerning the underwater protection of the ship.

Samples of copper sheathing recovered from beneath iron ballast pigs have clearly identifiable front and back surfaces; the front having diagonal file markings and a corrosion pattern consistent with exposure to sea-water (MacLeod, 1990, pers. comm.) and the back bearing vertical striations (like the grain of soft wood), which may be lines of corrosion from wood acids (fig 13). A round hole (*c.* 5mm in diameter) had been punched from back to front through the folded edge of one copper piece and about 35mm away, a 5mm^2 hole (consistent with the sheathing nails) had been punched from front to back. Holes for the nails were commonly punched into each copper sheet by a small hand punch with a collar, which ensured that the hole was not too big for the size of the nail (Staniforth, 1985, 28). A major disadvantage of the technique, however, was that the holes punched for the nails could come directly over the head of a bolt and easily let in the water (Knight, 1973, 305).

From the collection, it was apparent that there were at least two gauges of copper sheathing, a 'thinner' and a 'thicker' variety. When the *Berwick* was coppered in January, 1782, sheets of 32, 28 and 22 ounces were supplied for the purpose (Henderson & Stanbury, 1988, 47). Three samples were selected for analyses to test for compositional differences which might be related to the functional use or origin of the copper sheets, and to further the study of metal corrosion on aggressive shipwreck sites (MacLeod, 1994).

Physical examination of the samples (SI 357, SI 465A and SI 491) indicated that they were similar, although one piece appeared thicker and tougher. Analyses showed that the chemical composition of two pieces (SI 357 and SI 465A) was identical, whereas SI 491 had a much higher percentage of the impurity arsenic (0.826%). It was known that there were 'good' and 'bad coppers' for sheathing purposes; impurities in the copper, particularly iron, making the copper less resistant to marine growth. Arsenic and lead were the two main impurities noted in the *Sirius* copper sheathing but the maximum amount of arsenic was considered to be at the lower end of the range for ancient alloys (Scott in MacLeod, 1994, 274) leading to the conclusion that the *Sirius* was sheathed with good quality copper sheathing.

The findings indicate that there were two distinct batches of copper sheathing on the *Sirius* at the time the ship was wrecked which may relate to different phases of coppering or repair. Taking into account the estimated loss of thickness due to corrosion, it was also shown that the samples represented three different gauges of sheathing — 0.6mm (SI 465A), 0.75mm (SI 491) and 0.9mm (SI 357) — approximately 22, 28 and 32 ounces per square foot. While representing the same batch of copper, the samples of identical chemical composition (SI 357 and SI 465A) differed in thickness, corresponding to 32 and 22 ounces respectively; sample SI 491 represented a second batch of heavy gauge copper of 28 ounces.

Whether the two batches of copper can be related to the initial coppering of the *Berwick* in 1782 and to the subsequent refurbishment of the vessel as the *Sirius* is debatable. The arrangements under which the Navy obtained copper in the early 1780s appear to have been rather complex, contractors to the Navy Board often being 'front men or just sub-contractors' (Harris, 1966, 559-60). Because of the escalation in the demand for copper when the Navy implemented its programme of coppering in 1783-84, many companies were unable to fulfil their contracts and the orders were taken over by competitors or partners in the 'contractual agreement' (Harris, 1966, 559). It could be argued, therefore, that the two different batches of copper from the *Sirius* came from two different foundries at the same time, although ideally the ships should have been coppered with sheathing from the same source.

Metallurgical analyses of the sheathing nails used for the *Sirius* indicate that they were cast from arsenical tin bronze which would have given them good corrosion resistance (MacLeod, 1994, 268, table 1, SI 465; Samuels, 1983). Samuels (1983, 77-78) found that the metallurgical quality of the nails examined by him was poor, reflecting the level of technology in the eighteenth century; none the less they seem to have performed their function satisfactorily.

Samuel's observations appear to be supported by the archaeological evidence where sheathing nails have been found in extreme states of preservation — some being excellent and others very poor (fig 14). In a study by MacLeod and Pennec (1990), it has been shown that, in the absence of any discernible differences in chemical composition, widely divergent corrosion rates in copper alloys can be rationalised in terms of metal microstructure and the stresses induced at manufacture or during the shipwrecking process. Analysis of a *Sirius* sheathing nail

14 Tin bronze sheathing nails (length 4 cm)
(Photo: Patrick Baker, WA Maritime Museum)

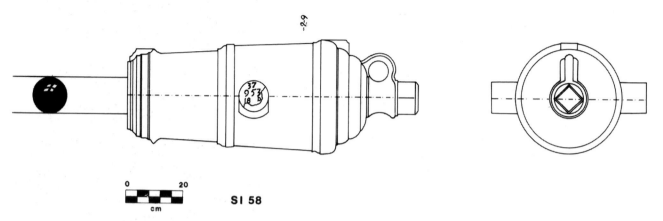

15 *Left* Trunnion carronade (SI 58) from HMS *Sirius* (*Photo: Patrick Baker, WA Maritime Museum*)

16 *Below* Trunnion carronade (SI 58) from HMS *Sirius* (*Drawing by M. Stanbury*)

17 *Bottom* Divers attaching a sacrificial anode to the second *Sirius* carronade (*Photo: Patrick Baker, WA Maritime Museum*)

SI 58

(SI 465) demonstrated that there was a fall in microhardness from the head of the nail to the tip indicating that it had been hammered in use, i.e. 'had been part of the vessel and not simply part of the cargo and they had been work-hardened' (MacLeod, 1994, 273).

Armament

It was stated earlier in this paper that one of the main roles of the *Sirius* was to defend the new colonies at Botany Bay and Norfolk Island against possible foreign incursion or insurrection. Whether the vessel had strategic capabilities 'appropriate' for this purpose is clearly an issue which is disputed by those who have referred to the *Sirius* as a 'pygmy battle ship of twenty guns' (Irvine, 1988, 40); the issue requires some clarification.

When the *Berwick* was recommissioned as the 6th Rate naval frigate *Sirius*, the classification had nothing to do with the vessel's fighting power and was made as a 'sociological move' (Lyon, 1992). Arthur Phillip, chosen by the Home Office to become Governor of the new settlement at Botany Bay (Frost, 1987b, 142-3), was a sea officer of Captain's rank with considerable seafaring experience. In recognition of his status the *Sirius* was made a post ship and Captain John Hunter appointed as the second captain. This left Phillip free to remain at the settlement and supervise affairs. Although Phillip requested the rank of commodore in order to ratify his superior authority, naval protocol rejected his request (Frost, 1987b, 147).

It should be pointed out, however, that the *Sirius* was quite capable of carrying a heavy armament. The *Berwick* could safely carry twenty-four 9-pounder guns on the middle deck and six 4-pounders and four 18-pounder carronades on the upper deck — a total of 34 guns (Henderson & Stanbury, 1988, 49). During the vessel's employ as an armed storeship, however, it seems that the number of guns actually carried on board may have varied from time to time, perhaps in relation to the particular destination in North America or the West Indies. Certainly, this level of armament for coppered ships employed in 'insecure' trades in the early 1780s appear consistent with data analysed by Rees (1971-72).

The *Sirius'* commission stated that it would be armed with four 6-pounder carriage guns, six 18-pounder carronades and eight swivel guns; ten more 6-pounders were ordered later to increase the complement (Henderson & Stanbury, 1988, 64). All the guns, with the exception of two carronades which fell overboard after the masts were cut, were hauled ashore with their carriages in January 1791 during the salvage operations (Henderson & Stanbury, 1988, 87).

One of the carronades (SI 58) was raised from the site by the *Sirius* Project in 1985 and has been successfully conserved (figs 15 and 16); the second, (SI 626), recovered in March 1993 by Norfolk Island personnel was cathodically protected *in situ* for five years prior to raising by the attachment of an aluminium engine block, which served as a sacrificial anode (MacLeod, 1989, 8; figs 17 and 18). Both carronades are 18-pounder trunnion carronades similar to

18 Aluminium engine block set up for use as a sacrificial anode *(Photo: Patrick Baker, WA Maritime Museum)*

examples from Dover Castle and drawings in the National Maritime Museum (Lavery, 1989, 18). While both guns share the same overall length (1.02m; 3ft 4in) and bore (131mm; 5.16in), they differ in weight; one (SI 58) has the weight mark '9-2-9' (9cwt 2qr 9lbs; 483kg) stamped in to the reinforce and the other (SI 626) is similarly marked '8-2-23' (8cwt 2qr 23lb; 442.3kg). The latter gun also has an unusual set of figures, '5-6-8', stamped midway along the muzzle. A turned wooden tampion attached by a coir lanyard to a ball of plaited coir-fibre was found inside the bore, but no shot, showing that the gun was not loaded.

Indications from various sources (Baker, 1983; Blackmore, 1976; Hughes, 1969; Lavery, 1989) are that there was a considerable number of small variations in the length and weight of carronades during the period between 1780 and 1860 as efforts were made to develop and refine the working of the piece. Carronades of 1800 were about 10 per cent heavier than those of 1780 (Lavery, 1987, 107), but the fact that they were generally not listed by their length makes it difficult to assess the relationship of these variables over time. A serial number '37 933' on the left-hand trunnion of carronade SI 58 is consistent with the Carron Company's numbers for the period and may assist in providing more accurate dates for these 'short fat gun[s] with trunnions' (Lavery, 1989, 16).

Probably the most important contribution that the treatment of the *Sirius* carronade has made to maritime archaeology and conservation is the development of a series of equations and relationships relating to cast iron guns which enable their treatment times to be predicted, and the sea-water immersion time to be calculated when the date of the shipwreck is unknown: in other words, an unexpected dating method (Carpenter & MacLeod 1993).

Conclusion

This paper has attempted to give an historical overview of HMS *Sirius*, a vessel whose significance has long been neglected and whose archaeological remains have the potential for providing valuable information concerning the construction of merchant and naval ships in the late eighteenth century, and the advances being made in shipbuilding technology at this time. In addition, the archaeology of the shipwreck at Norfolk Island is providing support for new theoretical perspectives concerning the British Government's motives for establishing a convict settlement on the east coast of Australia. By showing that the *Sirius* was not a leaky old tub, as convict transports were generally assumed to be, supports the thesis that the settlements at Botany Bay and Norfolk Island were intended to develop into permanent colonial outposts.

The *Sirius* did not fall into the normal category of rated naval vessels which makes the analysis of the archaeological record both fascinating and challenging. As the principal naval consort of the First Fleet, defence of the convoy, and subsequently the new penal settlements, was a priority role for the *Sirius* — but the vessel was no battleship! The rated designation was made principally because the *Sirius* had to carry a sea officer of Captain's rank, and not because of the vessel's fighting power.

The transition or 'reconstruction' of the *Sirius* from a Baltic trader (the *Berwick*) to armed storeship, and to a 6th Rate naval ship may certainly not have given the *Sirius* the same qualities or characteristics as a purpose-built ship of war. But, rather than being unsuited for the 'arduous undertaking' that the vessel had to endure (King, 1787-1790, 19), historical and archaeological evidence is increasingly lending support to the fact that the *Sirius* was an appropriate choice — 'a very capacious and convenient vessel' and 'exceedingly well calculated for such a service [as the voyage to Botany Bay]' (Hunter, 1793, 2).

Acknowledgements

The work of the *Sirius* Project was made possible by financial help from the Government of Norfolk Island, the Australian Bicentennial Authority, British Airways, QANTAS, Air New Zealand, East-West Airlines and the Westpac and Commonwealth Banks. The support of the Norfolk Island community, the Director and Trustees of the Western Australian Museum, and colleagues in the Departments of Maritime Archaeology and Materials Conservation, Western Australian Maritime Museum, is also gratefully acknowledged.

References

Baker, H.A., 1983, *The crisis in naval ordnance*. National Maritime Museum Maritime Monographs and Reports, No. 56, National Maritime Museum, Greenwich, London.

Blackmore, H.L., 1976, *The armouries of the Tower of London. I Ordnance*. Her Majesty's Stationery Office, London.

Bradley, W., 1786-1792, *A voyage to New South Wales. The journal of Lieutenant William Bradley RN of* HMS Sirius *1786-1792*. Public Library of New South Wales and Ure Smith, Sydney, 1969.

Carpenter, J. & MacLeod, I.D., 1993, Conservation of corroded iron cannon and the influence of degradation on treatment times. (Submitted to ICOM - Conservation Group Metals Conference, Washington, 1993)

Cresswell, G., 1989, Oceanography of Norfolk Island and the *Sirius*. In Henderson, G., (comp.), *Norfolk Island Government Project. 1988 expedition report on the wreck of* HMS Sirius. Report - Department of Maritime Archaeology, Western Australian Maritime Museum, No. 37.

Davis, R., 1962, *The rise of the English shipping industry in the 17th and 18th centuries*. National Maritime Museum Modern Maritime Classics Reprint No. 3. David & Charles, Newton Abbot (1972).

Desmond, C., c.1919, *Wooden ship-building*. The Rudder Publishing Company, New York. Reprinted by The Vestal Press, New York, 1984.

Frost, A., 1980, *Convicts and empire: a naval question 1776-1811*. Oxford University Press, Melbourne.

Frost, A., 1987a, Towards Australia: the coming of the Europeans 1400 to 1788. In Mulvaney, D.J. & White, J.P. (eds.) *Australians to 1788*. Fairfax, Syme & Weldon Associates, New South Wales: 389-411.

Frost, A., 1987b, *Arthur Phillip 1738-1814 his voyaging*. Oxford University Press, Melbourne.

Frost, A., 1994, *Botany Bay mirages. Illusions of Australia's convict beginnings*. Melbourne University Press, Carlton, Victoria.

Gesner, P., 1988, The *Pandora* project: reviewing genesis and rationale. *Bulletin of the Australian Institute for Maritime Archaeology*, 12.1: 27-36.

Gesner, P., 1991, Pandora. *An archaeological perspective*. Queensland Museum, South Brisbane, Queensland.

Gillen, M., 1982, The Botany Bay decision, 1786: convicts, not empire. *English Historical Review*, 97: 740-66

Harris, J.R., 1966, Copper and shipping in the eighteenth century. *The Economic History Review, Second Series*, 19.3: 550-568.

Henderson, G., (comp.), 1989a, *Norfolk Island Government Project. 1988 expedition report on the wreck of* HMS Sirius. Report - Department of Maritime Archaeology Western Australian Maritime Museum, No. 37.

Henderson, G., 1989b, The *Sirius* past and present. *Bulletin of the Australian Institute for Maritime Archaeology*, 13.2: 5-6.

Henderson, G. & Stanbury, M., 1988, *The* Sirius *past and present*. Collins, Australia.

Hughes, B.P. 1969, *British smooth-bore artillery. The muzzle loading artillery of the 18th and 19th centuries*. Arms and Armour Press, London.

Hunter, J., 1793, *An historical journal of the transactions at Port Jackson and Norfolk Island with the discoveries which have been made in New South Wales...* John Stockdale, London (Australian Facsimile Editions No. 148. Libraries Board of South Australia, Adelaide, 1968).

Irvine, N. (ed.), 1988, *The* Sirius *letters. The complete letters of Newton Fowell Midshipman & Lieutenant aboard the* Sirius *flagship of the First Fleet on its voyage to New South Wales.* The Fairfax Library, Sydney.

Jeffery, W.F., 1989, Mapping the wreck site. In: Henderson, G., (comp.), *Norfolk Island Government Project. 1988 expedition report on the wreck of* HMS Sirius. Report - Department of Maritime Archaeology, Western Australian Maritime Museum, No. 37:24-30.

Jones, S., 1984, The builders of Captain Cook's ships. *The Mariner's Mirror,* 70.3: 299-302.

Kimpton, G., 1992, Construction of replica anchor stocks and a carronade carriage for display of artefacts from HMS *Sirius* (1790). *Bulletin of the Australian Institute for Maritime Archaeology.* 16.2: 31-38.

King, P.G., 1787-1790, *The Journal of Philip Gidley King, Lieutenant RN, 1787-1790.* Fidlon, P. & Ryan, R. (eds.), Australian Documents Library, Sydney, 1980.

Knight, R.J.B., 1973, The introduction of copper sheathing into the Royal Navy, 1779-1786. *The Mariner's Mirror,* 59.3: 299-309.

Lavery, B., 1984, *The ship of the line. Volume II: design, construction and fittings.* Conway Maritime Press, London.

Lavery, B., 1987, *The arming and fitting of English ships of war 1600-1815.* Conway Maritime Press, London.

Lavery, B., 1989, Carronades and Blomefield guns. Developments in Naval ordnance, 1778-1805. In Smith, R.D. (ed.) *British naval armaments.* Royal Armouries, Conference Proceedings 1. Trustees of the Royal Armouries, London: 15-27.

Lyon, D., 1992, Evidence old and new: the post-Medieval warship. Paper presented to *The Archaeology of Ships of War* Conference, 31 October-1 November 1992, National Maritime Museum, London.

McKay, J. & Coleman, R., 1992, *The 24-gun frigate* Pandora *1779.* Conway Maritime Press, Great Britain.

McGowan, A.P., 1979, Captain Cook's ships. *The Mariner's Mirror,* 65.2: 109-118.

MacLeod, I.D., 1985, Conservation report, 1985 *Sirius* expedition — Norfolk Island. In Henderson, G. & Stanbury, M., *et al., Report to the Australian Bicentennial Authority on the 1985 Bicentennial Project expedition to the wreck of* HMS Sirius (*1790*) *at Norfolk Island.* Report — Department of Maritime Archaeology, Western Australian Maritime Museum, No. 24: 44-65.

MacLeod, I.D., 1989, The application of corrosion science to the management of maritime archaeological sites. *Bulletin of the Australian Institute for Maritime Archaeology,* 13.2: 7-16.

MacLeod, I.D., 1990, Conservation of materials from the wreck of HMS *Sirius* (1790) - 1990. Report to the Government of Norfolk Island. Unpublished report.

MacLeod, I.D., 1994, Conservation of corroded metals: a study of ship's fastenings from the wreck of HMS *Sirius* (1790). In Scott, D.A., Podany, J., Considine, B.B., (eds.) *Ancient & historic metals. Conservation and scientific research.* The Getty Conservation Institute: 265-78.

MacLeod, I.D., & Pennec, S., 1990, The effects of composition and microstructure on the corrosivity of copper alloys in chloride media. In ICOM *Committee for Conservation Preprints 9th Triennial meeting, Dresden.* Vol. 2, 732-38.

Mills-Reid, N., 1985, Conservation report. WAM File, MA 143/82.

Oldham, W., 1990, *Britain's convicts to the colonies.* Library of Australian History, Sydney.

Rees, G., 1971-2, Copper sheathing an example of technological diffusion in the English merchant fleet. *The Journal of Transport History. New Series* 1: 85-94. Leicester University Press.

Samuels, L.E., 1983, The metallography of some copper-alloy relics from HMS *Sirius. Metallography,* 16:69-79.

Samuels, L.E., 1992, Australia's contribution to archaeometallurgy. *Materials characterization,* 29.1-41.

Stanbury, M., 1991, Scientific instruments from the wreck of HMS *Sirius* (1790). *International Journal of Nautical Archaeology,* 20.3: 195-221.

Stanbury, M., 1994, HMS Sirius *1790. An illustrated catalogue of artefacts recovered from the wreck site at Norfolk Island.* Australian Institute for Maritime Archaeology, Special Publication No. 7.

Staniforth, M., 1985, The introduction and use of copper sheathing - a history. *Bulletin of the Australian Institute for Maritime Archaeology,* 9.1 and 2: 21-48.

Syrett, D., 1988, The fitting out of HM Storeship *Elephant. The Mariner's Mirror,* 74.1:67-73.

Syrett, D., 1989, HM Storeship *Porpoise,* 1780-83. *The American Neptune,* 49.2: 91-95.

Whitmont, T., 1992/93, Voyage of discovery. *The Bulletin,* 114.5852: 91-94.

Peter Gesner (Curator, Queensland Museum)

Managing Pandora's Box:
an exercise in eco-archaeometry

Introduction

My introduction to the *Pandora* shipwreck will be brief: it is the wreck of a 24 gun Porcupine class frigate which the Admiralty sent to the South Pacific to recapture the *Bounty* and bring to justice Fletcher Christian and his fellow mutineers. After a partially successful search lasting four months, the *Pandora* was returning to England carrying fourteen prisoners whom had been captured in Tahiti. On 29 August 1791, the frigate sank after running aground on an isolated reef outcrop while attempting to find a passage to the Torres Strait through unchartered waters to the north of the Great Barrier Reef. She took with her thirty-one of her crew and four of the *Bounty* prisoners (fig 1).

The wreck was discovered in 1977 in 33 metres of water during a search organized by the documentary film maker John Heyer. It was listed as a protected historic shipwreck in 1979 and is now being managed by the Queensland Museum under the auspices of the Australian Historic Shipwrecks Program. Since 1983 there have been a number of archaeological campaigns, however, after three seasons of

1 Eastern Australia showing the *Pandora* wreck site

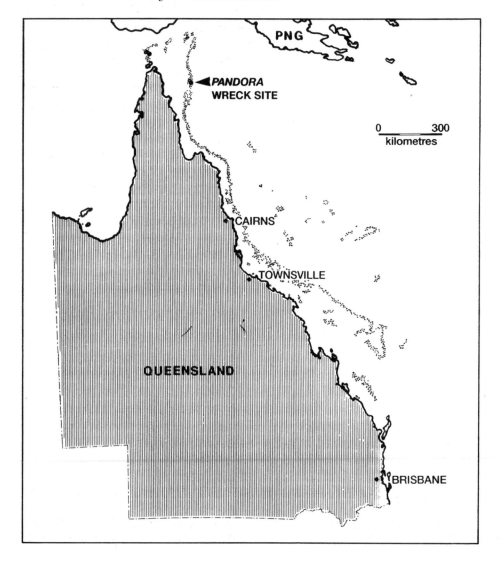

230

major excavation this programme has been put under review (Gesner, 1988, 27-36; 1990, 41-46; Henderson, 1986, 129-142).

As part of this review, an archaeological expedition will be carried out to determine the biological condition of the wreck and to delineate as definitively as possible, with remote sensing equipment (a 3.5khz sub-bottom profiler), its exact physical extent and condition.

The main aim of the expedition will be to gather environmental data which will provide information to help determine how the *Pandora* site can best be managed in the likely event that resources will not be available to continue the programme of excavation in the near future. As an adjunct to this objective, the Museum will arrange the ceremonial on-site placement of a memorial obelisk containing the skeletal remains of one of *Pandora*'s crew recovered during the 1986 excavation season (Gesner, 1991 43). To consecrate the obelisk the Museum has arranged for a Royal Australian Navy chaplain to conduct a 'Service for Burial at Sea' (fig 2).

The expedition will operate under the motto 'Managing Pandora's Box. The term 'A Pandora's Box' is probably familiar to most, but in case it is not, the following may help to refresh memories. It derives from Greek mythology and refers to the story in which Pandora, the darling of the gods, is sent by Zeus to marry Prometheus' brother Epimetheus. After finding a container (i.e. Pandora's Box) Pandora takes it to her husband who realizes that it contains all of the world's known evils. Pandora is not told what is in the box, but she is instructed not to open it under any circumstances.

Unable to restrain her curiosity, Pandora ignores the injunction and peeks into the box. Although she only lifted the lid a tiny fraction, the inevitable happened: evil and misery burst out, forever unleashed into an innocent world.

According to another version of the myth the box also contained blessings. After it had been opened, Hope was the only blessing to remain; all the others escaped. Had the

2 Crew abandoning the *Pandora*. Engraving based on an original drawing by mutineer Peter Haywood
(*courtesy Queensland Museum*)

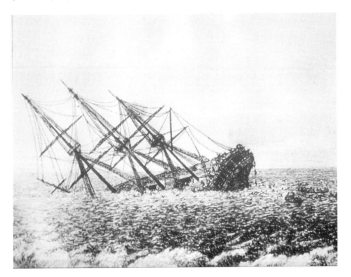

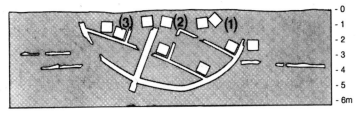

3a Predisturbance situation: artefact assemblages (1) (2) (3). etc, and hull remains sealed from oxygenated water by compact sediment layer of between 0.5-1m thick

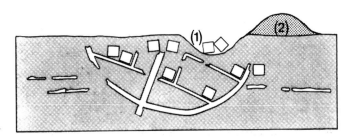

3b Excavation of artefact assemblage (1); sediment layer gradually removed and deposited on spoilheap (2) artefact assemblage (1) recorded in three dimensions and retrieved over a period of 4 to 5 weeks

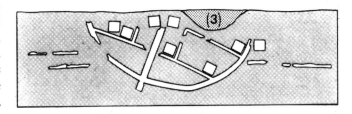

3c Back-filled excavation area (3) using sediment from spoil-heap

blessings remained, they would be there for the benefit of humankind, but as a result of Pandora's curiosity they too escaped and were lost. Whichever version was accepted, its purpose and meaning were clear, and, in its day, adequately accounted for all the woes of the world.

When the expression is used today its meaning is different. Now we mostly use it to refer to a potential situation or event which may have consequences that cannot be predicted or which may prove difficult to manage.

In the modern sense then, the analogy of Pandora's Box, when applied to our work, is particularly apt. Not only is there the obvious parallel with the ship's name, but also because, during her last voyage, the *Pandora* was carrying a temporary fixture known as 'Pandora's Box'. This was the small wooden gaol constructed on the quarter-deck in which the fourteen Bounty mutineers were imprisoned during their transport back to England to stand trial. Although it seems only its occupants used the term Pandora's Box to describe their gaol, it is likely that their gaolers also considered it an appropriate expression because, as far as they were concerned, the Bounty prisoners represented an evil which had to be contained at all costs.

Possibly this explains the Admiralty's orders to *Pandora*'s captain, Edward Edwards, to keep the mutineers in close confinement. Edwards appears to have interpreted these instructions literally; clearly he was concerned lest the

4 *Above* Diver recording measurements of the hull remains in the midships trench. The edge of the *Pandora*'s copper sheating is clearly visible in the middle ground
(photo: G. Crainitch, Queensland Museum)

5 *Right* Divers at work on the *Pandora*
(courtesy Queensland Museum)

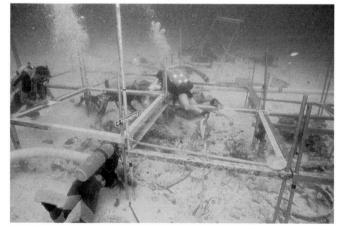

prisoners' previous actions inspire similar behaviour in his own crew.

Finally, the expression is particularly apt because the Museum's three previous excavations have, so to speak, lifted the lid on the remains of the wreck.

1993 Queensland Museum expedition
The principal purpose of the 1993 expedition is to gather data that will allow us to determine what destabilizing effects our lifting of the lid may have had on unexcavated artefacts and hull timbers which are known to be situated in deeper areas of the site and which appear to be in exceptionally good condition (Gesner, 1991, 48-49). As a results of our previous work, environmental conditions may have been created in which marine worms, borers and other agents of biological decay, are able to thrive and thereby accelerate the processes of deterioration within the wreck. We also need to know the effect of sediment disturbance on bacterial activity; specifically the relationships between the various microbiological

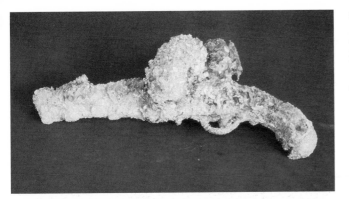

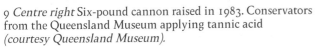

6 *Left* Concreted flintlock pistol (*courtesy Queensland Museum*)

7 *Below left* Conserved fob watch with silver casing and gold filigree workings (*Jon Carpenter, courtesy Queensland Museum*)

8 *Below* Earthenware jars (*courtesy Queensland Museum*)

9 *Centre right* Six-pound cannon raised in 1983. Conservators from the Queensland Museum applying tannic acid (*courtesy Queensland Museum*).

10 *Lower right* Some of the medical equipment that was found under the cannon in fig 9. Left to right: a tourniquet clamp, a syringe, a marble mortar and a glass bottle which contained traces of clove oil (*courtesy Queensland Museum*)

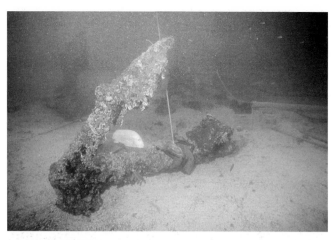

11 *Left* One of *Pandora*'s main anchors
(courtesy Queensland Museum)

12 *Below* Sand-timer glasses used to determine the speed of the
vessel *(courtesy Queensland Museum)*

13 *Opposite* The portable fireplace from the captain's cabin or
the great cabin on the upper deck
(Brian Richards, courtesy Queensland Museum)

organisms and the degree of preservation of the buried
timbers and their associated artefact assemblages. Also,
have we altered the metabolic rates of the different
bacteria, or indeed, have we disrupted the balance and
composition of the species, and, if so, will the situation,
over time, return to pre-disturbance levels? In short, have
we - to pursue the analogy - unleashed biological evils on
to the site? These are questions that must be answered as a
necessary first step to devising a strategy for the long term
conservation of the wreck.

It is proposed that we should attempt to answer these
questions by a comparative analysis of sediment samples
extracted from various locations on the site. These will
include locations which are 1) entirely undisturbed, 2) have

been excavated and back-filled, and 3) have been excavated
and back-filled more than once.

The analysis will be carried out at the University of
Queensland's Department of Microbiology under the
supervision of a Commonwealth Scientific & Industrial
Research Organisation (CSIRO) microbiologist at the CSIRO's
Marine Laboratories in Brisbane. A research plan was
discussed based on the premise that the wreck's excellent
state of preservation can be attributed to 'the maintenance
of anoxic conditions within the sediment' (pers. comm
David Moriarty). If the analysis of sediment samples
indicates that our back-filling method (fig 3) has increased
the level of oxygenated sediment (and thereby enlarged the
micro-environment capable of supporting organisms which

are detrimental to organic remains), then immediate counteractive measures will have to be considered to prevent or slow down further deterioration.

In a technical sense, this type of analysis of a site environment falls within the sub-discipline of 'eco-archaeometry': a relatively recent addition to the family of archaeological sub-disciplines. It has been defined as that branch of environmental science which "deals with studies of fundamental physico-chemical phenomena which lead to deterioration of ancient materials", or, put in other terms, it is concerned with understanding and quantifying harmful environmental processes which, once identified, can lead to finding "cost-effective ways to protect the cultural heritage" (Burns, 1991, 660).

References

Burns, G., 1991, Deterioration of our Cultural Heritage, *Nature*, Vol. 352, 658-61

Henderson, G., 1986, *Maritime Archaeology in Australia*, University of Western Australia Press

Gesner, P., 1988, The Pandora Project: reviewing genesis and rationale, *The Bulletin of the Australian Institute for Maritime Archaeology*, Vol. 12, no. 1 Fremantle.

Gesner, P., Situation Report: HMS *Pandora*, *The Bulletin of the Australian Institute for Maritime Archaeology*, Vol. 14, no. 2, Fremantle.

Gesner, P., 1991, *Pandora, an archaeological perspective*, Queensland Museum Press, Brisbane.

Addendum

Preliminary results of the 1993 expedition

Sediment samples were gathered from various locations on-site. It is too early to draw definitive conclusions about the effects of disturbance on the preservation of buried artefacts and hull remains. Surprisingly, preliminary indications seem to suggest that biological deterioration is occurring within anaerobic sediment layers. At this point however, it is not possible to assess the rate of bio-deterioration nor to measure its effects.

A trench was excavated in the midships area of the site which uncovered frames and planking along the starboard side of the hull. Although only exposed over a small area, these timbers appeared to be well preserved. More importantly, the trench also revealed the top edge of the *Pandora*'s copper sheathing indicating that the hull is likely to survive from about water-line level to the keel (fig 4).

The situation in the midships trench resembled more or less exactly the situation encountered during 1986 in the stern trench which exposed the hull over a larger area. In this light it is tempting to conclude that the hull remains are intact and continuous along the stern and midships sections of the hull. Assuming this is the case, then it appears that the depth of deposit of the hull remains are between two and two-and-a-half metres in the stern and midship areas.

This interpretation conflicts dramatically with the information gathered by remote sensing. The findings from

the sub-bottom profiler suggest that in the bow area the depth of deposit is between four and five metres and between three and four in the midships.

Clearly, the only reliable means of resolving this contradiction is to continue excavation and uncover the entire hull remains. This would not only provide information on the exact extent of the hull remains, but also it would make possible a precise determination of the hull's condition. Answers could then be given to such questions as, is the hull in a partial state of collapse? Are internal partitions still standing? Are some of the decks still intact?

Ann Birchall (formerly Assistant Keeper, Department of Greek and Roman Antiquities, British Museum)

HMS *Colossus*

The first *Colossus* was a 74-gun ship built by Cleveley at Gravesend and launched in 1787.[1] The draught-sheer-plan in the National Maritime Museum gives her vital statistics as: gun-deck length 172ft 3ins; extreme beam 48ft; hold depth 20ft. 8 1/4ins; burthen 1,717 tons. Her name immediately brings to mind the colossal statue of the sun-god Helios set up on Rhodes near (quite definitely not astride!) the harbour between 294-282 BC. Cast in bronze and about 110ft tall, it became one of the Seven Wonders of the ancient world (Higgins, 1988). Like the Colossus of Rhodes, toppled by an earthquake c.226 BC, the ship also had a brief career.

She first saw active service in 1793 when, during the Napoleonic War, she was among the vessels under Vice-Admiral Hood engaged in the siege and subsequent operations at Toulon. In 1795, as one of the fleet commanded by Admiral Lord Bridport, she was again in action against the French. An engagement off Isle Groix, although discontinued by Lord Bridport, nevertheless brought 3 French prizes with only light English losses, *Colossus* having 3 killed and 30 wounded. Her Captain, John Monkton, was a Scot who, it was said, had sent a kilted piper up into the maintopmast staysail netting to play throughout the three-hour long battle.

In 1797, now captained by George Murray, *Colossus* fought in the fleet commanded by Admiral Sir John Jervis against the Spanish in the Battle of St Vincent. There she was ordered to lead the van, but her fore-topsail yard carried away and she became serviceable only on one tack; she then became exposed to raking fire but was protected by *Orion* which lay

1 Plan of wreck site (*A.L. Allinson after Roland Morris*)

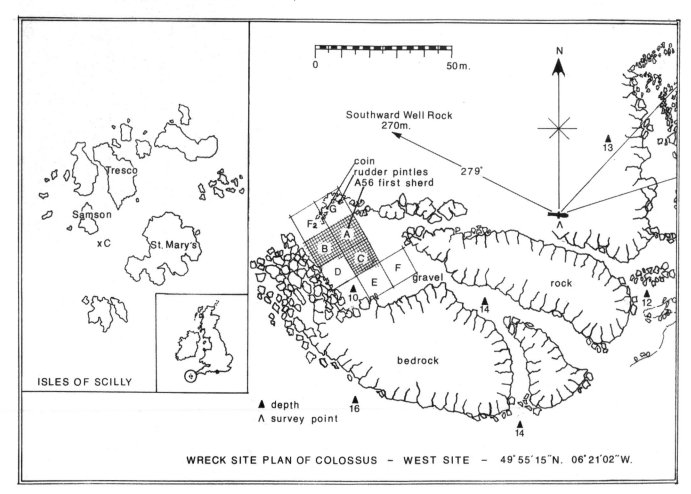

by to cover her until the danger had passed. The whole engagement ended in a great victory for the English: four Spanish ships were captured, including two by Commodore Horatio Nelson. Spanish losses were heavy, the English light - *Colossus* had 5 wounded. The victory brought several individual honours and formal votes of thanks from both Houses of Parliament.

For the rest of that year *Colossus* remained in the Mediterranean off Cadiz and Tagus. In October, still captained by George Murray, she was one of a squadron under Rear-Admiral Lord Nelson, in his flagship *Vanguard*, which blockaded Malta whilst it was occupied by the French; the result was the capture of Gozo.

It was in 1798 that *Colossus* made her last voyage. On 25 November she set sail from Lisbon in convoy, carrying, in addition to her cargo, sick and wounded from the Battle of the Nile. This was late in the year for such a voyage and the vessel itself was barely seaworthy, having been gradually stripped of gear for the use of other warships still in service. On 6 December, with a strong wind blowing along the English Channel from the east, *Colossus* headed for the Isles of Scilly and on the 7th was brought safely into the main anchorage at St Mary's. Late on the 10th, when the wind had veered to the south-east and risen to gale force, the best bower cable parted; two smaller anchors were unable to hold her and she was driven relentlessly on to Southward Well Reef, a shoal of rocks 18-24ft under water to the south of the small island of Samson (fig 1). By the small hours of the 11th, *Colossus* was lying on the seabed stern-on to the reef. A little later the brave islanders came to the rescue in their fishing boats, first taking off the sick and wounded. The ship was lost with only one life, that of the quartermaster who had apparently fallen overboard whilst taking soundings.

The sequel was the usual official and unofficial salvage. For some time *Fearless* was stationed at Scilly by the Admiralty to salvage stores (ten weeks' supply of food had been taken on at Lisbon), rigging, and guns - an operation doubtless entered into wholeheartedly, if clandestinely, by locals as well. Also salvaged was the embalmed body of Admiral Lord Shuldham in a coffin, shipped home as cargo so as to avoid arousing superstitious fears amongst the crew.

On 19 January 1799, at the customary formal inquiry,[2] the verdict attributed the loss of *Colossus* to the 'badness' of the weather and the 'rottenness' of the best bower cable; also the ship's poor condition, even before leaving Naples, emerges from the defects listed by her carpenter on arrival in Scilly.[3] In the event, all the officers and crew were exonerated from blame; indeed Captain Murray continued at sea serving with such distinction that, in 1815, he was knighted.

Gradually, interest in *Colossus* faded and she might have been completely forgotten (after all, the seabed off the Scillies is littered with wrecks of all kinds and periods) but for one unique factor - her cargo included part of Sir William Hamilton's Second Collection of ancient Greek vases.

William Hamilton (fig 2) was born in 1730, the youngest son of Lord Archibald Hamilton and a grandson of the third Duke of Hamilton. Brought up largely at the English

Court — becoming a close friend of the future King George III whom he always called 'foster-brother' — he served first in the army and then entered Parliament. In 1758 he married his first wife, an heiress, Catherine Barlow of Lawrenny Hall, Pembrokeshire. However, owing to her delicate health, Hamilton sought a position abroad in a more equable climate. And so he entered the world of foreign diplomacy. Between 1764 and 1800 he was British Minister to the Court of the Two Sicilies in Naples. Over the years he became the personal friend of King Ferdinand and

2 Portrait in oils of Sir William Hamilton by (or from the 'Studio of') Sir Joshua Reynolds National Portrait Gallery, 680; courtesy of the Trustees. Hamilton wearing the red riband and star of the Order of the Bath of which he had been created a Knight in 1772, holds a volume by d'Hancarville open on his knees; around him are vases from his First Collection and Vesuvius is shown smoking in the background

Queen Maria Carolina (sister of Marie Antoinette) enjoying a high reputation as a diplomat, music-lover, patron of the arts, scholar and connoisseur. Nowadays, however, he is generally remembered as the 'husband of Nelson's Emma', a judgement which seriously underestimates him.[4]

In the XVIIIth century a diplomat's duties were not onerous and at Naples Hamilton found ample time to pursue his own wide interests - music, painting and especially, in his own words, 'the antiquities and natural curiosities of the country'. He frequently visited the excavations at Pompeii, often serving as guide to distinguished foreign visitors like the Emperor Joseph II of Austria. He was also fascinated by the volcanic activity of Mount Vesuvius which he climbed innumerable times and on whose eruptions he wrote invaluable eye-witness accounts. He was also an avid collector of pictures, volcanic minerals and classical antiquities, and undertook some exceptionally fine publications, notably those commissioned from d'Hancarville (1767) and Tischbein (1791).

During his years in Naples Hamilton formed two large and important collections of antiquities. In 1772 during a visit to London, when he was created Knight of the Bath, Hamilton sold his First Collection to the British Museum for whom it was a major acquisition in the field of classical antiquities, marked by a bicentennial exhibition in 1972 (Birchall, 1972). The Collection comprised 6,000 coins and 3,000 other antiquities: marble sculptures, objects in bronze, amber, terracotta, glass, bone, ivory, and, of course, vases. Hamilton was, above all a 'vase-man', and his 730 Greek vases were to form the nucleus of one of the best Museum collections anywhere in the world today (Birchall, 1972, *passim*).

When Hamilton returned to Naples he started to collect again. By 1796 he had amassed a Second Collection of 1,000 vases. In 1798 during the Napoleonic War, when Italy faced the threat of imminent invasion, Sir William and his second wife, Emma, joined the Court in fleeing Naples. Hamilton's collection was hastily crated — apparently without inventory — for dispatch by sea to England. In due course, part arrived safely on board *Foudroyant*; but the rest went down with *Colossus*, eight cases of his best vases. In a letter dated 22 March 1799, Hamilton wrote: ' . . . you do me justice in thinking and knowing me to be a Philosopher, but my Phylosophy has been put to the Trial by the loss of the Colossus. You give me but little hopes, but I have heard that the body *insolvent* of Adml. Shuldham has been saved from the Wreck ... damn his body, it can be of no Use but to the Worms, but my Collection would have given information to the most learned ...'.[5]

In June Hamilton learnt that 'about ten vases and pateras' had been recovered from the wreck (present whereabouts unknown) but probably little more. Interest in *Colossus* stemmed not from the Greek pottery but her own gear, for which further salvage attempts were made from time to time. Most successful, probably, was that by John Deane, the celebrated diver who invented the copper diving helmet. In about 1827, employed by the Admiralty, he raised a quantity of rigging blocks and several guns from the wreck. Gradually interest in the old warship faded, leaving the sea - and the ground seas of W. Cornwall and Scilly are exceptionally severe - to continue the breaking up process over the next century and a half.

In 1939 *Colossus* again attracted the attention of salvors - this time of the late Roland Morris, then a 'hard-top' diver, later well-known for salvage work on a number of wreck

3 Diver measuring a cannon on the wreck site

sites around the Scillies and for his private Maritime Museum at Penzance. By virtue of a Ministry of Defence Agreement of 1966, he and a professional diving team had followed up painstaking documentary research into the loss of *Colossus* with 171 hours of underwater searching. In 1974, the team located the site of a wreck off Southard Well Reef which they believed to be that of *Colossus*; in the following spring they made formal application to the Department of Trade and Industry for the site to be 'designated for protection from unauthorised interference' under the provisions of the Protection of Wreck Act, 1973.

The Ministry's Advisory Committee on Historic Wreck, under the chairmanship of the late Viscount Runciman of Doxford, made the designation not on the grounds of the ship itself but because of the great archaeological importance of its cargo, part of Sir William Hamilton's Second Collection. A licence was granted to a company formed of Roland Morris and three highly experienced professional divers, Mike Hicks, Mark Horobin and Slim Macdonnell (the latter an underwater cameraman of international reputation), to carry out a pre-disturbance survey of the area; the work was to be carried out under my archaeological supervision, and a report made by the end of July 1975. The survey's main purpose was to identify the wreck positively as that of *Colossus*.

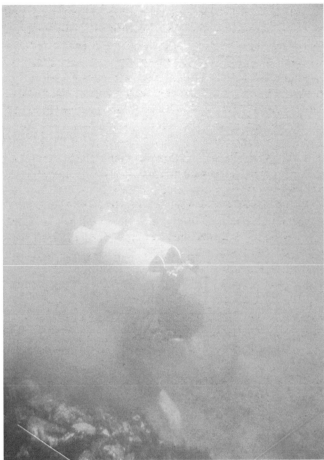

4 *Top* Shot box marked 'G3R' (i.e. King George III) found on the wreck site

5 *Above* The first Greek potsherd found on the *Colossus* wreck site (c5377); it shows the head of a satyr and comes from an Attic red-figured column-krater, date c.430 BC. Scale 3:4

6 *Right* Diver working on the site

In spite of various difficulties - the heavy growth of kelp and seaweed, poor visibility from plankton and occasional high winds - the team set up a survey grid over the site using several cast-iron guns (fig 3) and some large copper ship's fastenings as convenient reference points; they then swim-searched an area of over 10,000 sq.metres. Gradually evidence accumulated which showed the wreck to be that of a British man-of-war of the late XVIIIth century: keel pins, several musket-shot, a pin with the Admiralty's broad arrow, a shot box marked 'G3R' (i.e King George III) (fig 4), and some coins, the latest being Portuguese and dated 1794. But it was only after the area had been appreciably extended to the west (an area henceforward termed 'West Site') that the first fragment of Greek pottery was found (fig 5) - with incredible timing, only a few days before the July deadline! The fragment, from an Attic red-figured column krater depicting the head of a satyr (later numbered c5377), proved beyond all doubt that the wreck site was that of *Colossus*. The Advisory Committee now granted the team a licence to excavate, with myself as archaeological director and Mr Harold Barker, Keeper of the Conservation Department at the British Museum, as conservation adviser.

Underwater work began by clearing the West Site of weed and setting up a new grid centred on the find-spot of the Greek potsherd. Initially, two squares 10m by 10m, lettered A and B respectively, were laid out using special fluorescein-treated, floating nylon lines held in position by lightweight concrete blocks. Each 10 metre square was further subdivided, by specially made underwater tapes of non-stretch design, into single metre squares, numbered 1 to 100. Thus the find-spot for the first sherd became A56 (fig 5, see also fig 1).

Once excavation began, the simplest method of working proved the most effective. The three divers worked each within a single grid square (fig 6) but at sufficient distance from each other that visibility was not affected: the sand was fanned away gently with the hand to reveal the sherds (fig 7); these were then placed in a plastic box, labelled with the grid reference (fig 8). Clearance of each square was followed by sifting with a gentle 4-inch airlift, the outflow leading into a fine wire sieve so as to trap any very small sherds. At the end of each day the divers completed specially printed day-sheets giving all relevant details of the diving, sea conditions, etc., and of the grid square excavated. In accordance with the terms of the licence, excavation was restricted to the classical pottery: nothing else was raised except for a very, very few ship's items needing immediate

7 *Top* Diver on site with a sherd: actually part of vase C61, cf. figs 23-24

8 *Above* Diver on site putting sherds into a box

9 *Opposite top* In the temporary laboratory set up in Penzance sherds were washed to remove the soluble salts absorbed during nearly two centuries' immersion in sea-water

10 *Opposite bottom* Some of the thousands of classical Greek potsherds recovered during the first season

conservation treatment. Full lists of finds were forwarded to the official Receiver of Wreck.

Once ashore, the boxes of potsherds were transferred by helicopter to Penzance where a temporary laboratory had been set up. In a series of shallow sluice-tanks, made out of marine ply, the sherds lay for about ten days with fresh water passing continuously over them, washing out the soluble salts absorbed during nearly 200 years' immersion in sea-water (fig 9). The sherds, always kept in batches marked

with the relevant grid references, were then spread out to dry. After discussion with Mr Barker, it was decided to leave for the time being some problems of iron-staining, surface-flaking, incrustation and concretion.

The first season closed after 456 man-hours underwater, with diving taking place on average for 3-4 hours per day; about 300 cu.ft. of air per day per diver was used. The long periods spent lying full length on site meant that wet suits quickly became damaged at the knees and elbows and needed constant patching or reinforcing. Conditions under water were fairly constant, with depth at about 10m and visibility varying from 4m to 8m depending on the state of the tide; lack of tide meant suspended sediment with poor visibility. Undersea current was generally no problem unless very strong when it bounced the divers along the bottom.

The end of season's total was over 8,000 fragments of ancient Greek pottery (fig 10). As a Greek vase-specialist examining the sherds during my regular (and exciting!) site visits, I identified a wide variety of vase-shapes in fabrics which included Corinthian black-figure, Attic black-figure, Attic red-figure and South Italian red-figure, all dating between c.600-300 BC. An archaeologist must be an optimist almost by nature, but it did not seem too optimistic to hope that some of Hamilton's Second Collection, which had included fine painted Greek vases of great importance to classical archaeology, and long lost, might now be recovered, even though in fragments - archaeologists in the field are lucky if they get anything else!

Hamilton's passion for collecting - whilst he could 'command a farthing' - was clearly a compulsion which stretched his financial resources to the limit. By the time of another home leave in 1783 he was obliged to sell off some pieces from his Second Collection. One such was the exceptionally fine Roman vase, carved from blue and white cameo glass and now known as the Portland Vase, which the British Museum eventually acquired in 1945 (Haynes, 1964). By 1796 when the Second Collection had grown to 1,000 vases and Hamilton was negotiating its sale, unsuccessfully, to King Frederick-William II of Prussia, it was, he wrote, 'far more beautiful and complete than the series in London'. Privileged visitors had occasionally been shown it in Naples. One visitor in 1787 was the poet Goethe who was also entertained by a private performance of Emma's 'Attitudes', dramatic poses inspired by Hamilton's classical antiquities. In his *Italienische Reise* Goethe records that Emma wore a Greek costume which Hamilton had had made for her. A series of plates engraved by Tommaso Piroli (1752-1824), published in Rome in 1794, after drawings from life made by Friedrich Rehberg in Naples, show that Emma's theatrical props included an occasional Greek vase, undoubtedly borrowed from the Second Collection (Birchall, 1972, no. 6). Goethe was accompanied on his tour by Wilhelm Tischbein later appointed Director of the Neapolitan Academy of Fine Arts. When Hamilton was preparing to publish his Second Collection he commissioned Tischbein to illustrate a selection of vases by making fine outline drawings, usually at full scale (Tischbein, 1791-95). Many of these published drawings

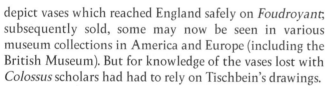

11 *Above left* Diver using a lifting-bag to clear rocks from the site

12 *Above* Divers Mark Horobin, *left*, and Slim Macdonnell, *right*, with Roland Morris examining some of the sherds recovered from the *Colossus* wreck site

13 *Left* Amongst the early finds from the *Colossus* site two Attic red-figured fragments from vase C15 identified as part of a vase drawn by Tischbein: *left*, part of the head of the wine-god Dionysos; *right*, part of the body of the smith-god Hephaistos; actual size

Next came the process of 'matching': matching sherds one with another on stylistic grounds as part, with or without joins, of one vase, and then, of trying to match such groups with any of the Tischbein drawings - not as easy as it sounds but often quite thrilling!

Joins - the fitting together edge to edge of fragments - could be, and frequently were, made during any of these processes. With few exceptions joins were made 'academically' not physically with adhesives; the latter process, it had been decided, should wait upon any final re-assembly. The exceptions were made in response to wide public interest after the showing of a BBC TV documentary on the early stages of the excavation (November 1975), when three vase-groups were put on exhibition in July 1976 in the British Museum's refurbished Front Hall.[8]

Research over the 1975-76 winter produced a list of Tischbein drawings of vases believed lost on *Colossus*. These drawings were to prove invaluable in many cases, serving as 'key' to an as yet unknown number of jig-saw puzzles; but problems remained. As only the picture had been drawn, the shape of the vase had to be deduced from the drawing, which is not always possible; and although many of the vases would have had figured scenes on both sides, rarely had both been drawn. Soon, however, 18 sets of sherds had been identified and matched with Tischbein drawings, thus creating 18 vase-groups. This total was supplemented by a further 80 which, not found in the published volumes, offered the bonus of hitherto unknown vases.

In June 1976, following renewal of the licence, the same team began a second season under water. The new season brought severe technical problems, involving the lifting of over 200 tons of rock and boulders, using air-filled bags

depict vases which reached England safely on *Foudroyant*, subsequently sold, some may now be seen in various museum collections in America and Europe (including the British Museum). But for knowledge of the vases lost with *Colossus* scholars had had to rely on Tischbein's drawings.

In January 1976, for logistic reasons and with the kind permission of the British Museum authorities who were now giving financial support to the excavation[6], I arranged for the transfer to the Museum of all the potsherds so far recovered. In the Greek and Roman Sherd Room - appropriately enough! - I set up the '*Colossus*-Unit', a team of voluntary assistants to begin marking and analysing the first season's final total of 8,184 fragments. A Register, recording the diver's day-sheet, sorting and conservation details for each sherd, was also compiled.[7]

The Unit's next task was sorting - sorting into basic categories of handle, rim, base or body fragments, and of figured, plain or patterned, red-figure or black-figure. Then came identification - whether from open or closed pots, which shape and fabric: in the case of red-figure, whether Attic (made in Athens) or South Italian, made in the Greek colonies of South Italy where several schools of vase-painters carried on the mainland tradition from the later Vth to IVth centuries BC.

(fig 11), and sieving through more than 15 tons of conglomerate of sand and silt. The three divers logged a total of 368 hours under water, a prodigious effort and one which enabled the grid area to be extended over two further 10m squares, C and D (fig 1), and an enormous quantity of sherds to be recovered. As a result, and as the Museum was also becoming increasingly involved with the whole project, all the pottery finds were taken direct from Scilly to the Museum for treatment in the Conservation Department. This second season proved dramatically successful, the divers raising a further 20,000 sherds (fig 12).

The sherds, once washed and dried, were transferred to the 'Colossus-Unit' for marking, registering and sorting as before. The fresh material added progressively more fragments to the various vase-groups, both to the 18 already matched with Tischbein drawings, and to our hitherto unknown ones; the latter now comprised 3 Corinthian black-figure, 16 Attic black-figure, 20 Attic red-figure and 60 South Italian red-figure,[9] including some fine examples of Paestan and Apulian.

Amongst the Attic material, attention centred on vase-group no. 15 (C15), a few fragments (fig 13) of a particularly fine red-figured bell-krater (i.e. a wine mixing-bowl), actually the first I had identified in Tischbein (vol. III pl. 9) (fig 14). As more and more sherds from this one vase were collected, it was interesting to note how widely they had been scattered on the seabed. This fact was repeated with other vase-groups. In other words, the action of wind and water on the wreck site scattered sherds from the same vase quite far

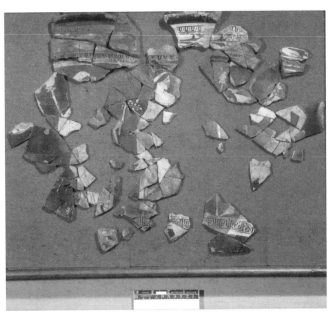

14 *Top left* Early fragments of vase C15 placed on the full-scale drawing by Tischbein (vol. III, pl. 9); it illustrates the Greek myth of the *Return of Hephaistos to Olympos*; cf. figs 26-27

15 *Above* The main side of vase C15 in November 1977; see fig 16

16 *Above right* The reverse side of vase C15 also in November 1977 - two maenads and a satyr

afield - even those which later proved to be 'joining' sherds. Though this was no surprise to the highly experienced divers they still kept strictly to the agreed system of diving and recording according to the grid squares.

By the end of 1976, the divers' success in Scilly was complemented by success in the *Colossus*-Unit. Many vase-groups were expanding in a most satisfying way and, in particular, the C15 krater was making astonishing progress. Over 300 fragments had been identified as belonging to it, now going well beyond the known scene into that on the other side and - even more difficult - into the purely black-glazed areas; a further discovery was the letter *epsilon* on the main side - part of an inscription unnoticed by Tischbein. The main picture shows *The Return of Hephaistos* - the story of the wine-god Dionysos, with satyrs and maenads, bringing a reluctant smith-god Hephaistos back home to Olympos, the whole party being very much under the influence of drink (fig 15)! The sherds identified as belonging to the reverse side (which had not been drawn by Tischbein), also depict a satyr and maenads, the traditional attendants of Dionysos (fig 16). Now the growing number of sherds from this one bowl offered the exciting possibility of totally re-assembling the vase (an augury perhaps of others to come), and of attributing it.

To 'attribute' a vase means to decide who was the individual artist who created it, thereby affording a vase-specialist particular satisfaction. On the basis of Tischbein's drawing, the great scholar J.D. Beazley had attributed our Attic bell-krater to the Group of Polygnotos (Beazley, 1963, 1061, 157). Now with the actual vase, albeit fragmentary, in front of me I felt able to attribute it to the Peleus Painter (one of the chief artists in the Group), who was active c.440 BC - the time when Sophocles was producing his *Antigone* and Pheidias building the Parthenon (Birchall, 1978, 72-73; also *Lexicon*, 162d - entry on *Hephaistos*).Other vase attributions followed, most notably that of another red-figured bell-krater, C20. This one, however, is not Attic but Paestan, and was not drawn by Tischbein. The main scene shows three men at a banquet; they recline on a couch under which sprawls a papposilen. It is by the great early Paestan vase-painter Python, c.350-325 BC (figs 17 and 18); this attribution flashed into my mind one night on the sleeper returning from Penzance! (Birchall, 1978, 72-75; see also Trendall, 1987, 148, no. 247, and illustrated in part on pl. 93c.).

With renewal of the licence yet again in 1977, work under water was resumed in June.[10] The new season got off to a slow start: winter storms bringing a lot of ground movement had resulted in the site being flooded with silt and debris which, with the addition also of considerable sea growth, entailed many hours spent simply on clearance (fig 19). Throughout the season the weather made diving conditions and excavation difficult: high winds, ground seas, poor visibility, the growth of plankton and unusually cold temperatures. An additional problem was that of marine concretion. Nevertheless, when diving ended the team had put in a remarkable 493 hours on site and fulfilled all our agreed objectives. These were to clear again the four grid squares (A to D), extend southwards (into E), and systematically search an area covering a quarter of a mile in radius from the main grid to confirm that sherds were not to be found so far afield.

Over 2,400 sherds were recovered in 1977, about one-fifth being found embedded in concretion (fig 20). This was found to be concentrated in great, solid masses and estimated to weigh overall at least 3 tons. It was necessary to break it up manually on the seabed, with hammer and chisel, so as to raise it in more manageable form for further treatment. This was undertaken in Penzance by Roland Morris who had developed a successful method of dealing with it (Morris, 1976, 333-343). The result was the extraction of some very fine sherds. The washing and drying of all the season's fragments was also carried out again in Penzance this season (fig 21), with the exception of a few taken into the Museum's Conservation Department to explore ways of removing some iron-staining.

The work in the *Colossus*-Unit continued apace in 1977, especially after the move in May to a much more spacious room, well fitted with shelves and trestle tables, at 9 Bedford Square (then one of the Museum's peripheral premises). Here we could really spread out our vase-groups (fig 22).

During my last visit to Scilly before the season closed and after several weekend training sessions at Fort Bovisand, I made two dives on the site myself.[11] This gave me the opportunity to see at first hand the nature and extent of the wreck site, experience the physical working conditions and appreciate the problem of the great quantities of concretion.

A final season, with two divers, took place in 1978.[12] 206 hours were logged, resulting in a further three squares being opened (F, F2 and G) (fig 1); compass-swim searches were carried out over the whole grid area and swim-searches on its northern periphery. The year, however brought changes both to the excavation in Scilly and the work at the British Museum. The total number of sherds was considerably down - about 1,000, and of markedly less good quality overall then previously. Immediate conservation was carried out yet again in Penzance, the Conservation Department in London

17 *Above* Diver on site holding a sherd, actually part of Paestan red-figured bell-krater, C20, cf. fig 18

18 *Opposite top* Paestan red-figured bell-krater, C20, at the end of the excavation. *Above*, rim fragments; *below right*, from the reverse side: parts of two maenads and a satyr (possibly Dionysos); *below left*, from the main side: three men recline on a couch, underneath a papposilen; the men are at a banquet and are probably enjoying a game of *kottabos* - the game in which dregs of wine are flung at a target. The vase is attributed by the author to the artist Python, date c.350-325 BC

dealing only with material specially selected for exhibition in the autumn. Unfortunately, for reasons beyond my control, no further work was done in the *Colossus*-Unit after May. The major *Colossus* exhibition scheduled as part of the Museum's 1978 Special Exhibitions programme, was also cancelled. However, at the request of the President of the International Association for Classical Archaeology (the XIth International Congress was to be held in London in September), the Museum's Trustees agreed to a minor display.

Eight vases went on exhibition in the Front Hall: the only vase found intact - a tiny Attic red-figured perfume pot - and seven others partly or completely reconstructed in the

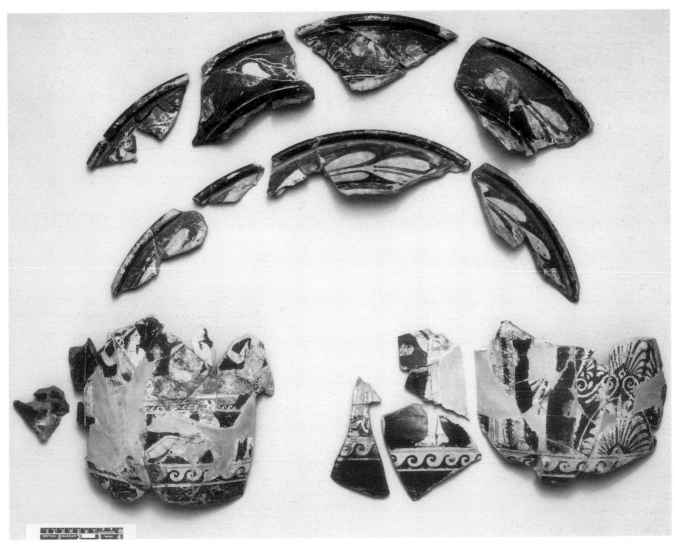

19 Diver clearing marine growth from the wreck site

20 A *Colossus* sherd embedded in marine concretion

21 *Top left* Sherds spread out to dry after washing

22 *Top right* Voluntary assistants Zosia Symanska and Philip Attwood working in the *Colossus*-Unit set up in Bedford Square

23-24 *Above* Apulian red-figured volute-krater, C61, partly reconstructed from 175 fragments; *23*, reverse side, scene of mourning: a man and a woman at a *stele* (grave monument). *24*, main side incorporating the sherd illustrated in fig 7, *naiskos* scene: a woman and a man bring offerings to a shrine which contains the figure of a deceased man. Placed by the author in the area of the Baltimore Painter, date c.330 BC

Conservation Department; in pride of place was the Attic bell-krater which had been brilliantly re-assembled by the late Nigel Williams[13] (figs 23-27). After computing its overall original shape, he built up a clay matrix on to which were set more than 520 fragments. The final removal of the matrix made a dramatic end-piece to the new, award-winning BBC TV documentary.[14]

At this point work on *Colossus* and some 32,000 fragments of classical Greek pottery was brought to an end and I myself left the Museum in October 1978. The material was finally incorporated into the Museum's collection in 1981 but, owing to a variety of vicissitudes, it was some years again before work resumed on it. Recently, some Hamilton material, which includes the re-assembled Attic bell-krater and a few objects from the First Collection, has been put on display (Room 11). A publication programme has now also been initiated.[15]

When Sir William despaired of the salvaging of his lost vases in 1799 he wrote: '... but come to the worst I have had the precaution of publishing the best that are supposed to be lost - and I have many living witnesses that the originals existed.'[16] Now, as the bicentenary of the wrecking of

25 Top picture *Left*, C56, Apulian red-figured epichysis reconstructed from 20 sherds, max. ht. 16cm; maenad with thyrsos; date c.330 BC

Centre, C21, Attic red-figured squat lekythos: woman running; this tiny perfume pot was the only vase found more or less intact, lacking only the handle and lip; max. ht. 4.9cm, date c.430 BC

Right, C58, Apulian red-figured mug reconstructed from 37 sherds, max. ht. 9.6cm; woman's head in profile; date c.330 BC

26 *Above left* Attic red-figured bell-krater, C15, as finally reassembled from over 520 fragments; reverse, Dionysiac scene - two maenads and a satyr

27 *Above right* The main side of C15 as finally reassembled: the *Return of Hephaistos to Olympos*. Attributed by the author to the Peleus Painter; max. ht. 46.5cm, date c.440 BC

Colossus approaches, may the British and international public alike find some of the originals existing once more.

Acknowledgements

I dedicate this paper with the deepest gratitude and admiration to Mike, Mark and Slim.

My sincere thanks to several other individuals are recorded in the *Notes* to the text.

I am also indebted to A.L. Allinson for his re-drawing of the site-plan (after Roland Morris). Underwater photography by Slim Macdonnell. Studio photography of the pottery courtesy of the Trustees of the British Museum.

Notes

1 There was a second *Colossus*: a 74-gun ship launched at Deptford in 1803; amongst other actions she took part in the Battle of Trafalgar (21 October 1805).

2 Captain Murray's Court Martial: Public Record Office ADM/1/5348 ERD/7793

3 List by J. Loney: Public Record Office ADM/1/2136 26846 Cap.M.383.

4 For an excellent biography see Fothergill, 1969.

5 Letter of 22 March 1799: British Library Add.MSS. 42071, f.14.

6 Many Trustees, Sir John Pope-Hennessey (Director) and the late Mr Denys Haynes (Keeper) had taken a keen interest right from the start; it was deeply appreciated by us all. Dr (later Sir) David Wilson succeeded as Director (1977-1992) and Brian F. Cook as Keeper (late 1976-early 1993).

7 Principally the late Mrs Barbara Gibson and Mrs Valerie Smallwood, joined for varying periods (up to May 1978) by graduate students from British and foreign universities: Philip Attwood, Marie-Louise Collard, Camilla Loewe, J. Gavronski, Robert Hannah, Robert MacGuire, Josephine van Prag, Walker Rucker, Zosia Symanska, Ceri Walker; Wing Commander A.V. Pim typed the Register compiled as far as sherd no. 18,306. To all of them I owe an enormous debt of gratitude.

8 Some loose sherds, a piece of marine concretion, and fragments from three vase-groups: Attic r-f bell-krater, attributed to the Peleus Painter (C15); Paestan r-f bell-krater, attributed to the artist Python (C20) and Apulian r-f volute-krater, attributed to the area of the Baltimore Painter (C61). The attributions are mine.

9 All figures quoted are taken from my annual Excavation Reports to the Runciman Committee; they are fluid as registering was incomplete in 1978 and some vase-groups may eventually merge.

10 The diving team for 1977 consisted of Mike Hicks, Mark Horobin and Mark Groves; Slim Macdonnell had withdrawn from the excavation.

11 Fort Bovisand Underwater Centre, Plymouth; to the director Lt. Cdr Alan Bax, RN, and my inexhaustibly patient trainers Linda and Nick Ashmore my deepest thanks.

12 Mike Hicks and Mark Groves; occasionally Mark Horobin. 1977-78 proved difficult all round; changes of staff at the Museum had brought a change in official attitude whilst in Scilly the team came under increasing financial pressure.

13 Completely restored: Attic r-f bell-krater (C15), Apulian r-f epichysis (C556), Apulian r-f mug (C58); partly restored: Attic b-f neck-amphora (C67), Attic r-f neck-amphora (C25), Paestan r-f bell-krater (C20) and Apulian r-f volute-krater (C61). Also exhibited: Attic r-f squat lekythos recovered more or less intact (C21). To David Akehurst, Conservator in the Department of Greek and Roman Antiquities and to all the staff in the Conservation Department, my deepest thanks.

14 A documentary film on the early stages of the *Colossus* excavation, produced by Tony Salmon was shown on BBC TV in November 1975. Another documentary, in two parts, *Colossus: the ship that lost a fortune*, was first shown on BBC TV in June 1978 and then world-wide. Excellently produced, again by Tony Salmon, it was awarded a Certificate of Merit by the British Association for the Advancement of Science.

15 I am grateful to the present Keeper, Dr Dyfri Williams, for access to the material in its new Reserve. Publication of the Attic pottery by Mrs Valerie Smallwood (voluntary assistant in the *Colossus*-Unit from the outset) and of the South Italian pottery by Dr Susan Woodford is in hand. Strangely, the special exhibition at the British Museum in 1996, *Vases and Volcanoes: Sir William Hamilton and his Collection*, with *Catalogue* by Ian Jenkins and Kim Sloan, entirely ignored the substantial Museum involvement in the *Colossus* excavation and virtually ignored its results.

16 Continuation of the letter of 22 MARCH 1799; British Library *Add.MSS.* 42071 F.14-15.

References

Beazley, J.D. 1963, *Attic Red-Figure Vase-Painters*, Oxford

Birchall, A., 1972, *The Hamilton Collection: A Bicentenary Exhibition*, London.

Birchall, A., 1978, 'The Story of Colossus', *The Illustrated London News*, September, 71-75.

Fothergill, B., 1969, *Sir William Hamilton*, London.

d'Hancarville (Hugues, P.F., called Baron), 1767, *Antiquitiés étrusques, grecques et romaines, tirées du Cabinet de M. William Hamilton*, 4 vols, Naples.

Haynes, D.E.L., 1964, *The Portland Vase*, London.

Higgins, R.A., 1988, 'The Colossus of Rhodes', in P. Clayton and M. Price (eds), *The Seven Wonders of the Ancient World*, London and New York.

Lexicon Iconographicum Mythologiae Classicae, 1988, Zurich and Munich.

Morris, R.M., 1965 'The formation of marine organic and detrital concretion in Cornwall and the Scilly Isles'. *International Journal of Nautical Archaeology*, 5.4: 333-343.

Tischbein, J.H.W., 1791-95, *Collection of Engravings from Ancient Vases ... now in the possession of Sir Wm. Hamilton*, 4 vols. with a fifth unpublished, Naples.

Trendall, A.D., 1987, *The Red-Figured Vases of Paestum*, Rome.

Mensun Bound and Hector Bado

Nelson's *Agamemnon*

He was an *Agamemnon* man . . . having served under Nelson when still captain in that ship immortal in naval memory . . .

Herman Melville
Billy Budd, Sailor

In *Agamemnon* we mind them not (i.e. heavy seas). She is the finest ship I have ever sailed in.

Letter from Nelson on the
Agamemnon outside Toulon

When she sank in Maldonado Bay, Uruguay (fig 1), in 1809, the 'old' *Agamemnon* was famous throughout the world, while in Britain, her country of origin, she had become an object of affection, revered both within the navy and by the public at large for her links with the great hero of the Nile, Copenhagen and Trafalgar. She had been Nelson's first flagship, she had fought under him or beside him in many engagements, and of course, it was upon her decks in the Bay of Naples that he had entertained Lady Hamilton. The *Agamemnon* was Nelson's favourite ship. When abandoned in the distant River Plate the newspapers of the day presented a picture of grizzled tars blubbering like babes as they scrambled down her sides for the last time.

Construction

The *Agamemnon*, the first of three vessels to be so called, was named after the Mycenaean Greek who was King of Mycenae and Argos. The story is told in Homer's *Iliad* of how, as commander-in-chief, he led the Greek forces to Troy to bring back Helen who had been stolen by Paris. Before leaving he sacrificed his daughter Iphigenia to appease Artemis. On his return he was murdered by his wife Clytemnestra and her lover Aegisthus.

The construction of the *Agamemnon* (fig 2) was ordered by the Admiralty in 1777. She was to be of the third rate *Ardent* class designed by Thomas Slade, that is to say a two-decker of 64 guns (fig 3). Her artillery comprised 26 24-pounders on the gun deck, 26 18-pounders on the upper deck, 10 9-pounders on the quarter deck and 2 9-pounders on the fo'c'sle deck. She had a keel length of 131ft 10in, a gun deck length of 160ft 2in, a beam of 44ft 5in and had a tonnage of 1,384. Her crew numbered 500. She was built by Henry Adams (fig 4) at Buckler's Hard, a rural shipbuilding centre on the Beaulieu River in Hampshire (Holland, 1993). According to the maritime museum at Buckler's Hard (fig 6), about 40 acres of 100-year-old oaks (2,000 trees), 100 tons

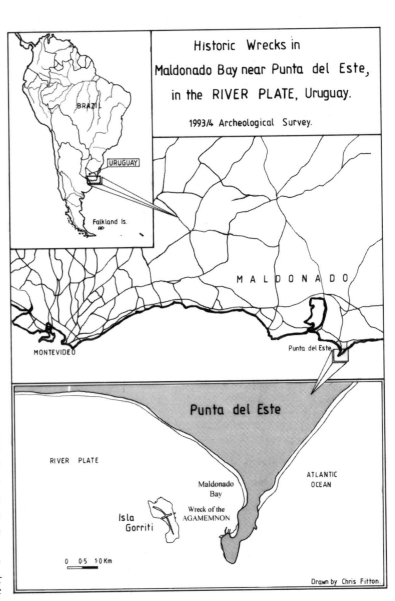

1 Maldonado Bay, Uruguay, where the *Agamemnon* was lost in 1809 (*Chris Fitton*)

of wrought iron and 30 tons of nails and copper rivets were used in her construction. The cost of the ship was £28,579.

She was launched on 10th April 1781, which the *Hants Chronicle* recorded as a 'blustery day when the rain fell in torrents so that only a few people were present'. It then took the riggers four days to tow her to Portsmouth where they installed her lower masts and bowsprit (fig 7).

The *Agamemnon* before Nelson

The *Agamemnon* was commissioned on 28th March 1781 (fig 8). Her first captain was Benjamin Caldwell. One of Caldwell's officers was Thomas Masterman Hardy, who, 24 years later, as flag-captain of the *Victory*, would be with Nelson at the time of his death. Before the year was over the *Agamemnon* had seen action as part of a squadron of 12 ships of the line under Rear-Admiral Richard Kempenfeldt with his flag in the *Victory*. They engaged a large French convoy with an escort of 19 ships of the line. After a short, fierce action, about 150 miles south-west of Ushant, they captured 15 merchantmen full of naval and military supplies destined for the West Indies.

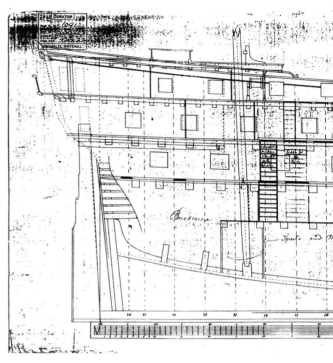

2 *Below* Model of the *Agamemnon* in the maritime museum at Buckler's Hard where the vessel was built in 1781 (*courtesy National Motor Museum*)

3 *Right and opposite* The *Agamemnon* was one of the Ardent class designed by Thomas Slade (*courtesy National Maritime Museum Picture Library, London*)

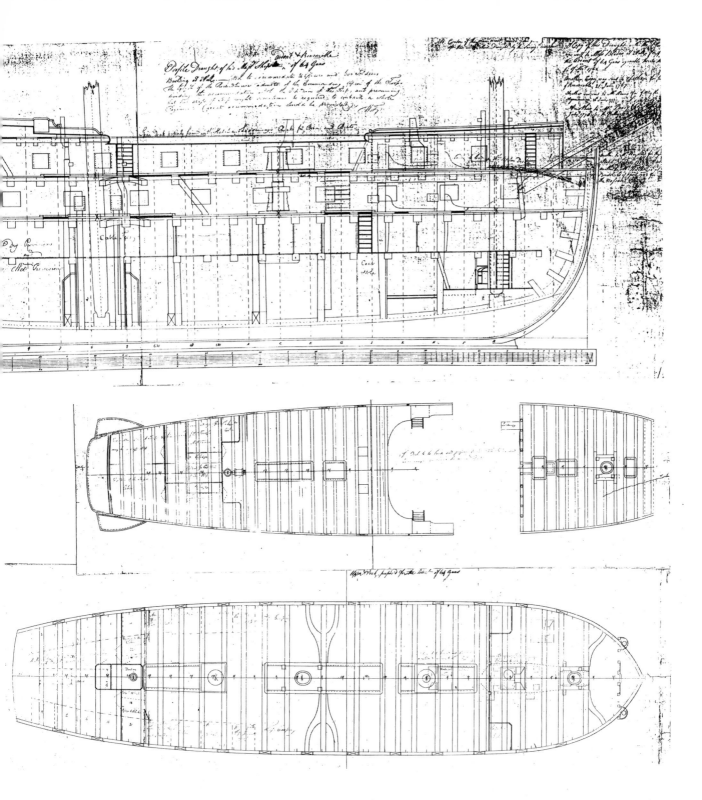

The following year she sailed for the West Indies where in April she took part in Sir George Rodney's victory over De Grasse in the Battle of the Saints, an engagement that was spread over three days and resulted in the capture of five French ships and four more in the chase that followed. 28 of her men were killed or wounded. For its innovative use of tactics this battle was described by Professor Lewis (1948, 513) as the most epoch-making fight since Barfleur. Strategies used for the first time during the Saints were later employed at Trafalgar by Nelson, who himself said that if the Battle of the Saints had been properly followed up, it would have been 'the greatest victory that our Country ever saw' (Cowburn 1966, 148). Another vessel that was involved in this battle was the frigate *Endymion* (see pp. 203-216)

The *Agamemnon* remained on the West Indies Station until the end of the American War of Independence, at which time she returned to England where her crew was paid off. She then lay out of commission at Chatham for ten years.

4 *Top* Portrait of Henry Adams, 1713-1805, builder of the *Agamemnon*. Adams was a shipwright at Deptford until 1744 when he was appointed naval overseer at Buckler's Hard. Three years later he left the Royal Service and took over the shipyard. The master builder's house in which Adams lived is still standing. His sons Balthazar and Edward continued to build ships at Buckler's Hard, thus perpetuating a tradition that lasted over a hundred years *(courtesy National Motor Museum)*

5 *Above* Portrait of Horatio Nelson as a 23-year-old post-captain by J. F. Rigaud, R.A.

The Nelson years

On the entry of Britain into the War of the French Revolution in 1793, the *Agamemnon* was recommissioned and put under the command of Captain Horatio Nelson (fig 5). Her first assignment was convoy duty in the Channel but soon after she joined a fleet of 51 ships in the Mediterranean under the command of Vice-Admiral Lord Hood with his flag in the *Victory*. Here she took part in the Siege of Toulon and the subsequent operations. It was soon after this that the *Agamemnon* was dispatched to Naples where Nelson entertained on board the King of Naples and met for the first time Sir William and Lady Hamilton[1]. In October 1793, the *Agamemnon* fought with the *Melpomene* off Sardinia. In April of the following year, while still under the command of Captain Nelson, she played a leading part in the 37-day siege and surrender of Bastia, Corsica, in which 4,500 men surrendered to 1,200 seamen and marines. In June the same year she participated in the 51-day Siege of Calvi which cost Nelson the use of his right eye. After a refit at Leghorn (Livorno), she returned to cruising and escort duties, and then in March 1795, as part of Admiral Hotham's fleet, she was first into action off Genoa against 15 French ships. During this engagement she devastated the man-of-war *Ça Ira* (fig 9) and helped capture the 74-gun *Censeur*. In July 1795, she was involved in an indecisive action against the French fleet near Hyères, and the following year, partook in actions near Vado, Liguria. In April 1796, as part of Sir John Jervis's squadron, the *Agamemnon* led a small detachment of four ships which captured four French transports that were anchored under shore-based batteries at Loano Bay. Later the same year she took part in the blockade of Genoa and soon after narrowly escaped capture when she was pursued by a French squadron.

By 1796 the *Agamemnon* was in a poor state so Nelson transferred his flag to HMS *Captain*. *Agamemnon* returned to Chatham for repairs where she was fitted with the capstan of the sunken HMS *Illustrious*. In 1797 she was one of the ships involved in the Mutiny at the Nore. It is believed that a majority of her crew and marines were not in favour of the revolt but were forced to show solidarity with the mutineers by three other vessels who had their guns trained upon her. When the Mutiny collapsed, she sailed to Sheerness to surrender. Those of her crew who were tried were pardoned. Many from other vessels were hanged or flogged from ship to ship.

In 1801, the *Agamemnon*, under Captain Robert Devereux Fancourt, was part of the North Sea fleet of 21 ships, 7 bombs,

6 *Opposite top* The 64-gun *Agamemnon* during construction at Buckler's Hard, by Harold Wyllie *(courtesy National Motor Museum)*

7 *Opposite centre* The *Agamemnon* alongside the sheerhulk at Portsmouth having her masts installed, by Harold Wyllie *(courtesy National Motor Museum)*

8 *Opposite bottom* The *Agamemnon* leaving Portsmouth on her maiden voyage in 1781. Her captain was Benjamin Caldwell. One of her officers was Thomas Masterman Hardy, later flag-captain of the *Victory* at Trafalgar *(Harold Wyllie; courtesy National Motor Museum)*

9 On 14th March 1795, the *Agamemnon* under Captain Nelson disabled the French man-of-war *Ça Ira*

2 fireships and 6 gun-brigs commanded by Vice-Admiral Lord Nelson who, following the Battle of the Nile, had been elevated to the peerage and promoted. At the Battle of Copenhagen (fig 10) in April 1801, she ran aground early in the action and thus was unable to make any active contribution to the victory. It was during this battle that Nelson (with his flag in the *Elephant*) raised a telescope to his blind eye and declared that

10 Battle of Copenhagen, March 1801, by Nicholas Pocock (*courtesy National Maritime Museum Picture Library, London*)

he did not see his commander-in-chief's signal from four miles away to disengage the enemy. The *Agamemnon* was not in action again until July 1805, when, under Captain John Harvey, she took part in Sir Robert Calder's action 120 miles off Cape Finisterre against a Franco-Spanish fleet commanded by Vice-Admiral Villeneuve and Admiral Gravina.

Calder's fleet consisted of 15 ships and 2 frigates; that of the enemy, 20 ships and 6 frigates. The *Agamemnon* lost three men and had her mizzen topmast and fore topsail yard shot away. It was another British victory but Calder was much criticized in the press for not having pursued the action. He demanded a court martial for cowardice at which he was acquitted, but severely reprimanded for not fighting to the finish.

The *Agamemnon*'s most famous action came on October 21st of that year, when, under command of Sir Edward Berry, she fought at Trafalgar (fig 11). The British fleet consisted of 27 ships and 4 frigates while the Franco-Spanish fleet numbered 33 ships and 5 frigates. The British attacked the enemy line in two columns, one under Vice-Admiral Cuthbert Collingwood, the other under Nelson in the *Victory*. The *Agamemnon* was number 8 in Nelson's weather column, as a result of this placement she was slow to engage and when she did it was with the Spanish van. She lost ten

killed or wounded. Battle began at noon. At 13.25 Nelson was mortally wounded while walking the quarter deck with his flag-captain, Thomas Hardy. Nelson died at 16.40 having learned of the thorough nature of his victory. The British lost 449 men; the allies about 7,000, as well as 18 of their ships (17 captured, 1 exploded). Of the 17 prizes, 2 sank, 2 were retaken and 6 were wrecked in the storm which followed the battle.

After Nelson

Following Trafalgar the *Agamemnon* was engaged in the blockade of Cadiz. After the blockade was raised she joined Sir John Duckworth's fleet of 11 vessels in the West Indies where, in February 1806, while still under Berry, she took part in a running action against a French fleet of nine vessels off San Domingo. The battle ended when the French Admiral, with one other vessel, ran ashore. Both vessels were burned and three further ships were captured. *Agamemnon* was slow into action and lost 14 killed or wounded.

In March 1806, the *Agamemnon*, in company with the *Carysfort*, captured the French 18-gun sloop *Lutine* and later the same month, while in company with the *Heureux* off Barbados, took the notorious 17-gun French privateer *Dame Ernouf*.

In 1807 Denmark sided with Napoleon against Britain. A fleet of 65 ships under Admiral Gambier was dispatched to lay siege to Copenhagen. The *Agamemnon*, by this time under Captain Jonas Rose, joined the British force during the second week. On August 28th a flotilla of two bombs, mortar boats and gun-brigs attacked the city's seaward defences while the army attacked from land. The Danes capitulated and surrendered their entire fleet of 70 vessels.

Later the same year the *Agamemnon* took part in the blockade of Lisbon after which, still under Rose, she went on the South American station.

Condition of the vessel

By 1809 she truly was the 'old' *Agamemnon*. Twenty-eight battle-laden years had passed since she slid from the stocks at Buckler's Hard. She was now sluggish, strained and leaking badly. At Rio in March her defects were listed by her captain and carpenter; they were read out later that year at the court martial following her loss (PRO ADM1/5399; the original spelling and syntax have been retained):

1st. Some of the standard knees and hooks work considerably which requires and additional fastening

2nd. The riders in general work much (some of them from the labouring of the ship) have worked themselves ¼ of an inch in the ceiling

11 Battle of Trafalgar, 21st October 1805, by T. Hellyer. The *Agamemnon* was number 8 in Nelson's column (*courtesy National Maritime Museum Picture Library, London*)

3rd. The ship shews her weakness in general and particularly in the wings when blowing fresh

4th. Several of the old bolts are apparently broke, and the beams work much in the clamps and the scarfs of some of them work much, which adds to the general weakness of the ship

5th. Each deck swags much and worn very thin, the sail heads (when labouring in the sea) leaks much, occasioned from the decay between wood and wood

6th. The pawl rim of the capstan is broke and wants replacing

7. The water cocks and pipes want replacing

8. The second pintle from the head of the stern post works much up hill upon the brace and makes the rudder work heavy

9. Taylors and Nobles hand pumps are much shook which occasions them to blow and deliver but little water

10. The copper pumps are worn very thin at the lower parts and wants repairs

11. The decks of the fore and after cockpits are worn very thin and wants replacing

12. The facing piece of the bitts is much worn

13. The after hoods on the stern frame of the tuck are much decayed and one chain plate in the larboard fore channels wants replacing

14. Several of the lower deck ports are very much decayed and leak considerably when blowing fresh at sea

15. Carried away and wants replacing the cross jack yard

Signed: Jonas Rose Es. Captain
        Geo Robbins Carpenter

The cross-examination of the witnesses at the court martial confirmed her poor condition. Particular attention was drawn to her hawsers that had been much eaten by rats.

Circumstances of her loss

In May 1809, Rear-Admiral Michael De Courcy arrived on the South American station in the frigate *Diana* carrying intelligence that a French squadron was on its way to the River Plate. The *Foudroyant*, *Bedford*, *Elizabeth* and the *Agamemnon* together with the sloops *Mistletoe* and *Mutine* were dispatched under De Courcy to intercept and engage. Nothing was ever seen or heard of the French squadron, but it was as the *Agamemnon* was entering the estuary on the Uruguayan side of the Plate that she went upon a shoal in Maldonado Bay, beside Punta del Este, and was lost.

The precise circumstances of what happened are contained within her logs which are held by the Public Records Office, London, but the most concise and evocative account is to be found in a letter to the Admiralty (PRO/ADM1/5399) written by Rose and which was read out at the court martial:

Agamemnon, Sunday Evening 18th June 1809 in Maldonado Roads

Sir,

I am under the painful necessity of stating to you the particulars of the loss of His Majesty's late ship the *Agamemnon* under my command, which got on shore in Maldonado Roads on Friday morning the 10th instant after using every effort in my power with the ready assistance I received from the squadron to get the ship afloat, which I lament proved ineffectual.

After having your permission to run into the roads of Maldonado, I trust it will be found that I shortened and furled sails in proper time so as to anchor the ship in the best situation according to the Spanish chart, and that of Capt. Ross Donnelly's survey, but finding that we shoaled the water and being on the weather side of the bay (wind about NE) I bore up with only the jib, finding the water to shoal fast from five fathoms to a quarter four and the ship only drifting to leeward, and having the best bower busy streamed with hands by that Anchor, I was induced to let it go, confident that the ship would come head to wind instantly, but we had drifted and was so suddenly in shoal water that the ship took the ground abaft and lay with her starboard side to the shoal, with the wind rather abaft the larboard beam, but laying very quick. The Boats were instantly got out and the kedge Anchor placed on the larboard quarter, by the Pinnace (in the direction the ship had drifted) on which we have some strain and moved the ship; immediately afterwards the Stream Anchor was carried out by the launch in the same direction, and hove on also, but some severe puffs of wind coming off the land at the moment, both the anchors came home; at this time (about half an hour from her first touching the ground) the ship had not made any water, but by the time the *Mistletoe* had come near enough and carried out the small, Bower Anchor, she had made considerably more water than the pumps could deliver.

The purchase that was got from the main mast on the small bower anchor, and the shores to keep the ship upright from heeling not having the effect, I thought it best in such situation to save as much of the stores as possible, therefore, employed the crew in clearing the boatswain's store room of sails and cordage, and the tiers of the cables, both of which we have nearly accomplished but not until the water had risen to the combing of the lower deck, and which is now as high as the main deck ports.

Nothing more being possible to be done I have disposed of the crew agreeable to your orders, and shall myself remove immediately with all the officers to the *Bedford*.

I take the liberty to enclose herewith the defects of the ship given in last March, and altho' it does not relate to the ships getting on shore, yet I trust it will have some weight in presuming that she might have been got off without injury had she not been in so decayed and bad a state.

I cannot in justice close this without mentioning the highest approbation of the exertions and the assistance I received from all the officers and nearly every individual of the crew.

I have the honour to be

Signed Jonas Rose

With the *Agamemnon* sitting on the bottom, but with her upper structure above water, a decision had to be made as to whether or not the vessel could be refloated, and, if it could, was it worth it? Survey reports (all dated 17th June 1809) were prepared by the masters, carpenters and captains of the *Foudroyant*, *Elizabeth*, *Bedford*, *Agamemnon* and *Mutine*). They respectively concluded:

… that it would be an useless effort and attended with much loss of time to attempt to save the ship in her present situation, she being bilged and her Main Deck scuppers under water, and likewise a great heel to starboard.

… It is our opinion that in case the *Agamemnon* can be righted and brought on an even keel that it is possible to stop the leak and clear the ship of water ... but we are further of opinion that with any superficial repairs we could make on her here she never could be Sea Worthy.

... It is our opinion that ... any attempt to heel her the contrary way so as to stop the leak is not likely to be attended with effect, and if effected, would not answer the purpose of saving the ship, and therefore recommended that every exertion should be used for the saving of her furniture or stores.

The clear consensus was that although it was possible to refloat her, she could not be made seaworthy and that, therefore, she should be abandoned.

Court martial

On 7th August 1809, Captain Rose faced court martial on board HMS *Bedford* in Rio de Janeiro for the loss of the *Agamemnon*.

The Honourable Henry Curzon (Captain of His Majesty's ship *Elizabeth* and second officer in command of His Majesty's ships and vessels on the Brazil station) presided over a panel that consisted of Captains Adam MacKenzie, Charles Marsh Schomberg, Richard Turner Hancock and James Lucas Yeo.

The minutes of the court martial are held by the Public Records Office, London (ADM 5399). It is a long repetitive document in which Rose, who conducted his own defence, posed the same questions to each of his sworn officers. The questions concerned his anchoring procedures, his efforts to refloat the vessel, the state of the ship, wind conditions, signals, etc. Finally, he asked each of the captains of the other vessels who were with him at the time in Maldonado Bay, whether, given identical charts, would they have anchored at the same location. Their replies were always favourable. Nothing contentious emerged from the proceedings and one has the sense that it was all no more than a formality. After a brief consultation the panel returned the following verdict:

The Court having carefully and deliberately weighed and considered the evidence on the part of the Crown as well as in defence of the Prisoner, were of opinion that His Majesty's late ship *Agamemnon* was run upon the shoal owing to the incorrectness of the chart or a bank recently thrown up, and that no blame attaches to Captain Jonas Rose; that he, the officers and ship's company appear to have done their utmost to get the ship off, and afterwards to save her stores. In consequence thereof the Court acquitted Captain Jonas Rose, the officers and company for the loss of the said ship.

Discovery and survey of the *Agamemnon*

In the early 1990s the wreck of the *Agamemnon* was discovered by a group of Uruguayan divers under the leadership of Héctor Bado. In 1993 Mensun Bound and Gianluigi Sacco of Oxford University MARE joined Bado and his colleagues to conduct a brief, preliminary nondisturbance survey of the *Agamemnon*.

The wreck was found to be situated in 8-10m of water on a fairly firm sandy bottom to the north of Gorriti Island close to the position indicated on a map in the Public Records Office. At the time of the visit currents were strong and visibility, which is usually no more than 3m, was down to a metre.

The site consisted of a long ballast mound reflecting somewhat the shape of the lower hull. Within and around the mound a number of items were seen: two sounding leads of different size, a tap, part of a bilge pump, a bronze inkwell, buckles, many pieces of copper sheathing and copper strips. Some of the latter were stamped with the broad arrow. Copper fastenings were everywhere to be seen and some of these were also marked with the broad arrow. One strip of copper (388 x 126mm) which had an edge turned down to form a lip, had been stamped:

1a dHI

9 NPR H3

(some of the letters in the top row might have been misinterpreted). Several cannon-balls and at least one cannon were visible. At places, through gaps in her ballast, bottom timbers could be seen.

In collaboration with the Uruguayan archaeological authorities it is hoped to carry out a full detailed survey of the *Agamemnon*.

Acknowledgements

The authors are indebted to Sergio Pronczuk, Carlos Coirolo, Francisco von Kuhn, Elianne Martinez, Carmen Curbelo, Antonio Lezama, Max Meister, Scott Perry, Christine Anne Sarkis, Miguel Pereira, Simon Dobbs, Susan Tomkins (Archivist Buckler's Hard Museum), Chris Fitton and Bryan Smith for their help in the preparation of this paper.

Notes

1 For more on Sir William and Lady Hamilton see Birchall on the *Colossus* (pp. 236-248)

References

Cowburn, P., 1966, *The Warship in History*, MacMillan, London

Holland, A.J., 1993, *Buckler's Hard: a rural shipbuilding centre*, Kenneth Mason Ltd

Lecky, H.S., 1914, *The King's Ships*, Vol. III, London, 33-39

Lewis, M.A., 1948, *The Navy of Britain*, George Allen & Unwin, London

Michael Teisen (Curator, Norwegian Maritime Museum)

The loss of HMS *St George* 1811

Historical background

Denmark sits as a cork at the narrows of the Baltic, the only passage in and out being by way of the Sound and the Great Belt. For 428 years, from 1429-1857, a toll was levied by the Danes at Elsinore on all ships navigating the Sound. Use of the Great Belt as a thoroughfare was discouraged by the presence of a guard-ship and a toll. To help protect their interests, all surveys of Danish waters were kept a state secret, even though ships of a draught deeper than about 20 feet could not pass the bar in the Sound outside Copenhagen.

Since Medieval times, the Baltic trade had been of great importance to England, France and, above all, Holland. Not only did they all import vast quantities of grain and other bulk-foods from the Baltic, but, more importantly, they depended on the region for their principal supplies of oak, pine, flax, linen, tar, iron, copper, leather, wax, etc., all strategic commodities necessary for the building and maintaining of the fleets upon which these nations depended for their defence. To a certain extent they could look to their colonies for their needs, but travel to and from distant parts was unsafe and took a long time. More significantly, none of the colonies could supply a worthy substitute for oak, an essential of shipbuilding which had become scarce in Western Europe. Small wonder that the Dutch referred to their commerce with the Baltic during the 16th and 17th centuries as 'the mother of all trades'.

It must be borne in mind that up until 1814 Denmark and Norway comprised a multinational single state under the Danish king. From the North Cape to Altona on the Elbe the State exercised a stranglehold on the Baltic. For most of the 18th century, Denmark had remained a non-aligned nation profiting greatly from the conflicts of others. Claiming neutrality, she insisted on escorting all free ships in convoy through the Channel with Danish men-of-war. This put them on a collision course with England; by 1800 conflict between the nations was inevitable. The situation reached a crisis point when Denmark, Russia, Prussia and Sweden formed the League of Armed Neutrality and closed all continental and Baltic ports to British ships. To Denmark this was part of a policy intended to force Britain to recognize a set of neutrality principles which, it was hoped, would create optimum conditions for shipping and trade under Danish colours. To Britain it represented a threat to her command of the seas and her ability to wage naval warfare; it was seen as a more serious threat than that posed by the navies of France and her allies (Feldbaek 1980, 9) and led to the largest naval operations to be carried out by the British during the Napoleonic Wars.

St George: Construction and biography

St George was built at Portsmouth in 1785 as a 1950 ton 2nd rater with 98 guns. Gun deck length 177ft 6in, beam 50ft 3in, hold depth 21ft 2in. Her armament consisted of twenty-eight 32-pounders on the gun deck; thirty 18-pounders on the middle deck; thirty 12-pounders on the upper deck, eight 32-pound carronades on the quarter-deck, and two 12 pounders on the forecastle. About 738 persons manned this enormous war-machine which was comparable to, but slightly smaller than Nelson's more famous flagship HMS *Victory*, which today can be seen at Portsmouth.

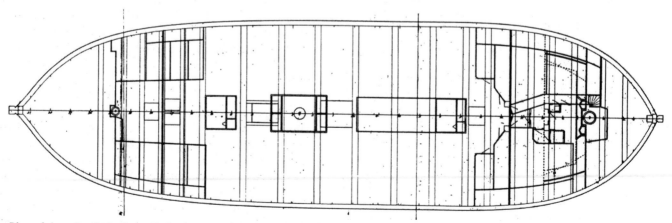

1 Plan of the orlop deck of HMS *Duke*, 1774. The *St George* was built after the same plans (*National Maritime Museum, Greenwich*)

St George was built as one of several ships on the plans of HMS *Duke* of 1774 (fig 1). She was intended to be, and performed as, one of the great workhorses of the Royal Navy. She began her career with a long service as a guard-ship at Plymouth. In 1793, however, she was posted to the Mediterranean where, with four other ships, she took a French privateer of 20 guns. She was in action off Genoa on 14 March 1795, and again off Hyeres on 13 July of the same year. She ran aground on the Cachopo Shoals, south of Portugal, on 18 January 1797.

HMS *St George*, however, drew too much water to go into action at Copenhagen, so Nelson moved his flag to the smaller HMS *Elephant*, while *St George* stayed with Hyde Parker north of Copenhagen out of action.

After the battle *St George* visited Jamaica and the Leeward Islands. 1805-7 was spent on station in the Channel. From 1809 to 1811 she was back in Baltic service. The political situation had changed after Britain had demonstrated her supremacy at sea in 1801 and again at Copenhagen in 1807, the latter time by bombarding the city

2 HMS *St George* under jury-rig at the Battle of the Glorious First of June 1794. She resembled this when wrecked in 1811. By G.B. Lawrence (*NMM, Greenwich*)

The Nelson interlude and after

At the Battle of Copenhagen in 1801, HMS *St George* was selected as Lord Nelson's flagship. He did not hold her in high regard and in a letter to Lady Hamilton wrote:

"I never intend, if I can help it, to set my foot outside the ship, but she is so completely uncomfortable you can have no conception how miserable she is. By Hardy's account he has been on board two days endeavouring to make my place a little decent, but it is neither wind nor watertight, but I shall religiously stay on board, as you like me to do so, and I have no other pleasures . . . I am certainly much better for leaving off wine; I drink nothing but water at dinner and a little wine and water after dinner. I believe it has saved me from illness" (Pope, 1972, 165).

The same day Nelson wrote to his wealthy friend, Alexander Davison, an army contractor:

"The ship is in a truly wretched state. I had rather encounter the newly painted cabins[1] than her dreary dirty leaky cabin, the water comes in at all parts and there is not a dry place or a window that does not let in wind enough to man a mill . . . I shall take my silverplate with me; sink or swim it goes with me" (Pope, 1972, 165).

and sailing off with the Danish Navy, leaving only the very small ships behind. After this, Danish waters were controlled by the Royal Navy, thereby splitting Norway from Denmark and dividing the Danish-Norwegian double monarchy, never to be joined again. The Norwegians suffered severe deprivation during this period because virtually no grain was passing the British guard-ships stationed off Denmark.

The League of Armed Neutrality was no more and by 1810 the Swedes had acquired an ex-Bonaparte marshal, Bernadotte, as king. Swedish neutrality was, by then, of such a nature that the Royal Navy could use Swedish waters and harbours for replenishment and refitting whenever necessary.

Prelude to the disaster

In 1811 a convoy of more than 130 merchant ships and men-of-war gathered at Hanø Bay, Sweden, with *St George* as flagship under Rear-admiral R. C. Reynolds and Commander D. O. Guion. The convoy was scheduled to leave for Britain no later than 1 November, but because of adverse winds they did not get underway until the 9th. At Bornholm the convoy experienced unusually bad weather and lost some of its merchant ships. South of the Danish Isles a heavy

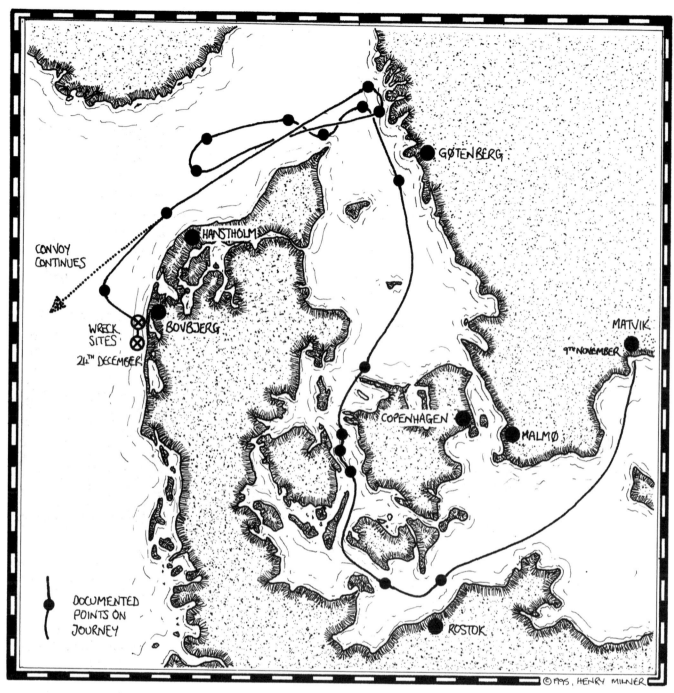

On the map: CONVOY CONTINUES · GØTENBERG · HANSTHOLM · WRECK SITES 24ᵀᴴ DECEMBER · BOVBJERG · MATVIK · 9ᵀᴴ NOVEMBER · COPENHAGEN · MALMØ · ROSTOK · DOCUMENTED POINTS ON JOURNEY · © 1995, HENRY MILNER

3 The route of the Baltic convoy of 1811. The positions have been taken from the log of HMS *Cressy*. *St George* and *Defence* wrecked at Thorsminde close to Bovbjerg *(drawing Henry Milner)*

thunderstorm blew from the NW so that anchorage had to be sought at Rodsand, Southern Denmark (see fig 3).

Safely in Gothenburg, Sergeant William Galey of the Royal Marines on board *St George* wrote on the 2 December to his wife at Milbrook in England:

"A dreadfull sky presented itself from the NW. At half past ten two watches were called to give the ship cable, as the wind at this time had increased to a perfect hurricane. We had not finished giving the ship cable, when we heard the piercing dismal shrieks of the crew of a large merchant ship, which was drifting on our bows and cutting our cables in two, as it sunk in a hollow of the mountainous sea. Our own danger was imminent: we found only 14 fathoms though we had anchored at 20. We hove out the best bower-anchor but it did not hold a moment, the wind and sea snapping off the ring as if it had been only a piece of wire. We now cast the sheet-anchor but it broke off in plowing the bottom of the ocean though it weighed 82cwt. The pilot informed us to cut away the masts. While the foremast was falling a heavy sea lifted the ship to the very heavens, from whence she was precipitated against a sandbank at 2 o'clock in the morning with a dreadfull crash that appeared to shake all her timbers to pieces. All hands were ordered to the pumps and employed in throwing overboard guns and everything else that could lighten us. Shortly after the mainmast was gone with another dreadfull crash. After repeated strikings against the bank the helm was torn from all its fastenings except the chains which burst at 5 o'clock. Otherwise the flapping of the helm would have knocked the ship to pieces and even as it was the stern was considerable damaged. About 10

260

o'clock the 17th we received assistance from the other ships (a Packenham emergency-rudder built on the *Cressy*, Fig 4) and fitted up with jury masts and bending sails. At 18th we were prepared to sail, except as to the rudder. Of the 120 sails which went from Hanø with us, we could only muster 76 on november 21st. We shall sail for England with the first fair wind. We have a fine ship to drag us along - the new *Cressy* - so that when we arrive to England the people may say - 'Here comes old *St. George* like a child in leading-string.' I resign myself however to the Almighty Disposer of all things, and doubt not that we shall arrive safe in England shortly after your receipt of this." (Naval Chronicle, 1812, 113 ff).

Sg. William Galey, along with about 850 of *St George*'s crew, never made it back to England.

At Gothenburg *St George* received temporary repairs and almost suffered another grounding. She was by that time in such bad shape, that a formal ship's council was convened to decide on whether or not she should be abandoned or returned to England. Abandoning the ship in a neutral harbour, however, was a serious matter which would have involved either scuttling the vessel or dismantling and burning her, so that she would be of no use to anyone else.

The loss of St George and Defence

On December 17 *St George* along with most of the original convoy left for England. In Skagerak a heavy storm was building from the NNW. HMS *Cressy* and *Defence* were ordered to remain with *St George* to offer assistance, while the rest of convoy headed direct for England. By 23 December, while off Jutland, *St George* was experiencing severe difficulty with the make-do Packenham rudder. The steering cables had parted and while efforts were being made to repair the damage, the north-westerly gales and southerly currents were all the time pushing the three ships towards the treacherous three sandbars off the coast of Jutland. Those on *Cressy* could see *St George* rolling heavily in the breakers under a reduced jury-rig. The situation was more than critical. On the *Cressy* a ship's council was convened during which the officers gave their unanimous opinion, in hastily written notes, that there was nothing that could be done to assist *St George*. To save themselves the *Cressy* turned before the wind. As they did so they passed close by the stern of *St George* but no signals were received from the latter requesting assistance.

Just before *St George* hit ground the remaining two anchors were released and the masts were cut away. This turned the bow into the sea, but when the anchors broke off almost immediately, there was no hope left.

Defence stayed with *St George* and observed her taking the ground but, as with the *Cressy*, she was unable to assist. Shortly after the *Defence* herself was wrecked, just a couple of miles north of *St George*. *Defence* was quickly beaten to pieces by the huge breakers; only six from a crew of about 560 survived.

Even though it was Christmas, a local salvage team was at the beach at the time, waiting for an opportunity to reach a wrecked Norwegian bark. They heard the gunshot distress-signals and rushed to the assistance, first of *Defence* and then *St George*. The local authorities were notified about

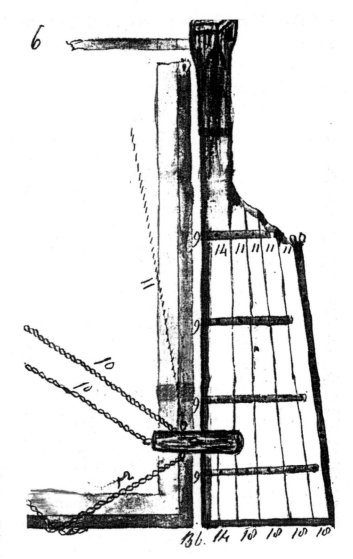

4 Commander Pater's Sketch of the Packenham rudder made on the *Cressy* for *St George*. It was held to the stern by chains and ropes. *(Public Records Office, Adm. 51/2216 capt. log HMS Cressy)*

the wrecking of the two hostile ships, but there was little anyone could be except drag the few survivors out of sea and give them temporary shelter in a tent on the beach.

The large hull of *St George* worked itself quickly down in the sand and within half an hour she had filled with water to the orlop deck. Everything on the weatherdeck, except the long-boat, was smashed and washed away. When cutting the mizzen-mast no axes were available so the sailors used their knives. As it fell a wave washed it away along with the entire poop structure and all who were on it.

The survivors who were still on board sought shelter on the deck by stacking the dead and unconscious in rows to make a barrier against the sea. The local salvors could only watch in horror as at 10 a m on December 24, a mountainous breaker sucked up the very sea-bed itself, and, carrying sand, gravel and stones with it in a thick brown mass, crushed down on *St George*. Local fishermen estimated that this wave washed away about 400 people. Only a couple of hundred were left (Frandsen, 1961, 111 ff.).

Of the total on board (about 865), only 12 survived. The 18 survivors of the about 1,425 persons who had been on both *St George* and *Defence*, were formally prisoners-of-war. In spite of the rather harsh war propaganda, the authorities and poor local fishermen did their best to treat the survivors well. This was customary behaviour to wreck survivors by the fishing population that lived beside the ship-hungry shores of Jutland. Similar hospitality was received by other British seamen wrecked at the Scaw (McDonald 1810).

Most of the 1,425 bodies were washed ashore along the coast of Jutland all the way down to Esberg. A few were identified and buried at local churchyards, but the churchwardens were afraid of numerous burials so the vast majority, according to the local tradition, was buried in the sand-dunes behind the beaches. These places are often named 'dead-man-hills' and to this day the occasional discoveries of human bones in these spots result in criminal investigations, until that is, the correct nature of the circumstances is understood.

The reaction in England

The Baltic convoy of 1811 was a disaster. It was not only *St George* and *Defence* that were lost, but also the *Hero*. She went down at Texel in Holland as a result of poor navigation, believing they were close to the English shore. Of *Hero*'s crew of about 550 only 8 survived. At Texel HMS *Grasshopper* was in such serious peril that it was decided to save the crew and the ship by going to Den Helder and surrendering to the Dutch. A large but unknown number of merchant ships from the convoy were also lost along the route from Hanø. More than 2000 British sailors were lost. This was more than all the seamen lost as the result of action during the Napoleonic Wars.

A parliamentary hearing was held in the House of Commons on 17 January 1812, and a lengthy debate was conducted in the pages of the Naval Chronicle of that year. At one point, an anonymous captain in the Royal Navy, stressed the fatal lack of modern navigational instruments in British naval ships, in particular chronometers for establishing longitudinal positions.

The tragedy also had a considerable impact in Denmark. It was described at length in the newspapers, official reports were compiled and condolences were sent to England. The Danish authorities eventually sent the few survivors back to England in exchange for twice as many Danish prisoners-of-war from the hulks on the Thames, with a preference for those from the district in which *St George* had been wrecked. A boy who witnessed the tragedy was so moved by the experience, that, in later years, he founded the Danish Lifeboat Institutions.

Salvage

Salvage work began as soon as the sea went down. Mostly these activities concentrated on the material that had come ashore, amongst which was an 18 pounder gun still on its carriage. Two more guns were salvaged, but adequate transport was so difficult to obtain that they were still on the beach ten years later. Some documents also drifted ashore; these eventually ended up in the Danish National Archives together with the official Danish reports of the wreck. As for *St George*, she quickly worked her way down into the sand so that very little of her structure was visible above water. Only two sails and some rope were salvaged from the vessel itself.

The wreck was forgotten until 1876 when a local salvage firm with a helmet-diver salvaged six small guns, some powder kegs and a large ship's bell which was donated to the nearby 'No' church (fig 5), and a smaller bell which is now at the *St George* memorial at Thorsminde.

In 1904 salvage recommenced. During a four day period 48 guns were recovered from a depth of about 10m. These were later sold to France as scrap-metal. A great box was the cause of much excitement; the diver who found it hoped that it might be the fabled half million pounds in gold that the vessel was reputed to be carrying - but it proved to be the carpenter's tool-box. The diver described how 'marvellous it was to see the remains of such a large ship. The two upper gun decks had been lost to natural decay. The lower gun deck, however, was free from sand and was about 1m above the sea-bed. The guns were still all lashed behind the gun-ports. I moved freely all over the gun deck but could not penetrate below as the hatches were all filled with sand. The lashing ropes were rotten where they touched the iron bolts. All the guns had tampions in the barrels and weighed about 4 tons including carriage'.

Even after recovery the guns were found still to be dangerous. As one of the tampions was dislodged it popped out with a bang, then, as one of the investigators took a closer look down the barrel by the light of a match, there was an explosion which burned away his beard (Normann, 1993.8).

The bottom of *Defence* was also found, but only a few copper bolts, marked with the broad arrow, were visible above the sand. Salvage was not thought worthwhile. This and later observations confirmed that *Defence* was broken to pieces soon after grounding.

5 The bell from *St George*, now churchbell in the 'No' church. *(Photo M. Teisen; drawing S.E. Ihle)*

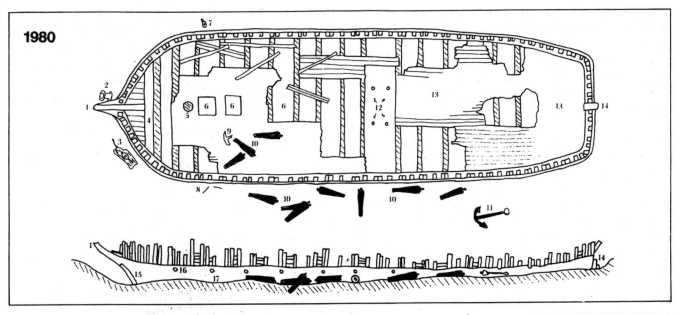

1980

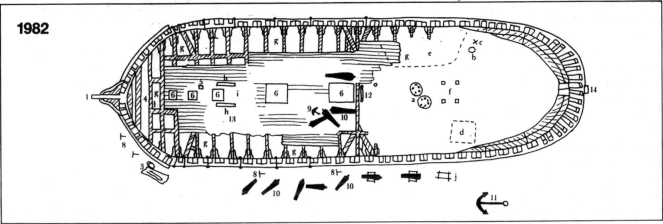

1982

6 A heavy storm in 1981 tore away the after half of the lower gun-deck. It is notable how several dives have improved the accuracy of the diver's sketch by Gert Normann Andersen

In 1940-41 a salvage firm briefly recommenced work on *St George*, removing copper bolts and a few guns. Dynamite was used in the bow but it apparently had little effect. To hide the precious copper bolts from the German occupation forces, they were cut down to stow in fish boxes and were then camouflaged with sea-weed. They also salvaged two small brass signal-guns, one of which is still in the possession of the son of the salvor; the other is at the Navy Union in Hirtshals.

Archaeological excavations

In 1970 local divers rediscovered *St George*. Only the fore-part of the lower gun deck was showing above the sand. An anchor found nearby the wreck was raised and is now together with the small ship's bell at the memorial at Thorsminde. The local Ringkøbing Museum had the anchor conserved and restored with a replica wooden stock of Admiralty long-shank pattern. The anchor was inscribed: '78 . 5 . 0 WL Plyme no 59' (i.e. 78cwt 5 quarters 0 pounds,

William Lemyn (mastersmith), Plymouth dockyard). On one fluke is inscribed 'Tho's' (i.e. the predecessor of Lemyn: Thomas Vaugh, or, maybe more likely, an assistant by the name of Thomas). Another anchor of about the same size was raised late in 1993.

In 1980, soon after heavy storms had accelerated local coastal erosion, divers found the lower gun deck to be completely exposed and the wreck standing 1-4m above the sea-bed. The gun deck had opened up in several places and it was possible to swim through the hatches into a clearing underneath the deck of about 1m. In the bow area of the orlop deck artillery equipment was seen behind the bulkheads. On the gun deck, four large guns and a kedge anchor were noted together with the remains of bitts and hatches. Iron concretions, containing all manner of items, could be seen everywhere. It was obvious that the wreck and its contents, in only 12m of water and unprotected by sand, were extremely vulnerable to wave action. The Department of Marine Archaeology at the Danish National Museum inspected the wreck late in 1980 and recognized its archaeological potential. As a wreck that was more than one hundred years old, it was protected by the Cultural Heritage Act, but this, however, would not serve to protect the site from the forces of nature. In 1981, while raising finance for a trial excavation, a hurricane illustrated the point by tearing off the after half of the gun deck (fig 6).

Along this part of the west coast of Jutland, reasonable conditions for excavation can only be expected for a few days at a time during the summer. Work is further hampered by bad visibility which is rarely over 1m. It is a site that requires experienced divers, professional back-up, good planning and sound funding. It was found that the extraordinary experience of diving inside an historic wreck attracted skilled divers who were prepared to work for low pay, even though they sometimes wondered about the strength of the deck above them, which was supporting the weight of four 32 pound guns.

In 1983 enough funds were raised to start excavation. The aims were: to document and record the wreck to such a standard of accuracy that it will be possible to monitor in detail the inevitable degeneration that will occur in the years to come. To record and map individual objects within and around the wreck. To recover and conserve those items threatened by either loss or decay.

To enable efficient, accurate mapping of structure and its associated objects, a centre-line was stretched from stem to stern. Position fixing was achieved by simple off-set measurements from the line. Men-of-war from this period are usually well documented with their plans, builder's surveys, equipment-lists, etc., still surviving in public records archives and museums. No major surprises were found on the *St George*, but minor anomalies resulting from refits, repairs, etc., such as the installation of iron knees, were observed.

The finds from the first year of excavation proved both the high number of items on board and their excellent state of preservation. While fund raising continued the project was given a more formal structure. The local Ringkøbing Museum became responsible for the excavation with assistance provided by the Danish National Museum in the form of a diving archaeologist and a diving conservator.

7 Excavation plan of *St George* with some of the major finds plotted. The fore part of the gun deck is in place. The after half of the orlop deck is open exposing the cable tiers. Also aft, officer's stores and 'carpenter's' walk to starboard, and Royal Marines stores to port *(M. Teisen)*

Local sportdivers joined the four or five professional divers to comprise a work-force of 10-12 people. An old tug-boat, rolling in the swell about 600m from shore provided a working platform over the site. The excavations which averaged about two weeks a year, continued until 1986. During this time work concentrated on the orlop deck.

The finds

The orlop deck was used for stowage and quarters. On the forward port side the boatswain had his stores and sailroom which contained reserves of rope, blocks and sheaves, sails, etc. In short, everything necessary for sailing the ship. Of particular interest were the reserve block-sheaves, situated in order of size, in rows, as they had been hanging when the ship went down. Some of them were of a new type with experimental bearings. They had all been stamped with the broad arrow and the year of manufacture (to enable the measurement of wear). The Boatswain's cabin was next to his stores.

On the forward starboard side the gunner had his stores and cabin. Samples of most types of gunnery equipment, such as rammers, spongeheads, worms, loading-trays, gun flints and leaden balls of different sizes for guns, muskets and pistols, were found. The latter were in small kegs. Almost all the equipment that could be stolen and resold, was marked with the broad arrow to indicate that it was state property; even the roves for clenching were marked.

The large anchor cables (21 inch), situated in the cable-tiers, took up much of the room in the midship area of the orlop deck. Compared with *Victory*, the cable-tiers of the *St George* were further aft and asymmetrically placed (fig 7).

Just aft of the port cable-tier, uniform-parts, brass emblems of the Royal Marines, bandoliers, boots, cartridge-boxes of wood covered with leather, muskets and pistols were found. Particularly spectacular was a small cutlass with guilded lion heads made by 'Prosser, Charing Cross, London.' (i.e. John Prosser 1797-1853, swordmaker for the King and Admiralty at 9 Charing Cross Road). Notable also were all the unused shoes, stacked on top of each other. These were of Royal Navy standard issue with no difference between left and right foot. They had to be worn into shape. Most of the shoes were of inferior quality with only scrap-leather used to fill the soles and heels rather than purpose

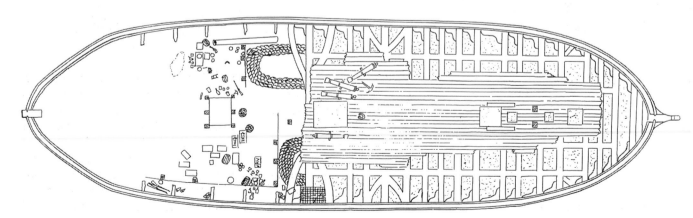

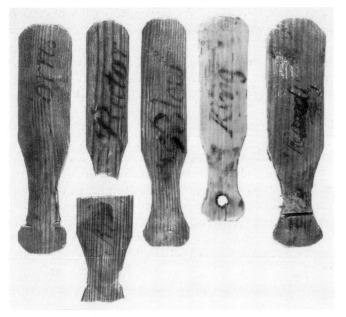

John Cleland, R. N.

8 *Above left* Wooden name-tags from the Royal Marines' stores. The names Morris, Rector, Blow, King and Hardy are still readable, length 8.7 to 17 cm *(Ringkøbing Museum)*

9 *Left* The stamp of the surgeon John Cleland, Royal Navy *(S.E. Ihle)*

10 *Below left* Port and champagne bottles from the officer's stores on the after starboard side of the orlop deck *(Jørgen Borg).*

11 *Above* Stoneware bottles for beverages for the officers *(S.E. Ihle)*

12 *Below* Medicine bottles *(Jørgen Borg)*

cut pieces. The Royal Marines also stored their knapsacks in this area; with them were a number of wooden tags which carried such names as Blow, Birch, Lucas, Smithurst, Peters, Morris, King, Rector, Giles, Rathcliffe, Clarke, Hand and Griffith, all of whom were listed in the Royal Marines musterbooks (fig 8).

At the after end of the orlop deck the surgeon had his dispensary and cabin, the cockpit itself acting as sick-bay and operation-ward in times of action. Two sets of surgical instruments nicely cased in wooden boxes were found here. One was for trepanation, the other for amputation. The steel had rusted away from these items, but the handles and the impressions in the cases, left no doubt as to their painful purpose at a time when anaesthetics as we know them today, were not available. The Irish surgeon's personal brass stamp, 'John Cleland, RN' confirmed the identify of the man who had used these instruments (fig 9). He also had earlier cured a certain McMahon for 'paralysis and incontinence of

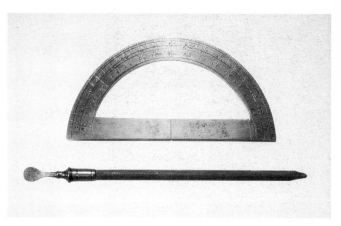

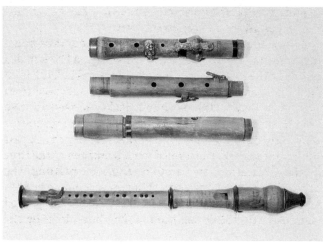

13 *Above left* Tea-set of Wedgwood basaltware *(S.E. Ihle)*

14 *Left* Flute made by Potter, Johnson's Court, London, Flageolet made by Bainbridge, Teacher and Inventor *(Jørgen Borg)*

15 *Below left* Octant made by Bradford Minories, London *(Jørgen Borg)*

16 *Above* Graduated arc and pencil for navigation *(Jørgen Borg)*

17 *Below* Two stone vases of Baltic porphyrite found near the officer's stores *(Jørgen Borg)*

18 *Opposite* Chandelier found on the orlop deck. Of likely Swedish origin *(Jørgen Borg)*

19 *Opposite below* Pottery from Bornholm. Probably sold by a 'bum-boat man' to somebody on *St George (Ringkøbing Museum)*

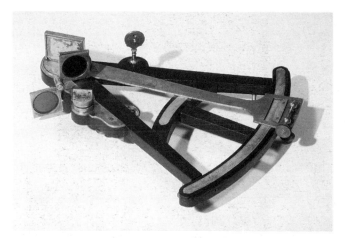

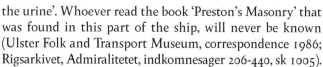

the urine'. Whoever read the book 'Preston's Masonry' that was found in this part of the ship, will never be known (Ulster Folk and Transport Museum, correspondence 1986; Rigsarkivet, Admiralitetet, indkomnesager 206-440, sk 1005).

The officer's stores were situated at the starboard after end of the orlop deck. Here was found a wine cellar containing hundreds of bottles. All the traditional bottle-shapes for claret, white-wine, port, champagne and gin were represented in large numbers (fig 10). Quite a few were still sealed with cork, their contents intact, but most had been contaminated with sea-water. A few bottles of port had retained the qualities of the drink. Glasses, shaped according to the type of drink for which they were intended, were

found stored next to the bottles. Stoneware jars (fig 11) and bottles were used to contain provisions of a more prosaic nature. Pepper seeds in some of the jars may perhaps indicate the former presence of pickled foodstuffs. Exotic perfume flasks were also found in addition to a vast quantity of English pottery, mainly of blue 'old willow' or brown flower decoration. Plain white soup-bowls and a coffee and tea-set of Wedgwood black basaltware, helped make possible a reasonably stylish and comfortable way of living for the officers (fig 13).

Drums and flutes - standard military instruments - were found in the same area. An almost intact flute, made by 'Potter, Johnson's Court, London' (fig 14), and a flageolet,

made by 'Bainbridge, Teacher and Inventor, 35 Holborn Hill, London' came from the cockpit. Navigation instruments were also recovered there; these included an intact Hadley's octant made by 'Bradford Minoris, London' (fig 15), a graduated arc (fig 16), gunters scales, rulers, and to write down the results, a pencil from the 'Strand, London'. A slate and slate-pencils within wooden boxes were also found.

Between the side of the ship and the bays ran the 'carpenters walk', a corridor that gave the carpenter and his assistants access to leaks anywhere along the sides. During the course of the loss, a few muskets and wine bottles had ended up here on the starboard side. The ship's cat had also sought safety here, but - as his bones tell - it was to no avail. As expected no human bones were found. Everybody had sought refuge on the upper decks and they had either died from exposure or had been swept away.

Some of the officers had earned large amounts of prize-money during the war, in particular while on the Jamaica station. In the Baltic one of them had invested in local, high quality souvenirs. Two heavy wooden boxes retrieved from the cockpit were found to contain, packed in sawdust, two 50cm high, beautifully polished, black-and-white porphyrite stone vases of likely Swedish manufacture (fig 17). A pair similar to these were auctioned in Copenhagen at the time of the excavation for around £80,000, baffling the excavation team who were working on a very low budget. Also of likely Swedish origin was a similarly packed chandelier (fig 18). It had been broken into pieces by the

20 Brushes for different purposes. One is marked "Crew, Portsmouth" *(S.E. Ihle)*

21 A tobacco pipe of porcelain with brass fittings *(S.E. Ihle)*

violence of the sinking, but nothing was missing and it was skilfully conserved and restored by the local county-conservation unit (who are also responsible for the almost 4,000 other items). A more modest purchase was a set of different pots and jars from Bornholm, these most likely came from a 'bum-boat man' (fig 19).

The primary purpose of excavating *St George* was to save the artefacts which otherwise would almost certainly have been destroyed by wave action. Much was saved during excavation, however some still remains, but no doubt this is being destroyed by winter storms and the continuing coastal erosion.

The wreck was sketched by a diver in 1980 when most of the gun deck was intact. In 1982 the same skilled diver made another sketch; this showed that the after half of the gun deck had been torn off and that the wreck was open to wave-action along the orlop deck. After ten years of careful monitoring by the same divers, we know that the sea has started eating away at the stern of the orlop deck, thus opening the hold itself to water action. This area of the ship is known to contain provisions, water barrels, shot-lockers, etc. At present the sea-bed is still level with XXI foot after draft-mark, approximately the old waterline.

In the course of our research we have been in close contact with the National Maritime Museum, Greenwich; HMS *Victory*, and the Royal Naval Museum, Portsmouth. From this we have learned that although much is known on paper about the various items of standard Navy issue during recent centuries, samples of the actual items themselves have usually not survived. This is one reason why the finds from the *St George* are so valuable. At another level they give us an important insight into everyday life and, in particular, the complex class and social structure that existed on a self-contained ship-of-the-line during the Napoleonic period.

As a result of the excavation the finds have been kept together as integral parts of an archaeological assemblage for research and display purposes. The material is now on exhibit at a new museum at Thorsminde. In time this museum will display finds from other wrecks in the area. This new museum integrates with the Ringkøbing Museum where items not on exhibition can be studied for research.

Note

1 The smell of fresh paint always made Nelson feel ill.

References

Archiv for Søevæsen 1829, vol. 3, Copenhagen 1829

Feldbæk, O., 1980, *Denmark and the armed neutrality*, Copenhagen

Frandsen, A.V., 1961, *St George og Defence forlis på den Jyske vestkyst 24.dec. 1811*. Hardysyssel årbog.

Kemp, P., 1970, *The British sailor*, London.

Longridge, N., 1955: *The anatomy of Nelson's ships*, London.

McDonald, J., 1810, *Travels through Denmark and Sweden*, London. *Naval Chronicle* vol. 27-28, London 1812.

Normann, G., 1993: *Dykninger ved vraget af St George*, Holstebro.

Pope, D., 1972, *The Great Gamble 1801*, London. (Danish Public Records Office)

Rigsarkivet. Admiralitetet 953, indkomne sager 206-440

Ryan, AN, 1964, *The melancholy fate of the Baltic ships in 1811*, Mariners Mirror vol. 50 p. 123-133, London.

Teisen, M. D., 1983, HMS *St George, dokumentation og prøveudgravning*, Roskilde.

Ulster Folk and Transport Museum, 1986, correspondence.

Uhd Jepsen, P., 1985, *St George og Defence*, Esbjerg.

Phillip J. Wright, (Center for Maritime and Underwater Resource Management, Michigan State University)

Armed schooners from the war of 1812: *Hamilton* and *Scourge*

Freshwater shipwrecks

The Great Lakes region has been occupied for over 10,000 years. Throughout this period, evidence representative of past events and people has been deposited as an archaeological resource on the bottomlands of these large bodies of water. Being immersed in fresh water, these deposits have survived the passage of time as a relatively intact three dimensional chronicle of past activities. This underwater record is quite diverse and includes not only shipwrecks, but also canoe spills, fish weirs, portages, middens, wharf areas, anchorages and inundated land sites.

The military actions on the Great Lakes during The War of 1812 also made a contribution to this underwater archaeological record as Britain and the United States fought to determine the boundaries of British North America. A naval action on Lake Ontario in the summer of 1813 was to lead to the sudden sinking, by natural elements, of two armed schooners, the USS *Hamilton* and the USS *Scourge* (figs 1 and 2).

1 Map of Canada and the United States showing the location of the wrecks in Lake Ontario

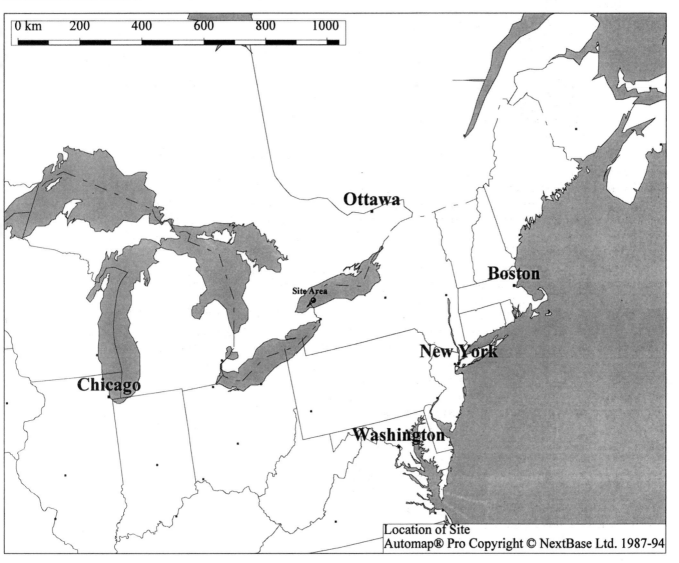

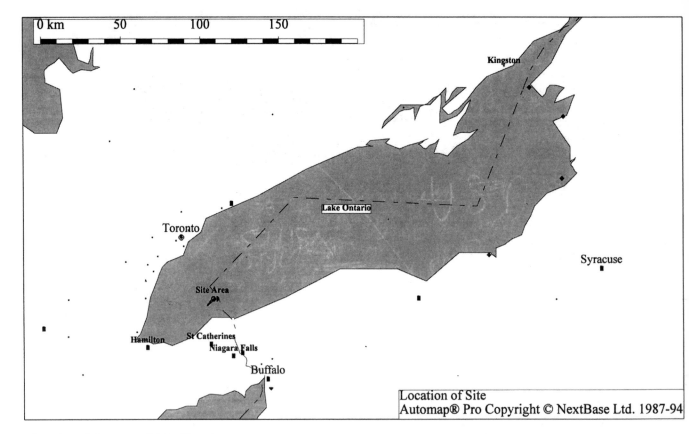

2 Location of sites around Lake Ontario

Today these two shipwrecks lie about 480m apart at a depth of approximately 90m in the western basin of Lake Ontario about 10 kilometres off Port Dalhousie, Ontario (Nelson, 1982a, 2). The *Hamilton* (fig 3) is estimated to have a deck length of 63ft and a maximum breadth of 17ft 9 inches. The *Scourge* (fig 4) is estimated to be 55ft in deck length with a maximum breadth of 16ft (Nelson, 1984). They sit upright on the bottom and their hulls appear not to have sunk that far into the mud. Their exposed decks exhibit only a moderate build-up of sediment. The lake bottom is flat and featureless in the site area. The vessels rest on a recently (in geological terms) deposited layer of mud that is 1 to 3 metres deep. Water clarity in October 1980, at a depth of 75 metres, was 4 to 5 metres and decreased to 1 to 1.5 metres below this depth (Nelson, 1982b).

The war on Lake Ontario

The two armed schooners were part of Commodore Chauncey's American squadron which was awaiting first light to undertake action against the British squadron commanded by Commodore Yeo. However, in the early hours of August 8 1813, both vessels were capsized and sunk by a sudden squall.

The *Scourge* was originally named the *Lord Nelson*. It was built at Niagara-on-the-Lake in Upper Canada in 1811 by Asa Stanard. A Lieutenant Woolsey captured it during an American embargo patrol on June 9 1812. The *Hamilton* was originally called the *Diana*; she was built at Oswego, New York in 1809 by Henry Eagle. Both schooners were purchased in the fall of 1812 by the United States Navy and converted for military use in this war (Cain, 1983).

On the 5 November 1812, Commodore Isaac Chauncey took command of the American squadron (which included the *Hamilton* and *Scourge*) on Lake Ontario. By August 1813, Chauncey had only three vessels (*Oneida, Madison, General Pike*) built specifically for naval purposes. The remainder of his force consisted of eleven converted merchant schooners. The three purpose-built warships had entirely different sailing characteristics from the merchant schooners. This difference in performance created a tactical problem for the American force. It was noted, for instance, that the converted merchant vessels made adequate gun platforms but in rough weather they were hard to keep steady. Under such conditions, Chauncey was forced to either put into port of maintain a close watch over the schooners. During blustery conditions some of the schooners often had to be taken in tow. The unresponsive nature of these vessels in unfavourable conditions slowed down his more powerful warships.

These performance problems became particularly apparent when, in 1813, the Royal Navy took over the Provincial Marine ships under the command of Commodore James Yeo. In a paper on Yeo, Frederick C. Drake (1987) stated that the British and American squadrons on Lake Ontario were seldom able to confront each other. Douglas (1987, 9-10) noted:

"Chauncey would engage only in calm weather, at long range, and near sheltered anchorages to gain the maximum benefit from his

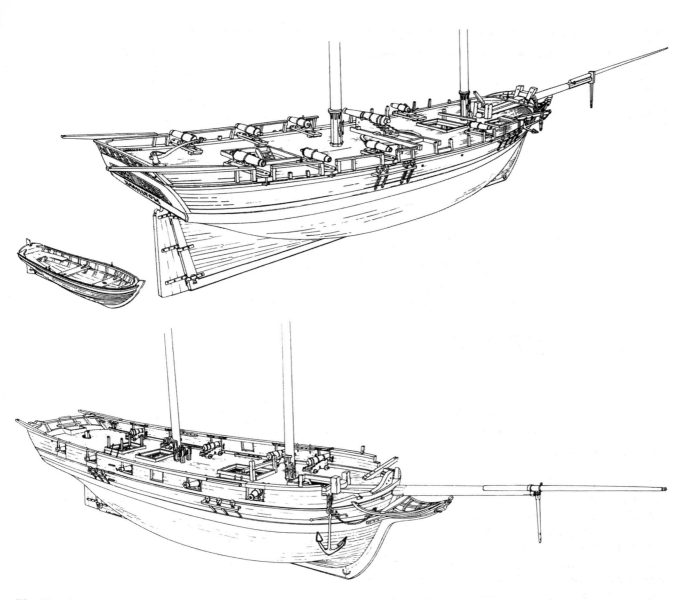

3 The *Hamilton* (ex-*Diana*). Built in New York in 1809. Deck length approximately 63ft

4 The *Scourge* (ex-*Lord Nelson*). Built in Canada in 1811. Deck length approximately 55ft

schooners and long guns. Yeo could only engage in rough weather, on the open lake where his greater co-ordination and superior sailing would enable him to come within a range close enough to offset his broadside disparity ... Rarely in the annals of warfare have tactical requirements contradicted strategic necessity so openly for both contestants with obvious results ... Yeo's purposes were served by such contradictions, Chauncey's were not ..." (Douglas 1987: 9-10)

Drake (1987) included in his study a table of armaments (as of August 1813) for those vessels purchased and renamed by the United States Navy before 5 November 1812. From this table, we learn that the *Hamilton* had a tonnage of 112, a crew of 50, one long 32-pounder pivot gun, one long 24-pounder pivot gun and eight long 6-pounders. The *Scourge* had a tonnage of 110, a crew of 50, one long 32-pounder pivot gun and eight short 12-pounders.

A documented sinking

The sinking of the *Hamilton* and *Scourge* during the early hours of August 8 1813, was a swift and dramatic event. At about two o'clock in the morning, with crews sleeping at their posts and not a breath of wind on the lake, a heavy squall line slammed in upon them from windward. The violence caught the vessels with canvas set. The two schooners were driven right over; water poured in and they sank. In a matter of minutes, a total of 53 men from both crews were lost; only 19 members survived.

An eye witness account of the event has survived. After the sinking, Yeo captured two of the American armed schooners, *Growler* and *Julia*. The *Julia* was the vessel that had rescued a certain Ned Myers, one of eight survivors from the *Scourge*. By chance, Ned Myers later gave his account of the sinking to the author James Fenimore Cooper (1852). Cooper incorporated his account into his 19th century naval classic, *Ned Myers; or A Life Before the Mast*, which was first published in 1843 (Cain, 1983).

It must be said that the sinking of these two vessels was not a significant event in the naval history of the War of

1812, but the importance of their loss in archaeological terms has proven to be considerable.

Searches, survey and photo opportunities

In 1971, Dr Daniel Nelson (research Associate, Royal Ontario Museum, [hereafter ROM]), Dr Doug Tushingham (Chief Archaeologist, ROM), and Dr P.G. Sly (Chief of Great Lakes Research, Canada Centre of Inland Waters - CCIW) began the search for these two vessels with a towed magnetometer and sidescan sonar. In 1973, after searching some 90 square kilometres of lake bottom they were located by Dr Nelson, the principal investigator (Nelson, 1981).

In 1975, the vessels were relocated using just the sidescan sonar. The 1975 imagery showed two vessels with intact hulls, masts and bowsprits sitting upright on the bottom. Later the same year, two dives were made on the stern area of *Hamilton* using CCIW's unmanned submersible, TROV I (Anon., 1978). These dives produced video images of the hull, rudder, spars, a ship's boat and human remains. Later analysis of the TROV video indicates that a platter was displaced by the submersible's manipulator and that an oar blade from the ship's long boat was damaged (Ames, 1987).

Based on the 1975 results, the *Hamilton* and *Scourge* Project Steering Committee was set up to determine the direction and suitability of further archaeological research. The Committee deemed that the establishment of legal title to the vessels was a priority concern. At the same time, the vessels were declared to be of national historic significance by the Historic Sites and Monuments Board of Canada.

In 1976, survey work was undertaken by the ROM and CCIW. Bad weather and equipment failures plagued this investigation but by 1978, CCIW had extracted sediment cores from the vicinity of the site, and recorded sidescan imagery of both ships and their surrounds.

A surface-suspended, unmanned television-photographic probe was deployed on the *Hamilton* in 1978. Bad weather and design problems resulted in only a very brief glimpse of the wreck. The results produced were of poor quality owing to light-back scatter.

Negotiations with the Secretary of the United States Navy resulted in an agreement, dated April 27, 1979, which transferred the wrecks to the ROM. The ROM then gave its 'rights, titles and interests in the contract with the Department of the United States Navy' to the City of Hamilton in a letter of agreement dated May 1 1980. The City of Hamilton was able to enter into this agreement through the passage of a bill in the Province of Ontario's legislature. Bill Pr21, 1979, enabled Hamilton to pass by-laws relating specifically to the historical vessels *Hamilton* and *Scourge* 'which are located outside the municipal boundary of the City of Hamilton'.

In 1980 an expedition from The Jacques Cousteau Society visited the Great Lakes. Under an archaeological licence issued to Karen Brazeau, the Jacques Cousteau Foundation deployed the diving saucer-submersible, *Soucuop*, from the research vessel *Calypso* to make video and photographic records of the stern, deck, bow, foremast and starboard side

of the *Hamilton*. The video coverage later revealed that the submersible had made a number of contacts with the wreck which had resulted in damage (Ames, 1987).

In 1982 the National Geographic Society cancelled an expedition to the shipwreck *Breadalbane* because of arctic ice conditions. This expedition was then diverted to the *Hamilton* and *Scourge*. The objective was to obtain detailed visual coverage of as much of the site as was possible. A remote operated vehicle (ROV), the Benthos RPV-430, was deployed. It carried photographic and video systems plus a sector scanning sonar. The latter made the approach to each wreck both accurate and safe. During the eight days spent on site, approximately 22 hours of video tape and 1,500 slides were taken. About half of the recorded visual imagery was considered to contain useful information (Aqua-Probe Inc., 1982).

While the expedition had initially been designed as an archaeological investigation, the results proved it to have been fundamentally a photographic mission. This was because the ROV was under the control of the photographer and the ROV pilot (Cassavoy, 1982, 36). Nevertheless, a preliminary archaeological report was prepared by the project archaeologist, Kenneth Cassavoy. His observations were based on viewing only 170 of the slides and a 25% to 30% analysis of the black and white video tapes. It was also noted that the survey's photographic-video coverage of the site was incomplete and that no reference points were established, or scales included, in any of the coverage. The report concluded that the data collected was only of visual value and that the report itself should be considered as a starting point for the design of a systematic approach to the investigation of the site (Cassavoy, 1982, 1-3).

The 1982 results indicated that the vessels are sitting on the bottom with marked lists to port. Aboard the *Hamilton* (fig 3) were seen eight iron carronades (12-pounders?) mounted on slides. A ninth gun (a long bronze 24- or 32-pounder) is mounted on a circular swivel amidships. All the ordnance that was seen appeared to be in more or less their original position. Spars, sweeps, blocks, deadeyes, cutlasses, ordnance equipment (power ladles, grape-shot canisters), wooden stocked anchors, and skeletal remains were also observed. The distribution of this material appears to reflect the vessel's list and the open state of its bulwarks which made it easier for material to fall over the side. Most of the extramural deposits were situated within five metres of the port side. Deposition would have taken place in two phases: the first at the time of the impact with the bottom; the second over a longer period of time as the lines decayed. It is assumed that many more items than those visible are concealed within the port side sediment.

The hull and associated structures seem to be in good condition with no evidence of significant damage. They appear to have retained much of their original strength and integrity. The total weight of ordnance can be taken as an indication of deck strength. The port anchor (estimated to weight 400 to 500 pounds) is supported by a small wooden timber/stanchion on the plank-sheer, and a section of a nearby wooden channel. Hull sections, deck structures and spars exhibit clearly defined edges. Individual smaller wooden artefacts appeared to be in equally good condition. Ferrous metal objects (both large and small) showed evidence of severe oxidization.

Three hatches were noted on the deck (one forward of the foremast, one between the fore and mainmasts, one aft of the mainmast). As mentioned, the bulwarks were opened for the entire length of the deck. Sweeps were stowed along the outside of the bulwarks resting on the outside edges of the carronade slides. The figure-head appears to have been carved from a soft wood and is believed to represent the goddess Diana.

Off the stern, sitting upright on the bottom, was the ship's longboat. The position suggests that it came to rest in its present location well after the sinking. Observations on its construction suggested that the boat's rudder could be attached to the bow to provide steerage when used to tow.

The *Scourge* (fig 4) had five mounted iron cannons (4- or 6-pounders) secured along each side. In addition, spars, sweeps, blocks, deadeyes, axes, cutlasses, ordnance equipment (rammers with worm(?), round shot), Fisherman (Rodgers) type anchors and skeletal remains were observed. The distribution of material followed the same pattern as that noted for the *Hamilton*. Despite the list to port the starboard guns were still secured in position by their cascabels. The *Scourge*'s closed bulwarks meant that a great deal of the displaced material ended up on the inside of the port bulwark. These items are mostly concealed by silt deposits that have collected there as a result of gravitational movement. It is felt that more material lies 5 to 10 metres off the port bow, side and stern.

Four hatches were observed on the deck of the *Scourge* (one forward and one aft of the foremast, two aft of the mainmast). The interiors of the bulwarks were planked. A key-shaped opening was thought to be a rowlock opening for a sweep. Small posts on the foremost gunports on both sides may have been used as thole pins for the sweeps. Bilge-pumps were located just forward of the mainmast. On the starboard side, just aft of the foremast, a circular object rose from the deck. It was thought to be the smoke-pipe from the galley stove below. The figure-head (fig 4) appears to have been made from a softwood and seems to be the walking figure of a gentleman (Lord Nelson?). It was also found that, like the *Hamilton*, she had suffered relatively little deterioration and that the strength and integrity of her structure appeared to be remarkably intact (Cassavoy, 1982, 4-23).

During the course of obtaining the photographic and video coverage, the ROV made accidental contact at various points on both shipwrecks. Most of these contacts resulted in only slight abrasions to surfaces (Ames, 1987). Damage occurred during a repositioning manoeuvre when a slack anchor cable removed the *Hamilton*'s foremast at a point about one foot above the deck and deposited it on the lake bottom beside the wreck (Cassavoy, 1982, Appendix I A, 1982 Survey Supplemental Report by D. Nelson).

5 The figure-head from the *Scourge*, believed to represent Lord Nelson after whom the vessel had been originally named (*drawing Helen Ford*)

As a result of the 1982 field season, an Ontario Heritage Foundation (OHF) committee made a series of recommendations. These urged that, in the public interest, the wrecks should be protected, and that a surveillance system be installed to monitor the site. It was also recommended that, before any thought could be given to raising the vessels, an exhaustive study of the conservation problems and a detailed investigation of the vessels themselves, their structural integrity and the nature of their contents, must be carried out. The committee also noted that, to meet these recommendations, an effective management team plus adequate resources were required.

The City of Hamilton received funds to install a surveillance system on the site in 1984. In addition, funds were granted to hire both an archaeologist and a conservation specialist. In 1985, a search for such professionals was undertaken but no suitable candidates were found. This dilemma was solved by the OHF establishing a Technical Study Team (TST) under the direction of a steering committee with the task of setting up a proper *Hamilton-Scourge* project.

The proposed plan for conducting the Hamilton-Scourge feasibility study

The 1986 steering committee represented three levels of government (i.e. that of Canada, Ontario and Hamilton). Owing to the past events, it took time to create a technical study team that could provide the necessary recommendations to the steering committee. The TST developed and endorsed a study plan and submitted it on October 27 1988, to the steering committee. The proposed plan documented the steps necessary '... to determine the feasibility of preserving, raising and conserving the *Hamilton* and *Scourge* for use as a heritage attraction in the City of Hamilton' (Storck, 1988, 2).

In developing this plan, the guiding principle adopted had been the protection and interpretation of the heritage value of the site. These dual priorities led and determined all major discipline (archaeological, engineering and conservation) activities associated with the wrecks. Protection was defined as being achieved 'through archaeological recording prior to, and in preparation for, disturbance or excavation, and/or by the prevention of physical intrusion into the site or a portion of it'. Interpretation was defined as being achieved 'by the advancement of knowledge of the site culminating in publication and other means of communication'. Heritage value was defined as 'the intrinsic potential of the site and the objects within it to inform us about the past' (Storck, 1988, 6-7).

This report outlined a number of deficiencies in the previously collected site data. These included the need for more precise locations of both vessels and the content and dimensions of the associated debris fields around and between the wrecks. This was required to establish off-site moorings and staging areas. There was also a need for more accurate information on the exact size (detailed plan drawings plus necessary elevations) of the ships, the nature of their associated material and the physical dimensions of the entire site area. In addition, there was a need for direct information (such as could be provided by recovered samples) on the site's state of preservation and integrity. Evidence required included the condition of the metals, wood and other organics plus data on such subjects as algae growth, water turbidity, and sediment. Finally, the nature and the extent of the past damage to the site needed to be recorded in order to monitor the impact of future dives and the progress of natural decay.

The feasibility study requested controlled scaled imagery of both vessels and the surrounding bottom so that a detailed, accurate map might be prepared. This was necessary not only for dive-planning, conservation and sampling strategies but also so that safe access corridors might be identified. Such a map was also deemed fundamental for a comparative study and interpretation of the remains. Once the foregoing had been completed, the next phase of the feasibility study called for the recovery of samples to answer conservation and structural questions.

The results of the above defined tasks would help determine the 'feasibility of preserving, raising and conserving the *Hamilton* and *Scourge* for use as a heritage attraction in the City of Hamilton' (Storck, 1988, 6-7).

The Jason Foundation For Education expedition

In the spring of 1990, Dr Robert Ballard undertook 'The Jason Foundation For Education, Great Lakes Project'. This was an educational programme that allowed students at various locations around North America, to participate in underwater 'scientific research' via live satellite transmissions, six times a day from a location on the bottom of Lake Ontario in the vicinity of the shipwrecks. This project provided an opportunity to employ appropriate underwater technology to collect data that could be used in addressing some of the issues identified in the 1988 feasibility study.

After negotiations, terms of reference were set up between the Jason Foundation For Education, the OHF, the City of Hamilton and federal representatives. The agreement stated that all activities conducted were to meet the standards of Canadian nautical archaeology, to protect the heritage value of the site and to promote the public's understanding and appreciation of marine heritage. An archaeological director was to be brought in to assess the proposed technology and its applications in the visual investigation and mapping of the wrecks with minimum site disturbances. This individual was also to formulate and execute the on-site operational protocols. These protocols were to be developed in co-operation with the Jason Foundation and the Canadian Centre of Inland Waters (CCIW). The agreement also pointed out that the data obtained during the course of this project was not to be considered part of the 1988 feasibility study, but would be of future use in it.

Dr Margaret Rule accepted the position of archaeological director and the project went ahead in April and May 1990. The Jason-Medea dual ROV system was used to collect the data. Medea is an underwater survey vehicle designed for large area coverage which is linked to Jason by a 100 metre, neutrally buoyant cable. Jason is a multi-sensory imaging and sampling platform designed for detailed work that requires a high degree of manoeuvrability. In spite of the poor visibility experienced during the project, a vast quantity of data was collected with no damage to the site.

The current task is how to process this vast amount of data. Efforts are underway to digest it in a fashion that will address the issues, tasks and recommendations outlined in the aforementioned feasibility study. The data obtained in 1990 represents a comprehensive body of electronic data for deep water shipwrecks. The tasks to be undertaken will take place over the next few years and will involve a number of individuals and institutions.

The tasks include the additional processing of data from the sidescan, the Spotrange point sonar, the Mesotech pencil-beam profiling sonar and the electronic stills camera (ESC). The Spotrange and Mesotech data can be used to develop quantitative models of the wrecks and to provide orientational and dimensional information on the hull forms. The Mesotech profile data and attitude data is to be used with individual ESC images to produce accurate measurements on the wrecks. Furthermore, photomosaic imagery can be produced. The Spotrange data can also be merged with navigation and SHARPS data and then used to review the video imagery.

Ironically, it has been the excellent state of preservation of these wrecks that has made their archaeological investigation such a long and circuitous task. These sites offer a unique opportunity to study the War of 1812 through the study of ship structures. Data relating to the ships' stores and the personal possessions (archaeologically defined as patterned artefact assemblies) will provide information relating to the needs and activities of the crews and shipboard life in general. The study of the armaments and their associated apparels will provide insights into strategies of naval conflict. These shipwrecks represent a single event that can be used to understand a particular early 19th century society while engaged in the enterprise of war.

References

Ames, J., 1987, *Hamilton-Scourge Project Artefact Inventory, Second Draft.* Manuscript on file with Hamilton-Scourge Foundation, Hamilton, Ontario.

Anon., 1978, *Side Scan Sonar Survey and Study of Red and White Targets in Lake Ontario - 1978, Report to the Hamilton-Scourge Committee.* Manuscript on file with Inland Waters Directorate, National Water Research Institute, Environment Canada, Burlington, Ontario.

Aqua-Probe Inc., 1982, *Report of the Photographic and Videotape Investigation of the Armed Schooners Hamilton and Scourge in Lake Ontario During May 1982.* Report presented by Aqua-Probe Inc., St. Catherines, Ontario.

Cassavoy, K.A., 1982, *Hamilton/Scourge, May 1982 Survey, Preliminary Archaeological Report.* Manuscript on file with Hamilton-Scourge Foundation, Hamilton, Ontario

Cain, E., 1983, *Ghost Ships.* Musson, Toronto.

Cooper, James Fenimore, 1852, *Ned Myers; or, A Life Before the Mast.* New Edition, Stringer and Townsend, New York.

Douglas, A., 1987, *The Historical Significance of a Midsummer's Night Dream.* Manuscript on file with the Ontario Heritage Foundation, Toronto.

Drake, F.C., 1987, *Command Decisions and Combined Operations: Commodore James Lucas Yeo.* Paper presented at the United States Naval Academy, 8th Historical Symposium, Annapolis, 24 September 1987.

Nelson, D.A., 1981, *An Approach to the Conservation of Intact Ships Found in Deep Water.* Paper presented to the ICOM Waterlogged Wood Working Group conference, Ottawa, September 15 to 18 1981.

Nelson, D.A., 1982a, *Deep Water Archaeology in Lake Ontario.* Paper presented to the First Annual Canadian Ocean Technology Congress, Toronto, September 11-14 1982.

Nelson, D.A., 1982b, *Hamilton-Scourge Project, Site Survey, July 1982, Design and Operational Manual.* Manuscript on file with Hamilton-Scourge Foundation, Hamilton, Ontario.

Nelson, D.A., 1084, *Homeward Bound, The Hamilton and Scourge Project, a Personal View.* Aqua-Probe Inc., St. Catherines, Ontario.

Storck, P.L. (Chairman), 1988, *A Proposed Plan for Conducting the Hamilton/Scourge Feasibility Study.* Document on file with Ontario Heritage Foundation, Toronto, Ontario.

James P Delgado (Executive Director, Vancouver Maritime Museum)

The wreck of the US Brig *Somers* (1842-1847)

Introduction

The wreck of the United States Brig *Somers* (1842-1847) was discovered off the coast of Vera Cruz, Mexico, in 1987. The brig foundered while blockading Vera Cruz during the United States' war with Mexico (1846-1848). A historically significant vessel with a notorious career in the United States Navy, the *Somers* represents a unique archaeological resource as the only American naval shipwreck from the Mexican War available for study. Characteristics of the vessel's sharp clipper lines and allegedly top-heavy rig could also be discerned. Additionally, *Somers* represents a diplomatic and political challenge as the United States and Mexico, while agreeing to preserve and study the wreck, dispute each others' claims to sovereignty over the site. The *Somers* case, like that of the Confederate raider *Alabama* in French waters (see Arch. of Ships of War, IMAS I, 90-102), is part of a recent U.S. government policy to assert its ownership over warship wrecks, while emphasizing a co-operative international approach to their preservation, study and interpretation. This approach is unique to the archaeology of warships.

Historical background

The mid-19th century was as much a time of change for the United States Navy as it was for the nation ashore. The change was particularly felt in the reorganization of the Navy into various bureaux and in the need for more suitable training for its officers. Matthew Calbraith Perry, then commander of the New York Navy Yard, was one of the more influential officers seeking an end to the haphazard education of young

1 Portrait of the *Somers*

midshipmen and an escape from the often degrading circumstances of training these impressionable youths in the rough and tumble, and often sordid circumstances that existed between the decks of an American man-of-war.

The solution Perry proposed, namely building brigs-of-war to serve as seagoing schools for midshipmen, was approved. The brig *Somers* (fig 1), designed by Samuel Humphreys was laid down at the New York Navy Yard, Brooklyn, and launched on April 16 1842. It was built to the Baltimore clipper model - sharp, fast and heavily sparred. *Somers* was 100ft long between perpendiculars, had a 25ft beam, an 11ft depth of hold and displaced 259 tons. Pierced for 12 guns, *Somers* carried ten 31-pounder carronades and two medium 32-pounders on her deck (Chapelle 1949:430).

Somers made one training voyage without incident under the command of Capt. Alexander Slidell McKenzie, Perry's brother-in-law. Her second voyage, again under McKenzie, involved running from New York to Africa, and thence back to the United States by way of the Caribbean, bearing dispatches for the Navy's African Squadron. The small vessel was crowded with a young crew of 120; many were teenagers. One of these youths was 19 year old Philip Spencer, the scapegrace son of the then Secretary of War John Canfield Spencer. Philip had a short but notorious naval career of drunken behaviour and brawls and thus was not welcomed aboard *Somers* by either the captain or his officers. None the less, Spencer remained aboard despite McKenzie's protests and sailed with *Somers* from New York on September 13 1842.

Throughout the voyage Spencer made a show of mocking the captain's authority and regulations, and spoke of piracy and mutiny. In a classic case of youthful immaturity - Spencer's - clashing with an overblown sense of duty - McKenzie's - the former reportedly told another crew member of his plan to murder McKenzie and the other officers and seize *Somers* for a piratical cruise. The crew member informed the ship's Lieutenant. Spencer was arrested and ironed. Two others, Bosun's mate Samuel Cromwell and seaman Elisha Small, were also arrested. Other crew members were implicated. Fearing the spread of mutiny on the small vessel, McKenzie ordered a court-martial. Spencer, Cromwell, and Small were convicted and hastily executed from the main yardarm on December 1 1842 (McFarland 1985).

Upon *Somers'* return to New York the news of the 'mutiny' spread. McKenzie was acclaimed; the New York *Herald* of December 18 noted 'We can hardly find language to express our admiration of the conduct of Commander McKenzie . . .'. Questions soon arose over the expediency of the executions, as well as their necessity. McKenzie unfortunately wrote that the executions were all the more necessary as Spencer, the son of a prominent man, most probably would have escaped justice ashore. Spencer had avowed it was all a joke. A damning letter in the Washington *Madisonian* of December 20 1842, probably penned by an angry and anguished John Canfield Spencer, summed it thus 'the mere romance of a heedless boy, amusing himself,

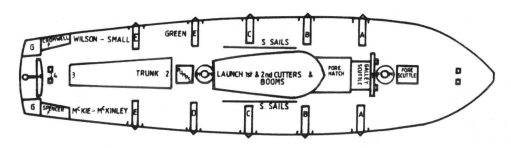

SECTION REPRESENTING THE SPAR DECK

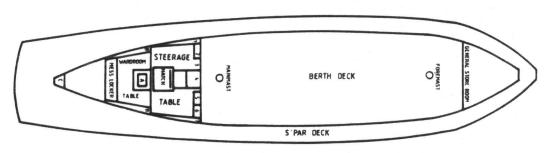

SECTION REPRESENTING THE BERTH DECK

2 Deck-plans of the *Somers*

INQUIRY

INTO

THE SOMERS MUTINY.

WITH A FULL ACCOUNT OF THE EXECUTION OF

SPENCER, CROMWELL AND SMALL.

NEW-YORK:
GREELEY & McELRATH, TRIBUNE BUILDINGS.
PHILADELPHIA: BURGESS & ZIEBER.
BOSTON: REDDING & CO.

Tribune Print.   160 Nassau-st.

3 An illustration from the New York *Weekly Tribune*, 21 January 1843

it is true, in a dangerous manner, but still devoid of such murderous designs as are imputed ... the result of unmanly fear, or of a despotic temper, and wholly unnecessary at the time ...'.

The subject was debated in the press, on the streets of New York, and throughout the nation. Anxious to clear his name McKenzie asked for and received a court of inquiry that lasted from December 28 1842, to January 28 1843, at the Brooklyn Navy Yard. The court of inquiry absolved McKenzie of wrongdoing, but not sufficiently so to satisfy him, his defenders, detractors, or the Secretary of the Navy, who favoured McKenzie's request for a court martial.

The court martial, on the charges of murder, illegal punishment, conduct unbecoming an officer, and general cruelty and oppression, lasted two months. It, like the inquiry, was closely followed by the press. Influential citizens rallied to McKenzie's cause, among them Richard Henry Dana, while others, notably James Fenimore Cooper, railed at McKenzie as a tyrant and murderer. The court martial acquitted McKenzie of all charges but as several historians have noted, the court of public opinion in the end, despite a strong and

continual defence of the captain, condemned not only McKenzie but the system he served. The matter is still debated in some circles, notably among the membership of Chi Psi, the national fraternity which Philip Spencer helped establish during a brief College career. *Somers* made no more training voyages. The system of training at sea was abolished in the wake of the '*Somers* Affair', and in 1845 the Secretary of the Navy established the United States Naval Academy at Annapolis, Maryland, in its stead. *Somers*, remaining in naval service, became an unwelcome subject of conversation among naval officers (Hayford 1959).

The most famous outcome of the affair was the interest of Herman Melville, whose cousin, Guert Gansevoort, was first officer board *Somers*. Melville made mention of the 'mutiny' in *White Jacket*, citing 'the well-known case of a United States brig ... a memorable example, which at any moment may be repeated. Three men, in a time of peace, were then hung at the yardarm, merely because in the captain's judgement, it became necessary to hang them. To this day the question of their complete guilt is socially discussed' (Melville 1850). Melville again employed *Somers*, and more directly so, in his last work, *Billy Bud*, published posthumously and with several parallels to the events of late November and December 1 1842 (Melville 1948).

With the outbreak of war with Mexico in 1846, *Somers*, assigned to the Home Squadron, sailed into the Gulf under the command of Raphael Semmes, an officer who later gained fame as a Confederate admiral and commander of the most successful commerce raider in history, CSS *Alabama*. Under Semmes' command, *Somers* helped enforce the United States' blockade of Mexico's most important Gulf port, Vera Cruz. *Somers*' war career was brief (fig 4). On December 8 1846, Semmes spotted a small vessel apparently trying to run the blockade. *Somers* gave chase as a squall blew up, striking the brig as she tacked. According to Semmes, 'Lieutenant Parker took the mainsail off her, and had got the spanker about half brailed up, when the squall struck us ... The brig being flying-light, having scarcely any water or provisions, and but six tons of ballast on board, she was thrown over almost instantly, so far as to refuse to obey her helm ...'. *Somers* was thrown on her beam ends, 'and the water pouring into every hatch and scuttle ... I ordered the masts to be cut away' (fig 5). The officers and men, who, with few exceptions, had by this time reached the weather bulwarks, immediately began to cut away the rigging'. However, 'this was a forlorn hope, the brig filling very fast, and her masts and yards lying flat upon the surface of the sea'. Then, 'when she was on the point of sinking beneath us, and engulfing us in the waves, I gave the order, "Every man save himself who can" (Semmes, 1851, 96-97).

Somers sank in 107ft of water in ten minutes, drowning 32 crew members. While entertained, the salvage of the

4 Map of the Gulf of Mexico with an inset showing where the *Somers* was lost

5 The last moments of the *Somers*

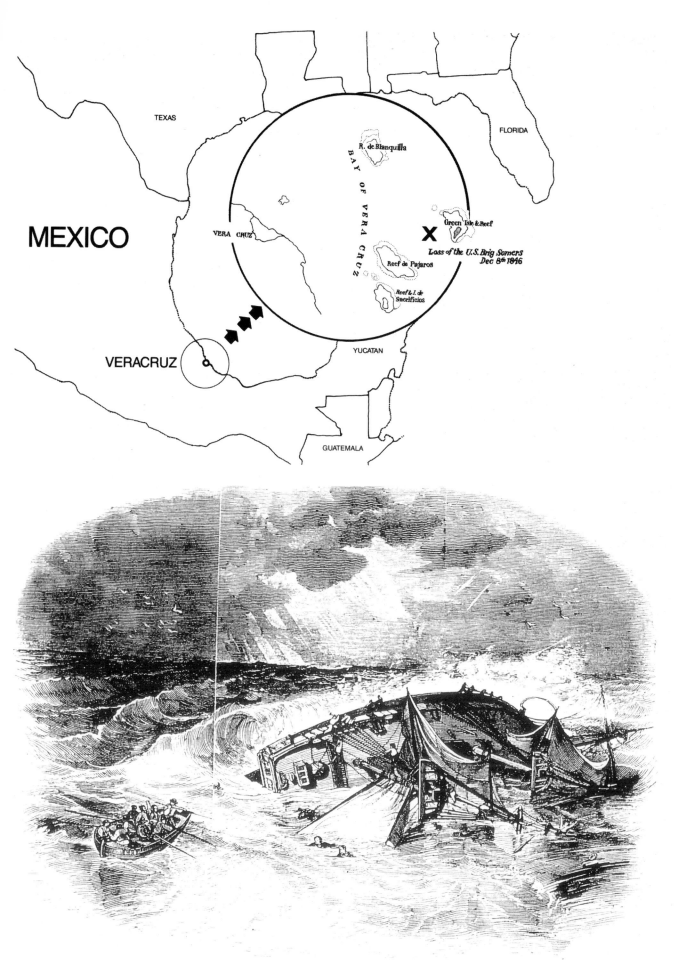

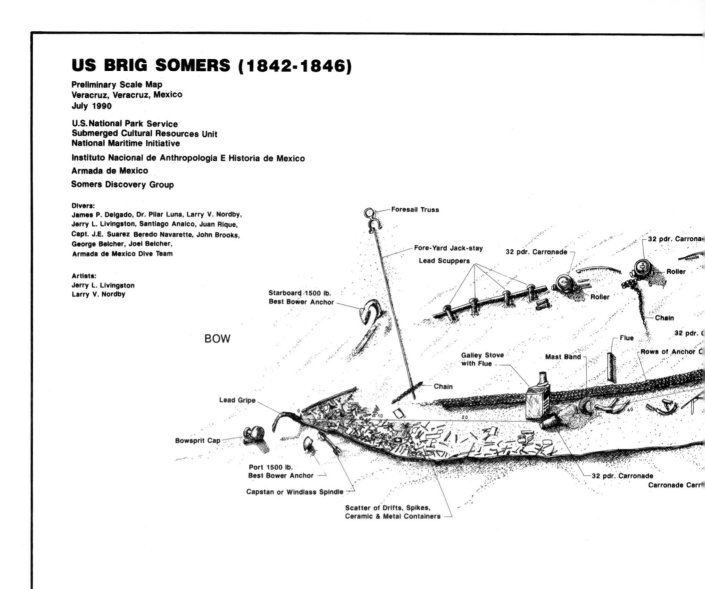

US BRIG SOMERS (1842-1846)

Preliminary Scale Map
Veracruz, Veracruz, Mexico
July 1990

U.S. National Park Service
Submerged Cultural Resources Unit
National Maritime Initiative

Instituto Nacional de Anthropologia E Historia de Mexico

Armada de Mexico

Somers Discovery Group

Divers:
James P. Delgado, Dr. Pilar Luna, Larry V. Nordby,
Jerry L. Livingston, Santiago Analco, Juan Rique,
Capt. J.E. Suarez Beredo Navarette, John Brooks,
George Belcher, Joel Belcher,
Armada de Mexico Dive Team

Artists:
Jerry L. Livingston
Larry V. Nordby

6 Plan of the wreck made in 1990

notorious brig was not acted upon, and *Somers* was left to the ocean, passing firmly into history.

Discovery of the wreck

The wreck of *Somers* was rediscovered in 1986 by an art dealer and explorer George Belcher of San Francisco. He had been requested by the then Governor of Vera Cruz, Acosta Lagunes, to carry out a search in the waters off Vera Cruz for historic shipwrecks that might provide material for the new state museum in Jalapa. In 1986, Belcher began his search by conducting a magnetometer survey of the area in which it was known that the *Somers* had gone down. On June 2 1986, as a squall obscured the sky, the magnetometer registered an anomaly in 110ft of water one mile off Isla Verde and close to where *Somers* was lost. Belcher, accompanied by his brother Joel, descended with scuba gear and landed on a wreck they strongly suspected was *Somers* (fig 6). A pale grey, glazed stoneware jar inscribed with

'Alexandria, D.C.' (Alexandria is now in Virginia but between 1789 and 1846 it was part of the District of Columbia) was recovered for the state museum (Belcher 1988, 93).

Anxious to secure protection for the site and insure scientific study of *Somers*, Belcher contacted various archaeologists and government agencies in the United States and Mexico. As a result of his efforts, the US Navy, the Department of State, and the National Park Service, which is the only federal agency with a working field team of maritime archaeologists, agreed to work co-operatively to seek a bilateral agreement with Mexico to survey and assess the wreck, which now lies in Mexican territorial waters. Belcher worked with both governments, seeking to help interpret the story of *Somers* through a documentary film.

Belcher privately funded a land and underwater film expedition to Vera Cruz in May 1987. At the same time, shipwreck archaeologist Mitchell Marken, who conducted

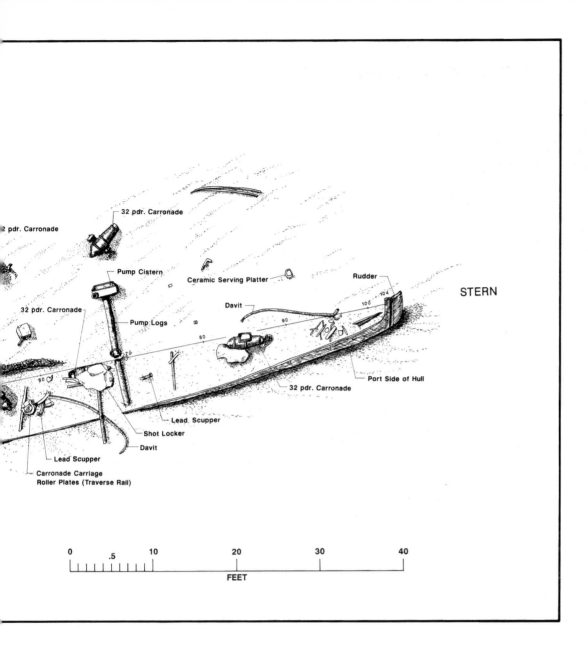

2 pdr. Carronade

32 pdr. Carronade

Pump Cistern

Ceramic Serving Platter

Rudder

STERN

32 pdr. Carronade

Pump Logs

Davit

80

70

90

100

104

Port Side of Hull

60

60

32 pdr. Carronade

Lead Scupper

Shot Locker

Davit

Lead Scupper

Carronade Carriage
Roller Plates (Traverse Rail)

0   .5   10   20   30   40

FEET

the first survey of the site, invited a National Park Service representative to Vera Cruz to see the wreck, help confirm the identification, and report to the various other US Government agencies. A site plan was prepared, several key features of the wreck were assessed, and the identification was confirmed. To ensure the integrity of the wreck and its associated artefacts, no excavating or even hand-fanning, was permitted.

Government interest and involvement

The discovery of *Somers* was announced in San Francisco on November 10 1987. The United States Department of State sent a note to the Mexican Government on November 18 1987, with additional notes in April, May, and June 1988, noting that the United States considers the *Somers* to be United States property, a war grave and an archaeological site of exceptional significance in U.S. history. The note and discussions with Mexican officials emphasized a co-

operative approach with Mexico, whereby an international team from both countries, consisting of the National Park Service, the US Navy, Mr. Belcher's group, and Mexico's Instituto Nacional de Antropologia e Historia (INAH), would complete a non-destructive documentation of the site and prepare a research design for future work. The latter would present proposals for the care and preservation of the site as well as consider the possibility of limited excavation and the study and display of any resulting artefacts. It was decided that any human remains would be returned to the United States. During negotiations, parties unknown located and looted the wreck; the chronometer, pistols and other artefacts were removed. The Mexican government has now ensured surveillance and protection of the site.

On November 27 1989, meetings between a U.S. delegation and the Mexican government in Mexico City resulted in an oral agreement to protect and to commence a joint study of the site. The first week of July 1990 was

Naval District. The Mexican Navy provided the 100ft patrol boat *Margarita Maza de Juarez* as a base of operations (fig 8). George and Joel Belcher guided the team to the site and participated in all activities.

Site description

The wreck is situated in 107ft of water three miles off Vera Cruz. It lies on its starboard side (practically on its beam ends) thus recalling the circumstances of her loss when, 144

7 *Left* Larry Nordby (USNPS) working on the draft site plan while Pilar Luna and Captain Santo Gomez Leyva look on

8 *Below left* The *Margarita Maza de Juarez* over the site (*John Brooks*)

9 *Below* Carronade, muzzle down into the bottom (*John Brooks*)

years ago, she was hit by a squall while on a starboard tack. The outline of the bottom of the hull is apparent on the exposed port side, and, to a small extent, at the bow and stern along the starboard side. The port side is nearly completely disintegrated, leaving only the keel and floors at the bottom of the hull. The rudder, intact to its second pintle, is canted to starboard. The sharp deadrise fore and aft reflects the wedge-like lower hull typical of a Baltimore clipper. The presumably more intact starboard side, buried in the soft bottom, will very likely provide a rare opportunity for a hands-on study of fast-hull design from the first half of the 19th century.

There is a considerable amount of wood on the site in the form of partially worm-eaten timbers, some of them are exposed on the starboard side. The hull was reinforced with iron braces and knees, a practice of this period for steamers, and warships carrying the heavy weight of guns on their decks. Several intact straps were observed, including an iron wale, or strap, at the main deck level. Stubs of straps that apparently connected to the ends of the hanging knees protrude from this wale. Masses of drifts, spikes, and other hull fastenings lie along the port side, indicating the consumed upper works of that side of the hull. Copper drifts four or more feet in length at the stern, indicate the heavily reinforced construction that tied large timbers of the

selected as the date for the inspection dives. Drawing from the resources of the National Park Service, notably the Submerged Cultural Resources Unit, the U.S. government assembled a four-person team - James Delgado, head of the U.S. delegation and principal investigator, archaeologist Larry Nordby, scientific illustrator Jerry Livingston, and photographer John Brooks.

Assembling in Vera Cruz on July 2, the U.S. team met their Mexican counterparts from the Armada de Mexico and INAH. The Mexican delegation was headed by Capt. Santos H. Gomez Leyva, from the Navy General Staff, Navy Secretariat, and Dr Pilar Luna Erreguerena, Chief of the Department of Underwater Archaeology of the National Institute of Anthropology and History (INAH). The project was hosted by Admiral Fernandez, commander of the Third

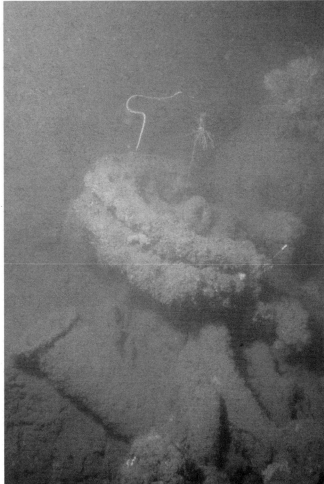

10 *Above left* Traverse roller from carronade carriage *(John Brooks)*

11 *Left* Traverse rail *(John Brooks)*

12 *Above* Pump log, broken at the point where it passed through the lower deck *(John Brooks)*

sternpost to the sternson and crutches. Broken lengths of iron straps also lie in the mass of wreckage inside the port hull. Additional wreckage presumably lies outside the hull, but sand has mounded up against the port side floors and the keel, burying them. Only the bow and stern are exposed to the depth of the keel as a result of scouring of the bottom by currents.

A number of fittings and equipment lie inside the area bounded by the port hull and the buried reaches of the starboard side. The site has been little disturbed so that the artefacts still reflect the vessel's original layout. Careful excavation and study of the distribution patterns will doubtless allow investigators to reconstruct those parts of the vessel that have been lost to natural decay.

Visible inboard features include the port quarter davits from which was suspended a 20ft boat - the only one to be launched from the stricken ship. It succeeded in ferrying several men and officers to the safety of nearby Isla Verde. Nine of the brig's ten 32-pounder carronades were observed, four to port and five to starboard. The port guns, while somewhat displaced, reflect their original alignment; the five starboard guns remain in a straight line, four with their muzzles pointing down into the seabed. Probing of the forewardmost port gun and aftermost starboard gun with an iron bar encountered a solid metal obstruction two feet inside each carronades' four foot bore. This indicates that at least two, and possibly all of the guns are loaded. This is to be expected because, at the time of her loss, *Somers* was clearing for action to halt a suspected blockade-runner. The remains of carriages were observed on or around each of the

lost *Somers* reportedly carried 500 32lb shot. Forward of the pump log is the brig's cast-iron galley stove, lying on its starboard side, with a section of flanged flue pipe lying immediately beside the flue which is still attached to the stove. The front flap of the stove is gone, but the drip pan and range grates remain in place (fig 14).

Lying across the stove and a 32-pounder is the spider-band and other possible rigging fittings from the foremast. Other

13 *Left* Pump cistern *(John Brooks)*

14 *Below left* Galley stove *(John Brooks)*

15 *Below* Diver examines anchor *(John Brooks)*

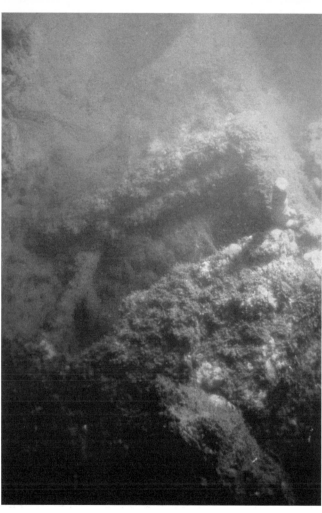

nine guns. Rollers for traversing the carronades were also seen (fig 10). A traverse rail was found lying next to one portside gun (fig 11).

The ship's metal pumps also survived. They were connected to the bilges, close to the port edge of the surviving hull. They bend to starboard and are broken close to the flanged junction that marks their passage through the berth deck (fig 12). The cistern is open (fig 13), with no other pump machinery readily apparent. Around the pumps are indications of what may be buried shot. When

rigging elements observed include the foreyard jack-stay, the foresail truss and the jib-boom band and martingale. The latter two items being situated off the bow, to starboard of the stempost. The rigging fittings lie on the bottom in the approximate positions they would have occupied within the rig, which is what we might expect if the brig came to rest on her starboard side and disintegrated without disturbance. All the metal fittings in the rig, from bands to clew-irons, grommets in the sails and sheaves in the blocks, should be present. This indicates the potential to document and reconstruct the rig of an 1846 clipper. It would provide the first detailed, material look at clipper rigging from this period and allow insight into the question of oversparring, a factor which some historians have suggested was a

16 *Below* Anchor cable, still payed out and stowed inside the hull *(John Brooks)*

17 *Above right* The remains of provisions in the bow *(John Brooks)*

18 *Below right* The author examines a plate *(John Brooks)*

19 *Bottom right* The author probes the muzzle of a carronade *(John Brooks)*

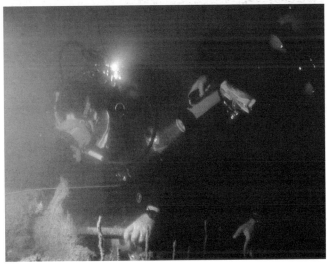

dangerous flaw in the Baltimore clipper brigs, particularly *Somers* and its sister ship, *Bainbridge*.

Off the port bow, lying against the hull, is the iron spindle, with two attached trundle heads, from the ship's wood and iron windlass. Adjacent to the spindle, and buried in the bottom so that only one arm and palm are exposed, is the port bower anchor (fig 15). To starboard, running parallel with the exposed side of the hull and with one arm and the shank showing, is the vessel's starboard bower. Its wooden stock has gone, but its form, close to the square of

the shank, has survived, as have the first stock-hoops. The position of the anchors indicates that they were catted when the brig sank; this is to be expected as the court of enquiry into the sinking established that Semmes was about to anchor when he spotted the vessel trying to run the blockade and commenced his fatal chase. The brig's first Lieut., M.J.L. Claiborne, testified that most of the port anchor cable was on deck when she was lost. This cable (chain) was not observed on site, which is to be expected since it would have fallen free and is now likely to be

20 Diver examines a scupper *(John Brooks)*

Conclusions

The project was a considerable success. It was the first international underwater archaeological project conducted jointly by two Western Hemisphere governments outside of the U.S. (other than two projects with the former Pacific trust territories). The collaboration on the preliminary documentation of the wreck was a clear demonstration of international goodwill and co-operation, all the more remarkable because the site represents a ship lost in a war between the two participating nations, a war in which the host nation lost over half of its national territory.

Hopefully, the *Somers* project will continue and that a more detailed plan than that featured here in fig 1 will be prepared. This survey, with the involvement of private citizens and two governments, demonstrates that there is a non-destructive, positive role that private citizens can and should play in shipwreck discovery and study. While the issue of ownership remains under discussion, the success of this project points the way to a positive future in which analogous sites abroad can proactively be protected and studied under bilateral agreements (similar, in fact, to the case with Confederate raider *Alabama*, see *Archaeology of Ships of War* (IMAS, 1, 90-102). While legally the property of each sovereign nation, regardless of where they lie, warship wrecks can rest within the national boundaries and hence under the control of foreign powers. Since warships often represent an international heritage, concerns other than a pragmatic need to preserve one nation's national interest in a wreck as a war grave or historical site, compel attention to projects such as the *Somers*.

situated beneath the wreckage of the collapsed port side. Rows of chain lie on the site, running at a slight angle and thinning to a single strand that runs in towards the exposed starboard bower anchor (fig 16).

Smaller artefacts were noted on the site, notably in the bow, which was the location for many of the ship's stores (fig 17). A ceramic jug was found in the area, as were three large vertebrae and a short bone, possibly a radius or ulna, that appeared to be from traditional cuts of either pork (*sus scrofula*) or beef (*bos*). The placement of these bones in the bow would indicate the stowage of salted meat; court of enquiry testimony established that *Somers* had nine barrels of salt pork and beef aboard. In the after area of the wreck, lying close to the sternmost starboard 32 pounder, were two white-glazed ceramic plates, one an oval, 12in platter, the other a slightly smaller, round serving plate (fig 18). No identifying marks were observed Nearby was the base of a black glass, alcohol bottle, with a high kick-up and pontil scar. A second glass artefact, a clear pane set in lead glazing, lies at the stern and may be from the skylights of the master's cabin or wardroom, or from windows in the transom.

References

Belcher, G., 1988, The US Brig *Somers* - A Shipwreck from the Mexican War, in *Underwater Archaeology Proceedings from the Society for Historical Archaeology Conference*, ed. J.P. Delgado, Society for Historical Archaeology, Ann Arbor, Michigan, 91-94

Chapelle, H.I., 1949, *The History of the American Sailing Navy: The Ships and Their Development*, W.W. Norton & Company, New York.

Hayford, H., 1959, *The Somers Mutiny Affair*, Prentice-Hall, Inc., Englewood, New Jersey.

McFarland, P., 1985, *Sea Dangers: The Affair of the Somers*, Schocken Books, New York.

Melville, H., 1850, *White Jacket, or The World in a Man-of-War*, Harper, New York.

Melville, H., 1948, *Billy Budd*, Harvard University Press, Cambridge, Massachusetts.

Semmes, R., 1851, *Service Afloat and Ashore During the Mexican War*, Wm. H. Moore & Co., Cincinnati.

John D. Broadwater (Manager, *Monitor* National Marine Sanctuary)

The Union Ironclad USS *Monitor*, 1862

Introduction

In March of 1862, early in the American Civil War, the ironclad warships USS *Monitor* and CSS *Virginia* fought a spectacular battle at Hampton Roads, Virginia. When the confrontation ended both ships were essentially undamaged, even though they had bombarded each other at point-blank range for more than four hours. Although the two vessels were quite different in design and appearance they actually shared several innovative traits: both were clad in wrought iron armour; both employed partially-submerged hulls to limit their exposure to enemy fire; both were powered by steam alone, with no masts or sails; both were driven by screw propellers; and both were designed to fight effectively with relatively few cannon. Not only were both vessels unique but their encounter at Hampton Roads was the first instance in which these new designs were tested against each other in combat. The result, which reached far beyond Virginia, was the rapid abandonment of conventional wooden, sail-powered ships-of-the-line and an escalation of naval weaponry and armour.

The innovative *Monitor* sank during a storm off Cape Hatteras, North Carolina on December 31 1862, while being towed south to join the Federal blockade of Southern ports. The *Monitor* was located in 1973 by a team of oceanographers and archaeologists employing remote-sensing equipment. Since her discovery, *Monitor* has been the subject of a modern naval technological revolution - that of undersea exploration. In the brief span of two decades, ocean technology has produced an array of new and better tools that have permitted the discovery, exploration and documentation of such famous deep-water shipwrecks as the CSS *Alabama* (Guérout, 1995; Watts, 1990), *Hamilton* and *Scourge* (Cain, 1983; also see Wright in this volume) and RMS *Titanic* (Ballard, 1987). The *Monitor* also inspired an innovative approach to historic shipwreck protection through the United States' National Marine Sanctuary Program. With improvements in ocean technology, the quality and efficiency of research at the *Monitor* site has also improved.

Arms versus armour

The important role played by the *Monitor* in the evolution of modern warships, as well as in the American Civil War, is best understood in the context of mid-nineteenth century naval technology. By the third quarter of the nineteenth century a new arms race was pitting offence against defence in a dynamic fashion. The smooth-bore cannon firing solid

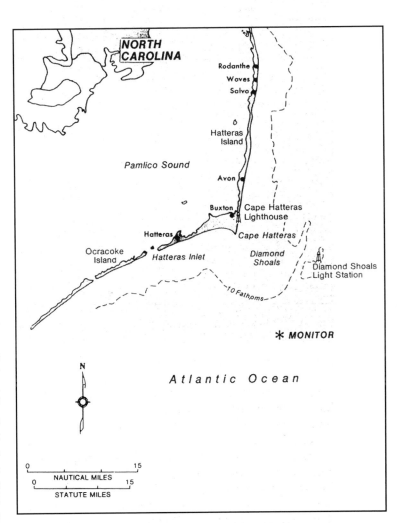

1 Location of the *Monitor* National Marine Sanctuary (*courtesy: NOAA*)

shot, the standard weapon ashore and afloat for centuries, was being supplanted by cannon with rifled barrels firing explosive and incendiary shells as well as solid round and conical shot. These new cannon were more accurate and more powerful than their predecessors and were capable of annihilating the wooden warships of the day. As a result, navies began experimenting with armour that could withstand these new weapons. The first armoured vessels were conventional sail-and-steam powered warships with plates of iron bolted to their sides. The American Civil War introduced two new and radical designs that altered naval combat forever.

2 Battle between USS *Monitor* and CSS *Virginia*, Hampton Roads, Virginia

3 One of the few photographs of the *Monitor*. Dents from the battle with the CSS *Virginia* can be seen in the turret. Towards the bow the pilot house can be seen
(courtesy of The Mariners' Museum, Newport News).

The Confederate ironclad CSS *Virginia* represented one novel approach to ironclad technology. The *Virginia* was commissioned on February 17, 1862 at the Gosport Navy Yard near Norfolk, Virginia. Her unique armoured casemate was constructed on top of the salvaged lower hull of the steam frigate USS *Merrimack*, which had been scuttled when the Navy Yard was abandoned by the Union Navy. This clever use of an existing hulk permitted the South to construct a formidable warship in a relatively short time, an especially important goal since the Confederate States Navy existed virtually in name only at the outbreak of hostilities (Broadwater, 1984, 103; Sharf, 1887, 17).

The USS *Monitor* was hurriedly constructed to counter the much-publicized threat of the *Virginia*. The *Monitor* was designed and built by the brilliant but controversial Swedish-American inventor John Ericsson. Employing a radical design and innovative construction methods. Ericsson was able to deliver the vessel in less than four

months. The *Monitor* was commissioned at the Brooklyn (New York) Navy Yard on February 25, 1862, barely a week after the commissioning of the *Virginia* (Miller, 1978:34).

The *Monitor* was unique in many respects, and was a striking contrast to the massive, hulking Confederate ironclad. In fact, the appearance was quite unlike that of any other vessel afloat, being almost completely submerged and with no superstructure except for her armoured 'tower' or gun turret amidships and a small raised pilot house forward. She was constructed primarily of iron, although her main deck and armour belt were of wood plated over with iron. Instead of a conventional battery of cannon lined along a gun deck, *Monitor*'s armament consisted of only two eleven-inch (28cm) Dahlgren smooth bore cannon, mounted side by side in her revolving turret. Skeptics - both North and South - doubted the prowess of this little 'cheesebox on a plank' (Miller, 1978, 34; Sharf, 1887, 167).

CSS *Virginia* proved that Northern fears were justified when, at Hampton Roads, Virginia, on March 8, 1862, she destroyed two powerful Union warships, *Cumberland* and *Congress*, suffering almost no damage to herself (Broadwater, 1984, 109-110) (fig 1). It appeared inevitable that *Virginia* would return the following day to decimate the remaining Union vessels. Instead, she was confronted on March 9 by the *Monitor* which, in a remarkable twist of fate, had entered Hampton Roads the previous night.

Monitor fought *Virginia* to a virtual draw during a four hour battle in which the two extraordinary craft bombarded each other at close range, seeking structural weaknesses but inflicting little damage (fig 2). The outcome of this naval engagement was widely reported and both sides claimed victory (Miller, 1978, 42-8). Although there remains disagreements as to the tactical and strategic results of the Battle at Hampton Roads, this first-ever confrontation between ironclad vessels dramatically demonstrated that wooden, sail-powered warships would soon be obsolete.

The Monitor: Lost and found

Although no one suspected it at the time, both ironclads had seen their finest hour. As Union troops overran the Hampton Roads area, *Virginia* soon found herself stranded without a friendly port in which to take refuge. This situation left her with few options: she could not escape into the Atlantic Ocean because she would have to pass under the powerful shore batteries at Fort Monroe and because she was not designed for the open sea. Nor could she steam up the James River to assist in the defence of the Southern capitol at Richmond because she drew too much water. As a result, she was scuttled and burned on May 10 at Craney Island, within sight of her battle arena of less than two months before (Broadwater, 1984, 113; Sharf, 1887, 221-238).

Monitor spent the spring of 1862 sitting idly at Hampton Roads (fig 3) under orders from President Abraham Lincoln to avoid a rematch with the *Virginia* (Lincoln was afraid that the *Monitor* might be sunk, thus thwarting the planned attack on the Southern capitol at Richmond). She participated in a brief, aborted attack in the upper reaches of

4 Loss of the USS *Monitor* off Cape Hatteras, North Carolina on December 31, 1862. The sidewheel steamer USS *Rhode Island*, which had been towing the *Monitor*, stands off while her boats attempt to rescue the ironclad's crew
(From a Harper's Weekly illustration)

the James River and was later sent to the Washington Navy Yard for repairs. Finally, in December, the *Monitor* received orders to join the Union blockade of Charleston, South Carolina. However, on New Year's Eve, while being towed south, *Monitor* sank in a severe storm off Cape Hatteras, North Carolina (Miller, 1978, 57-84; Watts, 1975, 310) (fig 4).

The *Monitor* lay relatively undisturbed, her exact location unknown until 1973 when she was located off Cape Hatteras by a scientific team aboard Duke University's R/V *Eastward*. The wreck lies approximately 16 nautical miles (25.8km) SSE of Cape Hatteras Lighthouse (Miller, 1978, 91-3; Watts, 1975, 312-314, 324-325).

Protection, management and research

The USS *Monitor* is one of the most famous and significant warships in the history of the United States Navy - indeed, in terms of naval technology, one of the most important ships in the world. The *Monitor's* discovery generated widespread interest and excitement. The first problem faced by researchers and historic preservation managers was how to protect this important historic vessel. Since her location was outside the territorial waters of the United States, and since the U.S. Navy had officially abandoned the *Monitor* in 1953, no simple means of protection was apparent (Watts, 1985, 315-16). It was soon recognized, however, that recent federal legislation, the Marine Protection, Research and Sanctuary Act of 1972, could be applied to a significant shipwreck such as the *Monitor*. Therefore, on January 30 1975, the *Monitor* was designated by Congress as America's first National Marine Sanctuary (Milholland, 1978, 20; Watts, 1975, 316). Twenty years later the *Monitor* remains the only shipwreck to be accorded National Marine Sanctuary status. However, historic and cultural resources within all twelve National Marine Sanctuaries are now protected and managed along with their natural resources (fig 5).

Since its designation, the *Monitor* has been protected and managed by the Sanctuaries and Reserves Division of the National Oceanic and Atmospheric Administration (NOAA), a federal agency. The *Monitor* is listed on the National Register of Historic Places, and has been designated a

5 Locations of NOAA's National Marine Sanctuaries
(courtesy: NOAA*)*

6 An isometric drawing of the *Monitor* as she appears on the
seabed, lying upside down and partially supported by her
displaced turret *(courtesy:* NOAA*)*

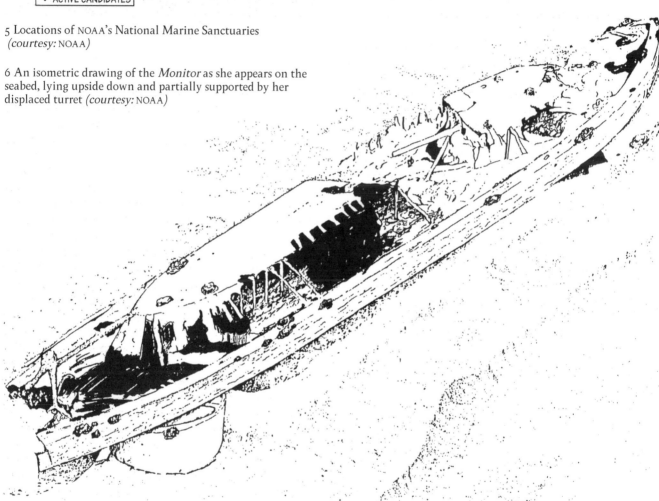

National Historic Landmark (Delgado, 1988). NOAA
published a management plan for the *Monitor* in 1982
(NOAA, 1982) and is currently in the process of revising the
plan to reflect the results of scientific research since the
wreck's discovery.

The *Monitor*'s inaccessibility is a major factor influencing
both management and research. She lies on a flat,
featureless, sandy sea-bed at a depth of 230 feet (70m). She
apparently rolled over as she sank, allowing her turret to fall
free, upside down. The hull then settled to the bottom, still
inverted, where it landed on the turret. The inverted hull
now rests partially buried in sediment with the stern port

quarter held above the bottom by the displaced turret (fig 6).
The lower hull, which is now the highest part of the wreck,
has collapsed forward of the midships bulkhead and the
stern armour belt and its associated structure has badly
deteriorated. The elevated port quarter creates a list to
starboard which has produced severe stresses within the
hull.

The *Monitor* suffers from extensive deterioration and
structural damage. The wreck reached its current state as a
result of three factors: damage that occurred at the time of
sinking, deterioration caused by more than a century of
exposure within a dynamic seawater environment, and

damage resulting from human activities. The wreck lies near the confluence of two major ocean currents, the cold southerly-flowing Labrador Current and the warm Gulf Stream, which follows the coast northward but begins to turn to the east when it reaches the coastal projection known as Cape Hatteras. These currents compete for dominance in the vicinity of the *Monitor*, creating confusing and often violent currents which can create tremendous stresses on the *Monitor's* hull and carry away parts of the hull and its contents. It is believed by some researchers that *Monitor* was inadvertently depth-charged during World War II, resulting in severe damage to the lower hull and, possibly, to the stern armour belt. In addition, there is evidence that the wreck has been damaged by illegal anchoring and fishing activities.

Since 1975, NOAA has gathered a considerable amount of data at the Sanctuary. The unique characteristics and location of the site have made it the object of studies by a wide range of specialists, including archaeologists, geologists, biologists, salvors and corrosion and structural engineers (Watts, 1985, 1987; Arnold *et al.*, 1991, 71-73; Arnold *et al.*, 1992, 46-58). Observations in recent years revealed an increase in the rate of hull deterioration. When NOAA began revising the sanctuary management plan in 1992, it was recognized that additional site data was needed in order for effective long-range management decisions to be made. Therefore, NOAA scheduled a scientific expedition to the site in 1993.

The 1993 MARSS Expedition

During July and August 1993, NOAA conducted the *Monitor Archaeological Research and Structural Survey* (MARSS) Expedition, under overall direction of the author. The major goals were to: (1) map and videotape the *Monitor's* hull in order to quantify and document site changes and deterioration; (2) deploy a permanent mooring; (3) locate, map and recover exposed, threatened artefacts, and (4) conduct test excavations and mapping of the *Monitor's* turret in order to assess the feasibility of is recovery.

It was recognized that the achievement of these goals, given the exceptional depth and adverse environmental conditions at the sanctuary, would require extensive planning as well as specialized training and equipment. A suitable vessel was not available for the expedition; therefore NOAA chartered the research vessel *Edwin Link* from the Harbor Branch Oceanographic Institution (HBOI) of Fort Pierce, Florida. HBOI had participated in several past *Monitor* expeditions, thus they had developed a high level of familiarity with the wreck site as well as operating conditions at the sanctuary.

The expedition was conducted during the period July 26 through August 11 1993 Dives were conducted from a NOAA open bell lowered from the deck of the surface vessel (fig 7 note 1). This procedure required the surface vessel to remain stationary over the site. The installation of a suitable temporary four-point mooring - a major effort in itself - was accomplished by the U.S. Navy submarine rescue vessel USS

7 R/V *Edwin Link* with NOAA diving bell *(courtesy:* NOAA*)*

Ortolan (ASR-22). Once the research vessel was secured in the mooring her position had to be adjusted so that the bell would descend precisely to a predetermined position near the *Monitor's* hull. This process involved aligning the vessel to the correct position using the ship's integrated navigational system, a sonar beacon placed near the wreck, and HBOI's manned submersible *Johnson-Sea-Link II* (*J-S-L II*). Extremely adverse weather conditions severely hampered operations, resulting in the completion of only nine submersible dives and three bell dives. In spite of these problems, several of the major objectives were met.

One of the primary goals of the MARSS Expedition was to continue long-term mapping efforts designed to further quantify site deterioration. A series of plastic reference stakes was to be placed at key intervals beneath the raised armour belt as a simple and inexpensive means of annual checks for hull movement. The measurements required only a flexible surveyor's tape and could be recorded by unskilled personnel. Stakes were to be placed beneath the armour belt at the bow, midships bulkhead and aft of the turret. Two measurements were to be made at each stake: first, the distance from the underside of the armour belt to the top of the stake; and second, the distance from the top of the stake to the sand. In that manner, it was possible to document any sag of the hull and changes in sand levels. In conjunction with these measurements, precise depth readings were to be taken at key points on the hull, armour belt and turret. These measurements were to be referenced to a datum point on the base of the turret from which all readings could be converted to relative site elevation data. Because of the poor diving conditions these stakes could not be installed at the time, but were installed and measured later by a privately-funded expedition (see below).

Another major accomplishment of the MARSS Expedition was the placement of a concrete mooring block at the sanctuary to provide a fixed location for divers to descend and a stationary ascent line for in-water decompression. This task was given high priority since it could not have been accomplished without the specialized equipment which would only be available during MARSS. The exact placement of the mooring block required the precise navigation and heavy lifting capability of the research vessel as well as observation reports from the submersible.

Using the *J-S-L II*, NOAA was able to study the turret more closely. Any plans to raise the turret will require information on whether or not the cannon are still inside and whether the turret is filled with silt. It is assumed that the *Monitor*'s two 11-inch (28cm) Dahlgrens and their carriages are still inside; however, the gunports are closed and the base of the turret is covered by a layer of sand and silt, thus obscuring the interior. A test excavation in the base of the turret (which is now the upper end, since the turret is inverted) was made in order to determine if the pine deck is still intact. The test, conducted under the supervision of an archaeologist in the submersible's pilot sphere, verified that the floor, or deck, of the turret has disintegrated; therefore, the turret must be filled with silt and debris from inside the *Monitor*'s hull. This information is essential for assessing the present condition of the turret and the feasibility of its future recovery, conservation and display.

A second test excavation, conducted outside the turret, verified that the buried portion of the turret is in very good condition.

The MARRS '95 Expedition

In August 1995, NOAA conducted the *Monitor* Archaeological Research, Recovery and Stabilisation Mission (MARRS '95), the broad purpose of which was to continue and expand the efforts begun two years earlier. The primary goal was to stabilize the *Monitor*'s deteriorating hull by moving its displaced skeg and recovering its propeller which had become unstable and was stressing the stern[2].

Work began on August 12 with the arrival in Hatteras of the NOAA dive team and the R/V *Elusive*. The mission, however, was interrupted by Hurricane Felix which forced the team to evacuate Hatteras on August 15. Work resumed four days later and, with support from the U.S. Navy salvage ship USS *Edenton*, the first NOAA self-contained dives were conducted on 24-25 August[3].

NOAA made two dives and the Navy made seventeen (fig 8) before operations were halted by the threat of new storms. A Kevlar strap was secured around the hub of the propeller and the incrustation and marine growths were removed from the junctures between the blades and the hull. Growths were also chipped from the portion of the shaft that was to be cut, but before the shaft could be severed the *Edenton* was forced by bad weather to return to its base in Little Creek, Virginia. The Navy will complete the task at a later date; when this has been done the propeller will be transported to The Mariners' Museum, Newport News, Virginia, where it will be conserved and placed on exhibit.

Private research and exploration

Since 1990 NOAA has issued permits to private-sector dive groups for research on the *Monitor*. These privately-sponsored teams use both compressed air and mixed gases to conduct deep, self-contained dives, employing techniques

8 Navy diver from USS *Edenton*, examining the *Monitor*'s encrusted propeller *(photo, Craig McLean, NOAA)*

that are commonly referred to as 'technical diving'. These 'technical' divers have photographed and mapped portions of the wreck, installed reference stakes and, under the supervision of a NOAA archaeologist, have recovered small artefacts that were in danger of being swept away by currents. The recovered objects included glass condiment and pharmaceutical bottles, a dinner plate and a pair of brass oarlocks. Research accomplished by private-sector divers in recent years has made a meaningful contribution to the body of knowledge concerning the *Monitor*.

Summary

In spite of weather problems, NOAA has been able to assess the deterioration of the *Monitor*'s hull, establish a permanent mooring, test the condition of the turret, record approximately 22 hours of high-resolution videotape and initiate the recovery of the propeller. Because recent research has revealed an increased rate of deterioration, NOAA is re-examining all management options, including the possible need for eventual recovery of additional major components such as the machinery and turret. The results of this on-going study are being incorporated into the Revised

Management Plan for the *Monitor* National Marine Sanctuary.

Acknowledgements
The *Monitor* National Marine Sanctuary is managed and funded through the Office of Ocean and Coastal Resources Management of the National Oceanic and Atmospheric Administration (NOAA). The 1993 dives were supervised by Dr Morgan Wells and Cliff Newell, chief of the NOAA Dive Office. The master of the R/V *Edwin Link* was Christopher Vogel.

The MARRS '95 expedition was developed by the author in association with Key West Diver Inc., Cliff Newell, Commander Craig McLean, Lieutenant Michael Hoshlyk and personnel from NURC/UNCW. Bill Deans served as mission dive supervisor and Newell participated as NOAA dive supervisor. The commanding Officer of the USS *Edenton* was John Paul Johnston and the master of R/V *Elusive* was Dan Aspenleiter.

Notes

1. The depth and frequently strong currents made it essential to develop a dive plan which would ensure both the safety of the divers and the accomplishment of goals. The dive plan was developed by Dr Morgan Wells, director of NOAA's Experimental Diving Unit. The NOAA Dive Office supplied additional personnel and equipment. The scientific dive team was made up of NOAA-trained divers headed by the author. Divers breathed a mixture of oxygen, helium and nitrogen that is generally referred to as 'trimix'. Because the proportion of gases was optimized for the depth and desired dive times at the *Monitor*, this mixture was designated NOAA Trimix I, or '*Monitor* Trimix' (NOAA 1993).

2. The author again served as project director. The participants were NOAA (Sanctuaries and Reserves Division and NOAA Diving Program); the U.S. Navy (Combat Logistics Group Two, Supervisor of Salvage and Diving, Naval Sea Systems Command); The Mariners' Museum, Newport News, Virginia; the National Undersea Research Center/University of North Carolina at Wilmington and Key West Diver Inc.

3. These dives utilized the same '*Monitor* Mix' as on the previous NOAA dives. In 1995, however, the divers were not tethered to the surface, instead they followed a buoy-line to the bottom and then followed a hand-line to the work area. These dives were conducted for assessment purposes with special permission from the NOAA Dive Safety Board, since some of the techniques employed fell outside its standard diving regulations. Navy divers conducted their dives from the *Edenton* using the Mk 21 diving system, (a Navy version of the Superlite 17 hat), surface-supplied mixed-gas, and a hot-water exposure suit.

References

Arnold, J. Barto III, *et al.*, 1991, USS *Monitor*: Update on Data Analysis from the 1987 Season. *Underwater Archaeology Proceedings from the Society for Historical Archaeology Conference*, John D. Broadwater (ed.), Richmond, Virginia, 1991, 71-3.

Arnold, J. Barto III, *et al.*, 1992, USS *Monitor*: Results from the 1987 Season. *Advances in Underwater Archaeology*, Society for Historical Archaeology, Vol. 26, Special Publication No. 4, 47-58.

Ballard, R.D., 1987, *The Discovery of the Titanic*, Madison Publishing Inc., Toronto, Ontario.

Broadwater, J.D., 1984, Ironclad at Hampton Roads: CSS *Virginia*, the Confederacy's Formidable Warship. *Virginia Cavalcade*, Vol. XXXIII, No. 3, 100-114

Cain, E., 1983, *Ghost Ships*, Muson, Toronto.

Delgado, J.P., 1988, A Symbol of American Ingenuity: Assessing the Significance of USS *Monitor*. Washington, D.C., Prepared for the National Oceanic and Atmospheric Administration by the National Park Service.

Guérout, M., 1995, CSS *Alabama*: Evaluation du site (1988-1992), *The Archaeology of Ships of War*, International Maritime Archaeology Series, Vol. 1, Mensun Bound ed., Anthony Nelson. 90-102

Milholland, J.A., 1978, The Legal Framework of the *Monitor* Marine Sanctuary, *The Monitor: Its Meaning and Future*, The Preservation Press (The National Trust for Historic Preservation), Washington, D.C.

Miller, M., 1978 USS *Monitor: The Ship that Launched a Modern Navy*, Leeward Press, Annapolis, Maryland.

National Oceanic and Atmospheric Administration (NOAA) 1982, *U.S.S. MONITOR National Marine Sanctuary Management Plan*.
1992, *Monitor National Marine Sanctuary Draft Revised Management Plan*.

Sharf, J.T., 1887, *History of the Confederate States Navy, from Its Organization to the Surrender of Its Last Vessel*, Rogers & Sherwood, New York: (Reprinted 1977, Fairfax Press).

Watts, G.P., 1975, The Location and Identification of the ironclad USS *Monitor*. *International Journal of Nautical Archaeology and Underwater Exploration*, 4.2, 301-329.

Watts, G.P., 1985, Deep-Water Archaeological Investigation and Site Testing on the USS *Monitor*. National Marine Sanctuary. *Journal of Field Archaeology*, Vol. 12, 315-332

Watts, G.P., 1987, A Decade of Research: Investigation of the USS *Monitor*. *Underwater Archaeology Proceedings from the Society for Historical Archaeology Conference*, Alan B. Albright (ed.), 128-139.

Watts, G.P., 1990, CSS *Alabama*: Controversial as Always, Yet Offering Opportunities for International Co-operation. *Underwater Archaeology Proceedings from the Society for Historical Archaeology Conference*, Toni L. Carrell (ed.), Tucson, Arizona, 75-80.

Daniel J. Lenihan (Submerged Cultural Resources Unit, United States National Park Service)

From Pearl to Bikini: The Underwater Archaeology of World War II in the Pacific

It is typical for societies to discard the tools of war when the conflict has ended. War weary nations focus on rebuilding and actively forgetting the carnage recently experienced. Special memorabilia of individuals or memorials to particularly traumatic or triumphant events excepted, the remainder is grist for recycling and rebuilding.

Beating swords into plowshares is a commendable practice, as is the covering over of battlefields with crops and housing projects; however, these post-war cleansing rituals do erase with amazing rapidity the physical remnants of events that shaped the course of future generations. Historians and archaeologists are faced with the task of reconstructing past events with greatly reduced access to their material residues.

In addition, the generation that fought the war, often finds several decades after the fact that they undergo a curious renewal of interest in their youthful role as warriors in the trenches or sustainers on the home front. They find the ability to reconnect with that past is often greatly diminished by the compulsive urge to order and rebuild that immediately follows war.

A notable exception is the scene of naval engagements. Unlike cultural landscapes that modern society modifies with frequency and fervor, the remains of great warships often lie on seascapes vulnerable to a slower, natural course of disintegration. An American archaeologist would say these vessels were subject only to natural site transformation processes; an English bard would say they have only "suffered a sea-change into something rich and strange".

The bottom of many Pacific harbors and atolls offer an incomparable museum of World War II naval engagements. The word museum is used loosely in this context: these ships lie where they fell and have never passed through the artful, yet artificial filter of museum technicians.

The United States was a latecomer to the conflict in the Pacific, much as it was in Europe. There had already been significant action against the Japanese from British and Australian Royal Navy contingents in the far Western Pacific, in addition to the long series of bloody land engagements in the Sino-Japanese theatre, before America was finally propelled into war with Japan following the raid on Pearl Harbor. For the United States, however, the trail from Pearl through the remainder of the war was an odyssey of epic proportions, and it is remarkable how soon so little is left to comprise a touchstone to that period except beneath the waves.

For example, Pearl Harbor. Sympathies of U.S. citizens in 1941 were overwhelmingly against Germany and Japan and stirred greatly by what was perceived as heroic British resistance, particularly at the conclusion of the Battle of Britain. The reluctance of American politicians and industrialists to commit to the war was not reflected in the myriad battles fought against the axis powers in the backyards of Iowa and Oklahoma and Texas by American farm boys with wooden rifles and paper Spitfires.

Meanwhile, more tangible support in the form of supplies, war material and eventually 50 reconditioned destroyers, were moving across the Atlantic in one direction, while fighter planes produced in American factories were making their way to the Royal Canadian Air Force and eventually across the North Pacific to the Russians, now involved in a building crescendo of conflict with their former German ally.

The new isolationism in America following WWI gave way steadily to a growing war fever, not a matter of if, but when. The Japanese provided the "when" on December 7 1941. Seen by Americans as a dastardly sneak-attack, indeed a day that would "live in infamy", Pearl Harbor was etched indelibly into the minds of several generations of Americans.

It is interesting to note, however, that if one visits Oahu today, the only visible reminders of the war on land are a few strafing holes in the barracks at Hickam field, a war museum on Waikiki, the occasional remains of a bunker, and a National Memorial cemetery. The rest of the great Pacific citadel has become transformed into wall-to-wall high-rise hotels and condominiums, the majority of which ironically now cater as much to Japanese tourists as Americans.

The striking exception is what remains on the bottom of Pearl Harbor. The USS *Arizona* and USS *Utah* rest where they sank, the former carried 1,147 men to their death and the latter 58. Most are still entombed in these rusting hulks; there are, for instance, more than 1,000 in *Arizona*. When our team of U.S. National Park Service (NPS) underwater archaeologists was assigned to examine the remains of these vessels in 1982, we were astounded at how little was known about the sites.

Although the *Arizona* was receiving 5,000 visitors a day to the memorial over the submerged hulk, and there was an active program of interpretation in the visitor center on land, knowledge of the actual historic fabric was almost non-existent. The NPS Submerged Cultural Resources Unit

(SCRU as the dive team is known) found the park and Navy had extensive files dealing with the appearance and condition of the ship before 1,000,000 pounds of explosives detonated in the forward magazine. This information and an incomplete salvage diary helped, but nothing could prepare the archaeologists for what they would find on their first dives.

Navy and civilian contractors had removed most of the *Arizona*'s superstructure during the war and what extruded above the choppy harbor water was primarily nondescript pieces of metal which the visitor could not relate to at all. Early dives by the NPSteam and a contingent of Navy divers assigned to assist them revealed startling finds, such as the entire forward 14-inch battery still intact in its turret and numerous rounds of live 5-inch shells lying under the visitors promenade. Furthermore, there was no torpedo entry hole where it should have been, if one of the prevailing theories of the *Arizona*'s demise was true.

Although the ship was not entered out of respect for its war grave status, color video footage obtained in 1983 by NPS

1 *Above* The hulk of the USS *Utah* lies where it sank in Pearl Harbor due to bombs from attacking Japanese planes December 7 1941 (*NPS Photo*)

2 *Left* Destroyer *Shaw* blowing up during Pearl Harbor attack (*NPS USAR Collection*)

divers revealed riveting ghostly images of the external features of the ravaged hull, teak decking still in place, hatchways yawning open with tropical fish milling about and portholes filled with air between the glass and their blackout covers. Honolulu television stations dedicated 2 to 3 minutes of each night's broadcast during the project to the data tapes shot during each day's survey activities, and soon the national networks picked up the story.

As the mapping operations proceeded, Memorial visitors were treated to the spectacle of a large scale drawing being pieced together each day, making sense of what had been an

3 *Above* US National Park Service and US Navy divers looking at model of USS *Arizona* built from data obtained from their mapping and photo-documentation project
(*NPS photo by Larry Murphy*)

4 *Left* Park Service and Navy divers working on USS *Arizona*
(*NPS photo by Larry Murphy*)

unrecognizable mass of metal beneath their feet. Using low-tech methods of string base lines, simple trilateration and hundreds of hours underwater, scaled drawings of the site from a planimetric view and from port and starboard elevations, emerged to create a very real sense of what remained of the most famous of American battleships.

In 1986 we returned to Pearl Harbor to address a different problem domain on the *Arizona* - that of determining what

processes of corrosion and deterioration were taking place. We were also directed to apply the same proven method of site recordation and documentation to that other great war artifact on the harbor bottom, the USS *Utah*. The *Arizona* had evolved by this point into a national lesson in submerged cultural resources management. It would become increasingly difficult to pursue the "out of sight, out of mind" philosophy that had before attended the study and care of underwater heritage sites.

To bring home to the preservation community the severity of the oversight that had taken place during the original National Historic Landmark evaluation for Pearl Harbor, a second study was undertaken. The original NHL designation, which is the highest level of recognition accorded a site for historical importance in the United States, had barely mentioned the two sunken ships. A National Park Service historian accompanied the archeologist on follow-up dives on the sites in 1988 and

nominated both ships as separate NHL's in their own right. The nominations were approved.

As National Park Service underwater archeological documentation activities moved west through the Pacific from the mid 1980s to the present, a great wealth of sunken heritage sites have been revealed or, in some cases, the importance of known sites finally recognized. Although many sites upon which SCRU archeologists concentrated were

5 *Top left* Wreckage of Japanese transport *Fujikawa Maru* at Truk (Chuuk) Lagoon *(NPS photo by Dan Lenihan)*

6 *Top right* NPS archeologist Jim Bradford videotaping site of Japanese transport sunk by US planes in Palau (now called Belau) *(NPS photo by Dan Lenihan)*

7 *Above* USS *Arizona* during test trials in East River, New York City *(NPS USAR Collection)*

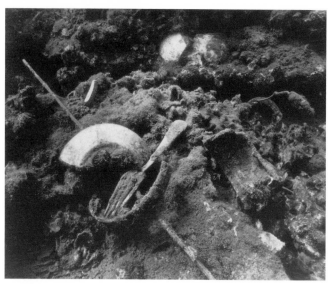

those areas, and the National Park Service, which is an Interior agency that retains the only federal team of underwater archeologists, had a clear mandate to work in these locations. Others, such as The National Geographic Society, examined sites in New Guinea and Woods Hole Oceanographic Institute pursued underwater survey and documentation activities in the Solomons at Guadalcanal.

Shipwreck remains in Guam, Truk (now Chuuk) Lagoon, and Belau have become the focus of increasingly active recreational diving use by American, Japanese and Australian divers. For the most part, Japanese transports, or "Marus", comprise the bulk of the sites at diving depths in

8 *Left* Eating implements found in galley of USS *Arizona* by survey team *(NPS photo by Larry Murphy)*

9 *Below* One of the atom bomb blasts at Bikini Atoll during Operation Crossroads *(Photo courtesy of National Archives)*

related to other maritime pursuits, such as whaling, general commerce and underwater components of prehistoric sites, WWII remains one of the richest areas for investigation.

Guam, Palau (now Republic of Belau), and the rest of Micronesia received the most attention from SCRU because these island groups were Trust Territories or, had once been held in Trust status by the United States of America. The Department of the Interior retains direct responsibilities in

these places. Truk and Palau were the targets of fierce air raids by Allied fast-carrier attack forces as the war neared its end. Most combatant ships escaped these raids but dozens of Japanese armed transports were sent to the bottom and now comprise vibrant artificial reefs of great interest to sport divers.

The occasional submarine or destroyer and a considerable number of patrol craft are included in these wreck populations, but for the most part larger warships were sunk in deep water beyond the range of recreational diving. One of the most compelling of these blue-water battles from which no documentation has been obtained is Midway, which would involve work in excess of 15,000 feet. Combatant vessels have been located, however, in 'Iron Bottom Sound' off Guadalcanal and should provide an intriguing archeological look at one of the more pivotal battles in the war.

Although they don't carry the same dramatic appeal to divers, from an archeologist's point of view, the transports may end up being the more important sites. Analysis of the cargo and the repair and refitting protocols of these vessels may offer the most valuable insights regarding social dynamics in war-time Japan. General principles of human behavior in high stress times will perhaps be evident from the manner in which these vessels were provisioned,

10 NPS diver Jim Miculka documenting tank turret remains at War in the Pacific National Historic Park in Guam (*NPS photo by Larry Murphy*)

11 *Above centre* US National Park Service divers documenting Japanese transport *Tokai Maru* sunk during WWII almost on top of German raider SMS *Cormoran* from WWI

12 BBC cameraman John Beck (left) discusses next dive on USS *Arizona* with Dan Lenihan. Navy personnel in background examine latest mylars from mapping operations (*NPS photo by Larry Murphy*)

13 NPS and Navy divers and shore exploration party scramble into a small boat during lull in the waves at Kiska Harbor, during the September 1989 expedition to the Aleutians

equipped and laden. Salvage behaviour, where transports are concerned, will also be revealing to anthropological investigation.

These ships continue into modern times as fascinating laboratories of human behavior. One of the biggest preservation problems at Truk Lagoon for example, is not the attrition of sport divers taking items from the vessels, but rather the continuing recycling of ships' cargo in the form of explosives for dynamite fishing. The natives of Chuuk find the ships' munitions cargoes a valuable source of high explosives, particularly antitank mines and certain easily opened projectiles. After having been dried out and reassembled into home-made bombs, these explosives are dropped back onto the WWII ships, which comprise the richest habitat for pelagic fish in the vicinity.

The result is tragic for the future of the islanders. The deterioration of the ships, (which, after all, are the most effective draw for a clean tourist economy) has been much hastened, and the rich biological communities which have formed on these unintentional artificial reefs have been heavily impacted. The National Park Service is now engaged in teaching the Historic Preservation Officers of these island nations to dive as well as encouraging them to increase their presence on, and assert their authority over, the historic shipwrecks which are situated within their areas of supervision.

The educational and symbolic value of some of the sites in Micronesia goes beyond just that of WWII. Perhaps one of the most striking examples is that of a site in Apra Harbor, Guam. Here the German raider SMS *Cormoran*, scuttled by its skipper in 1917, the day America entered WWI, lies keel to keel with the Japanese transport *Tokai Maru*, sunk by American submarines and torpedo planes prior to the reinvasion of Guam during World War II. The site, mapped by SCRU in 1983, is regularly visited by large groups of Japanese sport divers.

The cooperative effort between the U.S. National Park Service and the U.S. Navy to document far-flung underwater heritage sites in the Central and Western Pacific (known as Project Seamark), adopted a new course in 1989 and included sites in the North Pacific. NPS and Navy divers working from the Navy salvage ship USS Safeguard, explored the farthest reaches of the Aleutian Islands and documented some of the most remarkable remains of WWII on U.S. soil. The Aleutian campaign has often been overshadowed by the extraordinary, simultaneous happenings at Midway, the most pivotal of U.S. victories.

The 1942 Japanese invasion of U.S. territory in Alaska was met with great uproar by the American people, but its timing to coincide with Midway may have been one of the more significant Japanese blunders of the war. The loss of four Japanese carriers at Midway, while the U.S. lost only the *Yorktown*, marked the end of any real threat of a major Japanese offensive on the U.S. West Coast. The U.S. victory was a perilous one, however, marked by many instances of close calls and plain luck. It is hard to say what the outcome might have been if the two Japanese carriers that had been

14 *Top* Midget submarine still in its launch cradle, Kiska (*NPS photo by Larry Murphy*)

15 *Above* Bikini Atoll: Binnacle of USS *Saratoga* (*NPS photo by Larry Murphy*)

16 *Opposite top* Author videotaping propeller of Japanese battleship *Nagato* upside-down in Bikini Lagoon (*NPS photo by Larry Murphy*)

17 *Opposite bottom* Dan Lenihan photographing USS *Arkansas* (*Photo by Larry Murphy*)

assigned to attack the questionable targets of Dutch Harbor, Attu and Kiska, had remained with the Midway strike force.

Attu and Kiska today are very much like they were at the conclusion of the American and Canadian counterattacks which drove the Japanese from the islands in 1943. Bomb craters pockmark the tundra, Japanese gun emplacements still bristle with guns and hand-dug caves remain dangerous to explore because of booby traps. An almost intact midget sub still sits in a launch cradle in its pen, remote from human disturbance since the end of the war.

Closer to Russia than to mainland Alaska, even the U.S. Fish and Wildlife Service (the agency of jurisdiction) has difficulty finding the resources to visit their remote Aleutian holdings once a year. The NPS study conducted there in 1989 revealed a particularly rich bounty in history and artifacts on the harbor bottom. Among the ten odd targets on the seabed identified by side-scan sonar was a transport, a mine-layer and a Vickers class submarine which

the team was able to penetrate. Further survey is planned for future years, possibly in association with the Japanese.

Ironically, one of the greatest ship graveyards of the Pacific came into being not during, but after, the conclusion of the Second World War with the initiation of Atomic bomb testing at Bikini Atoll. Operation Crossroads gelled in the minds of the American military because, by the end of the conflict, it was becoming apparent that the hot war with Japan and Germany would soon be supplanted by a cold war with the Soviet Union. American supremacy in nuclear

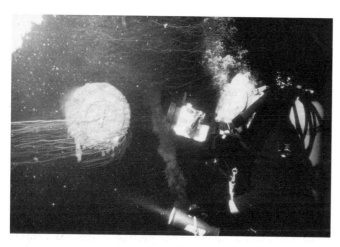

18. Dan Lenihan videotaping 16.1-inch gun of the *Nagato* (tampion still in place) 180 feet deep on floor of Bikini Lagoon (*NPS photo by Larry Murphy*)

warfare had been established with the destruction of Hiroshima and Nagasaki, but the U.S. military realized that effects of atom bombs on naval forces was still unknown.

The background research conducted by the NPS Submerged Cultural Resources Unit, in preparation and follow-up to its underwater survey work at Bikini Atoll, revealed the wealth of social historical insights that can devolve from studying the physical remains of recent history. Operation Crossroads took place in 1946 and involved the intentional detonation of two nuclear devices on a fleet of target ships that would have comprised the fourth or fifth largest Navy in the world at the time. It was an experiment of staggering proportions requiring the deployment of 46,000 men (and 36 women) and hundreds of test ships and support vessels.

The bikini tests resulted in the spectacle of mushroom clouds engulfing ships under the scrutiny of hundreds of cameras, photographs of sailors in shirt-sleeves 'cleaning' the radiation from ships' decks with brooms and mops within hours of atomic detonation, and a major collection of capital warships at diveable depths on the lagoon bottom.

During resurvey operations in 1989 and 1990, NPS divers mapped the USS *Saratoga*, a 900-foot aircraft carrier sitting on the lagoon bottom in 180 feet of water. Visits were also made to the battleship USS *Arkansas, Hijms Nagato* (Yamamoto's flagship), two Balao class submarines, destroyers, and during layovers in Kwajalein, reconnaissance work was carried out on the *Prinz Eugen.*

The remote atoll of Bikini in the Marshall Islands has

become the location of what is perhaps the greatest concentration of major WWII relics in the world. The target ships of Operation Crossroads have been recommended as the focus for the development of a marine park that will allow underwater site visitation. A contact station on the Island would educate visitors on various aspects of the nuclear age as well as the evolution from conventional to nuclear warfare.

This discussion has focused on the archaeology of WWII in the Pacific, but there is also a rich legacy of historic fabric from that conflict, and others, in the Atlantic. Scapa Flow is one of the first places that comes to mind. How soon we recognize the importance of these undersea components of our heritage, and afford them the attention and protection they deserve, will determine how many windows to the past will remain for our children to open.

Biographies

Héctor Bado Born Montevideo, Uruguay, 1958. Professional diver, researcher and maritime historian. Specialist in remote sensing techniques. Since 1985 has dedicated himself to wreck location, survey and recovery in the River Plate and off the Atlantic coast of Uruguay. Has found over 80 sites. In collaboration with Oxford University MARE has been excavating the wrecks of HMS *Agamemnon* (1809), *Sea Horse* (1728) and *Salvador* (1811) and sites off Cabo Polonia.

John Bingeman An amateur nautical archaeologist for many years and a Government historic wreck site licensee for 20 years. After diving on the *Mary Rose*, was given responsibility (for eight years) for the wrecks of the *Assurance* (1753), and the *Pomone* (1811) off the Needles, Isle of Wight. In 1980 identified and achieved designation for the wreck of the *Invincible* (1758) of which he remains the licensee. By profession, a chartered marine engineer, also had a career in the Royal Navy achieving the rank of Commander.

Ann Birchall W.F. Masom Scholar in Classics, London University; followed by doctoral research in the archaeology of the British and Continental iron Age at the Institute of Archaeology, London. Assistant Keeper, Department of Greek and Roman Antiquities, British Museum, 1962-1978; specialist in Aegean prehistory and Greek vase-painting. Has excavated in Britain, Greece and Syria; 1975-78 archaeological director of the HMS *Colossus* excavation. Since 1979 consultant on archaeology, including Archaeology Editor of The Illustrated London News, writing, lecturing and travelling extensively in the Mediterranean and Far East; broadcaster on radio and television; author of books, articles and excavation reports.

Mensun Bound Founder-editor of present series. Served in merchant marine before attending university in the USA. Former scholar of the Schepp Foundation and Institute of Commonwealth Universities. Director of Archaeology of Oxford University MARE. Has directed or co-directed wreck surveys or excavations off Giglio, Montecristo, Giannutri, Gorgona, Aeolian Islands, Ionian Islands, Gibraltar, Mahdia (Tunisia), Alderney, Turks and Caicos, Falklands, Straits of Magellan, Shetland Islands, Cape Verde Islands and Straits of Malacca. Most recent work on porcelain wreck off Vietnam and on Nelson's *Agamemnon* and the pocket battleship *Graf Spee* in the River Plate. Written or edited three books. Recently completed three-part series for television entitled *Lost Ships*.

John Broadwater Manager of the Monitor National Marine Sanctuary, National oceanic and Atmospheric Administration. During 1978-90, as Virginia's Senior Underwater Archaeologist, directed a study of shipwrecks from the Battle of Yorktown (1781) and developed a state-wide underwater archaeology programme. Member of the Advisory Council on Underwater Archaeology.

Javier Garcia Cano Professor of History at the Universities of Buenos Aires and Belgrano. Specialization: Underwater Archaeology and Preservation of Underwater Cultural Heritage. Project leader: HMS *Swift*; *Posadas*, underwater survey in the River Paraná; *Cayastá-Santa Fe La Vieja*, underwater excavations of the remains of the city Santa Fe La Vieja (1573); *Monje*, underwater survey of the remains of the Indian settlement 'San Bartolomé de los Chaná' (1616); *Las Encadenadas de Saavedra*, underwater survey of a litic period settlement (3000 b.p.). Active member of ICOMOS. Full member of ICUCH (International Committee of Underwater Cultural Heritage). Founding Member of the ALBENGA Foundation for the Preservation of the Underwater Cultural Heritage. member of the society of Maritime History of Latin America-Thalassa.

Michael Cates and **Diane Chamberlain** The East Kent Maritime Trust, a registered charity that administers the Museum Service in Thanet with support from the District Council. The Trust is responsible for the Maritime Museum in Ramsgate and the Seaside Museum in Margate and continually develops the aim of promoting and caring for the rich heritage of the area it covers. Michael, the Director and Diane, the Administrator of these Museums, have both worked with the Trust for over 14 years.

Jørgen Christoffersen Born 1946. Masters in prehistoric archaeology (European and Nordic). Since 1981 curator and researcher at the National Museum of Denmark, Dept. of Danish National Record of Sites and Monuments. Designer of databases for land and marine sites; field work on prehistoric and medieval sites and 17th century shipwrecks; research and publications on these topics.

James P. Delgado Served as executive director of the Vancouver Maritime Museum since 1991. Prior to that, was head of the U.S. Government's maritime preservation program, the National Maritime Initiative, in Washington, D.C. Trained as both a historian and archaeologist; has led or participated in shipwreck surveys and excavations in the United States, Canada, Mexico, and the Pacific. Author of 17 books and numerous articles; recently edited *The British Museum Encyclopaedia of Maritime and Underwater Archaeology* (1997).

Winifred Glover Curator of Ethnography at the Ulster Museum, Belfast, with responsibility for the non-Irish Collections which include the Spanish Armada. Publications on the collections include *The Land of the Brave* (1978), *Polynesia* (1987), *Travelling at Port Phillip* (1988) *and Realms of the Pacific* (1994). Has contributed many articles to historical and archaeological journals.

William Patrick Gosset learnt to dive in 1966 and through underwater archaeology acquired a keen interest in British Naval History. Author of *The Lost Ships of the Royal Navy 1793-1900*; is a chartered surveyor currently working as an Estates Manager for a company that owns in excess of 4000 public houses in England and Wales. Married with two children.

Bengt Grisell Born Stockholm 1942. Studied and trained in precision mechanics. Senior instrument engineer in departments of electron physics, accelerator technology and naval architecture at the Royal Institute of Technology, Sweden. For over 20 years worked with Anders Franzén (discoverer of the *Vasa*). In 1980 found, with Franzén and two others, the wreck of the *Kronen*. Active in the field of underwater remote sensing and photography. In 1991 awarded gold plaque by Swedish Academy of Engineering Science for his work in underwater technology and for his archaeological work on the wreck of the *Kronen*.

Max Guérout French navy captain (retired), founder member of the Groupe de Recherche en Archéologie Navale, a non profit-making association. Has directed archaeological operations since 1980. Is an associate member of the Laboratoire d'Histoire et d'Archéologie Maritime du CNRS, Paris IV-Sorbonnes, Musée de la Marine, and, as member of the International Scientific Committee of the UNESCO programme 'The Slave Route', is in charge of developing a programme of underwater archaeology on slave ships.

Daniel J. Lenihan Chief of U.S. National Park Service's underwater archaeology team known as the Submerged Cultural Resources Unit. Has supervised the NPS underwater programme since 1975. Is a member of the SHA Council on Underwater Archaeology and is the U.S. representative to the International Committee on the Underwater Cultural Heritage of ICOMOS. Obtained an MA from Florida State University in 1974 and has been an instructor in the sport and technical diving community since 1972. Besides the World War II projects listed in the article has conducted studies of shipwrecks in locations as diverse as the Great Lakes, California, and Florida.

Colin Martin Reader in Maritime Studies at the University of St Andrews. Since 1968 has been excavating shipwrecks of the early modern period off Scotland and Ireland, specialising in sites associated with the Spanish Armada. His research interests include ship construction and early artillery. At present is working on the wreck of a Cromwellian warship off Duart Point, Mull.

Manual Martin-Bueno Professor of Archaeology and Underwater Archaeology at the University of Zarazoga, Spain. Since 1971 has been Director of over one hundred archaeological excavations and projects in Spain and overseas: Gerasa (Jordan), Gulf of Aqba (Jordan), Cavoli (Sardinia), Livingstone Island (Antarctica), Gibraltar Strait (Spain), Denia (Alicante, Spain), Finnisterre (Galicia, Spain), etc. Is the author of numerous scientific papers and many books.

Svein Molaug Born 1914. Director of the Norwegian Maritime Museum for 28 years (1956-1984). The present museum building was realised during his directorship. Molaug is justly regarded as a pioneer of underwater archaeology in Norway. Was also the principal figure behind the now widespread awareness of maritime ethnology in his country. Via scholarly and popular books, articles and lectures, has made Norwegian maritime culture known to a wide public.

David Perkins A land archaeologist specialising in the archaeology of the Isle of Thanet. From 1978-1983 was much involved with Thanet Archaeology's diving team which discovered and carried out the initial survey of the Stirling Castle. Was the project's Finds Officer and Archaeological Advisor. Has published widely on the archaeology of the area.

Nigel Pickford A world authority on shipwreck history. Has been involved in a wide variety of discoveries ranging from 12th century junks to World War One freighters. Is the author of *The Atlas of Shipwreck and Treasure*.

Eric Rieth Research Director of CNRS, and head of the Department of Naval Archaeology at the Musée de la Marine, Paris. Is an archaeologist specialising in the history of ship construction from the Middle Ages to Modern Times. Since 1970, he has directed numerous underwater excavations of shipwrecks at sea and in rivers. Author of many papers and articles.

Bryan Smith Master Mariner, served as an Officer in the Merchant Navy (tramp ships and liner vessels) in the Australasian trade. Afterwards spent 22 years in Nigeria, first with the Nigerian Ports Authority and later with Shell International. Marine Archaeological experience includes a spell on the *Mary Rose*, then with Oxford University MARE on the Giglio, Panarea, Rhyl, Zakynthos, Alderney, *Nassau*, Cape Verde Islands, Mahdia and Uruguay projects.

Myra Stanbury Curator in the Department of Maritime Archaeology, Western Australian Maritime Museum, Fremantle, where she has been employed since 1972. Has worked on maritime archaeological excavations in Australia and overseas and is one of the principal investigators of the *Sirius* Project. In 1994 was awarded an Australian Academy of the Humanities Grant for the publication of the *Sirius* artefact research. Currently serving as Vice President of the Australian Institute for Maritime Archaeology and is editor of the AIMA Bulletin.

David C. Switzer Born Portland, Maine. Professor of history at Plymouth State College of the University System of New Hampshire. Received his BA from the University of Maine and his MA and PhD from the University of Connecticut. In addition to directing the excavation of the *Defence*, he co-directed the recovery of the bow of the clipper ship *Snowsquall* from the Falkland Islands and has worked with Colin Martin and George Bass. Is the Consulting Nautical Archaeologist for the State of New Hampshire.

Michael Teisen Born Copenhagen 1951. Degree in history/ maritime history from the University of Copenhagen. Assistant at the Royal Danish Naval Museum, 1975-80. HSE part I diver's licence from the Royal Danish Navy, 1979. Assistant at the Danish National Museum, Department of Maritime Archaeology 1980-85. Curator of the Loesø Museum, 1985-90. Curator at the Norwegian Maritime Museum, Department of Maritime Archaeology, 1990. Participated in underwater excavations in Denmark, Sweden and Norway.

Index